Koreans in North America

É
184
K6
M56
2013

Koreans in North America

Their Twenty-First Century Experiences

Pyong Gap Min

LEXINGTON BOOKS
Lanham • Boulder • New York • Toronto • Plymouth, UK

Published by Lexington Books
A wholly owned subsidiary of Rowman & Littlefield
4501 Forbes Boulevard, Suite 200, Lanham, Maryland 20706
www.rowman.com

10 Thornbury Road, Plymouth PL6 7PP, United Kingdom

Copyright © 2013 by Lexington Books

All rights reserved. No part of this book may be reproduced in any form or by any electronic or mechanical means, including information storage and retrieval systems, without written permission from the publisher, except by a reviewer who may quote passages in a review.

British Library Cataloguing in Publication Information Available

Library of Congress Cataloging-in-Publication Data
The hardback edition of this book was previously cataloged by the Library of Congress as follows:

Koreans in North America : their twenty-first century experiences / edited by Pyong Gap Min.
   p. cm.
   Includes bibliographical references and index.
     1. Korean Americans--History. 2. Koreans--United States--History. 3. Koreans--Canada--History. 4. United States--Emigration and immigration. 5. Canada--Emigration and immigration. 6. Korea--Emigration and immigration. I. Min, Pyong Gap, 1942-
E184.K6K6553 2013
305.8957'073--dc23
                                                                              2012040486
ISBN: 978-0-7391-7813-3 (cloth : alk. paper)
ISBN: 978-0-7391-8712-8 (pbk. : alk. paper)
ISBN: 978-0-7391-7814-0 (electronic)

∞™ The paper used in this publication meets the minimum requirements of American National Standard for Information Sciences—Permanence of Paper for Printed Library Materials, ANSI/NISO Z39.48-1992.

Printed in the United States of America

Table of Contents

Figures		vii
Tables		ix
Acknowledgments		xi

Chapter 1:	Introduction *Pyong Gap Min*	1
Chapter 2:	The Immigration of Koreans to the United States: A Review of Forty-Five Year (1965-2009) Trends *Pyong Gap Min*	9
Chapter 3:	Growth and Settlement Patterns of Korean Americans *Pyong Gap Min and Chigon Kim (Associate Professor at Wright State University)*	35
Chapter 4:	Changes in Korean Immigrants' Business Patterns *Pyong Gap Min*	57
Chapter 5:	A Comparison of Korean Protestant, Catholic, and Buddhist Religious Institutions in New York *Pyong Gap Min*	75
Chapter 6:	Explaining the Migration Strategy: Comparing Transnational and Intact Migrant Families from South Korea to Canada *Ann H. Kim (York University), Sung Hyun Yun, Wansoo Park, and Samuel Noh*	103
Chapter 7:	Transnational Interactions among Korean Immigrants in Toronto: Family Ties and Socioeconomic, Cultural, and Political Participation *Samuel Noh (The David Crombie Professor at University of Toronto), Min-Jung Kwak, and Joe Jeong Ho Han*	121
Chapter 8:	The Bifurcated Statuses of the Wives of Korean International Students *Se Hwa Lee (Doctoral Student, SUNY at Albany)*	135
Chapter 9:	Transnationalism and "Third Culture Kids": A Comparative Analysis of Korean American and Korean Chinese Identity Construction *Helene K. Lee (Dickinson College)*	157

Chapter 10: Authenticity Dilemma among Pre-1965 Native-Born Koreans 173
Linda S. Park (Doctoral Student, University of Wisconsin at Madison)

Chapter 11: A Four-Decade Literature on Korean Americans: A Review and Comprehensive Bibliography 195
Pyong Gap Min

Index 253
About the Contributors 259

Figures

2.1	Number of Korean Immigrants (by Country of Birth) to the U.S., 1965-2009	13
2.2	Mechanisms of Koreans' Immigration to the U.S., 1966-2009	17
2.3	Proportion of Women among Korean Immigrants (by Country of Birth), 1965-2009	23
2.4	Percentage of Status Adjusters among Korean Immigrants (by Country of Birth), 1965-2009	24
2.5	Annual Number of Korean Elementary and Secondary Students Who Went Abroad for Study	27
2.6	Number of Korean Visitors (Non-Immigrants) to the U.S., 1965-2009	28
2.7	Number of Korean Temporary Workers in the U.S., 1965-2010	30
3.1	Growth of Korean Population, 1970-2010	36
3.2	Changes in the Regional Distribution of Korean Population, 1970-2010 (%)	39
3.3	Ten U.S. States with Largest Proportions of Multiracial Korean Populations	42
3.4	Growth of the Korean Population in the Ten Largest Korean Population Areas (CMSA)	43
3.5	The Asian Population in Los Angeles City by Ethnic Group, 2010	49
3.6	The Asian Population in New York City by Ethnic Group, 2010	52
7.1	Family or Relatives Living in Korea by Age Group	127
7.2	Cumulative Percentage of Contacts using Telephone and Internet, Last Six Months	128

Tables

2.1	Percentage of Immigrants in Technical/Professional and Administrative/Managerial Occupations among Asian Immigrants by Country of Birth, 1965-2009	19
2.2	Number of Korean Adoptees Admitted to the U.S. as Immigrants by Country of Birth and Five Largest Source Countries of Adoptees, 1976-2009	21
2.3	Percentage of Status Adjusters among Korean Immigrants (by Country of Birth) Compared to Other Groups by Region of Origin, 2009	25
2.4	Annual Number of International Students for Top Three Countries of Origin	26
3.1	Place of Birth among the Korean Population, 2000-2008	37
3.2	The Asian Population by Ethnic Group in 2010	37
3.3	Numbers of Korean Americans in Fifteen Major Korean (20,000 or more) States, 2010	40
3.4	The Increase in the Korean Population (Single-Race and Multiracial) in Major Korean States between 2000 and 2010	41
3.5	Numbers of Korean Americans and Growth Rates in the Ten Largest Korean Population Areas, in 1990, 2000, and 2010	44
3.6	Selected Characteristics of the Korean Population (only Single-Race) by Place of Residence, 2006-2008	47
3.7	Population Change of Korean American Population in Los Angeles CMSA, 1990-2010	48
3.8	Growth of Korean Population in Three Major Los Angeles Suburban Areas, 1990-2010	50
3.9	Changes in the Korean Population in the New York-New Jersey CMSA, 1990-2010	51
3.10	Changes in the Korean Population in New York City by Borough, 1990-2010	53
3.11	Growth of Korean Population in Five Major New York-New Jersey Suburban Counties, 1990-2010	54
4.1	Changing Self-Employment Rates (%) among Korean Immigrant Full-Time Workers in the New York-New Jersey Consolidated Metropolitan Statistical Area in 1980, 1990, and 2000 by Sex	59
4.2	Korean Immigrants' Class of Workers by Sex, 1988 and 2005	61
4.3	Industries of Main Businesses owned by Full-Time Korean Immigrant Workers in the New York-New Jersey Area by Decade	64
4.4	Generation Differences (%) in Fluency in English and Occupational Patterns among Korean American Men in Labor Force (25-64 years old) in the New York-New Jersey Metropolitan Area in 2000	70
5.1	Korean Immigrant Respondents' Self-Reported Religions in Korea and New York (2005)	78

5.2	Korean Immigrant Respondents' Frequency of Participation in Religious Institutions	81
6.1	Demographic Information	108
6.2	Motivations for Migration, Children in School, and Social Class Background	110
6.3	Selected Characteristics of Families Prior to Migrating to Canada	113
10.1	Demographic Data (N=16)	176
11.1	Number of Books and Edited Anthologies Focusing on or Covering Korean Americans	198
11.2	Number of Articles and Book Chapters by Topic	199

Acknowledgments

I need to acknowledge a number of people whose assistance has made the publication of this book possible. First of all, I would not have been able to publish this book without five important chapters contributed by my colleagues, and I would like to extend my gratitude to the contributors for writing and revising their chapters in a timely manner. I also owe special thanks to Thomas Chung, the editor of the Research Center for Korean Community, for editing all manuscripts meticulously and formatting the final draft of the book manuscript to make it available for camera-ready printing. I also would like to thank Saehee Kim and Claire Kim for analyzing immigration and census data effectively. The results of their data analyses were my foundations for writing Chapters 2 and 3. In addition, Eun-been Lee, Saehee Kim, and Dong Wan Joo deserve my gratitude for spending many hours in preparing and updating the literature on Korean Americans. I also need to express thanks to Chigon Kim for replacing many tables in Chapters 2 and 3 with figures and changing several tables and figures in Chapters 3 and 7 by eliminating colors.

Four of the five chapters written by the contributors were originally presented as papers at a conference held in Flushing, New York City in 2010, and organized by the Research Center for Korean Community. Three of the five chapters I wrote were also originally presented as Research Reports for the Research Center. Financial support by the Research Center has been essential to organizing annual conferences and bimonthly seminars, as well as paying for Chung's editorial work and other student assistants' research activities. The Research Center for Korean Community was established at Queens College in Fall 2009, primarily to provide data and information about Korean Americans to the Korean community and the Korean government. The Research Foundation for Korean Community is the major supporting organization for the Research Center for Korean Community. I would like to express thanks to Dr. Yung Duk Kim and Elder Hae Min Chung, Co-Chairs of the Board of Directors, and other Board members for supporting the Center's various activities throughout the year. I also owe thanks to Incha Kim, Associate Director of the Research Center, and Dong Wan Joo and Young Oak Kim, the Center's research associates, for working many hours per week for the Center for meager monetary compensation. Finally, I should not forget to indicate that Young Oak Kim, my wife, has devoted many free hours to supporting my research activities, including editing this book, both at the college and at home.

Three of my own chapters included in this book were published in two journals in Korea. I would like to extend my thanks to the editors of the journals for allowing me to reprint the articles in this book. Chapter 2, "The Immigration of Koreans to the United States: A Review of Forty-Five Year (1965-2009) Trends," was published in *Development and Society* in 2011 (Volume 40, pp. 195-224). I owe my thanks to Prof. Shin-Kap Han, editor of the journal, for giving me permission to reprint the article. Chapter 5, "A Comparison of Korean

Protestant, Catholic, and Buddhist Religious Institutions in New York," was published in *Studies of Koreans Abroad,* a major Korean-English bilingual journal specializing in overseas Korean experiences, in 2009 (Volume 20, pp.182-231). Chapter 11, "A Four-Decade Literature on Korean Americans: A Review and Comprehensive Bibliography," was published in the same journal in 2010 (Volume 21, pp.15-132). I would like to thank Prof. In-Jin Yoon, editor of the journal, and Young Sam Yim, President of the Association for Studies of Koreans Abroad, the professional organization that publishes the journal, for allowing me to reprint these two articles.

Finally, I would like to thank Jana Hodges-Kluck, Associate Acquisitions Editor of Lexington Books, for recognizing value in this book and for patiently waiting for the final draft of the manuscript. Eric Wrona, Laura Reiter, and other staff members of Lexington Books worked quickly in getting this book published once they had the final draft of the manuscript. I have had only positive experiences in communicating with Jana and other staff members of the publisher. I hope to publish more via Lexington Books in the coming years.

Chapter 1
Introduction

by Pyong Gap Min

A Great Deal of Media and Academic Interest in Korean Americans

Abolishing the previous racist immigration law, Congress passed a liberalized immigration law in 1965. The Immigration Act of 1965 opened the door to people from all over the world for immigration to the United States. As a result of the enforcement of this new immigration law, more than 28 million immigrants have settled in the United States. More than 80% of the post-1965 immigrants have originated from Latin American, Asian and Caribbean countries. Naturally, the new immigration law has altered the racial and ethnic composition of the United States. The proportion of the non-Hispanic white population dropped from 87% in 1970 to 65% in 2010, with Latino and Asian populations respectively increasing from 4.5% and 0.7% to 14.7% and 4.8%. South Korea became one of the major beneficiaries of the liberalized immigration law. As will be shown in Chapter 1 in detail, South Korea sent more than one million immigrants to the United States between 1965 and 2010. As a result, the Korean population in the United States increased from about 70,000 in 1970 to more than 1.7 million in 2010. Despite a phenomenal increase over the past forty-five years, Korean Americans number-wise comprise the fifth largest Asian group, following Chinese, Filipino, Indian, and Vietnamese Americans. Among the six major Asian groups, Korean Americans outnumber only Japanese Americans, who consist mainly of native-born Americans due to a relatively low immigration flow from Japan in the post-1965 era.

However, the Korean immigrant community has probably attracted more local and national media and scholarly attention than any other Asian immigrant community. As analyzed in Chapter 11, about 140 monographs and edited books that focus on or cover Korean immigrants and their children have been published since the late 1970s. Also, close to 600 journal articles and book chapters focusing on or covering Korean Americans have been published. As evidenced by my frequent citation of articles in two of my books (Min 1996, 2008), English-language dailies have covered Korean immigrants with unusual frequency.

I believe there are two major reasons why Korean immigrants have received frequent media and scholarly attention. First, Korean immigrants were highly concentrated in several retail and service businesses beginning in the late 1970s. Immigrants' commercial activities in specific business types, whether serving co-ethnic or non-ethnic customers, usually attract more attention than their jobs in the general labor market. In particular, Korean merchants had more business-related conflicts with black customers, white suppliers, Latino employees, and government agencies regulating commercial activities than any other business-oriented immigrant group in the United States (Min 1996). For example, Greek immigrants in New York City have the highest self-employment rate, a slightly higher rate than Korean immigrants (Min 2008). However, being heavily concentrated in the restaurant industry, Greek immigrant business owners have not had much conflict with outside interest groups. By contrast, Korean greengrocers, grocers, and other retailers in New York City have had severe conflicts with black customers, white suppliers, and Latino employees, especially in the 1980s and early 1990s. Issues of the *New York Times* and other local English dailies published in the 1980s and early 1990s covered three or four Korean merchants' business-related conflicts almost every month. As shown in Chapter 11, more than a dozen books and over a hundred journal articles focusing on conflicts between Korean merchants and external interest groups were published in the 1990s and 2000s.

Second, Korean immigrants have attracted special media and research attention partly because of their active congregation-oriented religious activities. As will be discussed in detail in Chapter 5, approximately 60% of Korean immigrants are affiliated with Korean Protestant churches, with another 15% affiliated with Korean Catholic churches. Korean immigrants are the largest Protestant immigrant group in the post-1965 era. But both journalists and researchers have paid special attention to Korean Christian immigrants mainly because they are highly congregationally-oriented. There are approximately 550 Korean Protestant churches, along with twenty-five Catholic churches, in the New York-New Jersey metropolitan area alone. Both Korean Protestant and Catholic immigrants are active in participation in congregations. The *New York Times* has covered Korean immigrant churches many times. As shown in Chapter 11, several books and about eighty articles and book chapters have examined Korean Protestant churches and Korean Protestants for both immigrant and younger generations.

Introduction 3

The Need for a Comprehensive Anthology

Many acclaimed books and numerous informative and articulate journal articles focusing on particular topics related to Korean American experiences have been published. But there has been little effort to synthesize information about Korean immigrant or Korean American experiences in one book. The only book that provides general information about Korean American experiences is *Korean Americans* (1998), written by Won Moo Hurh. But even this book fails to cover many important issues related to Korean immigrant experiences. It is surprising that active research over the past forty years has not produced a few books that provide general information about Korean Americans.

I have prepared this anthology on Korean Americans in order to meet the need for comprehensive books that cover different aspects of Korean American and Korean immigrant experiences in the United States. The book begins with statistical data on Koreans' immigration and settlement patterns. It includes chapters focusing on Korean immigrants' business patterns, religious institutions, international students, second-generation Koreans' ethnic identity construction, and pre-1965 second-generation Koreans' identity construction. This book also includes a comprehensive annotated bibliography on Korean Americans.

In addition, it has two chapters that shed light on transnational ties among Korean immigrants in Canada. The immigration of Koreans to Canada also started in the 1960s when the Canadian government changed the immigration law. The total number of Koreans in Canada is approximately 150,000, about 8% of the Korean population in the United States. Both Koreans in Canada and those in the United States consist predominantly of post-1965 immigrants, but the two groups are somewhat different from each other in terms of characteristics. For one, international students, including early-study students, make up a much larger proportion of Korean immigrants in Canada than those in the United States. The two chapters focusing on Korean immigrants in Canada are important contributions to the literature on Korean Canadians, partly because there are a limited number of studies of Korean Canadians.

Most of the book chapters pay special attention to changes in Korean experiences in the twenty-first century. In addition to its comprehensiveness in covering different aspects of Korean American experiences, the other main strength of this book is the chapters' special attention to changes over time and their focus on Korean American or Korean Canadian experiences, particularly in the twenty-first century. Since Korean immigrant experiences in the 1980s and early 1990s were substantially different from their experiences in the 2000s, data collected twenty years ago do not help to understand Korean immigrant experiences now. In particular, the chapters authored or co-authored by this editor (see Chapters 2, 3, 4, and 11) examine changes over time in Koreans' immigration, settlement and business patterns, and trends in Korean American studies.

The other chapters also generally cover Korean experiences in the twenty-first century. For example, the number of international students, including early-study students, has exponentially increased in the twenty-first century. Also, since many 1.5- and second-generation Koreans have emerged as young adults, any comprehensive book on Korean Americans should have one or more chapters focusing on native-born Korean Americans' experiences and identities. This book has two chapters focusing on native-born Koreans' experiences.

The two chapters (Chapters 6 and 7) focusing on transnationalism among Korean immigrants in Canada are particularly important for this book because they contribute not only to the literature on Korean Canadians, but also to that on Korean Americans. As indicated in Chapter 11, several studies have examined transnational ties among Korean immigrants in the United States in connection with special topics, such as Korean adoptees, Korean women married to U.S. servicemen, and pre-war Korean Protestant immigrant leaders' independence movement against Japan. However, there is no survey study that has examined different elements of U.S. Korean immigrants' transnational ties to their homeland systematically. Some of the findings about Korean immigrants' transnational ties in Canada may be applicable to Korean immigrants in the United States.

Who May Benefit from This Book?

This book will be of great use to faculty members and graduate students who conduct research on Korean Americans. As a comprehensive bibliography and review of social science literature on Korean Americans in Chapter 11 suggests, the number of scholars who do research on Korean Americans has radically increased over the past three decades. As a sociologist, I am more familiar with scholars in the sociology discipline. There are over thirty sociologists who study Korean Americans. Moreover, many more people in Ph.D. programs in sociology and other social science disciplines are working on dissertations on Korean Americans. This book can provide important sources for these researchers of Korean Americans. In particular, an informed review of the literature on Korean Americans with a comprehensive bibliography in Chapter 11 will be immensely helpful to researchers who need to find research issues on and sources for Korean Americans. Systematic statistics on Korean immigration and settlement patterns in Chapters 2 and 3 also can provide important data for researchers studying Korean Americans, including doctoral students and community social workers writing proposals. This book is also likely to be an important resource for college libraries. Because of the comprehensive coverage of the topics, most college libraries are likely to purchase this book for faculty members and students. Approximately a hundred universities and colleges have established Asian American programs/centers. Most of them may like to keep this book in their own mini libraries. This book also has the potential to be adopted as a supplementary reader for Asian and Korean American courses. Many Asian American studies programs in the West Coast offer Korean American courses.

Summary of Each Chapter

A short summary of each substantive chapter is in order. Chapter 2 by Pyong Gap Min examines patterns of post-1965 Korean immigration in detail, based on statistical yearbooks issued by the immigration office. In particular, it focuses on changes in immigration patterns over time. Some of the significant findings are that roughly 75% to 80% of new immigrants during recent years had previously entered the United States with non-immigrant status and later changed their status to permanent residents. A significant proportion of these status-adjusted immigrants originally came to the United States as international students. Another important finding closely related to the dominance of Korean status-adjusted immigrants is that the vast majority of recent Korean immigrants are occupational immigrants and their dependents, with family-sponsored immigrants making up a very small proportion (20% or less). This is almost a reversal of the trend in the 1980s and early 1990s. This chapter also has systematic statistical data on the annual number of Korean adoptees.

Chapter 3 by Pyong Gap Min and Chigon Kim examines the growth of the Korean population and Korean Americans' settlement patterns in the United States and two metropolitan areas (the Los Angeles area and the New York-New Jersey area) between 1990 and 2010, using census data. The Korean population grew from approximately 70,000 in 1970 to more than 1.7 million in 2010. Korean Americans are heavily concentrated in Los Angeles, New York, the Washington DC-Baltimore area, and several other large metropolitan areas. Between 2000 and 2010, large Korean population centers such as Los Angeles, New York, Chicago, and Philadelphia lost their shares of the Korean population, while medium-size Korean communities, such as those in Atlanta, Dallas, and San Diego, experienced significant increases. Additionally, Korean Americans within major Korean population centers moved from the central cities to suburban areas during the period. This chapter also examines settlement patterns in the Los Angeles-Orange-Riverside County area and the New York-New Jersey area.

Chapter 4 by Pyong Gap Min examines changes in Korean immigrants' business patterns in the New York-New Jersey area. Korean immigrants in New York had a high self-employment rate (almost half of Korean immigrant households were self-employed) in the 1980s and 1990s, but their self-employment rate has dropped significantly since the early 2000s. The presence of many temporary residents and the participation of students-turned-new immigrants in the mainstream economy seem to be two major factors in the reduction of the self-employment rate among Korean immigrants. Also, the proportion of Korean-owned retail businesses has dropped, while the proportion of service-related businesses has increased greatly. Significantly, Korean immigrants' business-related intergroup conflicts with black customers and white suppliers that peaked in the 1980s and early 1990s have almost disappeared since the late 1990s. This chapter explains why business-related intergroup conflicts have disappeared. The major findings about changes in Korean immigrants' business patterns and business-related intergroup conflicts are applicable to other Korean communities.

Chapter 5 by Pyong Gap Min examines Korean immigrants' religious affiliations in Korea and New York, and the frequency of participations in religious institutions based on survey data collected in New York City. It explains the overrepresentation of Christians and the under-representation of Buddhists among Korean immigrants. It also explains why many Buddhists and those with no religion began to attend Korean Protestant churches in New York. More important, this chapter compares Korean Protestant, Catholic, and Buddhist religious institutions in terms of fellowship/ethnic networks, social services, and cultural retention. Many studies have examined the fellowship, social service, and cultural retention functions of Korean Protestant churches in the United States. However, there is not much data on the social functions of Korean Catholic and Buddhist religious institutions. Thus this comparative study provides useful information about Korean Catholic and Buddhist religious institutions.

Chapter 6 by Ann Kim and her associates compares Korean transnational migrant families and intact families in Canada. Transnational migrant families refer to Korean families who are split between South Korea and Canada, with the wives and children staying in Canada for children's education and the husbands working in Korea. Intact families refer to Korean husband-wife migrant families who live together in Canada. This chapter, which is based on a major survey, shows that a higher proportion of transnational families than intact families decided to leave Korea because of their dissatisfaction with the educational system in Korea. But more important, the authors found that the majority of both types of families considered a better educational opportunity in Canada the most important motivation for their migration decision. The chapter also shows that transnational families have on average a substantially higher family income than intact families. The chapter shows other significant differences between the two types of families.

Chapter 7 by Samuel Noh and his associates systematically examines several different dimensions of transnational ties to their homeland among Korean immigrants in the Greater Area of Toronto, based on survey data. Transnational ties examined include informal contacts with family and kin members using telephones and internet, organizational participation and activities, visits, economic ties, and emotional and psychological ties. Results of the survey show that approximately 20% to 50% of the respondents make telephone or online contacts with their family/kin members at least once a week. About 60% to 75% of adult immigrants were also found to send and receive from Korea either money or gifts. The chapter presents many other interesting findings about Korean immigrants' transnational linkages to their homeland.

Chapter 8 by Se Hwa Lee examines the effect of migration on spousal relations and the division of household labor among Korean international students and their wives. Lee's observations and findings are based on personal interviews of twenty-one wives and eight of their student husbands. Those Korean wives who accompanied their student husbands as homemakers became subordinated to their husbands and undertook almost all housework and childcare. In contrast, those wives who came to the United States as students or who met husbands as students here maintained far more egalitarian spousal relations and enjoyed more equal household labor and childcare responsibilities. The chapter is important because of the presence of so many Korean international students in the United States.

Chapter 9 by Helene Lee examines transnational identity construction among Korean Americans and Korean Chinese visiting their homeland, South Korea, based on personal interviews with thirty-three young Korean Chinese and thirty young Korean Americans in Korea. The major findings are that for Korean Chinese and Korean Americans, their experiences in Seoul reaffirm their connection with "Koreanness," but that nearly all informants conform to their own diasporic concepts of Koreanness (as embodied in Korean Americans or Korean Chinese) that are qualitatively different from South Koreans. The author claims that research participants generally inhabited their own hybrid Korean communities in Seoul, with Korean Americans flocking to other Korean Americans and Korean Chinese to other Korean Chinese, with little overlap with each other or with South Koreans.

Chapter 10 by Linda Park examines the authenticity dilemma a group of second-generation Korean Americans faced while living between two cultural worlds that are so prominent in their lives based on in-depth personal interviews with sixteen middle-aged native-born Korean Americans. The findings indicate that the informants had to negotiate their identity between trying to be white and comprehending their Koreanness. Participants' experiences with racial foreignness from their white peers only reinforced to them their Koreanness. These experiences helped participants to realize their Korean identity. Also, having two Korean parents, participants knew they are genetically and ethnically Korean. However, they experienced rejection as Koreans by their co-ethnic peers because of their loss of Korean language and culture. Whenever participants were in a Korean community setting (whether in the U.S. or in Korea), their co-ethnic peers identified them as cultural foreigners, and the message was that they were not "really Korean." They experienced confusion from being told by their parents that they were Korean, but also being told by their co-ethnic peers they were not. There was confusion from differing sets of expectations, without explanations from either side as to why they were not accepted as a Korean.

Chapter 11 by Pyong Gap Min provides an informed review of Korean American studies over the last four decades with a comprehensive bibliography. The chronological and topical reviews of the literature on Korean Americans divided into different topical categories are expected to help researchers understand the history and contemporary status of Korean American studies. Moreover, his discussions of significant works in connection with particular topics and his comments on neglected topics are likely to be useful to researchers in selecting research issues for future studies. In addition, the long bibliography is expected to greatly help graduate students and scholars to save time in conducting the literature review on particular aspects of Korean American experiences.

Chapter 2
The Immigration of Koreans to the United States: A Review of Forty-Five Year (1965-2009) Trends[1]

by Pyong Gap Min

Introduction

The Korean population, including multiracial Koreans, has grown to more than 1.7 million in 2010 in the United States. More than 95% of Korean Americans consist of post-1965 immigrants and their children. The influx of a large number of Korean immigrants to the United States since the late 1960s was made possible by the Immigration Act of 1965 that was in full effect in 1968. The new immigration law abolished the race-based discrimination in assigning immigration quotas and gave equal opportunity for U.S. immigration to all countries. The liberalized immigration law has resulted in the radical change in the source countries of immigrants. Before 1965, the vast majority of immigrants originated from European countries, with immigrants from Asian countries composing less than 5%. By contrast, about 75% of post-1965 immigrants originated from Latin America and Asia, with European immigrants making up less than 15% (Min 2002).

South Korea is one of the major beneficiaries of the new immigration law. As will be shown in this chapter, approximately one million Koreans immigrated to the United States between 1965 and 2009. But the Korean immigration flow has gone through changes over time since 1965 in size, immigrants' entry mechanisms, socioeconomic backgrounds, and the proportion of status adjusters. This chapter reviews changes in patterns of Koreans' immigration to the United States over the past forty-five years. It will focus on changes in patterns during the most recent years (2000 and after). Tables and figures presented in this chapter are based on *Annual Reports* and *Statistical Yearbooks,* published annually by the Immigration and Naturalization Service between 1965 and 2001, and *Yearbooks of Immigration* by Office of Immigration Statistics between 2002 and 2009. I consider this review of Korean immigration patterns with extensive statistics useful to scholars studying Korean Americans in the United States and Korea. It will also serve as an important reference source for Korean social workers and community leaders in the United States and policymakers involving overseas Koreans in Korea.

Major Contributing Factors to the Influx of Korean Immigrants

To explain international migration, social scientists have developed various theories, each of which emphasizes a particular factor. I consider the following four factors most useful to understanding changing patterns of Koreans' immigration to the United States: (1) the push-pull factors: (2) the immigration policy of the U.S. government and the emigration policy of the Korean government, (3) the military, political, and economic linkages between the United States and South Korea, and (4) globalization and easiness of population movement. These four factors, couched in four theories, complement one another to help us understand changes in patterns of Koreans' trans-Pacific migration the United States.

The push-pull theory is the oldest theory of international migration that focuses on individuals' motivations to leave their home country for a new country for temporary or permanent residence (Lee 1966; Todaro 1969). Common push factors include economic difficulty caused by famine or changes in industrial structure (economic migration), discrimination and even physical insecurity due to one's minority status, and a change in government or wars (refugee migration). The pull factors include better economic opportunities, better opportunities for children's education, and political freedom (refugee migration). The push-pull theory is particularly useful in explaining the massive exodus of Koreans for U.S.-bound migration between 1965 and 1990, as well as pioneer Korean immigrants' movement to Hawaii in the beginning of the twentieth century. Even now, the difficulty in obtaining a college education in Korea and the comparative ease of obtaining one in the United States are important contributing factors to the international migration of young and middle-aged Koreans.

Regardless, aliens, however motivated, cannot immigrate to the United States unless they are permitted to do so both by the U.S. government and by their home-country governments (Zolberg 1989, 2001). Thus the U.S. immigration policy and home countries' emigration policies partly determine how many and which particular aliens (what nationalities and what class background) are going to be admitted to the United States. Beginning with the 1882 Chinese Exclusion Act, the U.S. government took a series of measures to exclude Asians from immigration to the United States. But the passage of the Immigration Act of 1965 finally opened the door to all Asian countries for U.S.-bound emigration. The U.S. government established the liberalized immigration law in 1965 after the Korean military government had already formulated a liberal emigration policy as a means to controlling population pressure (Kim 1981). The Korean government even created more medical schools to export Korean medical professionals to the United States.

In addition, the U.S. government's military and political interventions in world affairs to counter leftist insurgencies, turn back community invasions or quell outbreaks of violence have contributed to the mass emigration of people from those countries (Massey 1999; Teitelbaum 1987). Militarily and politically, the United States has been deeply involved in South Korea since the breakdown of the Korean War in 1950. The fact that most Korean immigrants admitted to the United States between 1950 and 1964 were wives of U.S. servicemen or orphans—many of them war orphans—adopted by American citizens is testimony to the significance of the U.S.-Korean military and political linkages for the migration of Koreans to the United States. Post-1965 immigrants have included far more occupational immigrants than pre-1965 Korean immigrants. But the close military, political and economic relations between the United States and South Korea have continued to contribute to the mass migration of Koreans in the post-1965 period (Kim 1987). The migration of Korean women married to U.S. servicemen stationed in South Korea increased in the late 1960s and early 1970s. Moreover, strong U.S.-Korean ties and the continuous presence of American servicemen in Korea with its U.S. TV networks (AFKN) came to have a strong American cultural influence in Korea, which led middle-class Koreans to view America as a country of affluence and prosperity.

Finally, the globalization perspective is useful in understanding Koreans' international migration to the United States during recent years, especially a slight increase in both the annual number of Korean immigrants and a radical increase in the proportion of Korean status adjusters. In the 1980s, when the international movement of labor was expanding rapidly, a number of scholars tried to explain international migration flows within a global hierarchy (Portes and Walton 1981; Sassen 1988). In their view, international migration is linked to the development of the global economic system in which non-capitalist societies are gradually being inserted into the global markets. The penetration of capitalist economic relations into non-capitalist or developing countries creates a mobile population that is prone to migration to capitalist societies (Massey 1999). To maximize their profits, the owners and managers of capitalist firms in core countries also seek to get not only raw materials and consumers, but also laborers in peripheral countries.

As will be shown shortly, the proportion of employment-sponsored Korean immigrants in professional and managerial occupations has gradually increased since the early 1990s, accounting for a majority in the latter half of the 2000s. This indicates the usefulness of the globalization of economy to Korean immigration patterns. However, as Castle (2000, 2002) aptly points out, the globalization of international migration should pay attention not only to the globalization of the economic system, but also to that in other areas, such as the media, education, and travel. As will be shown later in this chapter, the proportion of Koreans who came to the United States as non-immigrants (international students, temporary workers, visitors, and so forth) and subsequently changed their status to that of permanent residents radically increased during recent years. This indicates that the globalization of education, travel, and the media has played as important a role as economic globalization.

Changes in Immigration Size

As shown in Figure 2.1, the annual number of Korean immigrants gradually increased beginning in 1965. It reached the 30,000 mark in 1976 and maintained an annual number of over 30,000 until 1990. Between 1976 and 1990, Korea was the third largest source country of immigrants to the United States, next to Mexico and the Philippines. To explain the expansion of Korean immigration to the United States in the 1970s and 1980s, we need to emphasize push factors from Korea. The low standard of living in Korea, characterized by lack of job opportunity, was the major factor that pushed many Koreans to seek emigration to the United States in the 1960s through the early 1980s. Per capita income in Korea was only $251 in 1970. It increased to $1,355 in 1980, but it was only about 1/8 of the per capita income in the United States in the same year (Min 2006b).

Political insecurity and lack of political freedom associated with military dictatorship between 1960 and 1987 in South Korea was the second major push factor to the massive Korean emigration to the United States. In addition, the military and political tensions between South Korea and North Korea, and fear of another war in the Korean peninsula also pushed many high-class Koreans to take refuge in the United States. Finally, various difficulties in giving their children a college education in Korea due to extreme competition in admissions and high tuitions played another important role in the exodus of many Koreans to the United States during the period.

Without a doubt, better economic and educational opportunities in the United States served as major push-pull factors in Korean immigrants' personal decisions for U.S.-bound emigration. But we cannot explain the mass migration of Koreans to the United States by Koreans' individual psychological motivations alone. As previously pointed out, we also need to pay attention to the fact that the strong U.S.-Korean military, political and economic linkages served as important structural factors that significantly contributed to Koreans' mass migration to the United States. South Korea probably has maintained closer military and political relations with the United States than any other Asian country, which has contributed to the influx of Korean immigrants. The continuing presence of the sizeable U.S. forces (approximately 40,000) in Korea until recently contributed to the migration of many Korean women through their marriages to American servicemen. The migration of Korean wives of U.S. servicemen provides the basis for subsequent kin-based immigration. Moreover, close U.S.-Korean ties, the presence of U.S. forces in Korea, and the postgraduate training of many Korean intellectuals in the United States popularized American culture in Korea.

Figure 2.1: Number of Korean Immigrants (by Country of Birth) to the U.S., 1965 – 2009

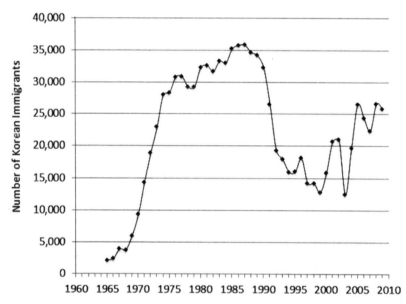

Sources: Immigration and Naturalization Service, *Annual Reports*, 1965-1978 and *Statistical Yearbook*, 1979-2001; Office of Immigration Statistics, *Yearbook of Immigration Statistics*, 2002-2009

Figure 2.1 shows that in 1991, there was a big reduction (almost 8,000 from the previous year), well below 30,000, in the annual number of Korean immigrants. The number continued to decline in the 1990s, reaching the lowest point (12,840) in 1999. By contrast, the total number of immigrants to the United States and numbers of immigrants from other Asian countries increased phenomenally in the 1990s compared to the previous decade. The increase in the U.S. immigration flow in the 1990s was due mainly to the effect of the Immigration Act of 1990 that raised the total number of immigrants to 675,000. This means that Korean immigrants became a smaller group relative to other major immigrant groups.

It is not difficult to explain why the Korean immigration flow declined drastically in the 1990s. To put it simply, the great improvements in economic and political conditions in Korea did not push too many Koreans to seek international migration in the United States or other Western countries. First of all, South Korea improved its economic conditions significantly, which is reflected by the per capita income of nearly $6,000 in 1990 (Min 2006d). Korea's per capita income reached almost $10,000 in 2000. The advanced economy in Korea was able to absorb college-educated work forces and even attract American-educated professionals and managers. South Korea also improved its political conditions through a popular election in 1987, putting an end to the twenty-six-year old military dictatorship. Before that, many American-educated Koreans had been reluctant to return to Korea for their careers due to lack of political freedom.

Also, as Korea improved its economic conditions, fewer and fewer Korean women married American servicemen beginning in the late 1980s. In addition, the media exposure in South Korea of Korean immigrants' adjustment difficulties in the United States discouraged Koreans from seeking U.S.-bound emigration. In particular, the victimization of more than 2,000 Korean merchants during the 1992 Los Angeles riots was widely publicized in Korea (Min 1996). Popularization of air travel enabled many Koreans to visit their friends and relatives in American cities and witness the latters' long hours of work under difficult conditions. By the early 1990s, Koreans' perception of the United States as a land of prosperity and security began to change.

The annual number of Korean immigrants steadily decreased in the 1990s, dropping to 12,840 in 1999. But it began to increase again beginning in 2000, and was hovering around 25,000 in the latter half of the 2000s, with the exception of the 2003 anomaly (only 12,512). The annual numbers of Korean immigrants in the later 2000s were substantially smaller than those of Korean immigrants during the peak years between 1976 and 1990 (30,000 and 35,000), but much larger than those in the 1990s.

I believe there are two major factors that contributed to the significant increase in the number of Korean immigrants beginning in 2000. One factor seems to be a high unemployment rate in Korea that started with the financial crisis in 1998. According to Korean real estate agents, a large number of people who had lost their jobs in Korea came to the United States in 1999 and the ensuing years to find jobs in Korean-owned stores or even to explore the possibility of starting businesses. Many of these temporary residents seem to have changed their status to permanent residents in later years.

The other and more important contributing factor is a radical increase in the number of temporary Korean residents in major Korean immigrant communities in the United States. Under the impact of globalization and by virtue of technological advances, relocation from one country to another has become much easier than before. During recent years, large numbers of Koreans visited the United

States for various purposes: to study, to get training and internships, to see their family members and relatives, for temporary work, for sightseeing and so forth. Many of them continue to stay here beyond the time period for which they originally intended to stay. Many others have changed their status to permanent residents. This will be discussed in more detail in the final section of this chapter.

We noted above that the economic and political problems in Korea that pushed many Koreans out of the country for emigration in earlier years were greatly mitigated in the early 1990s, which contributed to a significant reduction of the Korean immigration flow. But one thing that has pushed Koreans out of the country for emigration remains unchanged. That is the difficulty in providing their children with a college education. The number of colleges and universities has greatly increased in Korea during recent years. Thus, unlike twenty-five years ago, high-school graduates can now gain admission to a college if they choose one. But there is even more intense competition for admissions to decent universities than before, and without graduating from decent universities, they have little chance to find meaningful occupations in Korea. Therefore, many parents try to send their children to the United States and other English-speaking countries for a better college education than in Korea. Better opportunity for their children's college education and their own graduate education is now the most important motivation for Koreans' decisions to immigrate to the United States.

Korean Immigrants' Entry Mechanisms and Gender

According to the Immigration Act of 1965, aliens are eligible for immigration to the United States using one of three mechanisms: (1) family reunification, (2) occupational immigration, and (3) refugee/asylum status and other categories of aliens eligible for immigration by special measures. Koreans can become immigrants to the United States mainly using the first two mechanisms. The Immigration Act of 1965 has gone through three major revisions, respectively in 1976, 1986, and 1990. Among them, the Immigration Act of 1990 has brought about the most significant changes to the original immigration law passed by Congress in 1965. It raised the annual number of total immigrants to 675,000 and also the annual number of professional and managerial immigrants to 144,000, almost three times as high as before. In addition, it also allowed for admission of 195,000 temporary workers in specialty occupations, largely in professional and managerial fields, each year.

Figure 2.2 shows immigration mechanisms for total U.S. immigrants and Korean immigrants between 1965 and 2009 by year. The Immigration Act of 1965 determined immigration mechanisms for 1966 through 1991, while the

Immigration Act of 1990 affected mechanisms for 1992 through 2009. Under the Immigration Act of 1965, spouses and unmarried children of naturalized citizens (First Preference) and immigrants (Second Preference) were allowed to immigrate to the United States exempt from the numerical limitation of 20,000 immigrants per country per year. Naturalized citizens' married children (Fourth Preference) and siblings (Fifth Preference) were admitted subject to the numerical limitation. It assigned two categories to occupational immigration: Third Preference (professional/technical and administrative/managerial immigrants) and Sixth Preference (other occupational immigrants).

Figure 2.2 reveals that the majority of annual immigrants to the United States for most of the 1965-1991 years were immediate family members of naturalized citizens and permanent residents who were exempt from the numerical limitation. The second category of immigrants consisted of those who used two relative preference categories (naturalized citizens' married children and siblings). This category was smaller than that consisting of immediate family members, but much larger than that consisting of two occupational-preference immigrants. Occupational immigrants on the third column composed less than 10% of total immigrants to the United States for each year during the period.

The immigration mechanisms of Korean immigrants differ significantly from those of U.S. immigrants as a whole during the 1966-1991 period. In the late 1960s and the early 1970s, immediate family members of naturalized citizens and permanent residents comprised the majority of Korean immigrants. The immigration of large numbers of Korean adoptees and "war brides" during the period contributed significantly to this trend. Also, occupational immigrants accounted for a larger percentage of Korean immigrants than total U.S. immigrants during this period. This is due to the fact that many Korean professionals, especially medical professionals, entered the United States as immigrants during the period.

But Korean immigrants experienced changes in their immigration mechanisms after the mid-1970s. While the proportion of relative-preference immigrants (naturalized citizens' brothers and sisters) achieved a gradual increase after the mid-1970s, the percentage of occupational immigrants decreased to less than 10%. The increase in the proportion of relative-preference immigrants was due mainly to the fact that many Korean immigrants had become naturalized citizens by the mid-1970s and thus were able to invite their brothers and sisters. The 1976 Amendments to the 1965 Immigration Act that made it more difficult for alien professionals to immigrate to the United States.[2] is primarily responsible for the great reduction in the number of occupational immigrants in the late 1970s and the 1980s.

Figure 2.2: Mechanisms of Koreans' Immigration to the U.S., 1966 – 2009
(a) Total Immigrants in the United States

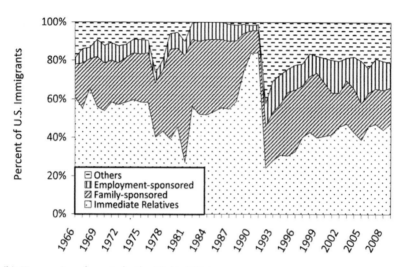

(b) Korean Immigrants in the United States

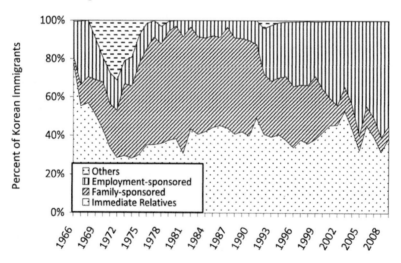

Sources: Immigration and Naturalization Service, *Annual Reports*, 1965-1978 and *Statistical Yearbook*, 1979-2001; Office of Immigration Statistics, *Yearbook of Immigration Statistics*, 2002-2009.
Note: Others include refugees/asylum adjusters, diversity immigrants, and non-preference immigrants for all years. Beneficiaries of Immigration Reform and Control Act were included in the immediate relatives category for 1966-1991, but in the other category for 1992-2009.

The Immigration Act of 1990 not only increased the total number of immigrants to the United States, but also changed entry mechanisms, especially by elevating the proportion of occupational immigrants. We can see the effects of the revised immigration law in U.S. immigration patterns during the 1992-2009 years. Before 1992, immediate relatives (spouses, unmarried children and parents) of U.S. citizens and those (spouses and unmarried children) of permanent residents were included in the same broad category that was exempt from the numerical limitation. But from 1992 onward, immediate relatives of U.S. citizens were included in one category, with those (spouses and unmarried children) of permanent residents, along with married children and siblings of naturalized citizens, included in another category. By separating immediate relatives of naturalized citizens from those of permanent residents, the Immigration Act of 1990 emphasized the importance of immigrants getting American citizenship.

As a result of this separation, the proportion of immigrants in the first category was reduced significantly from 1992 on. In turn, the family-sponsored preference category was supposed to increase, but did not. This means that the annual number of immigrants admitted through the mechanism of naturalized citizens' siblings decreased in the 1992-2009 period. Recently, the U.S. government seems to have discouraged American citizens' brothers and sisters from immigrating to the United States by making them wait longer, approximately twelve years. In the meantime, there was a substantial increase in the proportion of the third category, occupational immigrants. The proportion of refugee/asylum immigrants also increased significantly in the 1992-2009 period, which reflects the U.S. government's active military and political interventions in world affairs in the post-Cold War era.

An important aspect of the changes in Koreans' immigration mechanisms is that the proportion of family-sponsored preference immigrants, especially those based on the mechanism of U.S. citizens' siblings, decreased significantly in the 2000s, with a concomitant increase in the proportion of occupational immigrants. The proportion of Korean occupational immigrants and their family members doubled between 1991 and 1992, and continued to increase every year until it reached 60% in 2005. In all but one year between 2005 and 2009, occupational immigrants composed the majority of Korean immigrants. In every year between 1992 and 2009, the proportion of Korean employment-sponsored immigrants was much larger than that of total U.S. immigrants, by two to four times. It can safely be said that employment-sponsored immigration has replaced family-sponsored immigration as the dominant form of Korean immigration to the United States during recent years.

Table 2.1 compares Korean immigrants with other Asian immigrant groups in the proportions of the two highest-status specialty occupations (technical/professional and administrative/managerial). Most immigrants either did not have an occupation in their home countries or did not report it when they may have actually had them. Thus immigration data seems to have overestimated immigrants' occupational statuses, because those with lower-status occupations were less likely to have reported them. Nevertheless, the data roughly reflects their occupational backgrounds. The data seem to be useful especially for the purpose of comparing different Asian immigrant groups because overestimation of occupational statuses is likely to have uniformly influenced data for all groups.

Table 2.1: Percentage of Immigrants in Technical/Professional and Administrative/Managerial Occupations among Asian Immigrants by Country of Birth, 1965-2009

	China	India	Korea	Philippines	Taiwan	Vietnam
1965	16.3	59.7	59.8	41.4	--	--
1970	51.1	89.1	68.3	68.8	--	51.8
1975	47.3	82.9	51.5	60.6	--	53.0
1979	45.6	68.0	44.5	40.8	--	20.3
1985	29.5	62.2	45.3	42.7	65.0	10.7
1990	29.7	54.2	40.4	45.8	65.7	6.0
1995	33.0	66.9	48.3	51.3	65.6	4.6
2000	50.8	74.9	55.7	59.7	72.4	10.3
2001	69.1	84.9	61.3	56.1	78.1	9.5
2003	39.2	72.3	57.3	56.8	78.1	12.5
2004	55.0	81.4	60.2	57.3	79.2	13.8
2005	50.7	77.4	66.1	58.6	79.2	12.8
2006	27.4	57.2	64.8	57.8	70.5	12.7
2007	33.3	68.8	69.7	49.6	71.8	12.8
2008	35.7	70.7	77.5	43.0	77.3	15.0
2009	35.4	69.4	75.4	43.6	75.2	16.6

Sources : Immigration and Naturalization Service, *Annual Reports*, 1965-1978 and *Statistical Yearbook*, 1979-2001; Office of Immigration Statistics, *Yearbook of Immigration Statistics*, 2002-2009
Note: No data are available for occupations in 1980 and 2002. No data are available for Taiwanese immigrants for 1965, 1970, 1975, 1979 and Vietnamese immigrants for 1965.

The 1990 and 2000 Censuses showed that Indian and Taiwanese immigrants had the highest occupational and educational levels among all immigrant groups, substantially higher than those of other Asian immigrant groups (Min 2006c; Rumbaut 1996). But beginning in 2000 the proportion of Korean immigrants in two specialty occupational categories reached 60% and slowly increased over the years. Three major factors seem to have contributed to recent Korean immigrants' exceptionally high occupational levels. First, the Immigration Act of 1990 raised the numbers of immigrants and temporary workers in specialty occupations to make U.S. corporations competitive in the global labor market. Given that the proportions of Korean and other Asian immigrants in specialty occupations have radically increased with a concomitant decline in the proportions of family-sponsored immigrants during recent years, the U.S. government seems to have taken special measures to bring highly educated immigrants and to discourage family-sponsored immigrants. Second, the rapid increase in the number of Korean international students, including early-study students, during recent years also seems to have contributed to upgrading recent Korean immigrants' occupational statuses. As will be discussed in more detail in the next section, a significant proportion of Korean international students seem to have changed their status to permanent residents after they completed their education and found meaningful occupations in the United States. Third, the difficulty in finding professional and managerial occupations in Korea is likely to have pushed many Korean college graduates to enter the United States as temporary workers (with H1-B visa) or as occupational immigrants in specialty occupations. These two issues will be discussed in more detail in the next section.

The adoption of alien orphans by American citizens has become an important mechanism for the immigration of Korean children to the United States. During the Korean War, American servicemen began to adopt Korean orphans. The adoption of Korean children by American citizens was expanded after the Korean War. Annual Reports/Yearbooks of Immigration began to include statistics on adoptees beginning in 1976. As shown in Table 2.2, Korean adoptees composed the majority of adoptees by American citizens between 1976 and 1985. As South Korea improved its economic conditions, the number of Korean adoptees began to decrease in 1989, but until 1994 it was the largest source country of adoptees to the United States. Beginning in 1995, China emerged as the largest source country of adoptees by American citizens, with South Korea falling to third place. Even in the 2000s, South Korea remained as one of the five largest source countries of adoptees, but the number of Korean adoptees was reduced to about 1,000 in the last two years. Large numbers of Korean adoptees have been also sent to other Western countries, mostly to European countries, including France, Sweden, Denmark, and Netherlands (E. Kim 2010).

Despite the significant decrease in their entry during the most recent years, Korean adoptees still compose the largest alien group of adoptees to American families. Shiao, Tuan and Riezi (2004) estimated that approximately 100,000 Korean children had been adopted by American citizens by 2000. Using data released by South Korean Ministry of Health, Welfare, and Family Affairs, Eleana Kim (2010) reported that 109,242 Korean children were adopted to families in the United States between 1953 and 2008. This means that Korean adoptees have increased to over 110,000 at present. But Chinese adoptees soon will outnumber Korean adoptees in the United States, as a huge number of them have annually immigrated during recent years and will continue to do so in the near future.[3] It seems apparent that white American citizens prefer adopting East Asian children over other groups of children, which is why so many Korean and Chinese children have been adopted.

Table 2.2: Number of Korean Adoptees Admitted to the U.S. as Immigrants by Country of Birth and Five Largest Source Countries of Adoptees, 1976-2009

The Immigration of Koreans to the United States   21

Year	Total Number of Adoptees	Korean Adoptees	Korean Adoptees as Percentage of Total Adoptees	The Largest Source Country	The Second Largest Source Country	The Third Largest Source Country	The Fourth Largest Source Country	The Fifth Largest Source Country
1976	8,550	4,847	56.7	Korea	Vietnam (747)	Colombia (732)	Philippines (401)	Thailand (202)
1977	6,493	3,858	59.4	Korea	Colombia (575)	Vietnam (347)	Philippines (325)	Mexico (156)
1978	5,315	3,045	57.3	Korea	Colombia (599)	Philippines (287)	India (152), Mexico (152)	
1979	4,864	2,406	49.5	Korea	Colombia (626)	Philippines (297)	India (231)	Austria (141)
1980	5,139	2,683	52.2	Korea	Colombia (653)	Philippines (253)	India (319)	El Salvador (179)
1981	4,868	2,444	50.2	Korea	Colombia (628)	Philippines (278)	India (314)	El Salvador (224)
1982	5,749	3,254	56.6	Korea	Colombia (534)	Philippines (345)	India (409)	El Salvador (199)
1983	7,127	4,412	61.9	Korea	Colombia (608)	Philippines (302)	India (409)	El Salvador (240)
1984	8,327	5,157	61.9	Korea	Colombia (595)	Philippines (408)	India (314)	El Salvador (224)
1985	9,286	5,694	61.3	Korea	Colombia (622)	Philippines (515)	India (496)	El Salvador (310)
1989	7,948	3,552	44.7	Korea	Colombia (735)	India (677)	Philippines (481)	Peru (269)
1990	7,088	2,603	36.7	Korea	Colombia (628)	Peru (441)	Philippines (423)	India (361)
1991	9,008	1,817	20.2	Romania (2,552)	Korea	Peru (722)	Colombia (527)	India (448)
1992	6,536	1,787	27.3	Korea	Soviet Union (432)	Guatemala (423)	Colombia (403)	Philippines (353)
1993	7,348	1,765	24.0	Korea	Russia (695)	Guatemala (512)	Colombia (416)	Paraguay (405)
1994	8,200	1,757	21.4	Korea	Russia (1,324)	China (748)	Paraguay (497)	Guatemala (431)
1995	9,384	1,570	16.7	China (2,049)	Russia (1,684)	Korea	Guatemala (436)	India (368)
1996	11,316	1,580	13.9	China (3,318)	Russia (2,328)	Korea	Romania (554)	Guatemala (420)
1997	12,596	1,506	11.9	Russia (3,626)	China (3,295)	Korea	Guatemala (725)	Romania (558)
1998	14,867	1,705	11.5	Russia (4,320)	China (3,988)	Korea	Guatemala (938)	India (462)
1999	16,037	1,956	12.2	Russia (4,250)	China (4,009)	Korea	Guatemala (987)	Romania (887)
2000	18,120	1,711	9.4	China (4,943)	Russia (4,210)	Korea	Guatemala (1,504)	Romania (1,103)
2001	19,087	1,863	9.8	China (4,629)	Russia (4,210)	Korea	Guatemala (1,601)	Ukraine (1,227)
2002	21,100	1,713	8.1	China (6,062)	Russia (4,904)	Guatemala (2,361)	Korea	Ukraine (1,093)
2003	21,320	1,793	8.4	China (6,638)	Russia (5,134)	Guatemala (2,327)	Korea	Kazakhstan (819)
2004	22,911	1,708	7.5	China (7,033)	Russia (5,878)	Guatemala (3,252)	Korea	Kazakhstan (824)
2005	22,710	1,604	7.1	China (7,939)	Russia (4,652)	Guatemala (3,748)	Korea	Ukraine (841)

			of Total Adoptees			Country	Country	Country
2006	20,705	1,381	6.7	China (6,520)	Guatemala (4,093)	Russia (3,710)	Korea	Ethiopia (711)
2007	19,471	945	4.9	China (5,397)	Guatemala (4,721)	Russia (2,301)	Ethiopia (1,203)	Korea
2008	17,229	1,038	6.0	Guatemala (4,082)	China (3,852)	Russia (1,859)	Ethiopia (1,666)	Korea
2009	12,782	1,106	8.7	China (2,990)	Ethiopia (2,221)	Russia (1,580)	Korea	Guatemala (773)
Total	371,481	74,260	19.99	--	--	--	--	--

Sources : Immigration and Naturalization Service, *Statistical Yearbook*, 1979-2001; Office of Immigration Statistics, *Yearbook of Immigration Statistics*, 2002-2009
Note: Data on adoptees are not available for 1986-1988.

Figure 2.3 shows the change over time in the proportion of Korean female immigrants between 1965 and 2009. Women composed over 80% of all Korean immigrants in 1965, but it continued to decline, reaching less than 60% in 1975. We can explain women's overrepresentation among Korean immigrants by looking at particular mechanisms of Korean immigration, which is why this topic is discussed in this section.

Women composed the vast majority of Korean immigrants in the latter half of the 1960s and the first half of the 1970s because wives of U.S. servicemen, adoptees, and nurses made up the majority of Korean immigrants during the period. During this early period, the vast majority of Korean adoptees were girls (E. Kim 2010). But, as previously noted, these three groups of Korean immigrants grew smaller and smaller as time passed. Korean immigrants maintained a complete gender balance in 1981, but the proportion of women hovered around 55% between 1982 and 2009.

The major contributing factor to a slight gender imbalance in favor of women among Korean immigrants during recent years seems to be a greater tendency of Korean women both in Korea and in the United States to marry non-Korean American partners. Korean women's marriages to U.S. servicemen in Korea have been drastically reduced during recent years, as Korea has made a significant improvement in economic conditions. Also, the U.S. forces in South Korea have been scaled down to less than 20,000. However, many women in Korea have married American citizens in Korea and some of them have immigrated to the United States. Also, regardless of their generation, far more Korean American women than men have married non-Korean partners (Min and Kim 2009). This means that more Korean American men than women have brought their spouses from Korea.

Figure 2.3: Proportion of Women among Korean Immigrants (by Country of Birth), 1965-2009

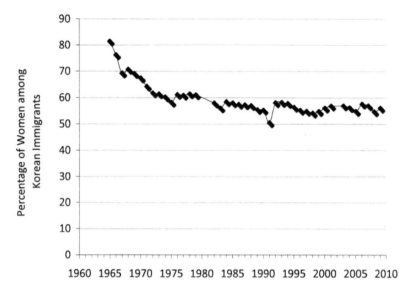

Sources: Immigration and Naturalization Service, *Annual Reports*, 1965-1978 and *Statistical Yearbook*, 1979-2001; Office of Immigration Statistics, *Yearbook of Immigration Statistics*, 2002-2009
Note: Data on gender are not available for 1980, 1981, 2002.

The Radical Increase in Status Adjusters

Annual immigrants in the United States consist of two groups: (1) new arrivals and (2) status adjusters. Status adjusters are those who entered the United States previously on another, non-immigrant status and changed their status to permanent residents in a given year. New arrivals are those who have been admitted as immigrants to the United States directly from a particular source country. Figure 2.4 shows changes over the years in the proportion of status adjusters among Korean immigrants.

Status adjusters comprised 20% to 35% of annual Korean immigrants during the period between 1967 and 1972. But the proportion declined gradually, reaching the lowest proportion (about 5%) in 1976. The 1967-1972 Korean immigrants included a fairly high proportion of status adjusters mainly because many Korean professionals, especially medical professionals, who had received graduate education or internship in the United States, legalized their status to permanent residents using the Preference 3 category of the Immigration Act of 1965. But the percentage of status-adjusted Korean immigrants decreased in the 1970s and 1980s because many state governments' laws in the early 1970s and ultimately the 1976 Amendments to the Immigration Act of 1965 made it difficult for professionals to immigrate to the United States. The financial crisis in the mid-1970s in the United States led U.S. policymakers to take measures to make it difficult for alien professionals to legalize as immigrants. Lobbies by medical professional associations also contributed to the change.

Figure 2.4: Percentage of Status Adjusters among Korean Immigrants (by Country of Birth), 1965-2009

Sources: Immigration and Naturalization Service, *Annual Reports*, 1965-1978 and *Statistical Yearbook*, 1979-2001; Office of Immigration Statistics, *Yearbook of Immigration Statistics*, 2002-2009
Note: Data on status adjusters are not available for 2003-2005.

The percentage of status adjusters among Korean immigrants gradually increased beginning in 1988 and skyrocketed in the new century. The radical increase in the 1990s and later seems to have been due mainly to the fact that many Korean international students changed their status after completion of their education in the United States. The 1990 Immigration Act tripled the number of professional and managerial immigrants. This act made it easier for Korean and other Asian international students to legally become permanent residents when they completed their undergraduate or graduate education.

As a result of globalization, the percentage of status adjusters has increased over the years for almost all major immigrant groups. But Table 2.3 shows that Korean immigrants have a substantially larger proportion of status adjusters (81%) than total immigrants to the United States (59%) and all Asian immigrants (56%). We need to explain why over 80% of recent Korean immigrants consist of status adjusters, compared to only about 55% for other major immigrant groups.

Table 2.3: Percentage of Status Adjusters among Korean Immigrants (by Country of Birth) Compared to Other Groups by Region of Origin, 2009

	Number of Total Immigrants	Number of Status Adjusters	Percentage of Status Adjusters
Korea	25,859	20,805	80.5
Asia	413,312	229,293	55.5
The Caribbean	146,127	76,345	52.3
Latin America	150,746	100,899	66.9
All Countries	1,130,818	667,776	59.1

Source: Office of Immigration Statistics, *Yearbook of Immigration Statistics*, 2009.

There seem to be two major reasons for an extremely high proportion of status-adjusters among Korean immigrants during recent years. One is the presence of a huge number of Korean international students in the United States, many of whom change their status after completion of their undergraduate and/or graduate education here. The other reason is the presence of many Korean short-term or long-term visitors to the United States, many of whom also change their status to permanent residents. The presence of extremely large numbers of Korean students and non-student visitors in the United States relative to the Korean population is possible mainly because of the strong long-term ties between the United States and South Korea.

As shown in Table 2.4, the number of Korean international students enrolled in U.S. undergraduate and graduate programs steadily increased since 1995, reaching 72,000 in 2009. It is estimated that approximately 86,400 Korean international students and their family members were in the United States in 2009.[4] South Korea is not far behind China and India in the number of international students, although the total Chinese and Indian populations are much larger than the Korean population, by more than twenty times, respectively. The statistics give us an idea of the overrepresentation of Korean international students in the United States. Korean students' visits to foreign countries for undergraduate and postgraduate education are not limited to the United States. There are large numbers of Korean college students in other English-speaking countries, such as Canada, Australia, and Great Britain. English-language skills and the rank of the college are probably the two most important factors for the job market in Korea. Thus parents are anxious to send their children to English-speaking countries for their children's college education as an alternative to a college education in second- or third-class colleges in Korea.

Table 2.4: Annual Number of International Students for Top Three Countries of Origin

	Total Inter-	Annual Number of	Annual Number of	Annual Number of

Year	national Students in the U.S. (A)	Chinese Students		Indian Students		Korean Students	
	N	N	% of (A)	N	% of (A)	N	% of (A)
1995/96	453,787	39,613	8.7	31,743	7.0	NA	-
1996/97	457,984	42,503	9.3	30,641	6.7	NA	-
1997/98	481,280	46,958	9.8	33,818	7.0	42,890	8.9
1998/99	490,933	51,001	10.4	37,482	7.6	39,199	8.0
1999/00	514,723	54,466	10.6	42,337	8.2	41,191	8.0
2000/01	547,867	59,939	10.9	54,664	10.0	45,685	8.3
2001/02	582,996	63,211	10.8	66,836	11.5	49,046	8.4
2002/03	586,323	64,757	11.0	74,603	12.7	51,519	8.8
2003/04	572,509	61,765	10.8	79,736	13.9	52,484	9.2
2004/05	565,039	62,523	11.1	80,466	14.2	53,358	9.4
2005/06	564,766	62,582	11.1	76,503	13.5	59,022	10.5
2006/07	582,984	67,723	11.6	83,833	14.4	62,392	10.7
2007/08	623,805	81,127	13.0	94,563	15.2	69,124	11.1
2008/09	671,616	98,235	14.6	103,260	15.4	75,065	11.2
2009/10	690,923	127,628	18.5	104,897	15.2	72,153	10.4

Source: Institute of International Education

Statistics on international students in Table 2.4 do not include early-study students who came to the United States for elementary and secondary education. As shown in Figure 2.5, more than 25,000 Korean elementary- and secondary-school students left Korea annually for studies abroad during recent years. Nearly 5,000 additional elementary- and secondary-school students also left Korea annually, accompanied by their parents who were dispatched abroad as exchange visitors, trainers, temporary workers or intra-company transferees. About one-third of early-study and parent-accompanied students (about 9,000 each year) seem to have come to the United States annually (Ministry of Education, Science and Technology 2010). Early-study students include those who came here with their mothers while their fathers stayed to earn a living in Korea. These internationally-split families are commonly referred to as *kirogi gazok* (geese families). Most early-study students return to Korea after a few years of education in the United States. But a significant proportion of them continue to stay here for a college education. When we include these early-study students, the total number of Korean international students and their family members in the United States in 2009 may have been over 110,000. They account for about 10% of the foreign-born Korean in this country.[5]

Figure 2.5: Annual Number of Korean Elementary and Secondary Students Who Went Abroad for Study

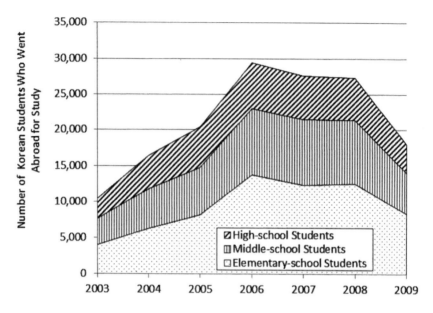

Sources: Center for Education Statistics, Korean Educational Development Institute, 2008 (Statistics on Elementary and Secondary School Students who went Abroad; http://cesi.kedi.re.kr)

A huge number of Korean international students contributed to the presence of an unusually large number of temporary residents in the Korean immigrant community. Korean international students who have completed their education in the United States have an advantage over college graduates in Korea in finding specialty occupations here. As shown in the previous section, the proportion of Korean occupational immigrants (and their family members) has increased since 1988, becoming the majority of annual Korean immigrants since 2005 (see Figure 2.2). Consistently, the proportion of Korean professional and managerial immigrants has steadily increased since 1990 (see Table 2.1). Moreover, many other Korean international students are likely to have become permanent residents through their marriages to Korean or non-Korean partners in the United States. Those Koreans who came to the United States at early ages and completed their undergraduate or graduate education here are more likely to change their status to live here permanently than Korean adult international students. Accordingly, the proportion of Korean status adjusters may comprise a higher proportion in the coming years.

The presence of many other Korean non-student visitors also contributes to the exceptionally high proportion of Korean status-adjusted immigrants. Due to close U.S.-Korean relationships, huge numbers of non-student Koreans visit the United States each year and many of them stay as temporary residents for short or extended periods of time. These non-immigrant and non-student temporary residents include exchange scholars and trainees, temporary workers, visitors for businesses or sightseeing, and intra-company transferees with their family members. Figure 2.6 shows that there were less than 5,000 Korean visitors to the United States in 1965. But the number rapidly increased, jumping to over 100,000 in 1985 and reaching almost 700,000 in 1995. It rose to 900,000 in 2009. The U.S. government accepted South Korea as a visa-waiver country in 2008. That most likely encouraged more Koreans to visit the United States. But economic recessions (in both South Korea and the United States) in 2008 and 2009 seem to have had a neutralizing effect on the visa-waiving advantage for Koreans' travels to the United States. More than one million Koreans are likely to have visited the United States in 2010, as the economy had improved in both countries.

Figure 2.6: Number of Korean Visitors (Non-immigrants) to the U.S., 1965 – 2009

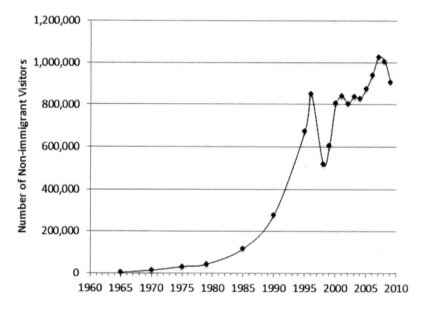

Sources: Immigration and Naturalization Service, *Annual Reports*, 1965-1978 and *Statistical Yearbook*, 1979-2001; Office of Immigration Statistics, *Yearbook of Immigration Statistics*, 2002-2009
Note: Data on non-immigrants are not available for 1980, 1997.

Members of all non-immigrant temporary resident groups have the potential to be status-adjusted immigrants in the future. Many Korean international students find jobs as temporary workers when they complete their undergraduate or graduate education, and then become permanent residents by legalizing their status through sponsorships by their employers. Middle-aged and elderly family members who were invited by their immigrant children can apply for green cards when their children become naturalized. Moreover, members of all groups of temporary residents can change their status to permanent residents by marrying Korean or non-Korean partners here.

The Immigration Act of 1990 raised not only the number of professional and managerial immigrants, but also the number of temporary workers (H-1B) in the same high-status occupations up to 195,000.[6] Computer-based professional occupations make up the majority of temporary-work specialty occupations. As shown in Figure 2.7, Korean immigrants included a small number of temporary workers in the early years. But the number jumped to over 5,000 in 2000 and continued to increase until it reached over 11,000 in 2007. South Korea has become one of the six or seven top source countries of temporary workers in the United States in specialty occupations, following India, China, the Philippines, Taiwan, Germany, and Canada.

Some H-1B temporary workers came directly from Korea to the United States. Others are international students in the United States who have changed their status to temporary workers. Still other temporary workers previously entered the United States as visitors for sightseeing and may have received temporary work visas. The implication of the increase in Korean temporary workers in specialty occupations is that temporary workers can change their status to permanent residents more easily than other groups of Korean temporary residents. Considering that such large numbers of temporary visas were given to Koreans in the decade of the 2000s, the immigration flow of Koreans in the 2010s is likely to rise beyond the 2009 level of 25,000.

Figure 2.7: Number of Korean Temporary Workers in the U.S., 1965 – 2010

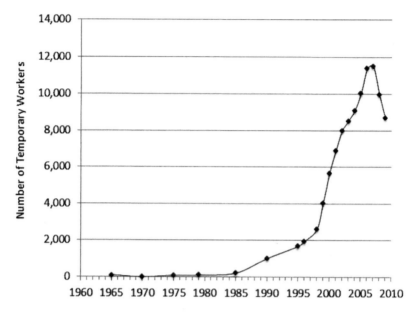

Sources: Immigration and Naturalization Service, *Annual Reports*, 1965-1978 and *Statistical Yearbook*, 1979-2001; Office of Immigration Statistics, *Yearbook of Immigration Statistics*, 2002-2009
Note: Data on non-immigrants are not available for 1980, 1997.

Summary and Conclusion

To summarize changes over time in patterns of Koreans' immigration to the United States, the annual number of Korean immigrants gradually increased for the first ten years, reached the peak between 1976 and 1990, gradually decreased in the 1990s, and slightly increased in the 2000s again. Lack of job opportunity, the difficulty in sending their children to colleges, and political and social instability served as major push factors for Koreans' mass emigration to the United States up to 1980s. Significant improvements in economic, political and social conditions in South Korea contributed to the reduction of Koreans' immigration to the United States in the 1990s. But the advantage of getting an English-language college education still remains a very important pull factor for Koreans' massive immigration and non-immigrant movement to the United States. In addition, the close U.S.-Korean military, political and economic linkages become a major factor that explains why South Korea sent the second largest immigrant group next to the Philippines among Asian countries between 1976 and 1990. And the movement of so many Koreans to the United States under the impact of globalization best explains a moderate increase in the Korean immigration flow in the 2000s.

At the end of the 1960s and early 1970s, professionals, especially medical professionals, composed a significant proportion of Korean immigrants. But the proportion decreased as the U.S. government took measures in 1976 to make it more difficult for professionals to immigrate. But, as Korean immigrants admitted in the late 1960s and early 1970s became naturalized citizens, they were able to invite their siblings for permanent residence in the United States, gradually increasing the proportion of Korean family-sponsored immigrants. However, as the Immigration Act of 1990 raised the number of professional and managerial immigrants by three times, the proportion of Korean immigrants in these specialty occupations gradually increased with a concomitant decrease in the proportion of family-sponsored Korean immigrants. Professional and managerial immigrants and their family members comprised the majority of Korean immigrants in four of the last five years. Korean international students who completed their education in the United States and college graduates in Korea fill up immigration quotas for specialty occupations. The immigration of large numbers of well-educated Koreans in specialty occupations during recent years has upgraded the socioeconomic background of Korean immigrants.

Korean international students enrolled in colleges and universities, early-study students, exchange visitors, employees of American branches of Korean firms, and other visitors comprise a much larger proportion of the Korean population in the United States now than thirty years ago. As a result, more than 80% of the 2009 Korean immigrants were status adjusters from these temporary resident statuses. The prevalence of status adjusters among Korean immigrants compared to other immigrant groups suggests that the Korean community has more non-immigrant temporary residents in proportion to the population size. Two interrelated factors, technological advances and globalization, have contributed to the radical increase in the non-immigrant temporary resident population for all U.S. immigrant groups. But, due to the close military, political, economic and cultural linkages between the United States and South Korea, the Korean immigrant community seems to have a substantially larger proportion of temporary residents than other Asian communities.

The Koreans who legalized their status to permanent residents through employment-sponsored categories in specialty occupations during recent years are generally young, with most of them having completed their undergraduate and/or graduate education in the United States. These young Korean immigrant work forces, unlike U.S.-born second-generation Koreans, are fluent in Korean and practice Korean culture actively here, while they are also fluent in English. As a result, the Korean community has many fluently bilingual young people who can bridge the gap between the middle-aged immigrant generation and the American-born second generation. The proportion of this fluently bilingual young immigrant generation is likely to continue to increase in the future. Moreover, the presence of so many international students and other temporary residents, in addition to these young fluently bilingual immigrants, has helped the Korean community maintain far more transnational ties with South Korea than before. Of course, technological advances are the other important contributing factor to Korean Americans' strong transnational ties to South Korea.

Notes

1. This chapter was presented as Research Report 3 for the Research Center for Korean Community at Korea Village-Open Center in Flushing, New York City in January 2011. It was also published in *Development and Society* 40 (2011): 195-223. I would like to express my thanks to Saehee Kim for analyzing immigration data efficiently for tables and figures included in this chapter.

2. Before 1976, foreigners with medical certificates were eligible for immigration to the United States. The 1976 Amendments to the 1965 Immigration Act required foreign medical professionals to get job offers from American companies to be eligible for immigration. They also needed to gain satisfactory scores in TOEFL to get medical licenses in the United States.

3. The one-child policy of China has recently led many Chinese parents with two or more children to give up their children for adoption by American citizens.

4. On average, one Korean international student has 1.2 household members including himself/herself.

5. It is estimated that single-race Korean Americans composed approximately 1.6 million in 2009. Assuming about 70% of Korean Americans were immigrants, there were approximately 1.1 million Korean immigrants in the year.

6. The U.S. government raised the number of temporary workers in specialty occupations in order to help American corporations become globally competitive by hiring needed workers in particular specialty areas quickly on a temporary basis and cheaply, and then discard them easily when they do not need them.

References

Castles, Stephen. 2000. "International Migration at the Beginning of the Twenty-First Century: Global Trends and Issues." *International Social Science Journal* 165: 269-281.
_____. 2002. "Migration and Community Formation under Conditions of Globalization." *International Migration Review* 36: 1143-1168.
Kim, Eleana. 2010. *Adopted Territories: Transnational Adoptees and the Politics of Belonging.* Durham, NC: Duke University Press.
Kim, Illsoo. 1981. *New Urban Immigrants: The Korean Community in New York.* Princeton, NJ: Princeton University Press.
_____. 1987. "Korea and East Asia: Remigration Factors and U.S. Immigration Policy." In *Pacific Bridges: The New Immigration from Asia and the Pacific Islands*, edited by James Fracett and Benjamin Carino, 327-346. Staten Island, NY: Center for Migration Studies.
Center for Educational Statistics, Korean Educational Development Institute. 2008. "Statistics on Elementary and Secondary School Students Who Went Abroad" http://cesi.kedi.re.kr.
Lee, Everett S. 1966. "A Theory of Migration." *Demography* 3: 47-67.
Massey, Douglass. 1999. "Why Does Immigration Occur? A Theoretical Synthesis." In *The Handbook of International Migration: The American Experience*, edited by Charles Hirschman, Philip Kasinitz, and Josh DeWind, 34-52. New York: Russell Sage Foundation.
Min, Pyong Gap. 1996. *Caught in the Middle: Korean Communities in New York and Los Angeles.* Berkeley: University of California Press.
_____. 2002. "Introduction." In *Mass Migration to the United States: Classical and Contemporary Periods*, edited by Pyong Gap Min, 1-19. Walnut Creek, CA: Altamira Press.
_____. 2006a. "Korean Americans." In *Asian Americans: Contemporary Trends and Issues*, edited by Pyong Gap Min, 230-259. Thousand Oaks, CA: Pine Forge Press.
_____. 2006b. "Asian Immigration: History and Contemporary Trends." In *Asian Americans: Contemporary Trends and Issues*, edited by Pyong Gap Min, 7-31. Walnut Creek, CA: Pine Forge Press.
_____. 2006c. "Major Issues Related to Asian American Experiences." In *Asian Americans: Contemporary Trends and Issues*, edited by Pyong Gap Min, 80-107. Walnut Creek, CA: Pine Forge Press.
_____. 2006d. "Patterns of Asian Immigration to the United States: History and Contemporary Trends." In *Asian Americans: Contemporary Trends and Issues*, edited by Pyong Gap Min, 14-45. Walnut Creek, CA: Pine Forge Press.
Min, Pyong Gap, and Chigon Kim. 2009. "Patterns of Intermarriages and Cross-Generational In-marriages among Native-Born Asian Americans." *International Migration Review* 43: 447-470.
Portes, Alejandro, and John Walton. 1981. *Labor, Class and International System.* New York: Academic Press.
Rumbaut, Ruben. 1996. "Origins and Destinies: Immigration, Race, and Ethnicity in Contemporary America." In *Origins and Destinies: Immigration, Race, and Ethnicity in America*, edited by Sylvia Pedraza and Ruben Rumbaut, 21-42. Belmont, CA: Wadsworth Publishing Company.

Sassen, Saskia. 1988. *The Mobility of Labor and Capital: A Study of International Investments and Labor Flows.* New York: Cambridge University Press.

Shiao, Jianbin, Mia Tuam, and Elizabeth Rienzi. 2004. "Shifting the Spotlight: Exploring Race and Culture in Korean-White Adoption Families." *Race and Society* 7: 1-16.

Teitelbaum, M.S. 1987. "International Relations and Asian Migration." In *Pacific Bridges: The New Immigration from Asia and the Pacific Islands*, edited by James Fracett and Benjamin Carino, 71-84. Staten Island: Center for Migration Studies.

Todaro, M. P. 1969. "A Model of Labor Migration and Urban Unemployment in LessDeveloped Countries." *American Economic Review* 59: 138-148.

Zolberg, Aristotle. 1989. "The Next Wave: Migration Theory for a Changing World." *International Migration Review* 23: 403-444.

_____. 2001. "Matters of State: Theorizing Immigration Policy. In *The Handbook of International Migration: The American Experience,* edited by Charles Hirschman, Philip Kasinitz, and Josh DeWind, 71-93. New York: Russell Sage Foundation.

Chapter 3
Growth and Settlement Patterns of Korean Americans

by Pyong Gap Min and Chigon Kim

This chapter analyzes census data to look at the growth of the Korean population between 1970 and 2010 and changes in Korean Americans' settlement patterns between 1990 and 2010. To examine Korean Americans' settlement patterns, we look at the distribution of the Korean population in major states and metropolitan areas. For understanding suburbanization of the Korean population over the decades, we focus on the Los Angeles and New York-New Jersey metropolitan areas, the two largest Korean population centers.

Growth of the Korean Population

Congress passed new liberalized immigration laws in 1965, abolishing the earlier race-based discriminatory immigration laws. The 1965 Immigration Act went into full effect in 1968. As a result of the enforcement of the new Immigration Act, the Korean population achieved a five-fold increase in the 1970s, from 69,150 in 1970 to 354,953 in 1980 (see Figure 3.1). It further increased to approximately 800,000 in 1990, achieving a two-fold increase in the 1980s.

Beginning with the 2000 Census, the U.S. Census Bureau allowed respondents with mixed racial and ethnic backgrounds (children of intermarried parents) to choose two or more racial and ethnic categories. As a result, we have two separate figures for the Korean population in 2000 and 2010, one for those who chose the Korean category alone ("Korean alone"), and another for those who chose the Korean category and one or more additional categories ("Korean in Combination"). In 1990 and before, children of Korean-other intermarried couples chose either the Korean, the other racial-ethnic category of the non-Korean parent, or "others." Thus, there must have been a moderate number of multiracial/multi-ethnic Koreans among the approximately 800,000 Korean Americans counted by the 1990 Census.

Figure 3.1: Growth of Korean Population, 1970-2010

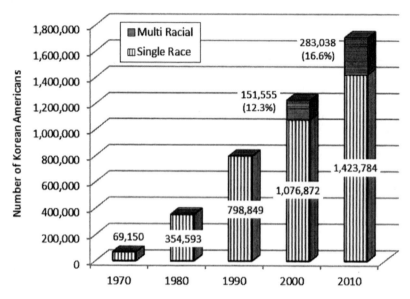

Sources: The 1970, 1980, 1990, 2000, and 2010 U.S. Censuses

The single-race Korean population in 2010 was more than 1.4 million, an increase of about 300,000 (27.4%) from 1,077,000 in 2000. Including about 283,000 multiracial Koreans, the total Korean population in 2010 was over 1.7 million. Multiracial Koreans composed 17% of Korean Americans in 2010, a significant increase from 12% in 2000. The proportion of multiracial Koreans will continue to increase as the majority of American-born Koreans have non-Korean partners. Both the Korean community in the United States and the Korean government tend not to accept multiracial Koreans as full members of the community. But they need to take them seriously because they will compose a larger and larger proportion of the Korean-American population in the future.

Table 3.1 shows the distribution of single-race and multiracial Koreans by birthplace for 2000 and 2008. In 2000, only 21% of single-race Koreans was native-born. By contrast, 75% of multiracial Koreans were native-born. The vast majority of multiracial Koreans were native-born because they were most likely to be children of Korean-other intermarried couples. While foreign-born Koreans have a very low intermarriage rate (Liang and Ito 1999), the majority of native-born Koreans engage in intermarriage (Min and Kim 2009). This means that the predominant majority of multiracial Koreans belong to the third- and higher generation Koreans. 25% of foreign-born multiracial Koreans were most likely to be children of intermarried couples between U.S. servicemen and Korean women who got married in Korea. In 2008, the native-born proportion among single-race Koreans increased to 26% while the foreign-born proportion among multiracial Koreans decreased to 16%. Since fewer and fewer Korean women are likely to marry American servicemen in Korea, the foreign-born proportion among multiracial Koreans is likely to decline even further in the future.

Table 3.1: Place of Birth among the Korean Population, 2000-2008

Nativity	2000		2008	
	Single-Race Korean	Multiracial Korean	Single-Race Korean	Multiracial Korean
Total	1,076,872 (100.0%)	151,555 (100.0%)	1,372,152 (100.0%)	160,033 (100.0%)
Foreign-born	79.1	25.5	73.6	15.6
Native-born	20.9	74.5	26.4	84.4

Note: Authors' compilation from 2000 and 2008 American Community Surveys (Ruggles et al. 2008).

Table 3.2 shows the Asian population size by ethnic group based on the 2010 Census. There were approximately 18 million Asian Americans in 2010, 3.5 times larger than the Jewish population in the United States (approximately 5.2 million). The largest Asian group is the Chinese, with almost 4 million. The Filipino and Indian groups closely follow the Chinese group in population size. Korean Americans comprise the fifth largest Asian ethnic group. The significant reduction of the Korean immigration flow since the late 1980s (see Min 2006a) has been the major factor for the slower increase in the Korean population relative to other Asian populations. The same trend will likely continue in the future as Koreans will have fewer incentives for choosing U.S.-bound emigration compared to other Asian populations.

Table 3.2: The Asian Population by Ethnic Group in 2010

Ethnic Group	Single Race	Multiracial	Total	% of Multiracial
Chinese	3,137,061	657,612	3,794,673	17.3
Indian	2,843,391	339,672	3,183,063	10.7
Filipino	2,555,923	860,917	3,416,840	25.2
Vietnamese	1,548,449	188,984	1,737,433	10.9
Korean	1,423,784	283,038	1,706,822	16.6
Japanese	763,325	540,961	1,304,286	41.5
Total	12,271,933	2,871,184	15,143,117	19.0
Other Asians	2,042,170	755,999	2,798,169	27.0
Asian Total	14,314,103	3,627,183	17,941,286	20.2

Source: The 2010 U.S. Census

Multiracial people comprise 20% of the total Asian American population. Japanese Americans show the highest proportion of multiracial people (41%), followed by Filipino Americans (25%). More than 70% of Japanese Americans are native-born, with the majority of the native-born Japanese belonging to third- or higher generations. By virtue of their higher generational status, proportionally more Japanese Americans are intermarried than other Asian American groups (who are comprised predominantly of foreign-born immigrants). This explains why Japanese Americans include a much higher proportion of multiracial people. Indian and Vietnamese groups have the lowest proportion (11% each) of multiracial people among the six major Asian groups because their native-born populations have the lowest intermarriage rates (32% and 40% respectively; see Min and Kim, 2009).

Distribution of Korean Americans in Four Regions and Selected States

Figure 3.2 shows changes in distribution of single-race Koreans in four different regions in the five given years (1970, 1980, 1990, 2000, and 2010). About 43% of Korean Americans were concentrated in the West in 1970. The proportion has not changed much over four decades. The lack of a decrease in the proportion of Korean Americans settled in the West between 1970 and 2010 contrasts with other Asian groups. Census data show that 71% of Asian Americans were concentrated in the West in 1970. By 2010, the proportion gradually decreased to 49% (Min 2010). Even in 2000, 73% of Japanese Americans and 68% of Filipino Americans lived in the West (Min 2006b: 32-33). But Korean Americans were much more widely dispersed in all regions of the United States than Asian Americans as a whole in 1970.

We speculate that a much wider distribution of Korean Americans throughout the United States away from the West compared to other Asian groups in 1970 was due mainly to the fact that the vast majority of Korean immigrants before the enforcement of the 1965 Immigration Act were Korean women married to American servicemen and children adopted by American citizens (Min 2006a: 13-14). Since both Korean women married to U.S. servicemen and adoptees followed their American husbands and adopted parents to wherever they were settled, unlike other Asian immigrants, they did not have the option (or limitation) to choose the West, the gateway to Asian countries.

The proportion of Koreans Americans in the Northeast has remained stable (around 20%) during the four-decade period. But the South has achieved a great increase in the Korean American population, growing from 18% in 1970 to 24% in 2010. Surprisingly, the South has a substantially larger proportion (3%) of the Korean population than the Northeast. As we will soon see, four Southern States defined by the Census Bureau—Texas, Virginia, Georgia and Florida—have experienced very high growth rates in the Korean population. In contrast to the

South, the Midwest suffered a big reduction in the Korean population, from 19% in 1970 to 12% in 2010. The Chicago area is the largest Korean center in the Midwest. The proportion of Koreans in the region began to decline in the 1980s, and it continued to decrease until it fell close to 12% in 2008. The decrease in the proportion of the Korean population in the Midwest and the increase in the South reflect changes in the U.S. general population. In the process of deindustrialization, many companies moved from the Midwest (the Rust Belt), to the South or the West (the Sun Belt).

Figure 3.2: Changes in the Regional Distribution of Korean Population, 1970-2010 (%)

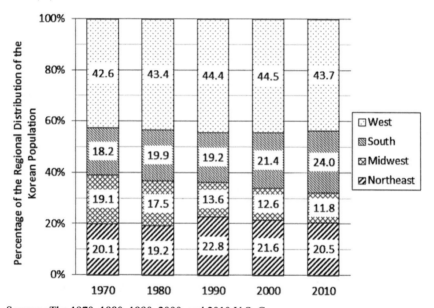

Sources: The 1970, 1980, 1990, 2000, and 2010 U.S. Censuses

Note: The 2000 and 2010 numbers include both single-race and multiracial Koreans

Table 3.3 shows the number of Korean Americans in fifteen major Korean states (states with Korean populations of 20,000 or more). A staggering 83% of all Korean Americans live in the fifteen largest Korean states, an indication of a high concentration of Korean Americans. Only 14% of Korean Americans in the fifteen largest states are multiracial Koreans, compared to 27% of Korean Americans settled in other states. Korean Americans outside of major Korean states have greater difficulty in finding Korean marital partners, thus they have a higher intermarriage rate than those who reside in major Korean states.

California has the largest number of Korean Americans, with more than half a million, accounting for 30% of the Korean population in the United States. New York and New Jersey follow California with about 154,000 and 100,000, respectively. The Korean population in California is larger than that in New York and New Jersey combined. The next three states—Texas, Virginia, and Washington—have similar numbers of Korean Americans (roughly 80,000). Nearly 60% of Korean Americans concentrate in these six major states.

Table 3.3: Numbers of Korean Americans in Fifteen Major Korean (20,000 or more) States, 2010

State	Single Race	Multiracial	Total	% of Multiracial	% Share in the Total Korean Population
CA	451,892	53,333	505,225	10.6	30.0
NY	140,994	12,615	153,609	8.2	9.0
NJ	93,679	6,655	100,334	6.6	5.9
TX	67,750	17,582	85,332	20.6	5.0
VA	70,577	11,429	82,006	13.9	4.8
WA	62,374	17,675	80,049	22.1	4.7
IL	61,469	8,794	70,263	12.5	4.1
GA	52,431	8,405	60,836	13.8	3.6
MD	48,592	6,459	55,051	11.7	3.2
PA	40,505	6,924	47,429	14.6	2.8
FL	26,205	9,424	35,629	26.5	2.1
HI	24,203	24,496	48,699	50.3	2.9
MI	24,186	6,106	30,292	20.2	1.8
MA	24,110	4,794	28,904	16.6	1.7
CO	20,433	7,744	28,177	27.5	1.7
Total	1,209,400	202,435	1,411,835	14.3	82.7
Other States	214,384	80,603	294,987	27.3	17.3
U.S. Total	1,423,784	283,038	1,706,822	16.6	100.0

Sources: The 2010 U.S. Census

New Jersey and New York have the lowest rates of multiracial Koreans with 6.6% and 8.2%, respectively. A large Korean population in the New York-New Jersey metropolitan area is one major contributing factor to an exceptionally low proportion of multiracial Koreans in the area. Korean Americans in the New York-New Jersey area do not have much difficulty in finding Korean marital partners, thus the intermarriage rate among Korean Americans in the area is likely to be very low, which accounts for a proportionately low birth rate of multiracial Koreans. The other important contributing factor is the overall low generational status of Korean Americans in the New York-New Jersey area. Although the Los Angeles area has a much larger Korean population than the New York-New Jersey area, it includes a larger proportion of multiracial Koreans (11%), because the Los Angeles Korean community has a higher proportion of native-born Koreans, including multigenerational Koreans, who have a much higher intermarriage rate than Korean immigrants. The Korean community in the New York-New Jersey area has a much smaller proportion of native-born Koreans, which has resulted in a lower intermarriage rate, and consequently, lower numbers of multiracial Korean children.

Table 3.4 shows the growth rate of the Korean population between 2000 and 2010 in the fifteen largest Korean states. The Korean population in the United States as a whole achieved a 39% increase rate between 2000 and 2010. Georgia achieved the highest rate of growth with 86%. Georgia was the eighth largest state in the 2010 Census count of the Korean population. But immigration data reveal that it was the fourth largest state in the proportion of annual Korean immigrants in 2009 and 2010. These figures suggest the popularity of Georgia as the destination of Korean immigrants during recent years.

Table 3.4: The Increase in the Korean Population (Single-Race and Multiracial) in Major Korean States between 2000 and 2010

State	Number of Koreans		Increase between 2000 and 2010	
	2000	2010	Number	Rate (%)
CA	375,571	505,225	129,654	34.5
NY	127,068	153,609	26,541	20.9
NJ	68,990	100,334	31,344	45.4
TX	54,300	85,332	31,032	57.1
VA	50,468	82,006	31,538	62.5
WA	56,438	80,049	23,611	41.8
IL	56,021	76,023	20,002	35.7
GA	32,660	60,836	28,176	86.3
MD	42,335	55,051	12,716	30.0
HI	41,352	48,699	7,347	17.8
PA	34,984	47,429	12,445	35.6
FL	23,790	35,629	11,839	49.8
MI	24,255	30,292	6,037	24.9
MA	19,469	28,904	9,435	48.5
CO	20,304	28,177	7,873	38.8
Total	1,028,005	1,417,595	389,590	37.9
Other States	200,422	289,227	88,805	44.3
U.S. Total	1,228,427	1,706,822	478,395	38.9

Sources: The 2000 and 2010 U.S. Censuses
Note: The bolded states achieved substantially higher rates of increase in the Korean population than the U.S. total rate.

Texas, Virginia, and Florida follow Georgia in terms of growth rate between 2010 and 2000. It should be noted that all four of these states are located in the South. By contrast, Hawaii and New York achieved much lower growth rates (18% and 21%, respectively) than the U.S. average. Among states in the Northeast, New Jersey and Massachusetts are the only two states that achieved substantially higher rates of growth in the Korean population than the national average. A significant Korean population growth in Massachusetts in the decade of the 2000s seems to do much with the increase in the number of Korean students enrolled in major colleges and universities in this state.

Figure 3.3 lists ten states with the highest proportions of multiracial Koreans. Hawaii ranks number one in the proportion of multiracial Koreans with 50%. As the home to pioneer Korean immigrants during the period between 1903 and 1905, native-born Koreans make up the majority of the Korean population in Hawaii, with the majority of native-born Koreans likely to be multigenerational (third- or higher-generation) Koreans. Moreover, intermarriage is more easily accepted in Hawaii than in other states. As such, Korean Americans in Hawaii have an exceptionally high intermarriage rate. Given these factors, it is not surprising that half of the Koreans in Hawaii are multiracial. The other states included in Figure 3.3 are relatively small states in terms of Korean population size, which means that finding Korean marital partners is not easy. Florida and Colorado belong to the fifteen largest Korean states, but they are newly emerging Korean states.

Figure 3.3: Ten U.S. States with Largest Proportions of Multiracial Korean Populations*

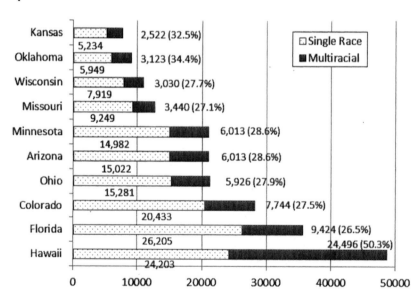

Source: The 2010 U.S. Census

*The ten states have been selected from states with Korean populations of 5,000 or more in 2010.

Distribution of Korean Americans in Selected Metropolitan Areas

Figure 3.4 and Table 3.5 show the growth and share of the Korean population in the ten largest Korean population areas (Consolidated Metropolitan Statistical Areas) in the three given years. We have selected the ten areas that had at least 10,000 Korean Americans in 1990. In 2010, 49% of Korean Americans were settled in the seven traditional immigrant gateway cities: Los Angeles, New York, Washington DC, San Francisco, Chicago, Philadelphia and Honolulu. Another 9% were concentrated in three newly emerging cities: Seattle, Atlanta and Dallas. Thus, about 58% were concentrated in the ten large gateway cities. However, this figure is a significant reduction from previous decades. In 1990 and 2000, 66% and 69% of the Korean population were concentrated in these metropolitan areas. The changes reflect the tendency of Korean immigrants to move from large metropolitan areas to smaller areas. We can see this trend more clearly when looking at changes in particular metropolitan areas below.

Figure 3.4: Growth of the Korean Population in the Ten Largest Korean Population Areas (CMSA)

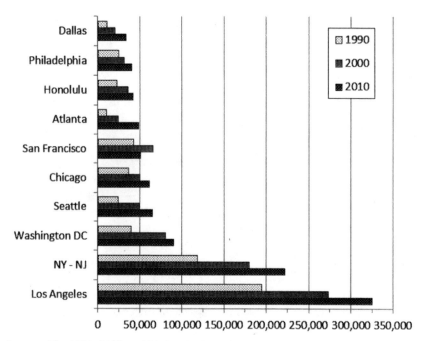

Sources: The 1990, 2000, and 2010 U.S. Censuses
Note: The 2000 and 2010 numbers include both single-race and multiracial Koreans

Table 3.5: Numbers of Korean Americans and Growth Rates in the Ten Largest Korean Population Areas, in 1990, 2000, and 2010

Metropolitan Area	1990 N	1990 %	2000* N	2000* %	2010* N	2010* %
Los Angeles CMSA	194,437	24.3	272,498	22.2	324,586	19.0
New York CMSA	118,096	14.8	179,344	14.6	221,705	13.0
Washington D.C. CMSA	39,850	5.0	80,592	6.6	90,157	5.3
Seattle CMSA	23,901	3.0	49,139	4.0	64,771	3.8
Chicago CMSA	36,952	4.6	49,972	4.1	61,229	3.6
San Francisco CMSA	42,277	5.3	65,218	5.3	50,867	3.0
Atlanta CMSA	10,120	1.3	24,232	2.0	48,788	2.9
Honolulu CMSA	22,646	2.8	36,069	2.9	41,689	2.4
Philadelphia CMSA	24,568	3.1	31,820	2.6	40,292	2.4
Dallas CMSA	11,041	1.4	20,140	1.6	33,593	2.0
Total in 10 Metropolitan	523,888	65.6	809,024	65.9	977,677	57.3
Total in the United States	798,849	100.0	1,076,872	100.0	1,706,822	100.0

Sources: The 1990, 2000, and 2010 U.S. Censuses

Note: Ten metropolitan areas with more than 10,000 Korean Americans, excluding multi-racial cases, in the 1990 Census are selected. a) The names of the metropolitan areas follow the 2010 definitions:
- Los Angeles-Orange-Riverside CMSA
- New York-Newark-Bridgeport, NY-NJ-CT CMSA
- Washington-Baltimore-Northern Virginia, DC-MD-VA-WV CMSA
- San Francisco-Oakland CMSA*
- Chicago-Naperville-Michigan City, IL-IN-WI CMSA
- Seattle-Tacoma-Olympia CMSA
- Philadelphia-Camden-Vineland, PA-NJ-DE-MD CMSA
- Atlanta-Sandy Springs-Gainesville, Atlanta CMSA
- Honolulu, HI MSA
- Dallas-Fort Worth, TX CMSA

In the 1990 and 2000 Censuses San Jose, San Francisco, and Oakland were included in the San Francisco CMSA. But San Jose was separated in the 2010 Census and Fremont was added to the San Francisco-Oakland CMSA.

* The 2000 and 2010 numbers include both single-race and multiracial Koreans

The Los Angeles CMSA (combining Los Angeles, Long Beach and Riverside) had nearly one-fourth of the Korean population in 1990 (24.3%). The proportion was stable through 2000 (24%), but it experienced a significant decline in 2010 (19%). With about 325,000 Koreans in 2010, Los Angeles is still the largest overseas Korean population center in the world. The presence of Asian populations in the 1960s, convenience of air travel to and from Korea, mild climate, and active trade relations between Los Angeles and Korea all contributed to the influx of post-1965 Korean immigrants to the LA CMSA (Min 1993).

The New York and Washington CMSAs rank as the second and third largest Korean population centers in the United States, with approximately 222,000 and 90,000 in 2010, respectively. Both areas marked an increase in the share of the Korean population between 1990 and 2000, but suffered a decrease in the next decade. The slight increase in the share of the Korean population in the New York-New Jersey area from 1990 to 2000 was mainly due to the rapid expansion of the Korean population in Bergen County, which will be discussed in the next section. The decrease in the same area between 2000 and 2010 is noticeable. We believe that economic difficulties in New York City pushed many Koreans in the area to move to Atlanta, Dallas, and various Western cities, which will also be covered in the next section. A great increase in the share of the Korean population in the Washington-Baltimore-Northern Virginia area from 5% in 1990 to 6.9% in 2000 was due mainly to the Census Bureau's incorporating the Baltimore metro area into the Washington-Northern Virginia CMSA. The San Jose-San Francisco-Oakland CMSA area, the fourth largest Korean population center in the United States, experienced a significant reduction not only in the share of the Korean population (from 5.3% in 2000 to 3% in 2010), but also in the absolute number between 2000 and 2010, mainly because the Census Bureau separated the San Jose area from the San Jose-San Francisco-Oakland CMSA area.

Hawaii in general and Honolulu in particular, home to the pioneering Korean immigrants in the beginning of the twentieth century, have continued to lose their shares of the Korean population since the post-1965 Korean immigration flow started. But, surprisingly, between 2000 and 2010, Honolulu achieved a modest gain in the share of the Korean population. We noted above that the state of Hawaii achieved the lowest proportion of increase in the Korean population among the major states with large numbers of Korean Americans between 2000 and 2010. The significant gain in the Korean population in Honolulu, despite a modest gain in Hawaii, between 2000 and 2010 suggests that many Koreans settled in small areas of Hawaii moved to Honolulu.

Chicago and Philadelphia are two major gateway cities that experienced significant declines in the share of the Korean population in both time periods (between 1990 and 2000, and between 2000 and 2010). By contrast, the metropolitan areas with medium-size Korean populations, such as Seattle, Atlanta, and Dallas, experienced significant increases in their shares of the Korean population. These areas were traditionally considered non-gateway cities, but they have become "newly emerging gateway cities" for Korean immigrants. Although not included in Table 3.5, San Diego, Denver, and Phoenix also achieved higher levels of increase in the Korean population than five "old" gateway cities.

There is enough evidence that large gateway CMSAs suffered modest decreases in the share of the Korean population with concomitant increases in medium-size Korean centers. How can we explain this change? We suggest that there are a few closely-related major factors that contributed to this change. One major factor is the economic difficulties that these traditional gateway cities experienced, along with high living costs. As already noted, deindustrialization and subsequent decreases in manufacturing jobs pushed people away from the Rust Belt cities of the Midwest and Northeast towards the milder weather and lower living costs of the Sun Belt cities of the West and the South. It should also be noted that this internal migration applies not only to Korean populations, but also to the general American population as a whole.

The other important factor, which is unique to Korean and other immigrants but inapplicable to the American general population, is the increasing conveniences of cultural and social life for Korean immigrants in medium-size Korean centers by virtue of increasing transnational ties between these cities and Korea. In the 1980s and the 1990s, Korean immigrants were willing to accept high living costs to settle in the Los Angeles, New York, Washington DC, and Chicago areas, partly because of the presence in those cities of strong ethnic media, many Korean restaurants, and other enclave businesses catering mainly to Koreans, which gave them advantages in maintaining full Korean cultural and social lives. But by the early 2000s, many other medium-size Korean communities, such as Atlanta, Dallas, and Seattle, had Korean populations large enough to provide similar Korean cultural and social amenities. Moreover, by virtue of technological advances and globalization during recent years, full-time Korean TV programs, large Korean grocery chains such as H-Mart, and many other Korean ethnic stores became available in these non-gateway cities with medium-size Korean populations. These days, Korean immigrants can enjoy most of the Korean cultural amenities in Atlanta that they could only previously find in Los Angeles. It is not difficult to see why so many of them would be willing to sell their houses to move to these less expensive Sun Belt cities.

Table 3.6 compares Korean Americans settled in the ten largest Korean gateway cities and those in other areas in the selected population characteristics based on the 2006-2008 combined American Community Surveys. We include only single-race Koreans for this comparison in population characteristics, but we include both single-race and multiracial Koreans mainly to determine the number of multiracial Koreans per 1,000 single-race Koreans. As expected, residents in the gateway cities include a larger proportion of the elderly population, while residents in non-gateway cities include a larger proportion of the younger population, which includes people below the age of 25. Korean elderly people prefer to live in large gateway Korean communities where they can live comfortably without speaking English. The non-gateway cities have a larger proportion of younger Koreans, partly because of the overrepresentation of Korean college students there. We need to remember that the U.S. Census refers to all foreign-born Koreans, including international students, as "Korean immigrants."

As expected, Korean residents outside of the gateway cities have higher proportions of multiracial Koreans, intermarried people, and English-only speakers than those in gateway cities. Surprisingly, more than one-third of married Koreans in non-gateway cities are intermarried. The majority of native-born Koreans engage in intermarriage (Min and Kim, 2009). Intermarried Koreans overwhelmingly speak English at home (Kim and Min, 2010), thus they do not have to live in gateway cities. These intermarried and multiracial Korean Americans are expected to compose an increasing proportion of the Korean population in the United States, as the intermarriage rate will increase over generations in the future.

Table 3.6: Selected Characteristics of the Korean Population (only Single-Race) by Place of Residence, 2006-2008

Population Characteristics	Place of Residence	
	Gateway	Non-Gateway
% of less than 25 years old	29.7	35.5
% of 65 years old and over	10.4	6.9
% of female	53.1	55.9
% of the first generation	56.2	50.5
% of the 1.5 generation	19.0	25.9
% of recent immigrants arrived within 3 years	6.7	14.1
Number of multiracial Koreans per 1,000 single race Koreans	51	185
% of speaking English only at home	15.2	28.6
% of intermarriage among the married people	13.9	38.3
%t of college of more educational attainment	39.5	34.5
% of managerial occupations among the employed	18.4	12.7
% of professional occupations among the employed	9.0	11.0
% of self-employment among the employed	21.5	16.6
% of home owners	55.9	62.5

Source: Authors' compilation from 2006-2008 American Community Surveys (Ruggles et al. 2008).

We also expect that Korean Americans settled in gateway cities have a higher self-employment rate than those in non-gateway cities. As more of them have their own businesses in large metropolitan areas, they are over-represented in managerial occupations, either in the general economy or for their own businesses, compared to Korean Americans in non-gateway cities. As expected, a higher proportion of Korean Americans in non-gateway cities have professional occupations than those in gateway cities. However, the difference is not as great as we expected. Since, as previously noted, the vast majority of residents in non-gateway cities still live in metropolitan areas, they are likely to have a wide variety of urban occupations. But we expect Korean Americans settled in small cities, like university towns, to have a high representation in professional occupations, such as medical professions and teaching jobs in higher educational institutions. For these Koreans, their professional occupations are most likely the main reason why they live in small cities. They are likely to have far more frequent social interactions with their white American neighbors and/or co-workers than those who live in gateway cities.

The Korean Population in the Los Angeles CMSA

Approximately 325,000 Koreans were settled in the Los Angeles-Orange-Riverside CMSA 2010. The Los Angeles area is the largest overseas Korean population center not only in the United States, but also among all Korean diasporic communities. Table 3.7 examines the change in the Korean population in the Los Angeles CMSA between 1990 and 2010. There are several reasons why the Los Angeles area has attracted more Koreans than any other U.S. metropolitan area. First, the Los Angeles area is physically closer to Seoul than metropolitan areas located in other areas. It takes about nine and a half hours to fly from Seoul to Los Angeles, which is four and a half hours shorter than the number of hours needed to fly from Seoul to New York. Second, a mild climate in Los Angeles is another factor that has attracted many Koreans to the area. Third, the presence of several prestigious state universities seems to be an additional factor for the influx of Koreans to the area. Finally, the settlement of so many Asians in the area may have led many Koreans to choose it as the destination. For the same reasons, the San Francisco and San Diego areas have attracted large numbers of Korean immigrants.

Table 3.7: Population Change of Korean American Population in Los Angeles CMSA, 1990-2010

	1990 N	2000* N	% Change 1990-2000	2010* N	% Change 2000-2010
Total	194,437	257,975	32.7	324,586	25.8
Los Angeles City	72,970	95,106	30.3	114,140	20.0
Suburban Areas	121,467	162,869	34.1	210,446	29.2

Sources: The 1990, 2000, and 2010 U.S. Censuses
*The 2000 and 2010 numbers include both single-race and multiracial Koreans.

The Korean population in the Los Angeles area had already reached about 200,000 in 1990. As previously noted above, the levels of the Korean population growth in the next two decades in LA CMSA were lower than those in other major Korean population centers. Even in 1990, far more Koreans lived in suburban areas (62%) than in the city of Los Angeles (38%). In the next two decades, Koreans in suburban areas experienced higher growth rates than those in the central city. As a result, Koreans in the city of Los Angeles accounted for a smaller proportion (32%) of those in the Los Angeles CMSA in 2010 than they did in 1990. This means that many Koreans settled in Koreatown and other adjacent areas in the 1970s and 1980s re-migrated to suburban areas. As will be shown in the next section, suburbanization of Korean Americans between 1990 and 2010 occurred far more radically in the New York-New Jersey area than in the Los Angeles area.

Figure 3.5 shows major Asian populations in the city of Los Angeles. Asian Americans comprised 13% of the population in Los Angeles City in 2010. The largest Asian ethnic group in the city of Los Angeles is the Filipinos with approximately 140,000. Korean Americans, numbering about 114,000, become the second largest Asian group. Surprisingly, the Chinese population is much smaller than the Filipino and Korean populations. Chinese immigrants in other metropolitan areas usually concentrate in the central cities, creating large Chinatowns close to downtown areas. But Chinese Americans in Los Angeles are exceptional to the tendency of Chinese to concentrate in the central cities with large enclaves. The original Chinatown in Los Angeles City has not expanded much while a large suburban Chinatown has been created in Monterey Park (Zhou and Kim 2003).

Figure 3.5: The Asian Population in Los Angeles City by Ethnic Group, 2010

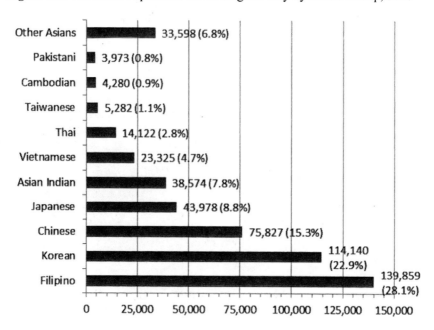

Source: The 2010 Census

Koreans in Los Angeles created Koreatown, a Korean enclave with a major

Korean business district. It is located approximately three miles west of downtown Los Angeles, covering about twenty-five miles (five by five miles). Koreans (N=46,664) composed 20% of the population in Koreatown in 2000, with Hispanics (predominantly Mexicans) accounting for the majority (51%) of the population (Yu et al., 2004). However, Korean residents in Koreatown accounted for over half of the Korean population in Los Angeles City. It is estimated that nearly 3,500 Korean businesses, with Korean-language signs, are located in Koreatown. Based on the 2001-2002 *Korean Yellow Pages*, Yu and his associates (2004) analyzed major Korean businesses located in Koreatown. They found 34 Korean book stores, 116 travel agencies, 193 law firms, 184 accounting firms, 410 medical offices, 204 acupuncture/herbal offices, and 41 nightclubs/bars in Koreatown. They also found that 41 of 66 Korean community service centers, 37 of 67 Korean bank branches, 23 of 33 Korean Buddhist temples were located in Koreatown. These figures point to the significance of Koreatown as the sociocultural, as well as the commercial, center of Koreans in Los Angeles.

Table 3.8 shows differential growth rates of the Korean population in the three suburban areas in the two decades. While the Los Angeles County area outside of the city of Los Angeles achieved moderate rates of growth in the two decades, Orange and Riverside Counties marked phenomenal growth rates. In particular, the Korean population in Orange County grew by more than 2.5 times during the two decades, from approximately 37,000 in 1990 to nearly 94,000 in 2010. By contrast, the Korean population in Los Angeles County suburban areas outside of the Los Angeles central city achieved only a 17% growth rate between 2000 and 2010, a lower rate than even Los Angeles City. Orange County has many upscale white neighborhoods and good school districts. Thus it is attractive to Korean immigrants who spent their first five or seven years of immigration in LA Koreatown and its adjacent neighborhoods. Creation of a suburban Koreatown in Garden Grove since the 1990s has further attracted Koreans to Orange County. This enclave, known as "Little Seoul," is the second largest Korean enclave in southern California, after LA Koreatown.

Table 3.8: Growth of Korean Population in Three Major Los Angeles Suburban Areas, 1990-2010

Counties	1990 N	2000* N	% Change 1990-2000	2010* N	% Change 2000-2010
Los Angeles County Outside of the City of Los Angeles	71,061	100,044	40.8	116,736	16.7
Orange County	35,684	58,564	64.1	93,710	60.0
Riverside County	3,701	6,274	69.5	14,384	129.3

Source: The 1990, 2000, and 2010 U.S. Censuses
* The 2000 and 2010 numbers include both single-race and multiracial Koreans.

The Korean Population in the NY-NJ CMSA

We have noted above that the New York-New Jersey Consolidated Metropolitan Statistical Area experienced a significant reduction in the share of the U.S. Korean population between 2000 and 2010. This area consists of twenty-nine counties, covering New York City, Long Island, Upstate New York, Northwestern New Jersey, and portions of Connecticut and Pennsylvania. Korean Americans in this area are highly concentrated in New York City, two long Island Counties (Nassau and Suffolk), two Upstate New York Counties (Westchester and Rockland), and Bergen County in New Jersey. Although the Korean population in the NY-NJ CMSA achieved a lower increase rate than in other metropolitan areas, the local differences in the growth rate of the Korean population are significant. Thus we need to examine Korean population changes in the aforementioned suburban counties of NY-NJ and the five boroughs of New York City.

Table 3.9 shows changes over time in the Korean population in the NY-NJ CMSA by separating New York City and suburban counties outside of the central city. In 1990, the majority (59%) of Korean Americans in the metropolitan area lived in New York City, heavily concentrating in Korean enclaves in Queens. But more and more Korean immigrants who had originally settled in Queens moved to suburban areas in Long Island and Bergen County in the 1990s. Also, many new arrivals from Korea settled directly in suburban counties, particularly Bergen County. Between 1990 and 2000, suburban counties experienced a 66% increase rate in the Korean population, compared to 29% in New York City. This suburbanization of the Korean population continued in the 2000s. While the Korean population in suburban counties recorded a 48% increase rate between 2000 and 2010, the Korean population in New York City increased only by 14%. In 2010, Koreans in suburban counties outnumbered those in the city by approximately 16,000.

Table 3.9: Changes in the Korean Population in the New York-New Jersey CMSA, 1990-2010

NY-NJ Area	1990 N	2000* N	% Change 1990-2000	2010* N	% Change 2000-2010
Total	118,096	170,509	44.4	221,705	30.0
NY Central City	69,718	90,208	29.4	102,820	14.0
Suburban Areas	48,378	80,301	66.0	118,885	48.0

Source: The 1990, 2000, and 2010 U.S. Censuses
* The 2000 and 2010 numbers include both single-race and multiracial Koreans.

Figure 3.6 shows the Asian population in New York City by ethnic group based on the 2010 Census. There were approximately 1.2 million Asian Americans in New York City, accounting for 14% of the city's population (over 8 million). Approximately half a million Chinese Americans comprise 43% of Asian Americans in the city. Chinese Americans, combined with Taiwanese Americans, outnumber Korean Americans in the city by about five times. Asian Indians comprise the second largest Asian group next to the Chinese. Indian Americans also outnumber Korean Americans by about 2.3 times. Korean Americans comprise the third largest Asian group in the city, but Filipinos and Bangladeshis closely follow Korean Americans in population size. These numbers give us ideas about the extent to which the Korean community has disadvantages compared to the Chinese or the Indian community in increasing their political power and taking other types of ethnic collective action using number power. Unfortunately, the demographic gap between the Korean community and other Asian communities in New York City and other areas is likely to increase as time passes.

Figure 3.6: The Asian Population in New York City by Ethnic Group, 2010

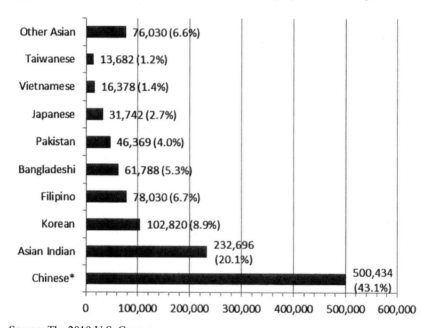

Source: The 2010 U.S. Census
Note: The Chinese-American population excludes Taiwanese.

Table 3.10 shows the differences among the five boroughs in the changes in the Korean population in the three given time periods (1990, 2000, and 2010). Queens has been the major Korean population center in New York City for quite some time, with Flushing serving as its Koreatown. In 1990, about 70% of New

York City Koreans lived in Queens. The proportion remained unchanged in 2000, but it was reduced to 64% in 2010. Surprisingly, between 2000 and 2010, the Korean population in Queens increased only by a little more than 2,000. The Korean population in the Bronx also experienced a decrease in the share of Korean Americans in New York City during the same period. However, Manhattan experienced a substantial increase in both decades, by about 4% between 1990 and 2000 and by 8% between 2000 and 2010. Between 1990 and 2010, the overall Korean population in Manhattan increased by three and a half times.

Table 3.10: Changes in the Korean Population in New York City by Borough, 1990-2010

New York City	1990		2000*		2010*	
	N	%	N	%	N	%
Bronx	4,908	7.0	4,076	4.5	3,101	3.0
Brooklyn	6,608	9.5	6,816	7.5	8,201	8.0
Manhattan	6,183	8.9	11,851	13.1	21,996	21.4
Queens	49,088	70.4	63,885	70.8	66,124	64.3
Staten Island (Richmond County)	2,931	4.2	3,580	4.0	3,398	3.3
Total	69,718	100.0	90,208	100.0	102,820	100.0

Sources: The 1990, 2000, and 2010 U.S. Censuses
* The 2000 and 2010 numbers include both single-race and multiracial Koreans.

We can cite two specific factors that contributed to a radical increase in the Korean population in Manhattan over the years. One is the big increase in the number of Korean international students who reside in Manhattan. They include graduate students enrolled at Columbia University, New York University, the CUNY Graduate Center and The New School, and undergraduate students attending various arts, music, and other specialized schools in Manhattan. The other contributing factor is the steady increase in the number of 1.5- and second-generation young Korean American adults who work for many companies located in midtown and downtown Manhattan. Due to the presence of so many young Koreans in Manhattan, it is extremely difficult to conduct phone interviews with Korean respondents in Manhattan. Young Koreans usually do not have home phones, especially with the advent of cell phones. Moreover, even if they have home phones, they are not likely to be at home during the hours that telephone interviews are usually conducted.

Table 3.11 shows changes in the Korean population in three time periods (1990, 2000, and 2010) in major New York-New Jersey area suburban counties where many Korean Americans are settled. Korean immigrants in New Jersey are heavily concentrated in Bergen County. Through the media and hearsay, Korean immigrants have heard about a radical increase in the Korean population in Bergen County over the last two decades or so, which has undoubtedly been a factor in the influx of Koreans into the county. But Table 3.11 shows more accurate statistics about growth of the Korean population changes in the county in the three time periods. In 1990, approximately 16,000 Korean Americans resided in Bergen County. The population increased by more than two times in 2000, and by 57% between 2000 and 2010. If the current trend continues, Korean Americans in Bergen County may outnumber those in New York City by the year 2020. This means that the two most prominent Korean suburban enclaves in Bergen County (Fort Lee and Palisades Park) have great potential for expansion in the future.

There are a number of factors that have contributed to the great increase in the Korean population in Bergen County over the past two decades or so. First, many Korean immigrants who had originally settled in Korean enclaves in Queens, such as Woodside, Flushing, and Elmhurst, re-migrated in the late 1980s and the 1990s to Fort Lee, Palisades Park, and other neighborhoods in Bergen County. They were attracted by the presence of better schools, lower crime rates, and good suburban amenities (Oh 2007: 82). When they re-migrated to Bergen County neighborhoods, they started new chains of subsequent Korean immigration from South Korea. Second, Bergen County's easy accessibility to Manhattan and other parts of New York City has also contributed to the expansion of the Korean population there. Many Korean residents in Bergen County commute to their businesses in Manhattan and other parts of New York City (Oh 2007: 84). Also, many Korean government employees working for the Korean Consulate General of Greater New York and other Korean government agencies located in Manhattan commute from Bergen County. Third, the relocation of many branches of Korean multinational corporations originally located in Manhattan to Bergen County in the mid-1980s initially contributed to the increase in the Korean population there. Finally, the development of suburban Korean enclaves in Fort Lee and Palisades Park in Bergen County since the late 1980s further attracted more Korean immigrants both from New York City and directly from Korea.

Table 3.11: Growth of Korean Population in Five Major New York-New Jersey Suburban Counties, 1990-2010

NY-NJ Suburban counties	1990 N	2000* N	% Change 1990-2000	2010* N	% Change 2000-2010
Bergen County, NJ	16,073	37,015	130.3	58,236	57.3
Nassau County, NY	5,704	8,769	53.7	14,338	63.5
Suffolk County, NY	3,320	4,697	41.5	6,461	37.6
Rockland County, NY	1,216	1,993	63.9	2,340	17.4
Westchester County, NY	3,572	4,857	36.0	6,184	27.3

Sources: The 1990, 2000, and 2010 U.S. Censuses
* The 2000 and 2010 numbers include both single-race and multiracial Koreans.

All suburban counties in New York included in Table 3.11 achieved substantially higher rates of growth in the Korean population between 2000 and

2010. But Nassau County in Long Island had the largest Korean population with nearly 11,000 in 2010 and achieved the highest rate of growth (64%) in the Korean population between 2000 and 2010. Nassau County in Long Island is attractive to Korean immigrants, including many early-study students directed from Korea, mainly because there are several good school districts with highly rated public schools. The neighborhoods where Korean immigrants are concentrated in Long Island, such as New Hyde Park, Great Neck, Port Washington, Syosset and Jericho, have many first-class high schools.

New York City's Korean immigrants have created their enclave in Flushing, the center of the Korean community. Approximately one-fourth of about 10,000 Korean Americans in New York City live in Community District 7 that encompasses Flushing, Whitestone, and College Point. They have established the Korean business district in Flushing, using distinctive Korean language commercial signs. The intersection of the Roosevelt Avenue and Union Street is the core of the Korean business districts that Koreans commonly refer to *Hanin Sangga*. Numerous Korean businesses that cater mainly to Korean customers with distinctive Korean cultural products are dotted along Union Street in nine blocks between 32th and 41st Avenues. Korean immigrants cannot expand their businesses west of Union Street because the next block, Main Street, is the heart of the business district of Flushing's Chinatown. Blocked from moving westward, Korans have expanded their ethnic businesses eastward two and a half miles (about eighty blocks) along Northern Blvd., up to 220th Street toward Bayside. This expansion reflects the residential concentration of Korean immigrants about two miles on both sides of Northern Boulevard between Flushing and Bayside.

References

Barringer, Herbert, Robert W. Gardner, and Michael J. Levin. 1995. *Asians and Pacific Islanders in the United States.* New York: Russell Sage Foundation.

Kim, Chigon, and Pyong Gap Min. 2010. "Marital Patterns and Use of Mother Tongue at Home among Native-Born Asian Americans." *Social Forces* 88.

Liang, Zai, and Naomi Ito. 1999. "Intermarriage of Asian Americans in the New York City Region: Contemporary Patterns and Future Prospects." *International Migration Review* 33: 876-900.

Min, Pyong Gap. 2006a. "Asian Immigration: History and Contemporary Trends." In *Asian Americans: Contemporary Trends and Issues, Second Edition*, edited by Pyong Gap Min, 7-31. New York: Pine Forge Press.

_____. 2006b. "Settlement Patterns and Diversity." In *Asian Americans: Contemporary Trends and Issues*, Second Edition, edited by Pyong Gap Min, 32-53. New York: Pine Forge Press.

_____. 1993. "Korean Immigrations in Los Angeles." In *Immigration and Entrepreneurship*, edited by Ivan Light and Parminder Bhachu, 185-204. New York: Transaction Publishers.

Min, Pyong Gap, and Chigon Kim. 2009. "Patterns of Intermarriage and Cross-Generational In-marriage among Native-Born Asian Americans." *Intergenerational Migration Review* 43: 447-470.

_____. 2010. "Growth and Settlement Patterns of Korean Americans." Research Report 2, The Research Center for Korean Community at Queens College.

Oh, Sook Hee. 2007. "Immigrant Communities and Ethnic Linkages: Suburban Koreans in the New York-New Jersey Metropolitan Area." Dissertation, New School University.

Ruggles, S. et al. 2008. Integrated Public Use Micro data Series: Version 4.0 [Machine-readable database]. Minneapolis, MN: Minnesota Population Center. http://www.ipums.org/.

Yu, Eui-Young, P. Choe, S. L. Han, and K. Yu. 2004. "Emerging Diversity in Los Angeles Koreatown, 1990-2000. *Amerasia Journal* 30 (1): 25-52.

Zhou, Min, and Rebecca Kim. 2003. "A Tale of Two Metropolises: Immigrant Chinese Communities in New York and Los Angeles" In Los Angeles and New York in the New Millenium, edited by David Halle, 124-149. Chicago: University of Chicago Press.

Chapter 4
Changes in Korean Immigrants' Business Patterns

by Pyong Gap Min

Post-1965 Korean immigrants had attracted a great deal of scholarly and media attention in the 1980s through the early 2000s mainly because of their exceptionally high rate of self-employment in small businesses and their business-related conflicts. Survey and ethnographic studies conducted in New York, Los Angeles, Chicago, and Atlanta showed in the 1980s and early 1990s that nearly half or the majority of Korean adult immigrant workers were concentrated in small businesses, such as grocery, liquor and produce retail, retail of Korean/Asian-imported manufactured goods, dry-cleaning service, garment manufacturing, and nail salons (Light and Bonacich and 1988; Min 1988, 1996, 2008; Kim and Hurh 1985). In particular, Korean immigrants depended upon various outside groups for their business operations: minority customers, white suppliers, Latino employees, and white, especially, Jewish landlords. The relationships between business owners and all of these parties often involve disputes and tensions because each side wants to maximize its economic interest. When Korean business owners depend upon non-Korean customers, suppliers, employees and landlords, business-related disputes can easily turn into racial tensions and conflicts. Thus Korean immigrant business owners had severe conflicts with black customers and white suppliers, and moderate conflicts with Latino employees and white landlords in the 1980s and early 1990s. A number of researchers examined Korean merchants' business-related intergroup conflicts using various theoretical perspectives (Abelmann and Lie 1995; C. Kim 2000; J. Lee 2002; Min 1996, 2008; Yoon 1997). I also documented Korean merchants' conflicts with white suppliers, Latino employees, white landlords, and various government agencies regulating small business activities (Min 1996, 2008).

Above, I pointed out that Korean merchants had severe or moderate conflicts with different outside interest groups in the 1980s and early 1990s. However, their business-related intergroup conflicts have almost disappeared since the mid-1990s. As will be discussed later in more detail, the near-disappearance of Korean merchants' business-related conflicts is partly due to factors external to Korean business patterns. But it is mainly due to changes in Korean immigrant business patterns. Although, as cited above, many scholars examined Korean-black conflicts, no other scholar has tried to explain why the conflicts have almost disappeared since the mid-1990s. In my book (Min 2008, Chapter 5), I have explained why black boycotts of Korean stores in New York City, which were prevalent in the 1980s and early 1990s, ended in the mid-1990s. In this chapter, I intend to show that changes in Korean immigrants' business patterns, along with changes in external factors, have contributed to the near-disappearance of Korean merchants' business-related intergroup conflicts in New York. Although this chapter focuses on changes in New York, I believe the same analyses are applicable to Los Angeles and other cities.

Decrease in Self-Employment Rate

One main change in Korean immigrants' business patterns is a substantial decrease in their self-employment rate. Census data are useful in examining a decrease or an increase in their self-employment rate in different decades. Table 4.1 shows changes in the self-employment rate among full-time Korean immigrant workers in the New York-New Jersey area by sex between 1980 and 2005-2007. The self-employment rate of Korean immigrants increased from 29% in 1980 to 34% in 1990. As more and more Korean immigrants established several lines of businesses, it became easier and easier for new immigrants to start their own businesses by getting business information and training from their relatives and friends. This means that Korean immigrants had greater ethnic resources for business establishment in the 1980s than they did in the 1970s. Thus it is not surprising that their self-employment rate increased by 5% between 1980 and 1990.

New Korean immigrants who arrived in New York in the 1990s had even greater ethnic resources for business establishment in the 1990s than those in the 1980s because Koreans had already controlled several lines of businesses by the early 1990s (see the next section). Moreover, Koreans who immigrated to the United States in the 1990s brought much greater class resources for business establishment, especially financial resources, because South Korea had improved economic conditions significantly by the early 1990s. The Korean immigration flow was substantially moderated in the 1990s mainly due to the greater economic improvement in South Korea in the decade (see Chapter 3). Many

Korean immigrants in the 1990s could afford to bring enough money to start their businesses in the United States. Moreover, the government also allowed new Korean immigrants to take significant amounts of money to the United States.

Table 4.1: Changing Self-Employment Rates (%) among Korean Immigrant Full-Time Workers* in the New York-New Jersey Consolidated Metropolitan Statistical Area in 1980, 1990, and 2000 by Sex

	Total	Men	Women
1980	28.5	35.6	16.2
1990	33.5	36.4	28.7
2000	25.3	29.3	20.3
2005-2007	27.2	29.8	23.6

Source: PUMS of the 1980, 1990, and 2000 U.S. Censuses, and the 2005-2007 American Community Surveys
*Immigrants 25-64 years old who worked 35 or more weeks and 35 or more hours per week in the previous years (1979, 1989, and 1999 and 2004, 2005, and 2006)

The above considerations suggest that the self-employment rate of Korean immigrants should be higher in 2000 than in 1990. However, Table 4.1 shows that the opposite is true. It indicates that the self-employment rate of Korean immigrants in 2000 dropped to 25%, 9% lower than that in 1990 and even lower than that in 1980. The self-employment rate of Korean immigrants increased slightly in the 2005-2007 years, but it never reached the level that it attained in 1980. To explain this unexpected finding, we need to pay attention to factors that may have reduced their motivation for starting businesses. One important factor is the significant increase in the proportion of non-immigrant temporary residents in New York and other large Korean communities. As discussed in Chapter 2 in detail, international students and other non-immigrant temporary residents have accounted for an increasing proportion of Korean residents. These temporary residents either have no job, or are employed as temporary workers in Korean-owned stores, American corporations (H1B visa), or branches of Korean firms.

Another factor that has contributed to a decrease in Korean immigrants' self-employment rate is that recently arrived Korean immigrants do not have as much of a language barrier as the earlier immigrants in the 1980s and 1990s. They have less of a language barrier than the earlier immigrants, partly because (as noted in the previous chapter) a large proportion of them entered the United States at earlier ages and completed their college education here. Moreover, even new arrivals directly from Korea can speak English better than the earlier Korean immigrants in the 1970s and 1980s, partly because they started the English education in early grade levels in Korea, and partly because they focused on spoken English with native speaking instructors.[1] And the change in the educational system focusing on spoken English started in the mid-1990s in Korea and has been recently enhanced. In 1990, 36% of Korean immigrants with a college education were self-employed, which suggests that their inability to find jobs commensurate with their educational levels pushed them to start businesses. But in 2000, only 21% of Korean college-educated immigrants were self-employed. In the 2005-2007 years, the self-employment rate of Korean immigrants increased to 27%. But those with a college degree had a low self-employment rate of only 22%, while 36% of non-college Koreans were self-employed. These figures suggest that recent Korean immigrants with a college education are more successful in finding meaningful occupations in the mainstream economy, and that this change has largely contributed to the reduction of Korean immigrants' self-employment rate.

The third important factor that seems to have contributed to the decrease in self-employment among Korean immigrants in the New York-New Jersey area is the radical increase in Korean-owned nail salons in the area. The president of the Korean Nail Salon Association estimated that there were about 1,400 Korean-owned nail salons in the early 1990s (Min 1996: 54). The number increased to approximately 4,000 in 2006 (Min 2008). Since each Korean nail salon usually has several employees, a very large number of Korean immigrant women, accounting for a significant Korean female work force in the New York-New Jersey area, work for nail salons. Many women who ran retail stores in the 1970s and 1980s have worked as employees in Korean-owned nail salons since the late 1990s, as the expansion of the Korean nail-service business has created the job opportunity for many Korean women. Table 4.1 reveals that the self-employment rate of Korean immigrant women sharply increased between 1980 and 1990, but dropped by 8% in the next decade. Much of the decline in the self-employment rate among Korean women can be explained by the shift from running their own retail businesses to being employed at nail salons.

Census data underestimate Korean immigrants' self-employment greatly mainly because in many cases, only the husband or the wife reports himself/herself as self-employed although both partners operate the family business. Statistics in Table 4.1 focusing on foreign-born Koreans also underestimate the self-employment rate of first-generation Korean immigrants partly because the foreign born include many 1.5-generation Koreans who immigrated to the United States at an early age. Since 1.5-generation Koreans have received their high school and college education in the United States, they can find meaningful occupations in the mainstream labor market. For this reason, they have a very low self-employment rate similar to the native-born second generation (Oh and Min 2011).

Independent surveys of first-generation Korean immigrants show much higher self-employment rates. My 1988 telephone survey of Korean married immigrant women in New York City[2] asked the respondents about the employment/self-employment status and types of employment (the ethnic economy vs. the non-ethnic economy) of themselves and their husbands. Table 4.2 analyzes working husbands' and wives' job types based on the results of the survey. 48%

of the married women respondents and 61% of their husbands were self-employed in 1988. These are much higher self-employment rates than shown in the 1990 Census. Since married persons have a higher rate of self-employment than unmarried young adults, results of the 1988 telephone survey of Korean married immigrant women may have slightly overestimated Korean male and female immigrants' self-employment rates. Nevertheless, survey data seem to reflect actual self-employment rates of Korean immigrant men and women in 1990 more closely than the 1990 Census. Results of my independent survey suggest that census data indeed severely underestimate the self-employment of Korean immigrants.

Table 4.2: Korean Immigrants' Class of Workers by Sex, 1988 and 2005

	Self-Employed	Employed in the Ethnic Economy	Employed in the General Economy	Total
1988				
Men	172 (61%)	69 (25%)	39 (14%)	280 (100%)
Women	102 (49%)	76 (36%)	31 (15%)	209 (100%)
Total	274 (56%)	145 (30%)	70 (14%)	489 (100%)
2005				
Men	56 (46%)	46 (38%)	20 (16%)	122 (100%)
Women	53 (34%)	71 (46%)	31 (20%)	155 (100%)
Total	109 (39%)	117 (42%)	51 (19%)	277 (100%)

Source: results of the 1988 telephone survey of married Korean immigrant women in New York City by the author; results of the 2005 telephone survey of Korean immigrants in the labor force in New York City by the author

Table 4.2 indicates that altogether 56% of the female respondents and their spouses were self-employed, with another 30% employed in Korean-owned businesses. Thus only 14% of them participated in the non-ethnic market. The heavy concentration of Korean immigrants in the Korean ethnic economy contributed to their cultural and social isolation. Although Korean businesses predominantly served non-Korean customers, neither Korean business owners nor employees had much social interaction with their customers due to their heavy concentration in retail businesses. Most of the time Koreans spoke Korean inside their stores. This means that Korean immigrants' heavy concentration in the ethnic economy also led to a slower acculturation process than other Asian groups, and more social segregation (Min 1995: 227-228). The affiliation with and active participation of most Korean immigrants in Korean churches and the active operation of Korean-language media further contribute to their cultural and social isolation (Min 1992).

Like census data, survey data in Table 4.2 also reveal that the self-employment of Korean immigrants dropped in the 2000s compared to earlier periods. Since only those in the labor force were included in the table's statistics, the results of the two surveys are comparable. In 1988, 56% of the working women respondents and their working husbands in New York City were self-employed. But the rate decreased to 39% in 2005. In 2005, more women were included in the table's statistics, although more men than women actually worked. When adjusting the men's underrepresentation, the self-employment rate of the total in 2005 would have been 43%, a little higher than the reported 39%. Nevertheless, it was substantially lower than that in 1988. The proportion of Korean immigrants in the general economy in 2005 was 19%, showing a 5% increase from the figure in 1988.

Changes in Types of Businesses

Korean immigrants' business patterns in New York have changed not only in the decrease in their self-employment rate, but also in a gradual shift from their concentration in retail businesses to personal-service businesses. Table 4.3 shows the main businesses of self-employed Korean immigrants in the New York-New Jersey area in four different time periods. The majority of Korean-owned businesses in the New York-New Jersey area were retail businesses (61%). In 1980, stores selling manufactured goods, such as wigs, clothing, shoes and costume jewelry, mostly imported from South Korea, comprised the majority of these retail businesses. They were the first important Korean businesses established in New York, as well as in other major Korean communities (Kim 1980: 121-143; Min 1984). Korean wholesale businesses, which accounted for 10% of all Korean businesses in the area in 1980, also sold these Korean-imported manufactured goods to Korean and Latino retailers. Korean immigrants in the 1960s and 1970s took advantage of the Korean export-oriented economy by wholesaling and retailing these Korean-imported manufactured goods. Retail businesses captured in the 1980 Census also include Korean greengrocery, grocery and seafood retail stores that began in the late 1970s.

Another structural factor that enabled Korean immigrants to purchase greengrocery, grocery and seafood retail stores since the late 1970s was the widespread retirement of many white American store owners who had previously controlled these retail businesses (Kim 1980; Min 2008)). Before a large number of Koreans began to immigrate to New York City in 1970, Jewish and Italian Americans controlled most of the grocery and greengrocery retail businesses. As old native-born Jewish and Italian retail business owners, especially in minority neighborhoods, retired in the 1960s and 1970s, their children did not inherit these labor-intensive small businesses. New Korean immigrants, highly motivated to work long hours for economic mobility, purchased these retail businesses from retiring white owners. They also preferred these retail businesses because they could start them with relatively small amounts of capital and operate them using their family members. Korean immigrants concentrated in retail mainly because these labor-intensive businesses were not attractive to native-born white Americans.

The proportion of Korean-owned retail businesses decreased to 44% in 1990, while personal-service businesses increased from 7% in 1980 to 19% in 1990. In the next decade (between 1990 and 2000), the proportion of retail businesses continued to decline, with a concomitant increase in that of personal-service businesses. To explain the gradual reduction of Korean-owned retail stores, we need to consider two structural factors that have made it increasingly difficult for Korean retail shopkeepers to survive. First, the emergence of retail mega stores, especially in lower-income minority neighborhoods, has made it difficult for Korean-owned small retail stores to survive since the late 1990s. Many Korean grocery, greengrocery, and fish retail stores were located in lower-income minority neighborhoods, such as Harlem (Manhattan), Jamaica (Queens), and Flatbush (Brooklyn), in earlier years. But the movement of large numbers of mega stores into minority neighborhoods, following the change in the zoning laws by the New York City government in 1996, forced many Korean retail stores to be closed (Min 2008). For example, the movement of Pathmark into Harlem nearly eliminated all Korean small grocery, greengrocery and fish retail stores. In 1991, there were four Korean-owned greengrocery stores, three grocery stores, and three seafood stores in the heart of Harlem (Min 2008). But I found that only one greengrocery store and a seafood store survived in 2006.

The other important reason Korean-owned retail stores decreased beginning in the latter half of the 1990s was the movement of many other non-Korean immigrants into minority neighborhoods for business ventures, especially in the retail of manufactured goods. These other immigrant groups include Chinese, Asian Indians, Middle Easterners, Dominican, and Caribbean/African black immigrants. These immigrants who originated from those countries with lower standards of living than South Korea were ready to run small businesses with lower profit margins. Thus Korean immigrants had difficulty in competing with them. In the late 1990s, Chinese and Indian immigrants in particular imported manufactured goods, such as clothing, hair-care items and wigs, from their home countries for substantially lower prices than Korean immigrants imported them from South Korea. This contributed to the reduction of not only Korean-owned retail stores, but also their wholesale businesses dealing in Korean imported manufactured goods. As shown in Table 4.3, wholesale trade businesses accounted for 10% of the total Korean-owned businesses in 1980, but it gradually decreased to 6% in 2000. The proportion of wholesale businesses increased to 11% in 2005-2007. But it was due mainly to emergence of other types of wholesale businesses, such as greengrocery, grocery, and fish wholesale store during recent years.

Table 4.3 reveals that the proportion of Korean personal-service businesses increased gradually, reaching 32%—the highest point—in 2000, and then slightly decreased to 23% in 2005-2007. Korean-owned nail salons and dry-cleaning shops comprise the vast majority of their personal-service businesses. The demand for more dry cleaning and nail services between 1990 and 2000 helped Korean immigrants to further expand these two ethnic niches. There were 1,500 Korean dry-cleaning shops in the New York-New Jersey area in 1991 (Min 1996: 54). Two Korean dry cleaners' associations in New York and New Jersey estimated that the number of Korean-owned dry cleaners increased to approximately 3,000 in 2006, accounting for about half of all dry cleaners in the area. The astronomical increase in the number of Korean-owned dry cleaners in the fifteen-year period indicates a change in American consumption culture in the direction of a greater dependency upon commercial dry cleaning, away from ironing at home. In the early 1990s and before, Korean-owned dry cleaners were concentrated in white middle-class neighborhoods. But many of them are now located in lower-income black and Latino neighborhoods as well. About 40% of Korean-owned dry cleaners are family businesses run by a husband-wife team. The others have one or two paid employees. Most of these dry cleaners have their own washing machines, with many of them having four to six employees, mostly Latino workers.

Table 4.3: Industries of Main Businesses owned by Full-Time Korean Immigrant Workers in the New York-New Jersey Area by Decade

Industry	Year			
	1980	1990	2000	2005-2007
Retail Trade	61%	44%	30%	29%
Wholesale Trade	10%	8%	6%	11%
Personal Services	23%	7%	19%	32%
Eating and Drinking Establishments	1%	5%	4%	3%
Finance, Insurance, and Real Estate	1%	3%	2%	7%
Professional and Related Services	8%	8%	10%	12%
Manufacturing	8%	7%	4%	3%
All Others	5%	9%	14%	22%
Total	100%	100%	100%	100%

Source: PUMS of the 1980, 1990, and 2000 U.S. Censuses, and the 2005-2007 American Community Surveys

The Korean Nail Salon Associations of New York and New Jersey estimate that there are approximately 4,000 Korean-owned nail salons in the New York-New Jersey area as of 2006, comprising the vast majority of nail salons in the area. This number was a three-fold increase from about 1,400 in 1991 (Min

1996, 54). Number-wise, the nail business is the largest Korean business line in the New York-New Jersey area. According to Ju Suk Pang, a former president of the Korean Nail Salon Association of New York, women alone own about 30% of Korean nail salons, with husband and wife teams co-running about 60%, and male owners with women managers making up the remainder. A nail salon usually has five to six paid employees, with a predominant majority of employees consisting of Korean women and the rest being Latino women. Thus, the nail salon business is significant for the Korean community in New York because it provides many jobs for Korean women, including illegal residents, wives of international students, and Korean women from China. Korean nail business leaders tout that Korean nail salons provide jobs for about 20,000 Korean women.

Theories of immigrant entrepreneurship have paid little attention to innovation as a major factor in the development and evolution of immigrant entrepreneurship. But the development of the nail business by Korean immigrants in New York City was made possible mainly because of their business innovations, responding to the increasing consumer demand for body-related services. Korean immigrants began to move into the nail business in the late 1970s after Korean women had learned nail skills through their employment in Russian-origin Jewish immigrant nail salons. Jewish-owned nail salons usually provided manicure (finger nail polish) and pedicure (toe nail polish) services. Korean-owned nail salons have innovated manicure and pedicure services by replacing the traditional acrylic gluing with linen or silk wrapping. Moreover, they have added two other important and popular body-related services—spa (washing and massaging feet) and skin care. Most recently, they have added different types of massage services—eye, shoulder and whole-body massages. As they have added other types of services, they have attracted male clients as well. According to the president of the Korean Nail Salon Association of New York, about 15% of clients for Korean nail salons are men. He optimistically predicts that male customers will continue to increase in the future, therefore the market in the nail business is unlimited. Approximately 500 Korean-owned nail salons in Manhattan do better than those in other areas of the city, because they can serve not only local residents, but also professional and managerial employees of corporations, and tourists.

The decrease in the proportion of personal-service businesses from 32% in 2000 to 23% in 2005-2007 does not indicate the decrease in the total number of these businesses during the six-year period. It is due mainly to a substantial increase in the total number of Korean-owned businesses during the most recent years. In addition to wholesale, finance/ insurance/real estate (FIRE) and professional businesses also achieved significant increases. Even many Korean businesses previously classified as small retail businesses have expanded to supermarkets and medium-size produce stores. These changes in business types during the most recent years suggest that Korean immigrants have gradually switched from labor-intensive small businesses to medium-size businesses involving managerial skills and professional knowledge. The substantial increases in the proportions of professional and FIRE businesses partly reflect changes in industrial structure in the United States as well as in other advanced industrial countries. But Korean immigrant-owned businesses seem to have experienced a higher level of transition from retail businesses to wholesale, FIRE, and professional businesses. It is due partly to many 1.5-generation young Korean Americans coming of age, and partly to exceptionally high educational levels of recent first-generation Korean immigrants.

Virtual Disappearance of Business-Related Intergroup Conflicts

Some alien minority groups served as middlemen in colonial and preindustrial societies by distributing merchandise produced by the ruling group to the consuming masses. Jews in Medieval Europe, the Chinese in many Southeast Asian countries, and Indians in Nigeria and Uganda were typical examples of middleman merchants (Eitzen 1971; Tinker 1974; Zenner 1991). A typical middleman minority was not likely to develop in the twentieth-century United States where the middle class comprised the majority of the population. Yet, Rinder (1958-1959) suggested that the United States might need a middleman minority to bridge the huge white-black racial status gap big status. He pointed out that in "the urban negro ghettoes, Jews have been prominent in venturing into this gap to service the commercial needs, even as they did for the Medieval peasant" (Rinder 1958-1959: 257).

As already pointed out, Korean immigrants in New York City moved into black neighborhoods for business ventures in the 1970s after Jews and other white business owners moved out. Korean-owned grocery, greengrocery and seafood retail stores, and gift shops selling Korea/Asia-imported manufactured goods were overrepresented in minority neighborhoods in the 1970s through early 1990s. Not only in New York City, but also in Los Angeles, Chicago and other cities, Korean immigrant merchants played the role of middleman merchants in black neighborhoods, distributing corporation-made grocery, greengrocery and liquor items to minority black customers (Min 1996, 2008). Middleman minority merchants in different societies were subjected to "host hostility," especially by minority customers they served, in the forms of boycotts, physical violence, arson, and riots. Korean merchants in black neighborhoods also encountered boycotts and other forms of rejection by black customers in the 1980s and early 1990s (Lee 2002; C. Kim 2000; Min 1996, 2008). Blacks' rejection of Korean merchants culminated in the 1992 Los Angeles riots, during which approximately 230 Korean-owned stores were destroyed. While Korean merchants in South Central Los Angeles experienced many cases of physical violence, those in black neighborhoods in New York City encountered six long-term boycotts and nine short-term boycotts (Min 1996, 2008: 76). Jamaica in Queens, Harlem in Manhattan, and Flatbush in Brooklyn were major black neighborhoods where long-term boycotts occurred frequently in the 1980s and early 1990s.

Korean merchants' "rude" treatment of black customers and their failure to hire black employees were frequent complaints among the black community, and disputes between Korean employees and black customers were immediate causes of long-term boycotts. However, black residents' severe underrepresentation in business activities in their own neighborhoods and the Black Nationalists' perception of Korean merchants as economically exploiting blacks were more fundamental causes of black boycotts of Korean stores (Min 1996, 2008). All major long-term boycotts of Korean stores were organized by Sonny Carson and other Black Nationalists. Black Nationalists usually rejected all Korean stores in the neighborhood when they were boycotting a particular Korean store in a black neighborhood. They also claimed that the U.S. government and American commercial banks helped Korean immigrants to establish businesses in black neighborhoods. Contrary to these claims, almost all Korean business owners depended upon their class and ethnic resources for establishment of businesses.

The last black boycott of a Korean store occurred in a hat store in Greenwich Village, a white neighborhood, not a black neighborhood, in 1995. Since that time, no black boycotts of Korean stores have occurred in New York City. What exactly contributed to the disappearance of black boycotts of Korean stores, which no one expected to dissipate in the late 1980s and early 1990s? To answer this question, we need to consider several important structural changes that have occurred in lower-income black neighborhoods since the late 1990s (see Min 2008: 89-96). As previously noted, one is the movement of many mega stores into black neighborhoods following changes in the zoning laws and urban renovations in 1996. Korean retail store owners could not compete with mega stores in terms of prices, and also could not survive rent hikes caused by urban renovations. Also, many members of other recent immigrant groups, such as Chinese, Indian, and Middle Eastern immigrants moved to black neighborhoods for business ventures. Thus the number of Korean-owned stores in black neighborhoods decreased to one third or one fourth of what the total number was in the 1980s and early 1990s.

There are currently significant numbers of immigrant business owners, including Koreans, in black neighborhoods. But these days, neither Korean nor other immigrant business owners encounter much rejection or hostility from black residents. Black residents can no longer consider immigrant-owned stores as invading their own territory because of significant changes in the racial composition of their neighborhoods. For example, in 1980, blacks composed 94% of the population in Central Harlem. The proportion of African Americans (the native-born black population) comprised only 68% of the population in 2000 (Min 2008: 91). By contrast, the proportion of Hispanics increased from 4% in 1980 to 17% in 2000. As of 2010, African Americans may still be the majority of the population in Central Harlem. But proportions of Hispanic, white and Asian populations are likely to have increased significantly. The racial diversity in Harlem has resulted in African American residents' loss of territorial claims made when they boycotted Korean stores. In this way, the New York City government's urban renovation plans and the racial diversity of the post-1965 immigrants has radically changed the structure of traditional black neighborhoods. In addition to Central Harlem, other black neighborhoods in Queens and Brooklyn have gone through similar changes in the racial composition of the population. A black boycott of immigrant-owned stores in black neighborhoods is unlikely to occur in the future.

The literature on middleman minorities does not provide much information about middleman retail merchants' conflicts with suppliers. However, Korean grocery, greengrocery and seafood retail store owners in New York City have had numerous conflicts with their distributors. In particular, Korean produce owners who had to visit Hunts Point Market to purchase greengrocery items suffered different forms of discriminatory treatment and physical violence by white managers and employees in the 1980s and early 1990s. Unfair treatment included getting rotten fruits which were hidden in the bottoms of boxes underneath fresh fruits, receiving no merchandise in the case of shortage of particular items even when they paid for it in advance, discrimination in parking, verbal threats, and beatings (see Min 2008: 58-61). Also, Korean produce retailers encountered armed robberies at Hunts Point Market early in the morning due to a lack of security measures.[3]

Initially, Korean produce owners at HPM felt powerless because they more or less depended upon white distributors for merchandise. Over time, however, they organized themselves to protect their economic interests against and to ensure their security from distributors through their association, Korean Produce Association of New York (KPA). As the number of Korean produce owners increased, the KPA realized that it could use the collective number power of Korean produce retailers to challenge the distributors. Among all forms of collective action it used against white suppliers, it found boycotting to be the most effective technique. Between 1977 and 1995, Korean Produce Association organized ten demonstrations and/or boycotts against white suppliers at HPM (Min 2008: 65). Half of the demonstrations/boycotts were in response to a Korean produce retailer being beaten. Since Korean produce retailers comprised a significant proportion or the majority of customers for most distributors at HPM in the late 1980s and afterwards, the targeted distributors were forced to accept most demands made by KPA within a week of each boycott.

An analysis of Korean newspaper articles shows that the last boycott organized by the KPA against a supplier at HPM was in 1995. When I interviewed the president and other staff members of Korean Produce Association in 2006 and 2007, they told me they had not had much conflict with suppliers since the late 1990s. They said that produce suppliers at HPM were very cooperative to

Korean produce retailers. If there was a minor problem with a particular supplier, a call and a warning would be enough to make it change services. Obviously, KPA's organization of several boycotts has made distributors change their attitudes towards Korean produce retailers. Many distributors have recently donated significant amounts of money for KPA's annual cultural festivals. Moreover, Korean greengrocers' improvements in English skills and experiences with dealing with suppliers also contributed to better relations with the latter, although KPA staff members did not emphasize these changes. In addition, white suppliers have made great efforts to satisfy Korean produce retailers since the late 1990s, partly because Korean greengrocers have become their more important customer base, even more so than before. Previously, American supermarkets were bigger customers than Korean produce retailers. But, as consumption of vegetables and fruits increased with a rise in health consciousness, supermarkets have begun purchasing large quantities of produce items directly from farms.

Koreans' Occupational Assimilation and Incorporation into American Society

Korean Americans as individuals and the Korean community in the New York-New Jersey area as a collectivity are more integrated into American society now than they were fifteen years ago. Their greater integration into the mainstream society is due partly to Korean immigrants' moderate occupational assimilation and partly to emergence of 1.5- and second-generation young adults. This chapter shows Korean immigrants' and younger-generation Koreans' occupational assimilation using census data pertaining to Korean Americans in the New York-New Jersey area. But most Korean Americans reside in smaller Korean communities than the Korean community in the New York-New Jersey area. They are likely to have achieved higher levels of occupational assimilation than Koreans in the area.

As noted above, as the self-employment of Korean immigrants has decreased since the late 1990s, more Korean immigrants work in the mainstream economy than before. Korean immigrants' moderate occupational assimilation means that more Koreans speak English at their workplaces and have more contact with white Americans and members of other minority groups for friendships and even dating. Moreover, the change in Korean immigrants' business types from retail businesses to service businesses has contributed to Korean business owners' and employees' increasing contact with non-Korean customers. A large number of Korean immigrant women work for Korean-owned nail salons either as business owners or as employees. As "emotional care" workers, both Korean nail salon owners and their employees have close personal interactions with their customers. To establish and secure regular clients, Korean nail salon owners and employees often ask white clients about their jobs, hobbies, and family backgrounds. Some even become friends with their clients, thanks to the nature of their services. Of course, they need to speak English all the time with their customers. Korean dry cleaners interact with their customers to a lesser extent than Korean nail workers. But they still communicate with their customers at a more personal level than Korean retail store owners.

Moreover, the vast majority of younger-generation Koreans, who have no language barrier and received their education in the United States, participates in the mainstream economy. As shown in Table 4.4, only 10% of 1.5-generation Korean male workers and 6% of U.S.-born male workers in the New York-New Jersey area were self-employed in 2000, compared to 31% of first-generation immigrant male workers. U.S.-born Koreans had a much lower self-employment rate than their Chinese American counterparts (9%), although Korean immigrants had a much higher self-employment rate than Chinese immigrants (11%) (Oh and Min 2011: Table 2). Younger-generation Koreans not only overwhelmingly participate in the mainstream economy, but also do well socioeconomically there. 63% of 1.5-generation Koreans and 62% of native-born Koreans had managerial or professional occupations, the two highest occupational categories (see Table 4.4). Again, this is a general pattern of intergenerational occupational transformations among Korean Americans applicable to other large Korean communities in the United States.

Table 4.4: Generation Differences (%) in Fluency in English and Occupational Patterns among Korean American Men in Labor Force (25-64 years old) in the New York-New Jersey Metropolitan Area in 2000

	1st Generation	1.5 Generation	Native-Born	Total
Number	31,056	3,762	1,739	36,557
Speaking English Very Well*	24.3	87.5	90.7	34.0
Managerial Occupations	18.5	23.3	20.2	19.1
Professional Occupations	18.2	40.0	48.1	21.9
Self-Employed	30.5	10.3	6.3	27.2
Mean Age	44	30	30	42

Source: U.S. Census of Population and Housing: 2000 PUMS published by IPUMS (2004)
*Those who speak English very well include those who speak English alone.

Younger-generation Koreans' participation in the mainstream economy does not merely contribute to their individual cultural and social assimilation. Their social networks with non-Korean co-workers also contribute to linkages of the Korean community to the larger society in a number of different ways. I can give one prominent example here. Many well established Korean social service organizations in the New York-New Jersey area hold annual galas as a way of collecting donations. Korean American Community Foundation is a foundation that was established in 2002 by immigrant and second generation Koreans. At present, 1.5- and second-generation Koreans control the leadership in the organization. About 1,000 people attended its annual donation gala held in October 2011 at Chelsea Piers in Manhattan at a cost of $400 a ticket. I learned that the majority of Korean participants were 1.5-generation and native-born Koreans, with non-Korean participants comprising a significant proportion as well. Second-generation leaders were able to use personal contacts at their companies to bring many representatives of American corporations to the gala. That helped the organization raise a fund of approximately one million dollars, a greater amount than any other Korean social service agency raised in 2011. Since Korean American Community Foundation distributes the fund to Korean social service organizations to help needy individuals and families, younger-generation Koreans' networks with their co-workers contribute to the welfare of the community as a whole.

Concluding Remarks

The Korean community is probably the most segregated from the mainstream society among the four major Asian groups in the New York-New Jersey area (Chinese, Indians, Filipinos and Koreans). One of the main reasons why it is highly segregated is the involvement of a predominance of Korean immigrants in the ethnic economy either as business owners or as employees of Korean-owned businesses. However, the Korean community is substantially less segregated from the mainstream society that it was twenty years ago partly because of changes in Koreans' business patterns. One major change in their business pattern is the decrease in their self-employment rate. A decrease in their self-employment rate means that more Korean immigrants participate in the general economy, more frequently interacting with non-Korean workers. Also, a gradual shift in business types from retail businesses to service businesses has contributed to Korean immigrants' more active personal interactions with their customers than before. This shift in business types has also partly contributed to the near disappearance of Korean immigrants' business-related intergroup conflicts, which were prevalent in the 1980s and early 1990. In addition, the participation of a predominant majority of younger-generation Koreans in the mainstream economy has further linked the Korean community to the mainstream society.

Notes

1. When we attended school in the 1950s in Korea, we started to learn English in the seventh grade. But they start to learn English in the second grade. We had English grammar, composition, and reading classes, but no English conversation class. However, elementary and high school students have to take one or more English conversation classes in Korea and native speakers usually teach English conversation classes.
2. For more detailed information about this survey, see Min (1997).
3. Most Korean produce retailers went to Hunts Point Market early in the morning, around 3:00 or 4:00 a.m.

References

Abelmann, Nancy, and John Lie. 1995. *Blue Dreams: Korean Americans and Los Angeles Riots.* Cambridge, MA: Harvard University Press.
Eitzen, Stanley. 1971. "Two Minorities: The Jews of Poland and the Chinese of the Philippines." In *Ethnic Conflict and Power: A Cross-National Perspective*, edited by D. Gelfand and R. Lee. New York: John Wiley and Sons.
Kim, Claire Jean. 2000. *Bitter Fruits: The Politics of Black-Korean Conflict in New York City.* New Haven, CT: Yale University Press.
Kim, Illsoo. 1980. *New Urban Immigrants: The Korean Community in New York.* Princeton, NJ: Princeton University Press.
Kim, Kwang Chung, and Woo Moo Hurh. 1985. "Ethnic Resources Utilization of Korean Immigrant Entrepreneurs in the Chicago Minority Area." *International Migration Review* 19 (1), 82-111.
Lee, Jennifer. 2002. *Civility in the City: Blacks, Jews, and Koreans in Urban America.* Cambridge, MA: Harvard University Press.
Light, Ivan, and Edna Bonacich. 1988. *Immigrant Entrepreneurs: Koreans in Los Angeles 1965-1982.* Berkeley, CA: University of California Press.
Min, Pyong Gap. 1984. "From White-Collar Occupations to Small Business: Korean Immigrants' Occupational Adjustment." *Sociological Quarterly* 25: 333-352.
_____. 1988. *Ethnic Business Enterprises: Korean Small Business in Atlanta.* New York: Center for Migration Studies.
_____. 1992. "The Structure of Social Functions of Korean Immigrant Churches in the United States." *International Migration Review* 26: 1370-1394.
_____. 1995. "Korean Americans." In *Asian Americans: Contemporary Trends and Issues*, edited by Pyong Gap Min, 199-231. Newbury Park, CA: Sage Publications.
_____. 1996. *Caught in the Middle: Korean Communities in New York and Los Angeles.* Berkley, CA: University of California Press.
_____. 1997. "Korean Immigrant Wives' Labor Force Participation, Marital Power, and Status." In *Women and Work: Race, Ethnicity, and Class*, edited by Elizabeth Higginbotham and Mary Romero. Newbury Park: CA: Sage Publications.
_____. 2008. *Ethnic Solidarity for Economic Survival: Korean Greengroceries in New York City.* New York: Russell Sage Foundation.
Oh, Sook Hee, and Pyong Gap Min. 2011. "Generation and Earnings Patterns among Chinese, Filipino, and Korean Americans." *International Migration Review* 45: 852-871.
Rinder, Irwin. 1958-1959. "Strangers in the Land: Social Relations in the 'Status Gap.'" *Social Problems* 6: 253-260.
Tinker, Hugh. 1974. *A New System of Slavery: The Export of Indian Labor Overseas, 1830-1920.* London: Oxford University Press.
Yoon, In-Jin. 1997. *On My Own: Korean Businesses and Race Relations in America.* Chicago: University of Chicago Press.
Zenner, Walter. 1991. *Minorities in the Middle: A Cross-Cultural Analysis.* Albany, NY: State University of New York Press.

Chapter 5
A Comparison of Korean Protestant, Catholic, and Buddhist Religious Institutions in New York

by Pyong Gap Min

Introduction

Korean immigrants in the United States significantly differ from other Asian immigrant groups in their religious background. While other Asian immigrant groups have transplanted "Oriental" religions such as Hinduism and Buddhism or Asianized Catholicism, the majority of Korean immigrants are affiliated with Korean Protestant churches. Compared to the population, each Korean community has an exceptionally large number of churches. It is also known that Korean Protestant immigrants participate in Korean churches very actively (Hurh and Kim 1990; Kim and Kim 2001; Min 2000). In fact, as will be shown later, Korean Protestant immigrants seem to be more active in church participation than any other religious immigrant group.

The active participation of Korean immigrants in Korean churches and the presence of several Korean Protestant immigrant scholars have contributed to a great deal of research on Korean immigrant churches over the past several years (Hurh and Kim 1990; A. Kim 1997; I. Kim 1981; J. Kim 1996; Kwon et al. 2001; Min 1991, 1992, 2000, 2008a, 2010; Shin and Park 1988). The second-generation Korean English ministry has also been subjected to great scholarly analysis (Alumkal 1999, 2001; Chai 1998, 2001a; Chong 1998; Ecklund 2006; R. Kim 2006; Min 2010; Min and Kim 2005; Park 2001). As a result, we have access to abundant data that shed light on the structure and socio-cultural functions of Korean immigrant and second-generation Christian congregations.

Protestant churches are the most important, but not the only, religious institutions in the Korean community. Significant proportions of Korean immigrants are Catholics and Buddhists. Korean Catholic and Buddhist immigrants have also established their religious institutions. However, not much academic research has been conducted on Korean Catholic or Buddhist institutions. To my knowledge, no published materials focusing on Korean Catholic churches in the United States are available. Materials on Korean immigrant Buddhist temples are available, but severely limited (Chai 2001b; Kwon 2003; Suh, 2003, 2004; Yu 2001), especially compared to those on Korean Protestant churches.

This chapter has two main objectives. One main objective is to provide a descriptive overview of three major religions among Korean immigrants in New York in their religious choices and participation in religious institutions. Studies of Korean Protestant immigrants and/or Protestant immigrant congregations have examined the social services, fellowship, and cultural retention functions of the church, as well as Korean immigrants' frequency of participation in the congregation (Hurh and Kim 1990; I. Kim 1981, Chapter 6; Kim and Kim 2001; Kwon et al.... 1997; Min 1992). The other major and more important objective of this paper is to compare Korean Protestant, Catholic, and Buddhist religious institutions with regard to fellowship, social services, and cultural retention functions of the institutions.

Data Sources

To examine New York Korean immigrants' affiliations with and participation in religious congregations, I use results of a telephone survey study of Korean, Chinese, and Indian immigrants in New York City conducted between March and May 2005. The survey was conducted as part of a larger study that compared Korean, Chinese and Indian immigrants in the effect of business involvement on ethnic solidarity (Min 2008b). I used the so-called Kim sample technique for the Korean sample. Kims comprise about 22% of the population in Korea (Korean National Bureau of Statistics 1977). Kim is a uniquely Korean name, and Kims represent the Korean population socioeconomically (Shin and Kim 1984). This means that a random selection of Kim households listed in public telephone directories will yield a representative sample of Korean immigrants.

We selected 800 Kim households listed in the 2004 public directories of five boroughs of the New York City. Many selected households were not eligible for the interview because they were either second- or 1.5-generation Korean households or did not have any worker at the time of the interview. Many other selected Kim households were unreachable either because they moved away or possibly due to both partners having worked long hours. Thus, only 537 (about two-thirds) of the 800 households were eligible or reachable households. Of them, 277 (52%) were successfully interviewed by Korean students. The questionnaire included more than forty items, but their responses to three questions—one on religion in Korea, another on religion at the time of the interview, and the third on frequency of participation at the time of the interview—were used for this chapter.

To compare the social service, fellowship, and cultural retention functions of the religious institutions, I conducted ethnographic research on the Shin Kwang Church of New York in Queens (hereafter referred to as the Shin Kwang Church) in 2003, and St. Paul Chong Ha Sang Roman Catholic Chapel in Queens (hereafter referred to as the Queens Catholic church) and a Korean temple located in Upstate New York, New York Bulkwang Zen Meditation Center, (hereafter referred to as the New York Korean temple) in 2001. The Queens Catholic parish is the largest Korean Catholic parish with more than 2,100 registered households. Although it was much larger than the Shin Kwang Church (approximately 300 households) and the New York Korean temple (430 households), its selection was inevitable because it was the only Korean Catholic parish in Queens at that time that was physically independent. Other Korean Catholic congregations in Queens are Korean ethnic congregations within American Catholic parishes. The Shin Kwang Church was a medium-size Korean Protestant church in New York, and there were several large Korean immigrant churches with 500 or more registered households. But I selected the medium-size Korean church because its senior pastor was very cooperative to my research. Although the selected temple was the second largest Korean temple in New York, it was much smaller than the Catholic church in membership and socio-cultural activities.

I conducted ethnographic research at the Shin Kwang Church of New York for four months in 2003. I observed the Sunday worship services, the Sunday lunch service and fellowship in the dining room, the Korean-language, and other socio-cultural activities in the church. I also interviewed the senior pastor, two associate pastors, two elders, the principal and teachers of the Korean language school, and several lay members. I also reviewed the church's annual directories, newsletters, and other documents. When I had questions about the church's worship services and other socio-cultural activities, I called the senior pastor and associate pastors for more information. For the Queens Catholic parish, I conducted personal interviews with four staff members in summer 2001. I also made observations of Sunday masses and various programs, including youth and Korean language programs, on four days. I conducted research on the selected Korean temple in fall 2001. I personally interviewed the abbot, an assistant priest, and a few members of the temple who are familiar with its activities and history. I also observed two Sunday services and a Friday lecture meeting. I also used newsletters and other documents relating to the three selected Korean religious institutions.

As part of a larger study, I had fifty-five tape-recorded personal interviews with Korean Protestant immigrants in New York conducted between December

2000 and August 2001. The interview questions focused on examining how Korean Protestant immigrants maintain their ethnicity through religion. I have used portions of these personal interviews to analyze Korean Protestant immigrants' participation in Korean churches and Korean churches' social functions. In January through March 2002, I also interviewed more than ten Korean Christian and Buddhist leaders in New York personally or on the phone to answer specific research questions that emerged while analyzing the two types of data described above. These interviews with Korean religious leaders are another data source used in this study.

The Overrepresentation of Christians among Korean Immigrants

Table 5.1 shows Korean immigrants' religions in Korea and at the time of the interview. The second column in the table indicates that 48% of the respondents were Protestants in Korea with another 13% being Catholics and only 8% being Buddhists. Thus the majority of Korean immigrants in New York City were Christians prior to their migration. But Christians made up less than one-third of the population (Protestants 20% and Catholics 7%) in Korea in 2003 while Buddhists comprised about 25% of the population (Korea National Statistical Office 2005: 539). Before 2003, Christians made up even a smaller proportion, as proportions of both Protestants and Catholics have gradually increased over the last forty-five years from 5% in 1962 (see Min 2010, Chapter 2). These figures suggest that Christians are heavily overrepresented among Korean immigrants to the United States while Buddhists are severely underrepresented. Survey studies conducted in the late 1980s (Hurh and Kim 1990; Park et al.... 1989) show that Christians, especially Protestants, had much larger proportions of Korean immigrants than the general population in Korea.

Table 5.1: Korean Immigrant Respondents' Self-Reported Religions in Korea and New York (2005)

	In Korea		In New York	
	Number	%	Number	%
Protestantism	133	48.0	162	58.5
Catholicism	35	12.6	39	14.1
Buddhism	36	13.0	22	7.9
Other	1	0.4	2	0.7
None	72	26.0	52	18.8
Total	277	100.0	277	100.0

Source: A 2005 Survey of Chinese, Indian, and Korean Immigrants in New York City

Three major factors explain this selective migration of Korean Christians to the United States. First of all, Christians are overrepresented among the middle-class people in Korea, and Korean immigrants are largely drawn from the middle-class segment of the population. Moreover, Christianity, especially Protestantism, is more popular in large metropolitan areas in Korea from which Korean immigrants are heavily drawn, while Buddhism is more prevalent in rural areas (Park and Cho 1995).[1] In addition, more Christians seem to have selectively chosen the path of U.S.-bound emigration than Buddhists or people with no religion because Koreans consider the United States as a typical Christian country.

The fourth column of Table 5.1 indicates that the proportion of Protestant respondents at the time of the interview was substantially larger than that of the respondents who were Protestants in Korea. The increase in the percentage of Protestants from 48% prior to their migration to 59% at the time of the interview suggests that a large number of Korean immigrants who were not Protestants in Korea have been Christianized after migration. This means that many Buddhists and non-Christian Koreans prior to their migration to the United States have participated in Korean Protestant churches. Non-Protestant Korean immigrants have attended Korean immigrant churches because the latter serve a number of socio-cultural functions for Korean immigrants and their children, such as immigration orientations, fellowship, provision of social services, and Korean language education (Hurh and Kim 1990; I. Kim 1981; Kwon et al.... 1997; Min 1992). Accordingly, it is difficult for Korean immigrants, most of whom have a language barrier, to survive without participating in a Korean church.

While the demand for Korean churches to provide communal bonds has contributed to the increase in the proportion of Korean immigrants participating in Korean Protestant churches, the supply of too many Korean Protestant churches has also led to a further increase in the Protestant population in the Korean community. Mainly due to the presence of many Korean immigrant pastors,[2] an exceptionally large number of Korean Protestant churches have been established. As of 2003, there were 520 Korean Protestant churches in the New York-New Jersey area with a population of approximately 200,000. To survive, each church needs to bring more members, which means that there has been strong competition among Korean Protestant churches to bring more Korean immigrants, including non-Christian Koreans, to their churches.

The effort to bring more Koreans to their churches is also consistent with their evangelical theological position that evangelizing other non-Protestant members is one of the main missions of Christians. The importance of the supply of so many Korean Protestant churches for explaining the increase in the number and proportion of Protestants in the Korean community is demonstrated by the fact that the proportion of Catholic respondents has not increased from Korea to New York City. There are only about 25 Catholic churches in the New York-New Jersey area, compared to about 540 Korean Protestant churches. Although, as will be shown later, Catholic churches serve almost the same socio-cultural functions, they have not brought many non-Catholic members because there are a relatively small number of Catholic churches. The number of Korean Catholic churches is small because Korean Catholics need permission from the local Catholic diocese to establish a new one. As a result, Korean Catholic churches have not been in strong competition to attract more Korean immigrants.

Statistics in Table 5.1 show that only 13% of Korean immigrants in New York City chose Buddhism as their religion in Korea, and that the proportion of Buddhists at the time of the interview further decreased to 8%. The results of the survey indicate not only that Buddhists were severely underrepresented among those who chose the U.S.-bound emigration in Korea; but also that about 40% of Korean Buddhist immigrants have stitched to Korean Christian churches, especially Korean Protestant churches, in New York. Many Korean Buddhist immigrants in New York in the 1970s and 1980s needed to attend Korean immigrant churches for immigration orientations and other services, because there were few Buddhist temples at that time and even those few temples did not provide social services. In particular, Korean Buddhist immigrants with their school-attending children may have needed to attend Korean Protestant churches for the benefit of sending their children to a Korean school established within a Korean church. Theologically, Korean Buddhists, like other Asian Buddhists, tolerate different religions and thus it was not difficult to switch their religious institutions.

As of January 2002, there were twenty-one Korean Buddhist temples in the New York-New Jersey area. According to my interview with the editor of *Modern Buddhism in America* (*Mizu Hyundae Bulgyo*), a Korean-language Buddhist magazine in New York, in the 1970s and early 1980s Korean Buddhist immigrants in New York, as well as in other Korean communities, had difficulty establishing temples mainly because of a shortage of priests. But since the early 1990s some priests in Korea have come to the United States to build temples for Korean immigrants and Americans. Also, many Korean priests who have recently come to the United States for religious studies at universities in the East Coast have served for Korean temples in the area. As the number of Korean Buddhist temples have increased during recent years, some Korean immigrants who switched to Korean Protestant churches in the early years have come back to Buddhist temples.

Korean Immigrants' Frequency of Participation in Religious Institutions

According to a survey study in Queens conducted by this investigator in 1997 and 1998, only 2 of the 148 Korean Christian respondents (one Protestant and the other Catholic) reported that they attended non-Korean churches. All Korean Buddhist respondents participated in a Korean temple. There are three major reasons why nearly all Korean Christian immigrants participate in a Korean congregation. First, as previously noted, there are more than enough Korean churches that provide Korean immigrants with native-language services. Another important reason why almost all Korean Christian immigrants participate in a Korean church is their cultural homogeneity characterized by a monolingual background and lack of regional differences. Needless to say of Filipinos and Indians, even Chinese immigrants suffer from internal divisions in terms of language and the place of origin. Yang (1999) has shown the difficulties a Chinese American church in Washington D.C. encountered, partly caused by the multilingual background of Chinese immigrants.

By contrast, Korean immigrants have only one language and their regional differences in culture are almost insignificant (Min 1991). By virtue of their monolingual background, Korean immigrants can participate in any Korean immigrant church and enjoy all kinds of cultural and social programs provided by each Korean church. Given that most Korean immigrants encounter a serious language barrier in English and that every Korean immigrant church offers Korean-language services, it is quite natural that Korean immigrants prefer a Korean church to a non-Korean church. Even professional Korean Christians who are fluent in English prefer a Korean church because it provides them with all kinds of social services and socio-cultural programs that a non-Korean church cannot offer. In fact, each Korean church plays the role of a Korean social and cultural center (Hurh and Kim 1990; I. Kim 1981; Min 1992).

Table 5.2 shows the frequency of Korean immigrants' participation in a congregation based on the 2005 survey of Korean immigrants in New York City. Ninety percent of Korean Protestant respondents go to church once a week or more often. The table shows that Korean Catholics participate in a congregation less frequently (77% every week) than Korean Protestants, but still with high frequency compared to other Christian immigrant groups. Other survey studies conducted in New York and Los Angeles (Hurh and Kim 1990; Min 1987: 54) show similarly high levels of Korean Christian immigrants' participation in an ethnic congregation.

Table 5.2: Korean Immigrant Respondents' Frequency of Participation in Religious Institutions

	A few times a year or less often	Once every two weeks or less often	About every week	Twice a week or more often	Total
Protestants	8 (5%)	8 (5%)	87 (54%)	59 (36%)	162 (100%)
Catholics	4 (10%)	5 (13%)	23 (59%)	7 (18%)	39 (100%)
Buddhists and Others	11 (46%)	7 (29%)	4 (17%)	2 (8%)	24 (100%)
Total	23 (10%)	20 (9%)	114 (51%)	68 (30%)	225 (100%)

Source: A 2005 Survey of Chinese, Indian and Korean Immigrants in New York City

The exceptionally high rate of Korean Christian immigrants' participation in a congregation becomes clearer when compared to those of non-Korean Christian groups in the United States. According to 1996-1997 Racial and Ethnic Presbyterian Panel Studies (Kim and Kim 2001: 82), 78% of Korean Presbyterian respondents participated in Sunday worship services every week, compared to 28% of white Americans, 34% of African Americans, and 49% of Hispanics. My 1997-1998 survey of Asian immigrants in Queens indicates that 44% of Indian Christian immigrants and 39% of Chinese Christian immigrants, compared to 83% of Korean Christian immigrants, attend church at least once a week.

How can we explain Korean Christian immigrants' exceptionally high level of participation in an ethnic congregation? Previous studies have emphasized Korean immigrants' psychological and social needs for regularly participating in an ethnic church (Hurh and Kim 1990; Kim and Kim 2001; Min 1992). That is, Korean immigrants go to an ethnic church with exceptional frequency partly to cope with their frustrations deriving from their difficulty adjusting to American society and partly to meet their practical needs for communal bonds and social services.

However, other Asian Christian immigrant groups with similar adjustment difficulties participate in a church much less frequently than Koreans. Given this, we cannot put too much emphasis on Koreans' psychological and social needs to explain their frequent participation in a Korean church. Moreover, several Korean Protestant pastors informed me that Christians in South Korea, whether Catholics or Protestants, are highly congregation-oriented, many participating in a church twice or three times a week. They told me that, since most Korean pastors in Korean immigrant churches graduated from a theological school in Korea, their emphasis on members' regular participation follows the Korean tradition.

This prompted me to check government documents on participation in religious institutions published in Korea. The results of "Social Statistics Survey 1991" reveal that 76% of Protestants fifteen years old and over in South Korea participated in church at least once a week and that 35% participated twice or more often (Korea National Statistical Office 1992: 301). Slightly higher church participation rates of Korean immigrants derived from survey studies here than the results of the survey in Korea seem to be due mainly to the older age of the Korean immigrant samples (usually twenty-five years old and over) than the sample used in Korea (fifteen years old and over). Thus, the exceptionally frequent church participation rate of Korean Protestant immigrants seems to reflect more of their religious practices in Korea than their adaptation to their immigrant situation.

Table 5.2 shows that Korean Catholic immigrants attend church slightly less frequently than Korean Protestant immigrants, but still attend it with a high level of frequency (77% attend it at least once per week). As previously noted, while Korean Protestant churches in New York are very congregation-oriented independent of denominational hierarchies, Korean Catholic churches are strongly tied to local dioceses. One implication of this difference is that priests in Korean Catholic churches do not emphasize participation in their own congregations in the way pastors in Korean Protestant churches emphasize. As one member of the Korean Catholic parish selected for my study said, "Our priest has always stressed our regular participation in mass, but he has never emphasized our attendance to his own church. He has often encouraged us to try to attend any Catholic congregation closest to us on a given day, whether it is a Korean or non-Korean congregation."

For Catholics, any Catholic congregation can be his/her congregation. By contrast, pastors in Korean Protestant churches emphasize regular participation in and loyalty to their own churches (see Kim and Kim 2001: 82-83). When considering the relatively loose affiliation of Korean Catholic immigrants to their own congregation is considered, their church participation can be considered fairly high. In particular, their participation is very high, compared to American Catholics. For examples, results of a 2004 national survey by the Center for Applied Research in the Apostolate show that only 28% of U.S. Catholics went to church at least once a week (Goodstein 2005), compared to 77% for Korean Catholic immigrants.

Table 5.2 shows that 25% of Korean Buddhist respondents attend temple once a week or more often. This rate is much less frequent than Korean Christian respondents' participation rates. The Buddhist temple selected for my study has 430 registered households (about 800 members) as of fall 2001. According to the abbot, the number of participants in each Sunday service fluctuated from 160 to 100, although the number exceeded 200 on important Buddhist holidays. He told me that more than half of the registered households did not participate in the Sunday service regularly while about 30% attended it with an average rate of twice per month, usually on the first and third Sundays each month. Most participants in Sunday services are middle-aged or elderly immigrants, with young people and children accounting for a tiny proportion of all participants. It is important to note that some Korean Buddhists are affiliated with two or more temples and thus they go to different temples for Sunday services in a given year. This suggests that Korean Buddhist immigrants' affiliation with a Korean temple is not as tight as Korean Protestant immigrants'.

Sociologists of religion have indicated that contemporary non-Christian immigrant groups in the United States, such as Hindus and Buddhists, have developed the congregational form of services to adapt their religious practices to the American context (Fenton 1988: 179; Warner 1994, 1998: 21; Yang and Ebaugh 2001). By referring to the development of "congregationalism" among non-Judeo-Christian immigrant groups, they have partly pointed to the increased participation of immigrants in formal religious institutions. However, as far as Korean Buddhist immigrants are concerned, this generalization should be accepted with caution. First of all, as noted above, Korean Buddhist immigrants' frequency of participation in a religious congregation (Sunday services in a temple) is much lower than that of Korean Protestant immigrants. Moreover, according to my interviews, congregationalism among Korean Buddhists was already developed in South Korea prior to their immigration. In answering my question of whether Buddhists go to a temple on Sunday in South Korea, the abbot of the temple selected for my study said:

In the 1960s and 1970s many Korean Buddhists converted to Christian religions, especially to Catholicism. In reaction, Zen Buddhist centers in large cities adopted some of the Christian styles of worship in the 1980s. Having regular services on the first and fifteenth days (by lunar calendar) of each month and using organs for singing Buddhist hymns are two of the major adaptations made for self-defense. As a result of the adaptation, the proportion of Buddhists has increased since the 1980s.

The editor of *Modern Buddhism in America* informed me that Buddhists going to temples twice a month for regular services is currently a common scene in Seoul and other large Korean cities, and that urban Buddhists modernized Buddhist music by singing *chanbulga* (Buddhist hymns) with pianos to melodies borrowed from Christian hymns (Baker 1997: 166).

In Korea, about two-thirds of Buddhists are women, mostly middle-aged or elderly married women. Because the majority of these women in Korea do not work outside of the home, they can attend a temple on the first and fifteenth days of the month no matter what days of the week the two days fall on. But most Korean immigrant married women in the United States (about 70%), as well as their husbands, work long hours and usually work for six days a week. Accordingly, Korean Buddhist temples in the United States need to hold services on Sundays. Many Korean Buddhist immigrants go to a temple twice a month, which is just about how frequently Korean Buddhists in large Korean cities attend. This indicates that one of the major adjustments Korean Buddhist immigrants have made in their religious practices is not their increased participation in the congregation, but rather participation on Sundays instead of the first and fifteenth days of the month by lunar calendar.

Fellowship

Korean Protestant immigrant churches enhance members' fellowship and ethnic networks through a number of mechanisms. We can see different mechanisms for ethnic fellowships and networks in the Shin Kwang Church of New York. First of all, the church facilitates members' social networks through the church directory. At the end of each year the church gives a copy of the church directory for the coming year to each family. Along with other basic information about the church, the directory includes the home and business phone numbers of, addresses, and names of all family members. Thus the directory serves as a vehicle for social networks and communications for all members.

The church provides three services for Korean immigrants on Sunday. It has two other meetings in addition to Sunday services: a one-hour service between 8:30 and 9:30 on Wednesday (with about fifty attending it) and a prayer meeting at 8:30 on Friday (about forty attending it). Approximately 350 to 400 members attend the main, 11:00 am service. The majority of church members attend the church once a week, the Sunday's main service. Immediately after the main service, the vast majority of the participants in the Sunday's main service eat free lunch in the dining room. Church members voluntarily pay for the Sunday's lunch on a rotating basis while the three women's missionary groups rotate preparing lunch in the cafeteria. Adult members usually eat lunch with their spouses and close friends, and the children eat with their own friends. While eating lunch, the church members usually talk about what happened over the past week. Meeting close friends and enjoying talking with them over lunch is the central component of fellowship in the Shin Kwang Church as well as in other Korean immigrant churches.

Many other Korean immigrant churches do not provide full lunch; instead they offer coffee/soda and snacks. Members of these churches often eat lunch with their close friends in Korean restaurants after the Sunday's main service. But the Shin Kwang Church and many other Korean churches, theologically conservative, discourage their members from eating in restaurants on Sundays to remain sacred.

Most members of the Shin Kwang Church also belong to one of the several missionary groups organized by age and sex and one or more functional committee. Each missionary group and each committee have meetings at least monthly. Church members' participation in monthly and weekly meetings and involvement in organizational activities also facilitate members' fellowship and social networks. Since members of each organization work for common goals and have extended formal and informal social interactions, they easily make friends with one another. For example, Kyung Man Hurh, a middle-aged Korean man who transferred from another church three years earlier, said that as a result of his active participation in church activities about 60% of his close friends are members of his church. He plays golf every Thursday with five or six close friends, all of whom belong to his missionary group. After playing golf, they usually eat at a Korean restaurant. He enjoys eating with his church members, especially because as "good Christians" they share his principle of not drinking beer or other liquor.

The church's other activities that contribute to members' fellowship are family retreat in July, one-day athletic activities for all members in May, and *hyodo kwankwang* (filial tours) for elderly members. "*Hyodo kwankwang*" may need a clarification here. One important aspect of the Korean Confucian ideology is "filial piety," children's respect for and obligations to their parents. As part of performing filial piety, adult children in Korea organize and fund filial tours for their parents on the occasions of their birthdays and wedding anniversaries. Many Korean churches in Korea and the United States provide "filial tours" for elderly members, usually organized and funded by a young members' group. This church has also established an informal filial tour program for elderly members. The program helps elderly members take two free tours per year, in spring and fall (see Min 2010 for detailed information). Young members also visit ill elderly members who cannot participate in the tour and give free gifts. Providing filial tours is only one of the many ways the church facilitates fellowship and friendship networks for elderly members. Not only the Shin Kwang

Church but also most other Korean immigrant churches play a significant role in the successful adjustment of Korean elderly immigrants through formal and informal friendship networks.

The Shin Kwang Church and other large and medium-size Korean churches have disadvantages, compared to small churches, in providing their members with opportunity for face-to-face, small-group interactions. But they have organized the *gooyuk yebae* (district services), a uniquely Korean style of small-group services created to facilitate face-to-face primary interactions among church members (see Kwon et al. 1997; Min 1992). The Shin Kwang Church has divided members into thirty-two districts, each consisting of six to eight households. They usually hold a two-hour district meeting at a district member's home once a month between 8:00 and 10:00 p.m. under the guidance of an elder assigned to the district and the head of the district.

After a short service (usually twenty minutes), the families eat dinner together, usually prepared by the host family but sometimes a potluck. They enjoy talking about their children's education, their businesses, politics in Korea, and others matters of mutual interest. New immigrant families receive help from the head and other members of the district in adjusting to American society. The district service enhances friendship networks among members of the district because it is a small-group meeting held at a private home with dinner. In fact, members of each district often become close friends to the extent that they exchange informal dinner invitations and help each other. Organizing district services is not unique to the church of my participant observation, but can be attributed to almost all Korean immigrant churches, which has been transplanted from Korea.

The Korean Catholic parish of my study has organized activities and programs, similar to the Protestant church, which contributes to its members' fellowship and co-ethnic networks. But a slight difference between the Korean Catholic and the Protestant churches is that the former does not give the church directory to all members so that each member can contact any other member for communications. This difference is true for all other Korean Catholic and Protestant churches. Another difference is that the selected Catholic church and other Korean Catholic churches usually provide snacks after the Sunday's main mass while most Korean Protestant churches offer full lunch after the Sunday's main service. These two differences suggest that Korean Catholic churches do not treat all church members as families as much as Korean Protestant churches do.

Like the Protestant church, the Korean Catholic church has many organizations (more than fifty) based on age, sex, and functions. Each committee usually holds a meeting monthly, often an outdoor meeting, which provides ample opportunity for fellowship for its members. Also, it organizes at least a three to four day summer retreat for all church members per year that enhances its members' friendship and solidarity. It, too, holds a major athletic meeting for all church members in summer in a park in Long Island.

My interviews with staff and lay members of the parish reveal that the activities within a particular functional committee or age group are most effective for facilitating fellowship and primary social interactions. I can elaborate the point using the elderly women's organization (*annahoi*) as an example. According to the former chairwoman, a significant proportion of the about 300 *annahoi* members, mostly widows living alone, meet one another at the church not only on Sunday but also on two other days to make Chinese dumplings (*mandoo*). They make Chinese dumplings to sell to church members to increase their fund for charitable funds. The chairwoman said the participants in the Chinese dumpling project feel happy not only because they engage in meaningful charitable activities, but also because they enjoy meeting their friends regularly. Moreover, the *annahoi* members enjoy a full-day meeting monthly on the same day the church provides free lunch for elderly Koreans in New York. They have a business meeting before lunch and usually engage in recreational activities in the afternoon. Also, most of the *annahoi* members participate in the annual out-of-the-city trip (*hyodo kwankwang*) organized by the young men's association. Finally, and most significantly, many members, divided into several informal networks, enjoy meeting in Korean bakeries, jogging in parks, and traveling to other cities. Because of their tight friendship networks and many church-related group activities, Yoon said, these women living alone in a foreign country do not feel lonesome.

In addition, the Catholic Parish has also organized the monthly "*gooyukmoim*" (district meetings) by dividing its members into eight different areas and dividing members in each area further into several different districts. In its organization and fellowship function, "*gooyukmoim*" for Korean immigrant Catholic parishes is exactly the same as *gooyukyebae* for Korean immigrant Protestant churches. They hold "*gooyukmoim*" monthly in a private home over dinner in the evening. While all Korean immigrant Protestant and Catholic churches hold district services or meetings, white American Christian churches in the United States are not known to organize a similar monthly meeting. It is important to note that both Korean immigrant Protestant and Catholic churches have transplanted the practice from South Korea. Many respondents to my personal interviews, both Protestants and Catholics, told me that district services organized by Korean immigrant churches are reproductions of district services practiced in South Korea.

Compared to Korean Protestant or Catholic churches, Korean Buddhist temples have disadvantages for providing fellowship and ethnic networks for their members in that the latter do not meet at the temple as often as Korean Christians do. Nevertheless, my ethnographic research on Korean Buddhist Center reveals that Korean temples do serve a moderate level of fellowship for the participants. The Korean Buddhist temple has the Sunday service between 11:00 and 12:30. After the service, participants eat Korean food together prepared by each participating family. When I attended the temple, about a hundred participants were eating lunch in the service room, barefooted and cross-legged on cushions. I found many people eating, sitting close to and talking with their friends. The participants in the Sunday service wear nametags on their shirts so that they can make friends with others easily.

The temple has not organized activities and programs comparable to annual retreat and a summer athletic meeting for Korean Christian churches. Yet, they have formal and informal small-group meetings that enhance their fellowship and informal networks. For example, it has organized a Buddhism lecture series on Fridays in which about twenty members participate every week. It also has a Saturday hiking club, while opening a *tai chi* class in summer. Women members who consist largely of wives of employees of branches of Korean firms have also established their association called *ilsimhoi*. They come to the temple in a group of four or five on weekdays on rotation, cooking and cleaning for monks and enjoying friendship with one another. However, the temple has not organized monthly district meetings popular in Korean immigrant churches. The abbot told me that it is impossible for his temple to organize such meetings because its members live widely scattered throughout the New York-New Jersey area. But he said that many members who live close to it maintain friendship networks informally. Buddhists in the Korean community may be able to make friends with one another easily because they belong to an invisible minority religious group in the heavily Christian Korean community (Suh 2004).

Retention of Ethnic Culture

As previously noted, both Korean Protestantism and Catholicism are Western religions that were popularized in Korea over the last forty-five years. Thus, neither of the Christian religions has incorporated Korean folk culture in the forms of food, holidays, dress, and music/dance, although both religions have incorporated Confucian and shamanistic elements (Baker 1997: 195-197). Accordingly, unlike Jewish Americans or Indian Hindu immigrants, Korean Christian immigrants in the United States cannot preserve their cultural traditions merely by practicing their religious values and rituals. They can maintain Korean cultural traditions mainly by practicing Korean culture in Korean churches. This means that their frequent participation in Korean congregations is a precondition for preserving their cultural traditions through religion. As previously noted, Korean Christian immigrants attend Korean churches regularly and spend a great deal of time there every week.

Korean churches also help Korean immigrants preserve ethnicity through cultural retention. The Shin Kwang Church helps its members retain their cultural traditions in several different ways. First of all, it enhances Korean culture by celebrating Korean cultural and national holidays. It celebrates two major Korean cultural holidays: the New Year Day and *Chooseok* (the Korean Thanksgiving Day on August 15 by the lunar calendar). To celebrate New Year's Day,[3] this church has two services, one on the New Year Eve and the other on the New Year's Day. After the main service on the New Year's Day, members eat *ttockguk* (rice-cake soup), usually served on New Year's Day in Korea. Some women and girls come to church wearing *chima jogori* (Korean traditional dresses for women). After lunch, the church reproduces the Korean custom of *sebae*. I watched the *sebae* ceremony one time. Ten children were lined up and gave deep bows to ten elderly members sitting in a room while parents watched them on the side. In return, elderly members gave candies to children, although in Korea they give money to children. All children and adolescents from kindergarteners to high school graders participated in this *sebae* ceremony on rotation.

The church also organizes special services to observe two major national holidays, the March First Independence Commemoration Day and the August 15 Independence Day. On the occasion of these national holidays, the senior pastor emphasizes Korean patriotism in his sermon by emphasizing the role of the earlier Korean Christians in the independence movement against Japanese colonization.[4] Many other Korean immigrant churches sing the March First Independence and August Fifteenth Independence songs to observe these national holidays. But, according to the senior pastor, to "remain sacred" this church does not sing these "patriotic songs."

The senior pastor emphasizes the role of the church in preserving Korean cultural traditions. As soon as the church moved to its new building in 1992, he established a Korean school to teach children the Korean language and culture. The Korean school provides three hours of classes between 9:30 and 12:30 on Saturdays, devoting two hours to teaching the Korean language and the remaining hour to an exhibition of *taekwondo, samulnori* (Korean traditional music/dance), and other traditional Korean folk cultural activities by experts. About 40 students, enrolled for the Korean school, each pay $140 per semester. In two months of summer, the Korean school has an expanded program that includes Korean dance, *taekwondo*, and English/math. Approximately 80 students—not only church members but also others—are enrolled in the summer program.

Teaching Korean roots is not limited to the Korean school. Partly to teach adolescents Korean cultural traditions and partly to enhance their religious belief, the church has arranged the Youth Group to have the Sunday's worship service bilingually together with adults at 11:00 a.m. once a month. To observe three religious holidays (Easter, Thanksgiving, and Christmas), the church has also arranged to have services with all children and adolescents together. A 47-year-old male member who had attended the church for 13 years reported that the arrangement to have services with adults helped his "children learn Korean etiquette and be proud of Korea." The senior pastor has also arranged Sunday School to have services bilingually to enhance the Korean cultural context for their worship services. Bilingual services and active social interactions between native-born and immigrant children/adolescents through church activities help the native-born learn the Korean language, customs, and values from the immigrant children.

The Queens Korean Catholic parish celebrates Korean traditional holidays in more authentic ways than the Queens Korean church. It replicates the traditional custom of giving deep bows to elderly people on the New Year day. After the Sunday mass immediately following the solar New Year day, participants, including children—some wearing traditional Korean costumes—perform the *sebae* (new-year bow) ceremony in the fellowship room. Making a group of about ten, adults give deep bows before the main priest and a few elderly members sitting in a row, wishing them good fortune in the coming year. In return, each bower is rewarded with two quarters. Children give deep bows to parents and other adults. During the Sunday masses following the lunar New Year day and the Korean Thanksgiving day, the Catholic parish has a memorial service similar to ancestor worship in Korea. Each participant writes the names of immediate ancestors and puts the list in an envelope. He/she then throws incense into a burner, gives a silent prayer, and drops the envelope into a box located close to the burner. Many Korean Catholic immigrants in the United States practice ancestor worship at home[5] while few Korean Protestant immigrants do it. This reflects another major difference in rituals between Catholics and Protestants in Korea.

The main priest emphasized the importance of Korean-American children's retention of ethnic culture and identity on the ground that no matter how much acculturated they would not be accepted as full American citizens. Therefore, he believed that it is important for the Catholic parish to provide programs for their retention of Korean culture. The church established the Korean School in 1977, which has offered Korean language, culture and history courses for kindergarten through 12th graders on Saturday. Teachers for Sunday schools and the Friday Bible study classes use both English and Korean languages to help children to learn Korean. They also try to teach Korean etiquette and manners while teaching the Bible and the Christian ways of life. Senior-high Sunday-school teachers have organized several workshops and lectures on the importance of maintaining ethnic identity and culture for high-school students and their parents. The church also has two *samulnori* teams (traditional Korean folk music and dance teams), one consisting of 1.5- and 2nd-generation young adults and the other consisting of elementary school kids. They have performed *samulnori* in many Korean and multiethnic festivals.

As previously noted, the Korean temple is not comparable to the Protestant or the Catholic parish in terms of its fellowship. The Buddhist temple's relative disadvantage in fellowship is due partly to its short history and small membership size, and partly to the nature of its religion. However, Korean Zen Buddhism can be more effective than Korean Protestantism or Catholicism for Korean immigrants' cultural retention because Korean cultural traditions have been far more successfully incorporated into it than in either of the two "Western" religions. The abbot of the Korean Buddhist temple emphasized in his *sulbop* (lecture about Buddhist doctrines) the strong linkages between Korean Buddhism and Korean culture:

> Unlike Western Christian religions, Buddhist missionaries propagated the religion to other countries without destroying local cultures. In its 1,600 years of

history, Korean Buddhism has become inseparably tied to Korean culture. It would not be an exaggeration to say that about 70% of the Korean cultural legacy is the Buddhist legacy. Due to their cultural worship of Western societies, many Korean immigrants have converted to Christian religions. But we Koreans need to recover our Buddhist cultural traditions to maintain our national identity. We can consider Korean Buddhism a major medium for Korean cultural transmission in the United States.

Although somewhat biased, the above statement by the abbot has many elements of truth. Koreans had exclusively used the lunar calendar before the end of World War II when they began to have active contacts with the Western world. The Buddhist temple still goes with the lunar calendar, with which Korean middle-aged and elderly immigrants feel comfortable. The temple celebrates two major Korean traditional holidays based on lunar calendar: the Lunar New Year day and *chooseok* (the Korean Thanksgiving day). On the Lunar New Year Day it performs ancestor worship with traditional Korean foods and fruits served. On the Sunday falling on or before April 15 by the lunar calendar, the temple has expanded services and rituals, often inviting an elderly priest from Korea for a dharma talk, to celebrate the birth of *Sokka*. July 15 by the lunar calendar is another important holiday for Korean Buddhists. Like other Korean temples, the temple holds *ch'ondoje* on the day, in which the abbot performs a special ceremony for its members to reduce their ancestors' sin committed in this world.

I attended two children's Sunday classes (elementary and junior high school students) at Korean Buddhist Center for participant observation. The class for elementary school students used English as the main language, but children memorized some Korean words for terms important for Buddhism, such as lotus and Buddha. The teacher for the junior high class used Korean as the main language, mixing with English vocabularies. The teacher emphasized the knowledge of the Korean language as a pre-condition for Korean children's learning basic Korean Buddhist rituals and sutras. For this reason, second-generation Korean-American Buddhists are more likely to learn the Korean language and culture than second-generation Christians. However, exactly for the same reason they need to use the Korean language and culture as a medium for practicing Buddhist rituals and chanting sutras, they also have more difficulty attending a Korean temple than attending a Korean church. The temple offers a class for senior high-school students on the first and third Sundays each month when it has more participants. But, since only five to six senior high students attend the Sunday service, the senior high class has been cancelled on many Sundays. A member of the temple told me that some high school children attend Korean Protestant churches while their parents participate in the temple.

Social Services

My 1988-1989 survey of Korean churches in New York City revealed that Korean immigrant churches provide a number of social services to their members in two different ways (Min 1992). First of all, the senior pastor and other church leaders help members informally on an individual basis by spending time and providing information and counseling for them. Second, Korean churches provide services for their members through a number of formal programs, such as Korean language schools, health clinics, and seminars. Smaller churches provide services through the pastor's and other staff members' informal and direct help of each member, while larger churches use more formal programs. As a medium-size church, the Shin Kwang Church provides both informal and formal services for its members.

The Shin Kwang Church spends a significant proportion of its revenue for the welfare of its church members. The church helps members with serious financial difficulty with an emergency relief fund and scholarships. Moreover, as already noted in the previous section, the church has established the Korean school, the summer school, and a kindergarten. These schools have been established to meet the purpose of services to church members, as well as the purpose of the educational mission of the church. The church also provides a number of informal services for members individually. Like most other Korean immigrant churches, the senior pastor and his wife, in close cooperation with the district chairs, help new immigrants with practical tasks: finding jobs, registering their children in schools, applying for social security numbers, renting apartments, and installing telephones. The five women exhorters, along with the senior pastor and his wife, take turns in visiting sick members and women with new babies. Members of a district and members of an age-based missionary group also visit their sick members and women with new babies. When newly-wed immigrants join the church, they help the couple to visit department stores for purchases of blankets, kitchen wares, and other necessities.

The list of this church's social services and donations to the Korean community, the United States, South Korea, and other countries, beyond its members, includes periodic one-time donations to help various victims of natural disasters, such as major flood victims in South Korea and Tsunami and Katrina victims, donation of turkeys to the Council of Korean Churches of Greater New York for the poor for Thanksgiving, a contribution of $10,000 to help blind people in South Korea to receive eye operations, and scholarships to a high school in the neighborhood. In an effort to solve Korean youth gang and juvenile problems, the Council of Korean Churches of Greater New York established the Korean Youth Center of New York in Flushing in 1989. The church has also donated a certain mount of money every year to the Council of Korean Churches of Greater New York for the youth center. The senior pastor and other leaders of the church tend to connect these social-service activities with their missionary activities. For example, when the men's missionary group visited the nursing home in Long Island, the members sang hymns for the elderly residents while the senior pastor read a verse from the Bible. The senior pastor expressed his long-term plan to establish a nursing home for Korean elderly people from his and other Korean churches.

Korean Protestant churches and organizations in the New York-New Jersey area have increased donations and services to the Korean community as a whole or for other social causes over the years. To cite a few examples, the Council of Korean Churches of Greater New York collected donations from many Korean churches in the 1980s to establish the Korean Youth Center. Since it was established in 1989, the Korean Youth Center of New York run by the Council has contributed to reduction of gang and other juvenile problems in the Korean community in New York. Several Korean churches have been actively involved in collecting donations of food, money, and clothing to help North Korea and refugees from North Korea. Most recently, many Korean churches have donated significant amounts of money to help establish the Korean Community Center in Flushing.

Nevertheless, many Korean social workers and community leaders have pointed out that Korean Protestant churches in New York still focus on helping their own members, neglecting to help other people in the Korean community and in the larger society. Most other Korean immigrant churches with a similar scale of revenue seem to have provided smaller amounts of services for the Korean community and the larger society than the Shin Kwang Church. Given that several Korean Protestant churches have respectively sent a dozen or more missionaries to foreign countries, they have financial and manpower resources to organize one or more programs to provide services for all Korean immigrants in New York. But none of them has established a community-wide social service program. Although some liberal Korean Protestant churches may be interested in creating a program to help all Korean immigrants, they are financially weak. Many large evangelical Korean churches are financially strong, but they are far more interested in evangelism than in providing services for the Korean community or larger society.

Results of the 1997-1999 Presbyterian Racial Ethnic Panel Studies also reflect Korean Christian immigrants' lack of interest in contributing for social causes relative to other Presbyterian groups. Data reveal that close to 20% of Korean Presbyterians gave no money for nonreligious causes in the month prior to the survey, compared to 4% of Caucasians, 5% of African Americans, and 15% of Hispanics (Kim and Kim 2001: 83). The strong evangelical background of Korean Presbyterian immigrants in the United States explains both their greater contributions to church than other groups of Presbyterians and their little interest in spending money for nonreligious social causes. Korean Protestant immigrants' or immigrant churches' low interest in welfare services for society and great interest in missionary activities reflect the reality in South Korea too. Some researchers have pointed out that American evangelicals are more concerned with participating in their own church communities than with wider social participation (Ecklund 2006; Wuthnow 1999). I believe that Korean churches' lack of concern with providing services for larger society in both Korea and in the Korean immigrant community here is mainly due to their heavily evangelical orientation.

Like the Queens Korean church, the Catholic parish selected for my study has a number of sub-organizations that provide services to needy members in different ways. First of all, the church has the Charity Committee (*Caritas*) to help members with serious financial or health problems. It has a special fund donated by members to help needy people. The Education Committee also locates and helps members who need scholarship for their children. Ten physicians and fifteen nurses, as members of the Charity Committee, provide blood, breast cancer, stool, and blood pressure tests free on first and third Sundays each month. Church members and non-members with no health insurance are eligible for free tests. The Charity Committee often helps those who suffer from serious illnesses to find American charitable organizations for free treatment.

More than 500 members of Region of Marie, service-oriented members of the church, visit elderly centers in Flushing and other areas of Queens to help Korean elderly people. They talk with lonely Korean elderly people, clean their rooms, and cook and pray for them. The Catholic parish also has a committee that helps its elderly members to buy burial sites and members with family deaths to arrange funerals. The committee has helped some poor members to get funerals free of charge from a New York City government agency.

The Korean Catholic Parish, under the leadership of particular committees and groups, has organized a number of lectures, forums, workshops, and classes to provide its members with counseling, education, and information. For example, it has organized a dozen lectures and workshops about parent-child conflicts over the past five years. In 1999, it had a three-day retreat in a motel in upstate New York for a workshop on successful marital adjustments to help members to moderate marital conflicts. The church has given a lecture on marital and sexual relations, and family planning every spring for newly-wed and prospective marital partners.

The Catholic parish established a credit union in 1979 as a self-help financial organization with voluntary services by a number of church members. They have turned it into a large banking system with eight full-time employees and an asset of eight million dollars. Not only members of this church but also those of other Korean Catholic communities in New York can join the credit union, whose membership increased to 3,500 as of December 2001. Members can take a loan with a lower interest rate than commercial rates and without going through a complicated credit check. The credit union currently provides other banking services, including personal checking accounts and credit cards, for its members.

We have already noted that members of Legion of Marie provide services for elderly Koreans, regardless of their membership to the church, by visiting elderly centers in Queens. The Catholic parish has other programs that target not only its members, but also all Koreans in New York. The Life Counseling Center (*saenghwal sangdamso*), established within the church, offers all kinds of counseling, information, and services: legal, medical, accounting, education, children's health, immigration orientations, mortgage loans, building regulations, and Chinese medicine. It also offers translation services. The center is open on Sunday between 12:30 and 2:00. The professionals who provide counseling and services at the center on Sundays on rotations include non-members as well as members of the church. And all Korean Americans in the New York-New Jersey area are eligible for services from the center. Another major community-wide service program the church provides is a free lunch program geared to all elderly Koreans in New York. It provides free lunch in combination with some entertainment once a month. Although most of the about 200 participants in the program are elderly members of the church, many other non-members use the services, enjoying lunch, entertainment and friendship.

As noted above, the Korean Catholic church has extensive programs to provide services for Korean Americans in New York as a whole, as well as for its members. The Korean Catholic Church's extension of social services to Korean Americans beyond its own members is noteworthy because contemporary Korean immigrant Protestant churches and other Asian immigrant churches, including Vietnamese Catholic churches, offer services largely to their own members (Ebaugh and Chafetz 2000; Min 1992; Zhou and Bankston 1998). However, it is not surprising at all, given that Catholic parishes in the United States traditionally played a major role in providing various social services not only for the needy in their neighborhoods, but also new immigrants and refugees in general (Dolan 1985; Links 1975). Catholic churches in South Korea, too, have made greater efforts than Protestant churches in helping poor and powerless people.

The New York Korean Buddhist temple has fewer programs to provide social services to its members. In fact, the only form of services it provides is information about immigration laws, welfare benefits for elderly people, health insurance, and other matters of common interest provided by medical doctors and other specialists. According to my interview with the abbot, both the lack of financial and manpower resources in Korean temples due to their small sizes and short histories, as well as the nature of Buddhism, are responsible for the absence of social service programs in his and other Korean temples. When I asked him whether the absence of social service programs gave Korean Buddhist temples disadvantages compared to Korean immigrant churches for attracting more Korean immigrants, he said:

> In order to focus on saving individuals from their life agonies, we Buddhists neglected to help other people with urgent practical problems. For social services we can learn a lot from Christians. When we leaders of Korean temples get together, we often discuss how to provide social services for Korean immigrants.

Since none of Korean temples in New York has financial and manpower resources for establishing a significant social service program by itself, the association of Korean Buddhist temples established a social service center called

Jabiwon in Flushing in 1999. Although the flier lists several types of services, including ESL and after-school classes and job referrals, it currently focuses on helping Korean elderly people with their paperwork for welfare benefits. The only staff member told me that the center plans to expand its services as it gets more donations from Buddhists in the Korean community and South Korea. In addition, Korean Buddhists in New York established the Buddhist Association for Mutual Help. With about 100 members, the association focuses on visiting the sick members and helping the members with family deaths to perform the Buddhist funeral ceremony.

I asked the editor of *Modern Buddhism in America* whether Korean Buddhist leaders in New York learned about the need of Korean temples to provide social services mainly from Korean immigrant churches. His response indicates that this is something they already learned from Christians in Korea prior to their migration:

> I cannot deny that Korean Buddhist leaders are pressured to provide social services because of Korean immigrant churches' active role in helping their members. But social service provision is not something new to them. In order to compete successfully with Christian churches, Korean Buddhist denominations began to develop social service programs from the 1980s on. I can tell you many examples. *Shinhungsa* (the name of a temple) in Sockcho established the largest kindergarten in the city in the early 1990s. The Buddhist College at Dongguk University established Department of Social Welfare to train Buddhist social workers. In the early 1990s, the Choge Order established Sharing House to help several former "comfort women" to live together.

To expand their missionary activities to successfully compete with Christian churches, by the 1980s Buddhist temples in large Korean cities had adopted not only the congregational mode of religious practice but also social service techniques from Christian churches. Thus, the transformation of Korean Buddhism was already developed in Korea in reactions to Christian religions before Korean Buddhist immigrants encountered American Christianity.

Summary and Conclusion

Findings from my ethnographic research shows that the selected Korean Catholic church serves the fellowship and cultural retention functions for their members in similar ways to the selected Korean Protestant church, and that members' frequent participation in both the Protestant and Catholic churches is central to facilitating fellowship and cultural retention. However, it reveals that the selected Korean Catholic and Protestant churches slightly differ in patterns of social services. While the Korean Protestant church offers services mainly to its own members, the Korean Catholic church provides services not only for its own members, but also for Korean Americans in New York as a whole. The Korean

Catholic parish's extension of services to the larger Korean community reflects the historical tradition that American Catholic churches played a major role in helping new immigrants and refugees. It also indicates the greater social concerns of Korean Catholic churches than Korean Protestant churches that focus on missionary activities.

The New York Korean Buddhist temple is much less active in providing fellowship and social services than the two Christian churches. The Buddhist temple's lower levels of fellowship and social services are caused partly by the nature of the religion and partly by its lack of financial and manpower resources due to its shorter history and smaller membership. Korean Buddhist temples usually did not pay much attention to members' fellowship and social welfare. But the abbot of the temple considers it important for his temple to increase its activities and programs for fellowship and social services. When the temple grows in membership and financial resources, it is likely to develop more activities and programs to enhance fellowship and social services for its members.

The Korean Buddhist temple, compared to the two Christian religious organizations, has disadvantages in developing programs for fellowship and social services due to their lack of manpower and financial resources. However, it has advantages in preserving Korean cultural traditions because Korean Buddhism is inseparably tied to Korean language, traditional Korean holidays, fine arts, music, dance, and architecture. Korean Christian immigrants can preserve Korean cultural traditions only by practicing Korean customs and values through their active participation in Korean churches. By contrast, Korean Buddhist immigrants can preserve Korean cultural traditions by practicing religious rituals. As Sharon Suh (2004) pointed out, Korean Buddhist immigrants believe that they represent "authentic Korean culture" while Korean Christian immigrants copy American or Western culture.

Notes

1. According to a pre-departure survey of the 1986 Korean immigrants conducted at the U.S. Embassy in Seoul, 56% Korean immigrants lived in Seoul and 71% lived in the four largest cities in South Korea at the time of the interview (Park and Cho 1955: 31).

2. The Korean immigrant community has too many Korean pastors partly because many Korean pastors have immigrated to the United States using the clergy category and partly because a number of theological seminaries established within large Korean immigrant churches have produced pastors. In New York alone, there are more than fifteen Korean theological seminaries established within Korean immigrant churches.

3. Following the Korean tradition, in the 1970s and early 1980s Korean immigrant churches in the United States celebrated Lunar New Year's Day. But, this church, like most other churches, celebrate New Year's Day by solar calendar, although they still observe Lunar New Year's Day in Korea.

4. On March 1, 1919, thirty-three Korean leaders announced the Declaration of Independence at a major park in Seoul, challenging the Japanese colonization. Sixteen of the thirty-three Korean leaders who signed for the Declaration of Independence were

Christian pastors and leaders. This indicates the magnitude of Korean Christian churches' contribution to the Korean independence movement at that time. Many Korean churches in different cities mobilized their members to participate in the marches protesting the Japanese colonization.

5. Many Korean pioneering Catholic leaders were martyred in the first half of the nineteenth century mainly because of their violation of the custom of ancestor worship. But Korean Catholics have been allowed to practice ancestor worship in a modified form since the early 1960s. They were allowed after John Paul VI announced, following the second Vatican meeting held between 1962 and 1965, that Catholics all over the world should be able to practice the religion consistent with their cultural traditions.

References

Alumkal, Antony. 1999. "Preserving Patriarchy: Assimilation, Gender Norms, and Second-Generation Korean American Evangelicals." *Qualitative Sociology* 22: 129-140.

_____. 2001. "Being Korean, Being Christian: Particularism and Universalism in Second-Generation Congregations." In *Korean Americans and Their Religions: Pilgrims and Missionaries from a Different Shore*, edited by Ho-Youn Kwon, Kwang Chung Kim, and R. Stephen Warner, 181-192. University Park, PA: Pennsylvania State University Press.

Baker, Donald. 1997. "Christianity." In *An Introduction to Korean Culture*, edited by John H. Koo and Andrew C. Nahm, 179-200. Elizabeth, NJ: Hollym.

Chai, Karen. 1998. "Competing for the Second Generation: English-Language Ministry at a Korean Protestant Church." In *Gatherings in Diaspora: Religious Communities and the New Immigration*, edited by R. Stephen Warner and Judith Wittner, 295-332. Philadelphia: Temple University Press.

_____. 2001a. "Beyond 'Strictness' to Distinctiveness: Generational Transition in Korean Protestant Churches." In *Korean Americans and Their Religions: Pilgrims and Missionaries from a Different Shore*, edited by Ho-Young Kwon, Kwang Chung Kim, and R. Stephen Warner, 157-180. University Park, PA: Pennsylvania State University Press.

_____. 2001b. "Intra-Ethnic Religious Diversity: Korean Buddhists and Protestants in Greater New York." In *Korean Americans and Their Religions: Pilgrims and Missionaries from a Different Shore*, edited by Ho-Young Kwon, Kwang Chung Kim, and R. Stephen Warner, 273-294. University Park, PA: Pennsylvania State University Press.

Chong, Kelly. 1998. "What it Means to be Christian: The Role of Religion in the Construction of Ethnic Identity and Boundary among Second-Generation Korean Americans." *Sociology of Religion* 58: 258-286.

Dolan, Jay. 1985. *The American Catholic Experience: History from Colonial Times to the Present*. Garden City, NY: Doubleday.

Ebaugh, Helen Rose and Janet Saltzman Chafetz, eds. 2000. *Religion and the New Immigrants*. Walnut Creek, CA: Altamira Press.

Ecklund, Elaine Howard. 2006. *Korean American Evangelicals: New Models for Civic Life*. New York: Oxford University Press.

Fenton, John. 1988. *Transplanting Religious Traditions: Asian Indians in America*. New York: Praeger.

Goodstein, Laurie. 2005. "His Flock; Catholics in America: A Restive People." *New York Times*, April 3.

Hurh, Won Moo, and Kwang Chung Kim. 1990. "Religious Participation of Korean Immigrants in the United States." *Journal for the Scientific Study of Religion* 29: 19-34.

Kim, Illsoo. 1981. *New Urban Immigrants: The Korean Community in New York*. Princeton, NJ: Princeton University Press.

Kim, Jung Ha. 1996. "The Labor of Compassion: Voices of 'Churched' Korean American Women." *Amerasia Journal* 22: 93-105.

Kim, Kwang Chung, and Shin Kim. 2001. "The Ethnic Role of Korean Immigrant Churches in the United States." In *Korean Americans and Their Religions: Pilgrims and Missionaries*, edited by Ho-Youn Kwon, Kwang Chung Kim, and R. Stephen Warner, 71-94. University Park, PA: Pennsylvania State University Press.

Kim, Rebecca. 2006. *God's New Whiz Kids: Korean American Evangelicals on Campus.* New York: New York University Press.

Korean National Bureau of Statistics. 1977. Population Composition by Surname: A Report on the Data from the 1970 Korean Census of Population. Seoul: Korean Economic Planning Board.

Korean National Statistical Office. 1992. *1992 Social Indicators in Korea.* Seoul: Korea National Statistical Office.

_____. 2005. *2005 Social Indicators in Korea.* Seoul: Korea National Statistical Office.

Kwon, Ho-Youn, Kwang Chung Kim, and R. Stephen Warner, eds. 2001. *Korean Americans and Their Religions.* University Park, PA: Pennsylvania State University Press.

Kwon, Victoria Hyonchu, Helen Rose Ebaugh, and Jacqueline Hagen. 1997. "The Structure and Functions of Cell Group Ministry in a Korean Christian Church." *Journal for the Scientific Study of Religion* 36: 247-256.

Kwong, Okyun. 2003. *Buddhist and Christian Korean Immigrants: Religious Belief and Socioeconomic Aspects of Life.* New York: LFB Scholarly Publishers.

Min, Pyong Gap. 1987. "Some Positive Functions of Ethnic Business for an Immigrant Community: Koreans in Los Angeles." Final Report Submitted to National Science Foundation.

_____. 1991. "Cultural and Economic Boundaries of Korean Ethnicity: A Comparative Analysis." *Ethnic and Racial Studies* 14: 225-241.

_____. 1992. "The Structure and Social Functions of Korean Immigrant Churches in the United States." *International Migration Review* 26: 1370-1394.

_____. 2000. "Immigrants' Religion and Ethnicity: A Comparison of Korean Christian and Indian Hindu Immigrants." *Bulletin of the Royal Institute for Inter-Faith Studies* 2: 121-40.

_____. 2008a. "Severe Under-representation of Women in Church Leadership in Korean Immigrant Churches in the United States." *Journal for the Scientific Study of Religion* 47: 225-242.

_____. 2008b. *Ethnic Solidarity for Economic Survival: Korean Greengrocers in New York City.* New York: Russell Sage Foundation.

_____. 2010. *Preserving Ethnicity through Religion in America: Korean Protestants and Indian Hindus across Generations.* New York: New York University Press.

Min, Pyong Gap, and Dae Young Kim. 2005. "International Transmission of Religion and Ethnic Culture: Korean Protestants in the United States." *Sociology of Religion* 66: 263-282.

Park, In-Sook Han, and Lee-Jay Cho. 1995. "Confucianism and the Korean Family." *Journal of Comparative Family Studies* 26 (1): 117-135.

Park, In-Sook Han, James Fawcett, Fred Arnold, and Richard Gardner. 1989. "Koreans Immigrating to the United States: A Pre-Departure Analysis." Paper No. 114. Hawaii: Population Institute, East-West Center.

Park, So-Young. 2001. "The Intersection of Religion, Race, Gender, and Ethnicity." In *Korean Americans and Their Religions: Pilgrims and Missionaries from a Different Shore*, edited by Ho-Young Kwon, Kwang Chung Kim, and R. Stephen Warner, 193-209. University Park, PA: Pennsylvania State University Press.

Shin, Eui Hang, and Eui-Young Yu. 1984. "Use of Surname in Ethnic Research: The Case of Kim in the Korean American Population." *Demography* 21: 347-359.

Shin, Eui Hang, and Hyung Park. 1988. "An Analysis of Causes of Schisms in Ethnic Churches: The Case of Korean-American Churches." *Sociology of Religion* 49 (3): 234-248.

Suh, Sharon. 2003. "To be Buddhist is to be Korean: The Rhetorical Use of Authenticity and the Homeland in the Construction of the Post-Immigrant Identities." In *Revealing the Sacred in Asia and Pacific America*, edited by Jane Naomi Iwamura and Paul Spickard, 171-192. New York: Routledge.

———. 2004. *Being Buddhist in a Christian World: Gender and Community in a Korean American Temple*. Seattle: University of Washington Press.

Warner, R. Stephen. 1994. "The Place of Congregation in the American Religious Configuration." In *American Congregations*, vol. 2: *New Perspectives in the Study of Congregations*, edited by James Wind and James Lewis, 54-99. Chicago: University of Chicago Press.

———. 1998. "Immigration and Religious Communities in the United States." In *Gathering in Diaspora: Religious Communities and the New Immigration*, edited by R. Stephen Warner and Judith Wittner, 3-36. Philadelphia: Temple University Press.

Wuthnow, Robert. 1999. *America and the Challenge of Religious Diversity*. Princeton, NJ: Princeton University Press.

Yang, Fenggang. 1999. *Chinese Christians in America: Conversion, Assimilation, and Adhesive Identities*. University Park, PA: Pennsylvania State University Press.

Yang, Fenggang, and Helen Rose Ebaugh. 2001. "Transformations in New Immigrant Religions and Their Global Implications." *American Sociological Review* 66: 269-288.

Yu, Eui-Young. 2001. The Growth of Korean Buddhism in the United States with Special Reference to Southern California. In *Korean Americans and Their Religions: Pilgrims and Missionaries from a Different Shore*, edited by Ho-Young Kwon, Kwang Chung Kim, and R. Stephen Warner, 211-226. University Park, PA: Pennsylvania State University Press.

Zhou, Min, and Carl Bankston III. 1998. *Growing Up American: How Vietnamese Children Adapt to Life in the United States*. New York: Russell Sage Foundation.

Chapter 6
Explaining the Migration Strategy: Comparing Transnational and Intact Migrant Families from South Korea to Canada[1]

by Ann H. Kim, Sung Hyun Yun, Wansoo Park, and Samuel Noh

Introduction

The separation of family members over geographic space and national borders for economic or educational goals is not a novel phenomenon. However, the historical and economic context in which it occurs determines its causes and consequences, and contemporary migration is distinct from past migration (Levitt and Jaworksy 2007). The transnational family currently encompasses an increasingly wider range of family structures that affects a wider range of cultures and nations. In the 1960s and 1970s, labour migrants from South Korea left spouses, mostly wives, and children for economic opportunities abroad, only to have their families re-connect with them in a more or less permanent move overseas.

More recently, South Korea's new position in the global economy has shifted family demography and strategies for social and economic mobility (Cho 2005). It is in this context that the transnational family has re-emerged and taken a new form; children are being sent abroad for educational opportunities, leaving one or both parents to work in South Korea, with the hope of re-uniting as a family either back in South Korea or in the place of destination. Presently, this type of transnational family, in contrast to the intact migrant family, remains little understood. In this chapter, we focus on the factors associated with these two types of migration strategies by comparing the similarities and differences in the motivations for migration and in the families' characteristics. In doing so, we consider push and pull factors, migration's gendered nature, the relevance of class position and socio-economic status in places of origin, social networks, and previous migration experiences using data from the *2011 Toronto Korean Families Study (TKFS)*.

Canada is our focus, as it has recently received large flows of migrants from South Korea, and these flows have become increasingly transnational in nature. The 2006 Canadian Census counted over 145,000 ethnic Koreans across Canada, with the largest concentrations in Toronto (39%) and Vancouver (31%). While the ethnic Korean population in Canada is much smaller than their counterparts in the United States, it is largely an immigrant population, with over 81% foreign-born, in contrast to the 74% foreign-born in the U.S. (Table S0201, 2010 American Community Survey, U.S. Census Bureau). There is also a substantial and growing "temporary" population of migrants from South Korea, those who are on temporary visas predominantly for study purposes. From 1999 to 2008, South Korea was the largest source of foreign student flows to Canada, with annual flows reaching over 20% of foreign students since 2002 (CIC 2010). These flows also appear to be getting younger in age in the recent period, jumping from 16% of study visas going to secondary school or younger students in 1999, to 47% in 2006 (CIC custom tabulation), and younger students comprised 59% of all international students in the Toronto District School Board (TDSB 2005). Figures reported for 2008 show that Canada was the third most common destination for foreign students at the primary and secondary educational levels, after the U.S. and Southeast Asia (Center for Education Statistics 2009).

Among ethnic Koreans, the temporary population (including the foreign students as well as paid workers) comprised about 17% of those born outside of Canada, in contrast to the 4% of the national foreign-born population in 2006. In addition to those with temporary status, we can include among transnational families those who arrive as visitors and enroll their children in short-term private language schools as well as those who arrive as permanent residents and have immediate family members living in or returning to South Korea. We can thus assume that there is a significantly larger transnational population than that counted by the census, and their growing presence in local communities across Canada is being noticed (Kim, Noh, and Noh 2012).

To be clear, we define intact families as families that consist of both parents living together in Canada with at least one child. Transnational families, recognized also as *kirogi*, or "wild goose" families, are defined as families whose parents live in separate countries, with one parent moving abroad with children, but who still consider themselves as a family unit. However, given the stigma associated with the term *kirogi*, transnational mothers have begun to reject its usage in their day-to-day interactions. As a result, we apply the term "foreign-student family" and transnational family interchangeably to refer to these split households.

We recognize that these types of families are only two of a myriad of possible family structures, and that family structure is never static but ever-changing. We also acknowledge that there are multiple strategies of migration for families —internal, circular, transnational, intact, etc.—and that our concepts belie the complexity and fluid nature of these strategies. However, with these limitations, we explore two possibilities and try to understand how families who follow these patterns differ at the time that they are engaged in the strategy. This will allow us to examine how the structure of opportunities, family resources, and past migration experiences factor into migration decisions. In this chapter, we begin with a brief discussion of the social and political context of transnational family migration from South Korea and then using survey data, we situate our empirical comparisons of transnational and intact families in the literature on migration motivations and on those dimensions understood to be important for structuring transnational opportunities such as motivations, social class background, gender and the division of household labor, and social networks and previous exposure.

The Context of Transnational Migration and Past Research

The role of states in a globalized economy figures prominently in setting the context within which international movements are facilitated and cross-border connections are sustained (Goldring and Krishnamurti 2007; Levitt 2001). States policies are also linked to the macro-structural political, economic, and cultural conditions in both sending and receiving contexts that shape migratory movements. The growth in transnational families in multiple sites can be attributed to unstable political and economic environments in sending countries (Silvey 2006; Tsang et al. 2003; Yamanaka 2005) and to the gap between what is culturally and economically desirable; parents may be economically successful in one place but want their children's education to take place elsewhere (Zhou 1998). It is further recognized that transnationalism is assisted by advances in technology (Basch et al. 1994). It is also understood to be a "flexible" response to inequality in the economies of different countries, and as facilitated by particular bilateral relationships (Basch et al. 1994; Cho 2005).

In addition to the South Korean government's globalization, or *segyewha* policy, in the late 1990s, mandatory English-language education expanded into the national public elementary school curriculum. These state-led initiatives sparked the growth of transnational movements as families bought into the discourse that English language skills were necessary for being competitive in a global market. Children's education, now dominated by the push for English language education, has come to be referred to as "English language mania" (Park and Abelmann 2004), and this mania has translated into a strong desire for overseas education and immersion, particularly in Western environments. A survey conducted in South Korea showed that nearly one-third of parents in Korea seriously considered sending their children abroad (Kim et al. 2005 as cited in Lee and Koo 2006).

The conditions in South Korea that have facilitated overseas movement for educational purposes have been complemented by favorable structural conditions in Canada. Immigration policies, educational policies, and currency exchange rates all shape migration patterns, transnational and otherwise. Signed in 1994, a bilateral agreement permitting visa-free short-term visits eased movement between the two countries and allowed families to visit Canada as part of their migration decision-making process. And as well as removing barriers to temporary visitors from South Korea, Canada offered greater opportunities for and speedier access to permanent residency status relative to the U.S. Moreover, migrants, depending on their status, have access to public and private educational institutions across Canada. There are established structures that accommodate students from abroad, from the placement of international students in local schools by public school boards to language courses offered by the unregulated private language industry. Finally, differences in currency exchange rates between the South Korean won and the Canadian dollar and the U.S. dollar, respectively, may also be an influencing factor shaping migration patterns. Han and Ibbott (2005) argue that this could explain, in part, the rise in immigrant flows from South Korea to Canada relative to the U.S. throughout the 1990s.

While the macro context is important for understanding the broader structural forces that shape education migration from South Korea to Canada in the recent period, it is inadequate for explaining why some families live apart and not others. Both intact and transnational families often identify their children's education as being the primary reason for migration to the West, and past research has shown the importance of individual and family characteristics for shaping transnational migration decisions (Cho 2008; Hiebert and Ley 2006; Huang and Yeoh 2005; S.C. Kim 2001; Waters 2007). However, the individual level factors that influence the specific migration strategy remain unclear, particularly for those from South Korea. Using survey data collected in Toronto, we consider what drives transnational and intact family migration to Canada, including migrant motivations such as the influence of children's experiences in schools, class position and socio-economic status in places of origin, gendered family relations and responsibilities for social reproduction, social networks, and previous migration experience.

Data and Methods

To identify differences in the two migration strategies along the dimensions mentioned, we used data from the *2011 Toronto Korean Families Study* (TKFS), a Korean/English bilingual survey that was administered to recent immigrant families with children from South Korea in the Greater Toronto Area from May

2010 to May 2011. The in-person, written, and structured survey took approximately one hour to complete and covered topics such as the motivations for migration, past migration experiences, social integration, health, civic participation, transnationalism, acculturation, marital relations, and children's experiences in schools, among others.

The survey is based on a non-probability sample of 422 immigrant families who arrived in Canada in the 2000 to 2009 period. To be included in the sample, respondents, who were located through purposive, snowball sampling techniques, had to have been married with a school-aged child at the time of arrival. We specifically targeted both intact and transnational families to ensure we would have sufficient sample sizes for comparative purposes, and interviewers screened potential respondents by asking about their family structures. Once a suitable family was identified, a trained bilingual interviewer completed a face-to-face interview with one of the parents. Our final survey resulted in a total of 155 transnational families and 267 intact immigrant families.

Of the 422 cases in the full sample, 398 are included in this analysis. We omitted those whose living arrangements could not be identified as either intact or transnational and those who were not married or living in common-law relationships. Table 6.1 presents the descriptive statistics for selected socio-demographic traits for the total sample as well as by migration strategy. Due to small frequencies in some cells and the potential for identifying these individuals, we suppress values that fall below ten cases. Additionally, due to missing data, not all of the variables will have a total of 398 cases. To test for associations, the results of chi-square tests or two-tailed t-tests for means are provided.

In terms of gender, participants consisted mostly of women (89.4% for the full sample), and this was true for both intact and transnational families. While we made some attempt to recruit male respondents from both types of families, women were more far more likely to be in Toronto and their spouses were more likely to be in South Korea, especially in the cases of transnational families. The mean age was 46.2 years, and there were no age differences between respondents from intact families and those from transnational families. The two main religions included Protestant and Roman Catholic, and again, we observe little difference in the two types of migrant families. With respect to their residency and migrant status, a greater percentage of respondents from intact families were citizens or permanent residents, and they have been here longer than respondents from transnational families. In other words, and as we would expect, transnational families on average have been residents for a shorter period of time, and they tend to be living under more temporary residential circumstances.

In the analysis that follows, we discuss our findings from a comparison of intact and transnational families along various dimensions, including the motivations for leaving South Korea and coming to Canada, social class background (Table 6.2), gendered division of labor, and previous migration experiences and social networks (Table 6.3). Taken together, these dimensions will shed light on helping to explain what shapes decisions about migratory strategies.

Table 6.1: Demographic Information

Variables	Intact	Transnational	Total	χ^2	p*
Gender					
Female	220 (84.6%)	--	356 (89.4%)	--	--
Male	40 (15.4%)	--	42 (10.6%)		
Age (n = 397)					
Mean (SD)	46.5 (5.3)	45.9 (4.0)	46.2 (4.9)	t=1.14*	0.256
Religion (n = 395)					
Protestant	159 (61.4%)	78 (57.4%)	237 (60.0%)	3.63	0.163
Roman Catholic	75 (29.0%)	36 (26.5%)	111 (28.1%)		
Other	25 (9.7%)	22 (16.2%)	47 (11.9%)		
Citizenship (n = 397)					
Canada only	82 (31.5%)	17 (12.3%)	99 (24.9%)	17.82	0.000
Other	178 (68.5%)	121 (87.7%)	299 (75.1%)		
Migration Status					
Permanent (or citizen)	222 (85.4%)	82 (59.4%)	304 (76.3%)	33.70	0.000
Temporary	38 (14.6%)	56 (40.6%)	94 (23.7%)		
Mean (SD)	7.1 (3.0)	4.8 (2.4)	6.3 (3.0)	t=7.56*	0.000

N = 398, unless otherwise noted.
* Two-tailed t-tests; for age, df=395; for years living in Canada, df=390.

Explaining the Migration Strategy

Motivations for Migration

For those who are not involuntarily displaced, motivations clearly factor into explaining patterns of migration for individuals and families. These motivations include economic and educational opportunities and family reunification. Improving the family's future and joining family or close friends were the two most frequently stated reasons for immigrating to Canada, and education was the third most common motivation (Statistics Canada 2005). For many, however, the goal of securing a future for the family may go hand in hand with seeking educational opportunities, as the acquisition of cultural capital through an overseas education is perceived to ensure the reproduction of families' middle-class status (Waters 2005).

By engaging in migration for education, both intact and transnational families from South Korea also hope their children will be in an advantageous position in the global economy, and will be able to secure or improve their families' social class position. The importance of English-language acquisition for educational and economic opportunities in South Korea is well-documented (Lee and Koo 2006), as is the highly competitive educational system that is captured in the expression, "if you sleep for three hours a day, you will pass the [*university entrance*] exam. Sleep four hours, you will fail" (Goh-Grapes 2009, "Phenomenon of Wild Goose Fathers in South Korea," The *Korea Times National*, February 22). It is this harsh system that families attempt to avoid by sending children overseas or by moving together as a family.

In the TKFS survey, respondents were asked in two separate questions to rank their reasons for leaving South Korea and for migrating to Canada. As expected among both types of families, the most common motivation for leaving South Korea and for coming to Canada was related to education (Table 6.2). However, despite this similarity among the migrant families, we observe some important and statistically significant differences in the top five primary reasons for migration.

Although the education system in South Korea was the most important reason to leave the country for both family types, a greater percentage of transnational families (58%) compared to intact families (50%) indicated it as their main reason for leaving. For transnational families, the need for their children to learn English was the second most common top-ranked reason (23%). Other less-frequently chosen, top-ranked reasons identified by several respondents included the lifestyle in South Korea and their children's performance in school. While no direction was indicated in the questions in terms of how their children performed, we can see from parental responses to questions about their two oldest children's performance and experiences in schools that most children did fairly well and performed above average and had few problems (Table 6.2). Limiting the sample to those who ranked their children's performance as the biggest driving force behind their migration suggests that families were motivated to move when their children did well in school in South Korea although the small sample size precludes us from drawing any firm conclusions.

While intact families also indicated somewhat similar motivations, the distribution of responses differed. In other words, lifestyle in South Korea was the second most common top-ranked reason for leaving among intact migrant families (21%), followed by the need for their children to learn English and limited economic opportunities. When asked to rank their reasons for migrating to Canada, respondents from intact migrant families were almost evenly split between ranking their children's education and a better future for the family as their primary reasons, 40% and 30%, respectively. This is in contrast to the overwhelming majority (71%) of respondents from transnational families who chose their children's education as the main reason for choosing Canada. Less than 10% indicated a better future for the family. Other reasons that ranked at the top for several respondents of both types of families include the relative ease of migrating to Canada, Canada's social welfare system, and the simple fact that their application to Canada was accepted.

Table 6.2: Motivations for Migration, Children in School, and Social Class Background

Variables	Intact	Transnational	χ^2	p
Motivations				
Main reason for leaving South Korea (n = 373)				
Education system in Korea	118 (50.0%)	79 (57.7%)	22.82	0.000
Life style	49 (20.8%)	11 (8.0%)		
Children's learning English	23 (9.8%)	31 (22.6%)		
Other	46 (3.8%)	16 (11.7%)		
Main reason for coming to Canada (n = 382)				
Children's education	99 (39.6%)	94 (71.2%)	39.31	0.000
Better future for family	76 (30.4%)	12 (9.1%)		
Relatively easier to immigrate to Canada	23 (9.2%)	12 (9.1%)		
Other	52 (20.8%)	14 (10.6%)		
Children in school in South Korea				
Children's academic performance				
Eldest child — above avg (n = 384)	172 (69.1%)	97 (71.9%)	0.32	0.571
Second child — above avg (n = 263)	97 (61.4%)	71 (67.6%)	1.06	0.303
Children's difficulties in school				
Eldest child — no difficulties (n = 388)	214 (84.9%)	112 (82.4%)	0.43	0.510
Second child — no difficulties (n = 269)	144 (87.8%)	96 (91.4%)	0.87	0.350
Social class background				
Household income in Korea before migration (n = 382)				
Less than ₩70,000,000*	170 (67.5%)	39 (30.0%)	48.57	0.000
₩70,000,000 or more	82 (32.5%)	91 (70.0%)		
Education**				
Respondent (n = 394)				
University degree or higher	195 (75.9%)	107 (78.1%)	0.248	0.619
Other	62 (24.1%)	30 (21.9%)		
Spouse (n = 392)				
University degree or higher	220 (85.9%)	126 (92.7%)	3.86	0.049
Other	36 (14.1%)	10 (7.4%)		

* In February 2012, this value was equivalent to approximately CAD 62,000.
** Education indicates the highest level of formal education attained outside Canada.

Like other migrant groups (Waters 2005), education for their children is the key reason for migration for many families from South Korea, and this has led to an increase in education emigration from South Korea since the early 1990s (D.H. Lee 2010). However, the results from the survey data, taken together, show that while education is the driving force behind many families' moves to Canada, motivations are often more complex and multifaceted. Furthermore, based on the findings, we observe the greater role that children play in the migration decisions of transnational families, and while children are important for intact migrant families as well, intact families' migration decisions appear to be focused more on the family as a unit.

The Importance of Social Class

Migration across national borders requires not only a motivation to move, but also resources such as financial and cultural capital. Historically, an overseas education was only accessible for the religious, technical, and intellectual elites (Shim 1994). However, the expansion of tertiary education and the rapid industrialization of South Korea beginning in the 1960s led to the growth of a large middle class by the 1990s (Koo 1991) who have been able to take advantage of opportunities abroad in multiple ways. Two such ways include the types of families that are of interest here.

To assess social class differences between the two types of families prior to migration, we asked respondents to indicate their household income levels before migrating to Canada and highest educational degree attained outside of Canada. As shown in Table 6.2, transnational families had significantly higher percentages in the higher income bracket prior to their move to Canada compared to intact families. Approximately 70% of transnational families had an annual household income of ₩70,000,000 or more (roughly CAD 62,000) compared to 33% of intact migrant families. These data suggest that social class is a determinant of the migration strategy and structure the types of migration opportunities available to families.

Interestingly, this is supported to some extent by educational characteristics. On the one hand, we do not observe significant educational differences between the respondents of the two types of migrant families, who were predominantly women, yet, on the other hand, there are significant differences in their spouses' level of education. These comparisons of household income and educational attainment show that transnational families, in general, are of a higher social class background than intact migrant families. Thus, while it seems a temporary stay overseas for the purposes of education appears to be more widely accessible, it still remains an opportunity primarily for those who have significant resources.

Gender, Migration Decisions, and the Division of Labor

The rise in transnational families from South Korea is a part of the global pattern in the increasing feminization of migration, which finds women not as dependent spouses but as leading the migration process. As "education managers," mothers from South Korea are at the frontlines of transnational familyhood (Park 2007). They assume a leading role in the migration decision-making process that involves a variety of activities from preparing and researching information about migration and schooling to dealing with adjustment issues in the destination country, managing children's daily activities, and attending language schools to maintain their own status after migration (S. Kim 2009). And in fact, our survey data reveal that while couples most often made the migration decision together, when we compare the two types of families that reported a sole decision-maker, either self or spouse, women from transnational families were 1.7 times as likely as women from intact migrant families to have made the decision instead of their spouses.

Despite having the power to make decisions regarding their children's education even if it means moving overseas and away from fathers, women in transnational homes often live in households that rely on a traditional division of labor. In other words, transnationalism among families from South Korea is made possible by a gendered division of labor and social reproductive practices (A.H. Kim forthcoming). As shown at the top of Table 6.3, survey results support this characterization. The data on the division of labor are presented for the women in the sample and for each area of responsibility, including domestic chores, finances, maintenance, and child-care, we report the percentage who indicated they had primary responsibility when living together with their spouse in South Korea. Overall, we observe traditional domestic roles for women from both types of families although women from transnational families were slightly more likely than women from intact migrant families to have primary responsibility for all four areas. For domestic chores, 84% of transnational mothers and 82% of mothers from intact migrant families had primary responsibility prior to migration. For household finances, the percentages were 75% and 71%, respectively. For household maintenance such as minor repairs around the house, auto care, and so forth, 23% of transnational mothers indicated having primary responsibility compared to the 16% of intact migrant mothers. We find similar gaps between mothers from the two family types with respect to child-care. Over 70% of transnational mothers and 67% of intact family mothers reported having primary responsibility for child-care. It is worth mentioning that the other response categories included spouse, a shared responsibility and someone else, and that for domestic chores and child-care, the second most common response for both types of families was that it was a shared responsibility.

Nevertheless, more than two-thirds of all women in the sample indicated they were responsible for domestic chores, finances, and child-care. It is likely that the greater decision-making power of transnational mothers with respect to the migration decision vis-à-vis intact migrant mothers is related to the distinction between migration and social reproduction. That is, temporary migration decisions related to children's education are seen as fulfilling the maternal role and expectations around social reproduction and they are not likely perceived as decisions about migration per se.

Table 6.3. Selected Characteristics of Families Prior to Migrating to Canada

Variables	Intact	Transnational	χ^2	p
Division of labour (females only)				
Domestic chores — Self ($n = 353$)	180 (82.2%)	112 (83.6%)	0.11	0.737
Household finances — Self ($n = 353$)	155 (70.8%)	100 (74.6%)	0.61	0.433
Household maintenance — Self ($n = 352$)	36 (16.4%)	31 (23.3%)	2.53	0.111
Childcare — Self ($n = 352$)	147 (67.1%)	94 (70.7%)	0.48	0.487
Social networks in Canada				
Knew someone living in Canada	174 (67.4%)	108 (78.3%)	5.13	0.023
Self or spouse has relatives in Toronto	92 (35.4%)	42 (30.4%)	0.99	0.320
Exposure through contacts in South Korea				
Knew Koreans who lived abroad ($n = 397$)	145 (55.8%)	85 (62.0%)	1.45	0.229
Knew Canadians or Cdn orgs ($n = 397$)	52 (20.1%)	27 (19.6%)	0.02	0.903
Lived in Canada before migrating				
Yes — Participants ($n = 394$)	30 (11.7%)	18 (13.1%)	0.18	0.672
Yes — Spouses ($n = 393$)	33 (12.8%)	10 (7.4%)	2.75	0.097
Yes — Children ($n = 391$)	40 (15.8%)	35 (25.4%)	5.26	0.022
Visited Canada before migrating				
Yes ($n = 397$)	126 (48.6%)	79 (57.2%)	2.67	0.103
Mean number of visits (SD) ($n = 187$)	2.0 (2.21)	1.64 (1.51)	t=1.21*	0.230

$N = 398$, unless otherwise noted.
* Two-tailed t-test, df=185.

Exposure through Social Networks and Previous Migration Experience

Explanations of migration have moved beyond the push-pull approach that framed much of the discussion on motivations above to viewing migration flows as a system (Castles and Miller 2009; A.H. Kim 2007). Whether through idealized images diffused through the mass media, information and stories through social contacts, or prior experience living in or visiting a place, greater exposure to a destination will encourage migration. In particular, the role of social networks for facilitating flows has long been acknowledged (Boyd 1989). Family members, friends, and community ties provide relevant social and financial aid and information which does not simply reduce the costs to migration but actively perpetuates movement and chain migration between places. Learning about overseas experiences from other families who have spent time abroad will influence a family's decisions about transnational familyhood, much like Jinu's Mother, in Park's ethnographic study, who sent her two sons to New Zealand for three months to study the English language after hearing about the daughter of a friend (Park and Abelmann 2004). Also related to exposure and information is previous migration to a place, which also facilitates future moves overseas. For example, a study by Lee and Koo (2006) found that transnational fathers in South Korea who sent their spouses and children to the U.S. had stayed there in the past to study or visit.

In the TKFS data, we find support for the importance of social networks in destinations. Our findings show that they are more important for transnational families than for intact migrant families. More than 78% of transnational families and 67% of intact migrant families had some contacts in Canada prior to their move (Table 6.3). Transnational families may be more likely to go where they have a contact as their needs must be met immediately and they may be more reliant on informal networks to help with settlement and enrollment. About one-third of each type of family had relatives living in Toronto, most often siblings, followed by grandparents. Beyond social networks in Canada, we also find that a majority of families had known others who had lived abroad and returned to South Korea (more than half of respondents from both family types).

Turning to the question of exposure to Canada through Canadians or Canadian organizations in South Korea, we find that while most respondents did not know Canadians or Canadian organizations, similar percentages of respondents from both family types did, falling at about 20% (Table 6.3). Among those who did know Canadians or Canadian organizations, they were most often English language teachers and immigration brokers.

Similarly, most respondents had not lived in Canada prior to moving to the country but of all the family members, children were the most likely to have lived in Canada previously with more than a quarter of children from transnational families having previously lived in Canada, and 16% of children in the intact family sample (Table 6.3). This highlights the more central role of children in the migration process relative to other family members, particularly among transnational families.

In contrast to previous long-term stays overseas, we find prior visits to Canada to be more common among the two samples studied. Approximately half of respondents from both family types indicated that they had visited Canada before their move and for an average of two visits (Table 6.3). There was no significant difference between the two samples on whether they previously visited Canada. Although these percentages seem low given the ease of travel in the contemporary period, it is not surprising with the plethora of alternative media of information, the most common sources among the respondents being the internet, books, magazines, and documentaries.

Discussion

In this chapter, we examined some of the key factors associated with migration flows, comparing families who engaged in a transnational migration strategy and other migrant families who were living together in Canada. We considered some of the motivations for migration, including the performance of children in schools, the social class background of families, the gendered nature of migration, and exposure through social contacts and prior visits or stays in Canada. We found that prior to migration to Canada, there were a number of similarities between transnational and intact migrant families: first, education was the main driving force behind migration for most families; second, the majority of families were characterized by a gendered division of labor in the home; and third, many respondents had social contacts in Canada and had visited the country previously.

However, the results also point to potential differences in the nature of migration between the two types of strategies, which structure how families engage in the migration process. In terms of motivations, children were identified as explicitly shaping migration trajectories, and more so for transnational families. For intact families, children were clearly important, but there was a greater recognition of the change in lifestyle and opportunities for the family as a whole. Transnational families tended to be of higher social class background than intact migrant families, and women had a greater decision-making role in transnational migration than in intact family migration, and finally social networks in Canada, while relevant for both types of families, appeared to be more important for transnational families.

The picture we develop from this analysis is that relative to intact migrant families, transnational families have the means and financial resources to engage in a process of education migration for their children that is expected to preserve and reproduce their social class status back in South Korea. In contrast, intact migrant families appear to have more limited means for upward mobility in South Korea and thus, they take advantage of migration to improve their families' opportunities and quality of life in another place. The more permanent nature of their stay allows them to rely less on social contacts in Canada as they can take time to settle and access formal services and programs. The short term nature of transnational families sojourn to Canada and tight timelines, however, requires them to rely on more informal networks. Finally, consistent with past work (A.H. Kim forthcoming; Park and Abelmann 2004), the greater decision-making power of women in transnational migration appears to be driven by the mothers' responsibilities for education and social reproduction. In other words, it appears to be less of a decision about migration, whereas for intact migrant families, in which mothers also take the lead on social reproduction, migration in and of itself takes primacy and requires a family decision.

Despite this characterization, we end with the caveat that the results are suggestive due to limitations in the data in terms of the small purposive sample from one city in Canada. We also argue that it is important to avoid purely instrumental explanations for the migration behavior of families from South Korea. In other words, while education and social mobility are clearly powerful motivators, decisions around migration are more complex and must be viewed in light of the structural and political context. Moreover, a number of empirical studies (Choi 2006; Jeong and Belanger 2012; S.S. Kim 2006; Kim and Chang 2004; Um 2002; Yeom 2008) have shown transnational migration to be an important social issue due to the separation of families and due to the range of effects on families, and thus an issue that requires greater attention.

Notes

1. Research reported here was supported by a Social Sciences and Humanities Research Council of Canada Standard Research Grant. The authors would like to thank Min-Jung Kwak, Eunjung Lee, Jeeseon Park, José Itzigsohn, Choong Ho Park and Young-Ah Kim.

References

English Language Literature

Basch, Linda, Nina Glick Schiller, and Cristina Szanton Blanc. 1994. *Transnational Projects, Postcolonial Predicaments, and Deterritorialized Nation-States.* Langhorne, PA: Gordon and Breach Science Publishers.
Boyd, Monica. 1989. "Family and Personal Networks in International Migration: Recent Developments and New Agendas." *International Migration Review* 23: 638-670.
Castles, Stephen and Mark J. Miller, eds. 2009. *The Age of Migration: International Population Movements in the Modern World* (4e). New York: The Guilford Press.
Center for Education Statistics. 2009. *Brief Statistics on Korean Education.* Korea: Korean Educational Development Institute.
Cho, Uhn. 2005. "The Encroachment of Globalization into Intimate Life: The Flexible Korean Family in 'Economic Crisis'." *Korea Journal* 45: 8-35.
Citizenship and Immigration Canada (CIC). 2010. *Facts and Figures: Immigration Overview, Permanent and Temporary Residents.* Pp. 124. Ottawa: Research and Evaluation Branch.
Goh-Grapes, A. (2009, February 22). "Phenomenon of Wild Goose Fathers in South Korea." The *Korea Times National.* Retrieved July 27, 2011, from www.koreatimes.co.kr/www/news/nation/2009/02/117_40060.html
Goldring, Luin, and Sailaja Krishnamurti. 2007. "Introduction: Contextualizing Transnationalism in Canada." In *Organizing the Transnational: Labor, Politics, and Social Change*, edited by Luin Goldring and Sailaja Krishnamurti. Vancouver: UBC Press.
Han, J.D., and Peter Ibbott. 2005. "Korean Immigration to North America: Some Prices That Matter." *Canadian Studies in Population* 32 (2), 155-176.
Hiebert, Daniel, and David Ley. 2006. "Characteristics of Immigrant Transnationalism in Vancouver." In *Transnational Identities and Practices in Canada*, edited by Vic Satzewich and Lloyd Wong, 71-90. Vancouver: UBC Press.
Huang, Shirlena, and Brenda S. A. Yeoh. 2005. "Transnational Families and Their Children's Education: China's 'Study Mothers' in Singapore." *Global Networks* 5: 379-400.
Jeong, Junmin, and Danièle Bélanger. 2012. "*Kirogi* Families as Virtual 'Families': Perspectives and Experiences of *Kirogi* Mothers." In *Korean Immigrants in Canada: Perspectives on Migration, Integration and the Family*, edited by Samuel Noh, Ann H. Kim, and Marianne S. Noh. Toronto: University of Toronto Press.
Kim, Ann H. 2007. "The Flow of Labor and Goods in Canada's International Migration System." *Canadian Studies in Population* 34: 241-268.
Kim, Ann H. Forthcoming. "Structuring Transnationalism: The Mothering Discourse and the Educational Project." In *Transnational Voices: Global Migration and the Experiences of Women, Youth and Children*, edited by Guida Man and Rina Cohen. Whitby, ON, Canada: de Sitter Publications.
Kim, Ann H., Marianne S. Noh, and Samuel Noh. 2012. "Introduction: Historical Context and Contemporary Research." In *Korean Immigrants in Canada: Perspectives on Migration, Integration and the Family*, edited by Samuel Noh, Ann H. Kim, and Marianne S. Noh. Toronto: University of Toronto Press.
Kim, Song-Chul. 2001. "'Weekend Couples' among Korean Professionals: An Ethnography of Living Apart on Weekdays." *Korea Journal* 41: 28-47.

Koo, Hagen. 1991. "Middle Classes, Democratization, and Class Formation: The Case of South Korea." *Theory and Society* 20: 485-509.

Lee, Doo Hyoo. 2010. "A Study of the Life and Culture of Young Korean Students Studying in the United States." *Educational Research and Reviews* 5: 78-85.

Lee, Yean-Ju, and Hagen Koo. 2006. "'Wild Geese Fathers' and a Globalised Family Strategy for Education in Korea." *International Development Planning Review* 28: 533-553.

Levitt, Peggy. 2001. "Transnational Migration: Taking Stock and Future Directions." *Global Networks* 1: 195-216.

Levitt, Peggy, and B. Nadya Jaworsky. 2007. "Transnational Migration Studies: Past Developments and Future Trends." *Annual Review Sociology* 33: 129-156.

Park, So Jin. 2007. "Educational Manager Mothers: South Korea's Neoliberal Transformation." *Korea Journal* 47: 186-213.

Park, So Jin, and Nancy Abelmann. 2004. "Class and Cosmopolitan Striving: Mothers' Management of English Education in South Korea." *Anthropological Quarterly* 77: 645-672.

Shim, R. J. 1994. "Englishized Korean: Structure, Status and Attitudes." *World Englishes*, 13 (2), 225-244.

Silvey, Rachel. 2006. "Consuming the Transnational Family: Indonesian Migrant Domestic Workers to Saudi Arabia." *Global Networks* 6: 23-40.

Statistics Canada. 2005. *Longitudinal Survey of Immigrants to Canada: A Portrait of Early Settlement Experiences.* Ottawa: Minister of Industry.

Toronto District School Board (TDSB). 2005. *Canadian and Korean Educators Connect: TDSB Partners with South Korean Educators to Develop Best EFL Teaching Methods.* News Release, April 29, 2005.

Tsang, A. Ka Tat, Howard H. Irving, Ramona Alaggia, Shirley B.Y. Chau, and Michael Benjamin. 2003. "Negotiating Ethnic Identity in Canada: The Case of the 'Satellite Children.'" *Youth & Society* 34: 359-384.

Waters, Johanna L. 2005. "Transnational Family Strategies and Education in the Contemporary Chinese Diaspora." *Global Networks* 5: 359-377.

Waters, Johanna L. 2007. "'Roundabout Routes and Sanctuary Schools': The Role of Situated Educational Practices and Habitus in the Creation of Transnational Professionals." *Global Networks* 7 (4): 477-497.

Yamanaka, Keiko. 2005. "Changing Family Structures of Nepalese Transmigrants in Japan: Split-Households and Dual-Wage Earners." *Global Networks* 5: 337-358.

Zhou, Min. 1998. "'Parachute Kids' in Southern California: The Educational Experience of Chinese Children in Transnational Families." *Educational Policy* 12: 682-704.

Korean Language Literature

Cho, Uhn. 2008. "The Contested Terrain of Class and Gender: Landscapes of Korean Family Politics in Globalization." *Korean Women's Studies* 24 (2): 5-37.

Choi, Yang-Suk. 2006. "The Phenomenon of 'Geese Families': Marital Separation between Geese-Fathers and Geese-Mothers." *Family and Culture* 18 (2): 37-65.

Kim, Seonmi. 2009. "A Qualitative Study on the Wild Geese Mother's Everyday Life Family Relationship and Social Networking." *Korea Journal of Family Resource Management* 13 (1): 41-59.

Kim, Sung-Sook. 2006. "The 'Kirogi' Fathers' Changes of Lives and Adaptation Problems." *Journal of Korean Home Economics* 24 (1), 141-158.

Kim, Yang Hee, and On-Jeong Chang. 2004. "Issue of Families that run Separate Households for a Long Time: The So-called 'Wild Geese Family.'" *Journal of Korean Family Relations* 9 (2), 1-23.

Um, Myung Yong. 2002. "Issues of Male Professionals Living Apart from their Families for a Long Time: The So-called 'Wild Geese Father.'" *Korean Journal of Family Therapy* 10 (2): 25-43.

Yeom, Ji-Sook. 2008. "The Light and Shade of Early Studying Abroad from Children's Experiences." *Journal of Korea Open Association for Early Childhood Education,* 13 (6): 241-259.

Chapter 7
Transnational Interactions among Korean Immigrants in Toronto: Family Ties and Socioeconomic, Cultural, and Political Participation[1]

by Samuel Noh, Min-Jung Kwak, and Joe Jeong Ho Han

Introduction

Transnationalism has been a buzz word in migration studies since it was first introduced by Schiller and her colleagues as "the process by which immigrants build social fields that link together their country of origin and their country of settlement" (Glick Schiller et al. 1992: 1). The concept represents a set of new perspectives of international migration that emphasize active and productive strategies of migration based on consciousness in the global capitalist system, in contrast to the old image of migration as a painstaking process of being ruptured or uprooted from one's home country. Over the last two decades, the field of transnational migration has become enriched with rigorous theoretical discussion and empirical findings. Yet, there has been little research conducted on Korean-Canadian transnationalism and even Korean-American transnationalism (Kwak and Hiebert 2007, 2010). This study presents descriptive results on the nature and extent of engagement in transnational activities among Korean immigrants in Ontario in Canada. It focuses on transnationalism in three domains:

informal social ties and contacts (cultural, emotional and financial ties) and organizational participation.

Transnationalism: Concepts and Research

Although transnationalism provides new perspectives of the contemporary patterns and processes of international migration, immigrants have always been engaged in cross-national activities and social exchanges. Pre-1965 immigrants also kept in touch with relatives and friends back home through letters and telegrams, and a large number of them returned home to settle permanently. In addition, migrant workers traveled back and forth between home and host countries looking for seasonal work (Levitt 2001). Indeed, transnational migration is not a new phenomenon (Foner 2001; Portes et al. 1991). Some researchers believe that transnationalism has become an overused term to explain nearly everything associated with migrants and migration, and has exaggerated the actual scope of immigrant transnational practice (Portes et al. 1999; Portes 2001, 2003). In fact, Portes (2001, 2003) found that transnationalism was only a minority phenomenon among Caribbean immigrants living in American cities, and argued that the classic position in immigration theory that emphasizes the assimilation of migrants to the host society was still valid. This is consistent with the critical analyses of transnationalism indicating that the concept of transnationalism is losing explanatory power (Kivisto 2001; Hiebert and Ley 2006; Levitt 2001).

Notwithstanding the radical criticism, there appear to be at least three important characteristics that separate contemporary transnational practices from those of the past (Levitt 2001; Portes et al. 1999). First, the contemporary concept of transnationalism recognizes critical en masse movement of money, commodities and people. Second, because of rapid technological development in telecommunications and transportation, information travels substantially faster than ever, and transnational activities have become enormously efficient, if not effective. Third, the impact of the grassroots level of transnationalism has prompted responses from government institutions and other organizations. Authorities have argued that these characteristics are sufficient to merit research on the transnational ties and practices of twenty-first century immigrants (Levitt 2001; Portes et al. 1999). In particular, the prevalence of *grassroots* transnationalism as a collective response to new global order seems to be a salient issue for many social science researchers.

Transnationalism from Above vs. Transnationalism from Below

Transnational ties and activities of grassroots immigrants have been the primary concerns of social scientists of migration studies. Grassroots movement has been considered as collective responses of the general public to social stratification and conflicts. In many writings on transnationalism, the term "grassroots" is conceived as diverse forms of collective identities that are led by ordinary migrants and different from the institutional transnational agents. Smith and Guarnizo (1998) and Portes et al. (1999) distinguish and further clarify two types of transnationalism—*from above* and *from below*—based on the level of institutionalization and initiating points. Institutional transnational actors typically include multinational corporations and national and international government bodies. Multinational corporations' direct investments in Third World countries and various efforts to expand global markets are prime examples of economic transnationalism from above. Some national governments have become interested in granting dual citizenship for their emigrants and made an effort to enhance cultural and economic ties with them by taking necessary political measures. The South Korean government has been known for making such efforts by establishing Overseas Korean Foundation. *Transnationalism from below* refers to various private transnational networks and cross-border interactions of individual migrants.

Examples of *transnationalism from below* include the business investments of Chinese-American entrepreneurial elites (Smart and Smart 1998, Willis and Yeoh 2002) in their home countries, as well as the efforts of undocumented migrants from Latin American countries (Levitt 2001; Mahler 1999; Bailey et al. 2002) to maintain transnational households by sending regular remittances. Fundraising for electoral candidates in home countries and promoting cultural events in ethnic/immigrant communities are also typical examples of *transnationalism below* (Portes et al. 1999). Adding to the existing transnationalism literature, the present study provides a snap shot of grassroots transnational ties and activities among a sample of Korean immigrants living in an urban setting.

Typology of Transnationalism

A number of scholars have attempted to sketch out actual patterns of transnationalism, paying particular attention to its shape, contours, structure, as well as the processes and agencies that sustain transnational trajectories and edifices. There have been many case studies that draw more or less different dynamics of TN activities. However, efforts to examine overall *transnational morphologies* and consequences have been mainly undertaken within the sociological and geographical disciplines. Portes' (1999, 2003) attempt to identify a general pattern of transnationalism (TN) between American host cities and three Caribbean home countries is a good example. Three sectors of transnationalism—economic, political, and socio-cultural—were observed, with each sector classified as having low or high level of institutionalization. Examples of economic TN at a lower level of institutionalization include informal, small scale trades and continuing circular labor migration. Highly institutionalized economic TN may include home country banking in the immigrant communities and organized tourism. In general, activities initiated and performed at the individual, family or local community level were considered as "low institutionalization." They typically overlap *from below* and *grassroots* transnational practices.

Based on a review of earlier studies of transnationalism among Asian immigrants in Canada (Waters 2003, Walton-Roberts 2003, Hyndman 2003, Ghosh and Wang 2003, Angeles 2003), Kelly (2003) noted that political, emotional, and social transnational linkages across the Pacific Ocean were deeply embedded in the everyday lives of Asian immigrants. Ley and Hiebert (2006) also found extensive transnational activities among most recent immigrants in Vancouver, Canada. They reported that many immigrants appeared to maintain informal social ties with family, relatives, and friends over years. However, transnational economic activities (e.g., business ownership), which was intensive at the early period of settlement, deemed to be fading over years.

Social Correlates

Among immigrants in the U.S., Portes (2001, 2003) found that the level of their economic, political, and socio-cultural transnational activities was associated with greater education, increased length of U.S. residence, and higher employment status. Findings from a large scale survey on transnationalism in Vancouver, Canada (Hiebert and Ley 2006) were substantially different from the results of Portes' (2001, 2003) study of transnationalism among Caribbean immigrants living in the U.S. For immigrants in Vancouver, the level of transnational activity was inversely associated with the length of residence in Canada, as recent immigrants tend to maintain stronger network than older immigrants with their country of origin. Socioeconomic status indicators, such as education and income, were not good predictors of transnational activities. For example, lower-income immigrants and those at lower educational level were more likely to own property in their home country, but less likely to own business property. Hiebert and Ley (2006) also noted that transnationalism in Vancouver seemed to represent an alternative source of social network and economic activities, and may exert an adverse effect on social and economic integration in Canada.

From the studies of immigrants in the U.S. and Canada, it is plausible to conclude that contexts of sending and receiving countries of immigrant groups determine the characteristics, intensity, and process of transnationalism. This paper provides data on associations of transnational ties among Korean immigrants in Canada with an array of social and demographic factors.

Korean Immigrants in Canada

A large scale of immigration of Koreans to Canada began officially in 1963, after Canada had removed discriminatory immigration policies and established diplomatic relationship with the Republic of Korea. The adoption of a 'point system' of immigrant recruitment in 1967 accelerated immigration from Korea. Except for the period from 1977 to 1986, Canada has experienced a steady growth of Korean-Canadians in each of the last five decades from the 1960s to the 2000s. Korean immigration flows to Canada was unprecedentedly high in the late 1990s. The Korean Ministry of Foreign Affairs and Trade (MOFAT) reported that the number of Koreans who directly emigrated from South Korea to Canada surpassed the number of those who reported emigration to the United States for the first time in 1999 and the trend lasted until 2003 (Korean MOFAT 2008). According to the Korean emigration data between 1999 and 2003, those who reported permanent migration to Canada and the U.S. were 32,310 and 23,536 respectively (ibid.). The U.S. has been the most favored destination of immigration among Koreans for almost thirty-five years with a large number of emigrants who directly moved from South Korea to the U.S. as well as a sheer number of those Koreans who adjusted their status while they resided in the U.S. Thus the figures may not be too meaningful for overall immigration statistics to the U.S. However, considering the fact that there has been no significant level of local landings among Koreans in Canada, the trend between 1999 and 2003 is noteworthy for the Korean immigration history to Canada.

According to Canadian immigration statistics, Korea was the fifth largest source country between 1999 and 2001, with an annual influx exceeding 7,000 (CIC 2006). Amendments to immigration policy in 2002 may have resulted in reduced annual landing statistics. Although Citizenship and Immigration Canada (CIC) reduced the threshold of passing points for skilled workers in the following year, the latest system still emphasizes high standards of educational qualification and proficiency in official languages (English and French), resulting in fewer Koreans being admitted to Canada. Changes to the business immigration programs also have impact. For example, those qualifying as entrepreneurs now need at least one year of actual business management experience (www.cic.gc.ca). As a result, the annual inflow has slightly dropped. Since 2004, approximately 5,000 to 6,000 Koreans have earned permanent residency status each year.

The revised policies, while reducing the scope of application for permanent migration from Korea, seemed to encourage more temporary migrants from Korea to apply for permanent residency rights while staying in Canada. Since 2002, more than 7,000 Koreans residing in Canada have reported their acquisition of permanent residency rights to local consulate general offices (Korean MOFAT 2008).[2] With a rapidly growing number of international students and visitors from Korea, the trends suggest that migrants with temporary permits will be an important source of future immigrants.

In terms of entry class, most recent Korean immigrants have arrived in Canada as economic immigrants rather than through the family reunification program or other programs. The economic class consists of four subcategories: "other independents" (skilled workers), "entrepreneurs," "self-employed," and "investors." The business program includes the last three of these subcategories. Since 1984, about 80% of the total Korean-Canadian immigrant population arrived as economic class migrants. The percentage climbed to 86% between 1996 and 2005 (LIDS 1980-2005). The number of Korean business class migration that processed between 2000 and 2005 is especially significant, accounting for 13% of the total business class migration. The annual number of Korean business class applicants has been large enough for Korea to be ranked as the fourth largest source country since 1981. This indicates that a large proportion of recent Korean immigrants is likely to be involved with business activities in Canada.[3] The already high propensity of self-employment among Korean immigrants in Canada will seemingly persist for some time (Ornstein 2000, Razin and Langlois 1996).

Source of Data

This study is based on results of a survey. The survey was a part of multi-site, international research project focusing on migration, ethnicity, culture, and depression. Data for this study were derived from a community-based survey of Koreans living in the Greater Toronto Area (GTA) (Canada). Data were collected through person-to-person interviews over a period of five months (January–May) in 2010. Most interviews were conducted in Korean, except a few cases that were conducted in English. We aimed to mimic the demographic profile of the Korean community in the GTA in our sample by obtaining balanced representations of gender, age, and higher education (i.e. university degree). We planned to recruit respondents from all regions of the GTA. Our sampling also considered proportionate representations of religious affiliations (Protestant, Catholic, Buddhism, and no religious affiliations) to reduce potential sampling bias.

A total of 274 adult respondents (20-72 years of age) provided written consent to participate in the study and completed a face-to-face interview. There were 130 (47.4%) male and 144 (52.6%) female participants. The age of the participants ranged from 20 years to 72. All age groups were well represented in the sample. A large majority of the participants immigrated prior to year 2000 (N=212, 77.4%); less than one quarter of the sample came to Canada on or after the year 2000 (N=62, 22.6%). About 43 % (N=119) of the sample reported having completed university education. The figure is consistent with the rate of university education found in previous research (Noh and Avison, 1996).

Informal Ties and Contacts

Informal or personal social relations are critical indicators of social behaviors. Many informal social relations are intimate, personal, and unorganized. Informal relationships are often long lasting, exemplified in intimate groups such as family and close friends. Informal relations are thus labeled as primary social relationships that involve 'whole' persons where forming personal bonds or connections are a goal in itself. This is opposed to secondary or formal social relations in which people engage with specific goals or benefits they intend to achieve through formal structures and rules. As such, secondary social relations involve exchanges of specific functions, capital or talents. Business transactions are typical cases of secondary or formal social relations. Transnational ties and contacts based on informal or personal relations and secondary relations typically represent *from below* and *grassroots* transnational practices.

Figure 7.1: Family or Relatives Living in Korea by Age Group

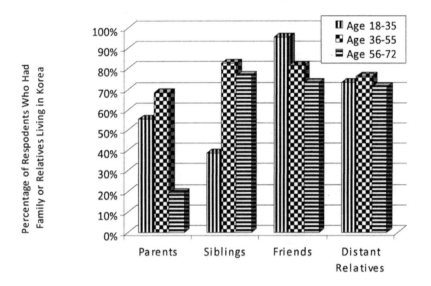

Informal Contacts

Figure 7.1 illustrates the percentage of respondents who had family or relatives living in Korea. Figure 7.2 presents cumulative frequencies of contact with parents, siblings, relatives, and friends living in Korea during the past six months prior to the interview. The solid lines show the frequencies of contacts on telephone, and the shaded lines are for the on-line contacts (e-mail, internet calling, chatting, etc.). First looking at the top-left corner of Figure 7.1, we found that of those who have parents living in Korea, about 45% talked to their parents on the telephone weekly or more frequently. The figure also shows that almost 80% had telephone contacts with their parents at least once a month. Thus, it seems as if Korean immigrants are in very frequent contact with their parents living in Korea.

Figure 7.2: Cumulative Percentage of Contacts using Telephone and Internet, Last Six Months

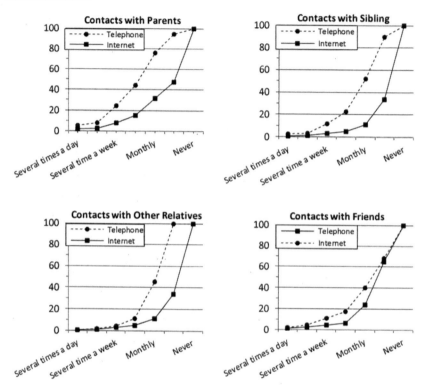

In contrast to telephone contacts, on-line communications with parents were substantially lower; about 50% reported that they have never used online mediums to contact their parents. But, about 30% used internet-based means to communicate with their parents in Korea once or more times per month.

Contact with siblings was considerably lower compared to the frequency of contacts with parents. About 25% of the sample contacted siblings on a weekly basis, and 50% talked on the telephone with siblings at least once a month or more. Online contact was also significantly lower. In total, only 30% had ever used online forms of contact. Contact with *extended family* and *distant relatives* was fairly low; during the last six months, less than 50% and about 35% had made contact via telephone and internet, respectively; only 10% reported making either telephone or internet contact at least once a month. Telephone and internet were used equally when contacting relatives. The participants contacted their *friends* in Korea slightly more frequently than they contacted their relatives, and the internet was used more frequently than telephone for this purpose.

The findings suggest most active transnational contacts are with parents, followed by contacts with siblings. A majority of our sample indicated that they have never been in contact with distant relatives; about 30% have never been in touch with friends in Korea during the past year. It is interesting to observe that the contacts with friends were made by using on-line means. The telephone use was limited as the means for contacting friends.

Men and women showed nearly identical data with respect to the frequency of transnational informal social contacts. With respect to current age, overall, young adults were most active in transnational contacts. Young adults (20-35 years old) contacted their parents significantly more frequently than middle-age and older-age adults. It is interesting to note that middle-age adults made the least contact with extended family members and relatives, compared to younger and older adults. We also found a trend showing that immigrants who had been in Canada for less than ten years were more active in maintaining their transnational contact with their kin than those who had been in Canada for ten years or longer.

Informal Exchanges

While the information about the ties and contacts is an important indicator of transnational practice, data on personal visits and exchanges of material resources provide another dimension of transnationalism. About one-third of our sample *visited* Korea during the past twelve months prior to interview, and a few (3.6%) visited more than once. Most visits to Korea lasted less than a month. Considering the distance between Korea and Toronto, the data appear to be indicative of strong transnational contacts among Korean immigrants living in the GTA. Twice as many immigrants exchanged gifts. Two-thirds of study participants reported that they have *sent money or gifts* to persons in Korea during the past year. Another 67% of respondents said they have *received money or gifts* from Korea. Our data demonstrated that the pattern of exchanges may be related to age. There was a trend indicating that young adults (20-35 years) are more likely to receive money or gifts compared to middle age and older age adults, whereas middle and older age adults are more likely to send money and gifts compared to young adults. Thus, exchanges of gift or money seem to flow from older members of the family to the younger regardless of the place of residence, Canada or Korea.

Cultural, Emotional, and Financial Ties

We have examined the extent of transnationalism in terms of informal social ties and activities. In this section, we report findings on transnational practice ties with respect to the utilization of cultural products of Korea (i.e. media), as well as emotional attachment to Korea. Furthermore, we will also examine financial assets the immigrants still keep in Korea. Although the information on these areas may not be direct indicators of transnational activities, they clearly provide salient information on transnational attachments at behavioral, emotional and financial aspects of life.

At the behavioral level, a large majority of respondents consumed cultural products of Korea. Over 80% of respondents watch Korean TV programs or films *often or daily*, and nearly 90% of respondents read news from Korea in newspapers, magazines, or on internet websites *often or daily*. We also collected data on *emotional tie* with Korea. To evaluate the degree to which Korean immigrants hold emotional attachment to Korea, survey respondents were asked to indicate how often they wished they were living in Korea. The results showed that almost 50% of our survey respondents prefer to re-migrate back to Korea. In addition, about one in eight respondents (11.7%) indicated that they wished they were living in Korea *frequently* or *all the time*; more than one third (37%) indicated that they *sometimes* wish they were living in Korea. Therefore, our data appear to suggest that extremely large proportions of Korean immigrants in the GTA are frequent users of Korean media and cultural programs, and they wish they were living in Korea. Furthermore, a large majority of Korean immigrants do possess wealth in Korea. Almost 75% of Korean immigrants have asset(s) in Korea (home, land, cash or stock, and business). One-third (33%) of the sample indicated that they own assets worth a total of more than $100,000 but less than $500,000. Nearly 14% of the current sample reported that they own assets worth a total of more than $500,000; 10% reported owing assets worth a total of over $1 million.

Overall, we find strong transnationalism among Korean immigrants in Toronto with respect to their attachments to family and personal ties. This is exemplified in frequency of long distant contacts, resource exchanges and visitations, cultural emotional ties as well as the extent to which the immigrants keep capital wealth and property over in Korea.

Organizational Participation

Our study had relatively fewer data on organized transnational activities. Specifically, our survey included two questions on the organizational participations in educational programs (for children) in Korea and personal involvement in Korean politics and election. Among married respondents of our survey, 7.5% said they sent a child or children during the past year to organized educational programs, such as summer language and history courses in Korea. The participation in educational programs was most prevalent among middle-age immigrants (36-55 years of age), with almost 10% of them participating in educational activities. Transnationalism in political activities was kept minimal; 3.3% of respondents voted in an election, 1% reported participation in a political organization or party. Therefore, compared to the social and cultural transnationalism, Korean immigrants' transnational activities regarding institutional or organizational sphere (transnationalism *from above*) was negligible.

Discussion

The present study aimed to provide descriptive profiles of transnational ties and activities among Korean immigrants living in the Greater Area of Toronto, based on data derived from a relatively small sample of adults. Overall, the findings of the study suggest that a substantial proportion of Korean immigrants report family members, relatives and friends living in Korea. About 20% to 50% of Korean immigrants seem to make telephone or online contacts with them at least once every week. It seems reasonable to conclude that transnational informal ties are prevalent among Korean immigrants living in Toronto, especially among younger and more recent immigrants. These findings are consistent with the patterns reported by Kelly (2003) and Ley and Hiebert (2006) with respect to immigrants in Vancouver.

In contrast to informal network contacts, participation in transnational politics and organized social programs is limited to a small minority of immigrants. However, strong transnational ties are evident in social and economic transnational ties. About 60% to 75% of adult immigrants of all ages send over and receive either money or gifts from Korea. Three out of four immigrants reported that they still keep assets in Korea. About one in ten have assets worth more than one million dollars; almost one in four have more than one half million dollars worth of assets. Koreans appear to invest in real estates in Korea which has appreciated in a significantly faster pace compared to the Canadian market. As proposed by Schiller and colleagues (Glick Schiller, Basch, and Blanc 1992), our findings suggest that immigrants adopt conscious and productive transnational strategies based on the perceived opportunities of the global capitalist systems. The trend is much stronger among recent immigrants, and the intensity dissipates as the immigrants extend their residency in Canada. This is also consistent with the findings of Canadian immigrants (Kelly 2003; Ley and Hiebert 2006), and inconsistent with the reports on Caribbean Americans (Portes 2001, 2003).

Are transnational ties and activities salient for the well-being of immigrants? Although it is beyond the scope of this chapter, preliminary analyses of our data (unreported) deemed to support the view. While affirmative implications must await complete analyses, a preliminary examination of data suggests that TN contacts with family members, relatives and friends were associated with a lower degree of acculturative stress, an increase in self-esteem, and a decrease in depressive symptoms. The results support the view that the distant transnational networks and capital provide salutogenic social support effects. Thus, it is possible that transnationalism may offer an alternative model of migration and social integration, and the concept of transnationalism provides an intellectual framework that is effective in understanding and explaining alternative migration strategies.

Our measure of emotional tie represented the degree to which immigrants wish they live in Korea. Some preliminary results (not shown in this chapter) indicated associations of emotional ties with increase in Korean ethnic identity, increased level of acculturative stress, lower self-esteem, and higher in depressive symptoms. Thus, the variable emotional tie as assessed in this study may represent an emotional reaction to settlement difficulties and frustration of living in Canada. There is a need for further investigation of measuring emotional ties.

Limitations of the current study include the non-probability sampling and small sample, as well as the use of non-standardized measures of transnationalism. Despite these limitations, the present study discovered a number of important and new findings, which suggested needs for more systematic approaches to empirical and theoretical studies of transnational migration and its impact on immigrant well being.

Notes

1. This paper was presented at the Conference focusing on "Korean Diasporic and Immigrant Communities' Transnational Ties to the Homeland" organized by the Research Center for Korean Community and held on October 9, 2010 at Korea Village-Open Center in Flushing, New York City.

2. The data for local landings are only available from 2002 when the Korean MOFAT became able to collect information through consulate general offices.

3. However, this does not necessarily mean that they are experienced entrepreneurs. As Ley (2006) found in his study of immigrant entrepreneurs in BC, Korean business migrants are less likely to have entrepreneurial experience in their country of origin. Unlike their counterparts from Hong Kong and Taiwan, most Korean principal applicants to the business program worked as managers in large corporations.

References

Angeles, L. C. 2003. "Creating Social Spaces for Transnational Feminist Advocacy: The Canadian International Development Agency, the National Commission on the Role of Filipino Women and Philippine Women's NGOs." *Canadian Geographer* 47 (3): 283-302.
Bailey, A., R. Wright, A. Mountz, and I. Miyares. 2002. "Reproducing Salvadoran Transnational Geographies." *Annals of the Association of American Geographers* 92: 125-144.
CIC. 1980-2005. *LIDS (Landed Immigration Data System)*. Ottawa. CIC.
CIC. 1998-2006. "Facts and Figures: Immigration Overview." Ottawa: Strategic Policy, Planning and Research.
Foner, N. 2001. "Transnationalism Then and Now: New York Immigrants Today and at the Turn of the Twentieth Century." In *Migration, Transnationalization and Race in a Changing New York*, edited by H. Cordero-Guzman, R. C. Smith, and R. Grosfoguei. Philadelphia: Temple University Press.
Ghosh, S., and L. Wang. 2003. "Transnationalism and Identity: A Tale of Two Faces and Multiple Lives." *Canadian Geographer* 47 (3): 269-282.
Glick Schiller, N., L. Basch, and C. Szanton Blanc. 1992. "Transnationalism: A New Analytic Framework for Understanding Migration." In *Towards a Transnational Perspective on Migration: Race, Class, Ethnicity, and Nationalism Reconsidered*, edited by Glick Schiller et al. New York: The New York Academy of Sciences.
Hiebert, D., and D. Ley. 2006. "Characteristics of Immigrant Transnationalism in Vancouver." In *Transnational Identities and Practices in Canada*, edited by Vic Satzewich and Lloyd Wong, 71-90. Vancouver: UBC Press..
Hyndman, J. 2003. "Aid, Conflict and Migration: The Canada-Sri Lanka Connection." *Canadian Geographer* 47 (3): 251-268.
Kelly, P. 2003. "Canadian-Asian Transnationalism." *The Canadian Geographer* 47 (3): 209-218.
Kivisto, P. 2001. "Theorizing Transnational Migration: A Critical Review of Current Efforts." *Ethnic and Racial Studies* 24: 549-577.
Korean MOFAT (Ministry of Foreign Affairs and Trade) 2008. *Korean Emigration Report 1962-2007*. Seoul: Overseas Koreans Cooperation Division. Also available at www.mofat.go.kr./webmodule/htsboard/. Retrieved March 23, 2008 (In Korean).
Kwak, M. J., and D. Hiebert. 2007. "Making the New Economy: Immigrant Entrepreneurs and Emerging Transnational Networks of International Education and Tourism in Seoul and Vancouver." In *Tourism, Ethnic Diversity and the City*, edited by Jan Rath, 27-49. London and New York: Routledge.
Kwak, M. J., and D. Hiebert. 2010. "Globalizing Canadian Education from Below: A Case Study of Transnational Immigrant Entrepreneurship between Seoul, Korea and Vancouver, Canada. *Journal of International Migration and Integration* 11 (2): 131-153.
Levitt, P. 2001. "Transnational Migration: Taking Stock and Future Directions." *Global Networks* 1: 195-216.
Ley, D. 2006. "Explaining Variations in Business Performance among Immigrant Entrepreneurs in Canada." *Journal of Ethnic and Migration Studies* 32 (5): 743-764.
Mahler, S. 1999 "Engendering Transnational Migration: A Case of Salvadorans" *American Behavaral Scientist* 42 (4): 690-719.

Noh, S., and W. Avison. 1996. "Stress Process in Asian Immigrants: A Case of Korean Immigrants." *Journal of Health and Social Behavior* 37: 192-206.

Ornstein, M. 2000. "The Specificity of Ethnicity." *Institute for Social Research Newsletter* 15 (1): 1-3.

Portes, A. 2001. "Introduction: The Debates and Significance of Immigrant Transnationalism." *Global Networks* 1: 181-193.

Portes, A. 2003. "Conclusion: Theoretical Convergencies and Empirical Evidence in the Study of Immigrant Transnationalism." *International Migration Review* 37 (3): 874-892.

Portes, A., L. Guarnizo, and P. Landolt. 1999. "The Study of Transnationalism: Pitfalls and Promise of an Emerging Research Field." *Ethnic and Racial Studies* 22: 217-237.

Razin, E., and A. Langlois. 1996. "Immigrant and Ethnic Entrepreneurs in Canadian and American Metropolitan Areas—A Comparative Perspective." *Canadian Issues* 18: 127-144.

Smart, A., and J. Smart. 1998. "Transnational Social Networks and Negotiated Identities in Interactions between Hong Kong and China." In *Transnationalism From Below*, edited by Michael Peter Smith and Luis Edwardo Guarnizo. New Brunswick, NJ: Transaction Publishers.

Smith, M. P. and L. E. Guarnizo, eds. 1998. *Transnationalism from Below*. New Brunswick, NJ: Transaction Publishers.

Walton-Roberts, M. 2003. "Transnational Geographies: Indian Immigration to Canada." *Canadian Geographer* 47 (3): 235-250.

Waters, J. 2003. "Flexible Citizens? Transnationalism and Citizenship amongst Economic Immigrants in Vancouver." *Canadian Geographer* 47 (3): 219-234.

Willis, K., and B. Yeoh. 2002. "Gendering Transnational Communities: A Comparison of Singaporean and British Migrants in China." *Geoforum* 33 (4): 553-565.

Chapter 8
The Bifurcated Statuses of the Wives of Korean International Students[1]

by Se Hwa Lee

Introduction

How does migration change gender relations and the division of household labor in migrant families? A great deal of research has attempted to answer this question. However, as previous studies have focused on the experiences of working-class immigrant women with low levels of education (Darvishpour 2002; Glenn 1983; Grahame 2003; Hertzog 2001; Hondagneu-Sotelo 1994; Kibria 1993; Menjivar 2006; Ong 2003; Parreñas 2001; Wong 2000), less attention has been paid to highly educated middle-class migrant women (for a critique, see George 2001). Although there are some studies that have examined the gender relations of middle-class migrant families, they have primarily focused on those who have immigrated to the United States on a permanent basis (Lim 1997; Min 1997, 2001; Moon 2003; Zentgraf 2002; Zhou 2000). Only a few studies, which focus on skilled labor migration, have been conducted on middle-class women who have migrated on a temporary basis (Weeks 2000; Willis and Yeoh 2000; Yeoh and Khoo 1998).

In these studies of skilled labor migration, the wives of professional migrants have often been described as "trailing spouses" or "tied migrants" who passively accompany their professional husbands to keep their family together, while prioritizing men's careers and education over their own (Man 2001; see the critique in Kanjanapan 1995; Yeoh and Khoo 1998). Although many migrant families adopt "household strategies" (Espiritu 2008; Glenn 1986; Grahame 2003; Kibria 1994; Pessar 1995; Willis and Yeoh 2000) to maximize the well-being of the family as a whole, international migration is a highly gendered process (Willis and Yeoh 2000) that produces different experiences for women and men. In particular, middle-class wives and husbands in migrant families may have different interests and goals and thus may experience gender conflict and struggle in their migration process (Lim 1997; Liu 1992; Man 2001; Min 2001; Willis and Yeoh 2000). Given this context, there should be more research that examines how middle-class temporary migrant families experience gender conflict and renegotiate power relations in their migration process.

To fill this gap in the literature, I explore the lives of international students' wives (ISWs), focusing on the changes in gender relations and the division of household labor in their families. So far, only four studies have been conducted on ISWs (Baldwin 1970; Liu 1992; Kim 2006; Weeks 2000). However, ISWs constitute an important segment of the middle-class temporary migrant women whose experiences should be explored for a variety of reasons. First, the flow of international students and their families into the U.S. has rapidly increased. International students comprised 3.4% of total U.S. college and university enrollment in the 2009/2010 academic year, and their number increased to 690,923, a 26% increase since the 2000/2001 academic year (2010 IIE). Furthermore, international students accounted for 10.3% of total graduate students in the U.S. in the 2009/2010 academic year (2010 IIE), and they received 27% of master's degrees and 33% of doctoral degrees conferred in science and engineering in 2009 (National Science Board 2012). In this chapter, I study Korean ISWs, whose country is the third leading place of origin following China and India, with 75,065 students, comprising 10.4% of the total international students in the U.S. in the 2009/2010 academic year (2010 IIE).

Second, Korean ISWs share the common experience with highly skilled migrants' wives from various countries. All of these women are "temporary" migrants whose legal status is dependent on their husbands, and they are prohibited from finding gainful employment because of the restrictive immigration policy (Kim 2006; Man 2001; Yeoh and Khoo 1998). Thus, by analyzing Korean ISWs, this paper not only sheds light on the underexplored middle-class temporary migrant women population in general, but also enhances understanding of the ways in which migrant women's temporary status and legal dependence affect their gender relations within the household in the migration process across their countries of origin.

Third, the study of ISWs provides a valuable opportunity to examine whether previous theories on the division of household labor can be applied to migrant families. Many studies of families contend that women's paid employment and high levels of education are critical resources for them to maintain egalitarian gender relations with their husbands in the division of household labor (Bianchi et al. 2000; England 2000; Hochschild 1989; Risman and Johnson-Sumerford 1998; South and Spitze 1994). However, it is unclear whether these resources can help middle-class temporary migrant women in the U.S. enhance their bargaining power given their legal dependence on their husbands, which seriously weakens the status of these women within the household. Therefore, I examine the ways in which Korean ISWs—who generally have higher educational attainment than other women in the U.S. (including women with U.S. citizenship) and had professional careers prior to migration—experience and address the changes in their status and spousal relations after migration.

Fourth, this paper attempts to fill the gap in the previous literature on ISWs in four ways: First, recent studies on ISWs have been based on relatively small samples; for example, Kim (2006) and Weeks (2000) studied only eleven and six wives, respectively. To gather richer information from wives, a bigger sample is necessary. My paper includes twenty-one ISWs and eight student husbands in the sample. Second, all previous studies on ISWs analyzed data at a single university. My paper includes respondents from two university settings, and thus has a better chance of obtaining a more diverse group of ISWs. Third, earlier studies on ISWs have paid attention mainly to the perspectives of ISWs, while overlooking their husbands. It is probably because researchers often lose sight of the fact that migrant men also deal with gender issues, when they focus on women (George 2001). To correctly understand the complex and relational gender dynamics in international student families, I explore the perspectives of both wives and their husbands.

Finally, although many ISWs hold a student status, previous studies have not fully captured the variation in the lives of these women. While Baldwin (1970) and Kim (2006) included wives who themselves held a student status in their samples, neither of them explicitly examined the differences between the students and the full-time housewives. Only Weeks (2000) did include a brief discussion of the experience of an ISW who was a graduate student. However, the student status of ISWs is important and deserves special attention at least for two reasons. First, migrant women's professional careers and student status can be important material and emotional resources for the renegotiation of the gendered division of household labor (Bianchi et al. 2000; Espiritu 1995, 2008; George 2001; Hondageu-Sotelo 1994; Kibria 1994; Ong and Azores 1994; Pesquera 1993; Pessar 1984; South and Spitze 1994; Zhou 2000). Second, the number of such Korean women has rapidly increased over the past thirty years.

Data and Methods

I conducted in-depth interviews with twenty-one Korean ISWs and eight husbands between March 2009 and December 2010 in two northeastern U.S. university settings: University at Albany, SUNY in New York and Harvard University in Boston, Massachusetts. To investigate the effects of ISWs' student status on the division of household labor, my sample consists of two groups of ISWs: fourteen full-time homemakers and seven graduate students. In addition, to make an overall comparison of each spouse's share of housework and childcare, I also interviewed eight male Korean students, who were husbands of ISWs. Interviews with both wives and husbands allowed me to construct a more comprehensive picture of the gender dynamics among Korean international student couples.

In Albany, I recruited the initial interviewees through the Korean Graduate Student Association (KGSA) and International Student and Scholar Services (ISSS) of the University at Albany. KGSA provided its members a list of Korean graduate students. The ISSS forwarded my recruiting e-mail to all Korean graduate students enrolled at the university. In Boston, I recruited the initial interviewees through my personal acquaintances. After recruiting the first interviewees in both areas, I asked them to refer to other Korean ISWs and their husbands who might be interested in and willing to participate in my study. In this way, I recruited a total of twenty-one wives and eight husbands (fifteen wives and six husbands in Albany and six wives and two husbands in Boston).

Interviews were based on a semi-structured interview guide with open-ended questions, lasted approximately one to two hours, and were audio-recorded. Interviews were conducted at locations where my interviewees felt most comfortable, such as a cafeteria, a playroom or the living room of their apartment, and at the time when they felt most convenient. I provided each participant with a gift card.

Some respondents were curious about what their spouses said about their relationship. Others were concerned that what they told me would spread among the Korean community, because I was involved in the Korean student community. By guaranteeing strict confidentiality, I overcame these difficulties during my data collection. In addition, I recognized that because of my female status, some husbands tried to make good impressions on me or were hesitant to talk about their spousal relationships. Thus, I carefully ordered my interview questions—I asked easier questions first, such as inquiries about school life, and then questions about more sensitive topics such as spousal relationships. Also, I expressed empathy to the participants. Further, through effective probing, I extracted more candid and vivid accounts from my interviewees. After transcribing each interview, I compared and analyzed the transcripts. In the excerpts used in this paper, all names are pseudonyms.

Characteristics of Korean ISWs

Certain characteristics were common among Korean ISWs in both the full-time homemaker group and the female student group. All of the wives in my study had at least a bachelor's degree. Among the fourteen full-time homemakers, ten held bachelor's degrees and four held master's degrees. Among the seven female students, six were currently doctoral students and one was a master's student. In terms of age, most wives were in their thirties, with two wives over forty and three wives under thirty. There were few differences in the duration of marriage or the length of stay in the U.S. between the full-time homemakers and the female students. The wives had been married between one and fifteen years, and had lived in the U.S. between one and fourteen years. Most wives attended a Korean church after migration regardless of their religion before migration. Finally, most wives received some level of financial support from their parents or parents-in-law, even if their husbands had a scholarship and/or assistantship. Two wives reported that their families were fully supported by their parents-in-law. Only five wives did not rely on any financial support from their parents because their husbands had held prestigious jobs (e.g., businessmen, public officials and a medical doctor) prior to migration.

Despite these similarities, there were differences between full-time homemakers and female students in six aspects: the presence of children, prior jobs before migration, the timing of marriage, the separation experience with husbands, the purpose of migration, and legal independence from their husbands. First, most of the full-time homemakers had children, while only two of the seven female students had children. Second, full-time homemakers experienced significant changes in their employment through migration, while female students did not. Most homemakers in the U.S. used to have professional careers prior to migration (e.g., businesswomen, teachers, and public officials); only two were full-time homemakers before migration. Nevertheless, with the exception of three women who took a leave and maintained their employment, all the wives in the homemaker group had quit their jobs to come to the U.S., and five of the homemakers had under-the-table jobs at the time of the interviews. In contrast, most female students had been students before migration and were lawfully working as graduate assistants. Third, most homemakers had migrated to the U.S. after marriage, while half of the female students had migrated to the U.S. alone as students and then got married to male students. Fourth, most homemakers had always lived with their student husbands, while most female students had lived separately or were living separately from their student husbands at the time of interviews. Fifth, the homemakers came to the U.S. to support and live together with their husbands, while female students came to the U.S. for their study. Finally, the full-time homemakers and the female students had different legal statuses. As F2 visa holders, full-time homemakers were legally dependent on their student husbands. They were allowed to neither obtain gainful employment nor study as full-time students in the U.S. In contrast, female students had F1 visas, were thus legally independent from their student husbands, and had half-time paid jobs at academic institutions. These characteristics played important roles in reconfiguring the spousal relationships and the division of household labor in Korean international student families. I discuss it more in detail in the next section.

Changes in Spousal Relationships

After migration, Korean ISWs were empowered in the following respects: First, wives were freed from the burdensome filial duties of a daughter-in-law.

In Korea, wives had to attend many familial events, even if they did not want to. Wives were also expected to be the primary person, and sometimes the only person, to serve the whole family on Parents' Day, New Year's Day, and Korean Thanksgiving Day, as well as at memorial services for ancestors. Due to the heavy burden of family duties, one ISW even confessed that she had felt like a slave to her in-laws when she had been living in Korea. After migration, wives no longer had to perform these filial obligations and family duties, which allowed many Korean ISWs greater comfort and freedom.

Because migration liberated the ISWs from the patriarchal control of their in-laws, these women could more forcefully ask their student husbands to share domestic responsibilities. At the same time, because the husbands were released from the surveillance of both other Korean men and their own families, they could participate more actively in housework with fewer concerns about threats to their masculinity. In sum, migration to the U.S. provided Korean international student couples with an opportunity to be liberated from the patriarchal gender role ideology.

Finally, the loneliness of life in a new society as temporary migrants heightened the value of the ISWs in the eyes of their husbands. In Korea, both wives and husbands had many social/familial roles, relationships, and obligations. However, after migration most student couples had only the roles of husbands and wives. The couples' social networks were also much smaller in the U.S. One wife even confidently said that she was the only friend of her student husband. Thus, student couples often devoted much more attention, energy, and time to their spouses. The fact that most Korean student couples had no one whom they could rely on in a new society also helped wives increase their leverage in the spousal relationship.

Although these factors increased the status of all ISWs, the spousal relationships of homemakers and female students were bifurcated: The marriages of full-time homemakers shifted to unequal spousal relationships after migration, whereas female students maintained egalitarian spousal relationships. Various factors led to this bifurcation.

Different Purposes of Migration

Homemakers and female students migrated for different purposes. Homemakers came to the U.S. to support and live with their husbands, although some had additional goals such as moving out of their parents-in-law's house, providing their children with American educational opportunities, or taking a break from their busy jobs. Many wives were also embedded in the traditional gender ideology that dictates men as the head of the household. Because they believed that their family would be happier if their husbands received a degree and obtained a good job, most wives willingly sacrificed their successful careers in Korea. Although some did not want to quit their jobs to accompany their husbands to the U.S., these wives could not resist the patriarchal pressure their parents-in-law placed on them to support their husbands. Whether or not they wanted to, once the homemakers migrated to the U.S. as students' wives, their everyday lives were organized around the schedules of their student husbands. Homemakers also did their best to ensure that their husbands were not distracted from their studies by housework and childrearing, because the wives' main goal was helping their husbands achieve a degree as quickly as possible. Therefore, homemakers did not ask for an equitable division of household labor, even if they felt the situation was unfair.

In contrast, female students came to the U.S. to pursue a degree rather than to support their husbands. Further, unlike the homemakers who came to the U.S. with their student husbands, half of the female students migrated to the U.S. as single women and got married afterwards. Thus, those who had not been married before they left Korea had never experienced the patriarchal control of parents-in-law. In addition, unlike the homemakers who sacrificed their careers, whether readily or forcibly, to accompany their husbands, many female students gave up living with their student husbands rather than sacrificing their own studies. At the time of the interviews, among the seven female students in the sample, four had lived separately and one was currently living separately from their student husbands. Only two female students had not experienced this type of separation. Because they had their own goals and careers in the U.S., female students had power to organize their everyday lives based on their own schedule, and to justifiably ask their student husbands to share housework more equitably.

Differences in the Legal Statuses and Paid Employment

Wives' legal independence and paid employment are critical for explaining the different paths of homemakers and female students. The full-time homemakers entered the U.S. on F2 visas, while female students entered on F1 visas. As F2 visa holders who were legally dependent on their husbands, homemakers were allowed to neither obtain paid employment nor enroll at academic institutions in the U.S. as full-time students (Kim 2006). Accordingly, most homemakers had not held a formal job after migration, even though most of them had had professional careers prior to migration. These wives lost the economic power and social status they had enjoyed prior to migration. In particular, those who had enjoyed professional careers that had provided them with a decent socioeconomic status, respect, and satisfaction more keenly sensed this change in their status and felt frustrated (for more discussion, see Liu 1992; Weeks 2000). One full-time homemaker, Heejin, who had to quit her job as a government official, expressed her frustration: "When I am alone at home, I feel often depressed. I have nothing but to wait for my husband coming home for all day. Due to my visa status, I cannot do anything freely. I cannot apply for any job even if I want to get a job in the U.S. I am so bored of being here." Heejin's frustration corroborates the findings of previous studies that emphasized the structural constraints that the host society places on migrant women and their status (Glenn 1983; Grahame 2003; Hertzog 2001; Kim 2006; Man 2001; Menjivar 2006; Min 2001; Perista 2000; Weeks 2000; Wong 2000).

Interestingly, despite the restrictions of U.S. immigration laws, five of the fourteen homemakers had under-the-table jobs. Some worked at a laundry shop or deli whose owners were Korean Americans. Others taught Korean children at home in subjects such as English, math, and art. Previous studies have emphasized working-class migrant women's increased economic contributions to the family, coupled with men's reduced economic power, as critical resources for women to challenge male dominance at home (Blumberg 1991; Hertz 1986; Hondagneu-Sotelo 1994; Kibria 1994; Pessar 1984; Pesquera 1993). However, paid employment of the Korean middle-class homemakers in my sample did not help them contest the unequal gender relations at home. Small incomes and the lower social status attached to their under-the-table jobs failed to provide a material and emotional basis on which most middle-class Korean ISWs—who had held successful careers with good salaries prior to migration—could request egalitarian gender relations after migration. Some housewives even hid their dead-end jobs from other Koreans because they did not want to "lose face" in the Korean community (not to mention the peril of deportation). In sum, full-time homemakers viewed their illegal part-time jobs solely as an ad hoc means to supplement family income, and not as a "path to fulfillment or upward mobility" (Espiritu 2008: 94). In this context, paid employment itself does not necessarily empower middle-class migrant women within the household. Rather, the social status and prestige attached to the jobs are more critical for increasing middle-class migrant women's power in their spousal relations.

In contrast to homemakers, female students with F1 visas were legally independent from their student husbands. Because of their legal independence, these women did not have to rely on their student husbands to handle everyday issues such as opening a bank account, which in turn helped these wives retain their leverage in their marital relationships. In addition, U.S. immigration laws allow F1 visa holders to have part-time jobs at academic institutions. Thus, most female students in my study had legal part-time academic jobs.

Interestingly, unlike the situation faced by full-time homemakers, paid employment greatly helped female students confront male dominance at home. In contrast to housewives' illegal jobs, the jobs of female students were a legally justifiable means of making a living. Whereas housewives were often ashamed of their dead-end jobs and wanted to hide them from other Koreans, female students highly valued their academic jobs as a way of obtaining research and teaching experience that would help them get a good job after graduation. Hence, using their earning power and equal status as F1 visa holders, female students were able to enjoy greater power than full-time homemakers in their spousal relationships.

Identities and Motherhood

While wives in the homemaker group shifted their identity to full-time housewives after migration, those in the female student group maintained their principal identities as students, rather than as housewives. This difference in identities led to differences in the power dynamics between the two groups. Because housework was not regarded as "real work" by most of the Korean wives and husbands in the sample, the performance of daily housework was invisible, and signified that full-time housewives were doing "nothing" after migration. The comment of Seyoung, previously a manager in a prestigious company in Korea, confirms this point: "When I was in Korea, I had an egalitarian relationship with my husband. However, after migration, I have been subordinated to my husband, because I no longer have economic and social activities… Now, I am just his wife and the mother of his child. I am losing my presence." Some wives even lost self-esteem and self-confidence as they became confined to the role of housewife. Hyomin, a teacher who was taking a leave of absence, reported being very frustrated when other people, who did not know that she had a good job in Korea, treated her as a housewife who passively followed her student husband and did not do any meaningful work. She confessed that after migrating she lost confidence in herself and that she would like to return to Korea as soon as possible to resume her own career.

While the work of housewives was not considered fulfilling, motherhood was a highly respected full-time occupation (Stone 2007) among the Korean ISWs in the sample. Hence, most full-time homemakers tried to compensate for their weakened status at home by becoming the mother. Through motherhood, full-time homemakers not only spent their suddenly increased free time more meaningfully, but also felt a sense of achievement that they could not obtain from their position as the wife of a student. In this context, some full-time homemakers who did not have children felt even worse about themselves because they believed that they had neither a meaningful role nor a job to which they could commit themselves. Nevertheless, the presence of young children made it even more difficult for most full-time homemakers to make productive plans for the future. Consequently, motherhood conferred emotional benefits to women at the price of a chance to recover their previous careers or statuses.

In contrast to homemakers, most female students did not depict themselves as housewives. Rather, they identified as F1 international students with independent legal and social status, and this identity gave them the confidence and power to voice their opinion in the household. In addition, because female students did not lose their formal and social status after migration, they found few reasons to strengthen their status at home through motherhood.

More important, however, female students' choice to delay having children was not always voluntary. Rather, the difficulty of meeting the conflicting demands of motherhood and student life forced many of these women to postpone having children. Because female students could not take care of their children while they were studying at the university, those who did have children needed help with childcare. However, most female students could not afford daycare, because international students usually have serious budget constraints. In addition, many female students lacked familial childcare support because their families resided in Korea. Thus, those who became mothers often had to sacrifice their studies. The story of Jayoung, who had taken care of her newborn baby alone for a year until she sent him to her mother-in-law in Korea, reflected the difficulties of female students who became mothers:

> My baby boy is now in Korea. Daycare here is expensive. It costs around a thousand dollars per month. With our small stipend, we could not afford to pay for the expensive daycare, because we also had to make a living. So, I took a leave for a year to take care of him. However, I wanted to resume my study. So, what did I have to do? I had no choice but to send my baby to Korea. Otherwise, I could not have studied....Now I study even harder, because I want him back. To bring my baby back, I have to be a (doctoral) candidate quickly. Thus, the only thing that I do now is study.

As Jayoung's case shows, if female students decide to have children, this decision slows the pace of their studies and delays graduation. Female students in my study understood this and therefore most postponed pregnancy and childbirth, hoping to have a baby after they obtained a degree or got a job. Only two of the seven female students in the sample were mothers, and these two women did not raise their children by themselves: One sent her one-year-old son to live with her mother-in-law in Korea, while the other asked her mother and mother-in-law to come to the U.S. and share her child-rearing responsibilities. This type of conflict between work and family was never mentioned by male students in the sample. Only women, regardless of whether they were full-time homemakers or students, were forced to make a decision on reproduction, and juggle the competing demands of work and family.

Differences in Social Networks

Full-time homemakers had much narrower social networks than female students in the U.S. Although for women in both groups their relationships with family members and friends in Korea became weaker during their time in the U.S., it was more difficult for the homemakers to build new social networks after migration than for female students. In contrast to female students who built independent social networks through a variety of sources including school, employment, and student associations, full-time homemakers generally made new friends through their student husbands. Further, due to the language barrier, the social networks of full-time housewives were often confined to Korean ISWs to whom they had been introduced by their husbands. Because homemakers were highly dependent on their husbands for socializing, their relative power at home was further weakened after migration.

Another route through which both groups of wives made new friends was church. Korean churches were extremely important places for most Korean ISWs to socialize and relieve their loneliness as temporary migrants in a new society. Korean churches greatly helped newly migrated ISWs settle into their new surroundings. For young children who were born in the U.S., church was the place where they learned Korean language and culture, and met other Korean friends. Some wives even moved to a new church to find better social networks that could provide more helpful information about life in the U.S. and more peers in their children's cohort.

However, the Korean church community was not always helpful to wives. First, peer pressure within the Korean church community sometimes forced student couples to reinforce their traditional gender relations. For instance, a female student, Soyoung, and her student husband, Daehee, maintained a quite egalitarian division of household labor. More accurately, Daehee did more housework than Soyoung. Daehee said, "Even yesterday, I prepared all the meals. My wife just came to eat when the meal was ready... Recently, I cooked more than my wife did. I also do all laundry, although my wife washes dishes more than I do. Regarding cleaning...although we don't do it frequently, we clean together when it is necessary." Daehee did not like to admit that he contributed more to the household labor than his wife. It was because he was very concerned that his admission would threaten his masculinity or manliness and make him lose face in the Korean church community, which was his main focus of socializing. Soyoung was also quite defensive about possible criticism from other Koreans regarding her failure to perform the role of devoted housewife, although she was very happy that her husband made an equal or even greater contribution to the household labor.

Second, it was not easy for wives to maintain consistent relationships within the Korean church community because of their temporary status in the U.S. Many wives reported that their social relationships were often disrupted when their friends either returned to Korea or moved to another city in the U.S. The patriarchal pressure from the Korean church community and the negative impact of inconsistent social relationships among Korean ISWs were greater for homemakers who lacked alternative sources for socializing. In sum, compared to female students who had broader and more independent social networks, full-time homemakers, whose social networks were confined to the Korean community and isolated from the mainstream society, tended to report weaker status in spousal relations after migration.

Changes in the Division of Household Labor

The division of household labor is a good measure of the power relations between spouses. However, previous studies on ISWs have for the most part overlooked this aspect of spousal relationships. To fill the gap, this section analyzes the ways in which migration altered the distribution of household labor between Korean international student couples. Interestingly, homemakers and female students presented different paths with regard to the division of household labor after migration.

Division of Household Labor: Full-time Homemakers

I first discuss the ways in which full-time homemakers experienced the changes in the distribution of household labor and childcare after migration. Most homemakers in this study held good jobs and performed little housework in Korea because of the high workload of their paid jobs. Their husbands shared a good deal of housework with these working wives. More than half of the homemakers told me that they used to have an egalitarian division of household labor in Korea. However, both women and men reported that wives' share of household labor and childcare had greatly increased after migration. For instance, half of the fourteen homemakers reported that they did more than 90% of the total housework and childcare, with three wives doing 80% and four wives doing 70%. All the five homemakers' husbands in my study also admitted that they shared only 20% of housework and childcare.

In terms of the types of housework and childcare, there was a clear gendered division. Homemakers did feminine and routine housework that could not be delayed such as cooking, cleaning, doing dishes, laundry, and grocery shopping. Some wives also reported that they did childcare alone. In contrast, husbands did masculine household chores that needed strength but did not have to be done so frequently such as removing trash bags, moving heavy stuff, and mowing the lawn. Even if husbands did some feminine works such as vacuuming, cleaning the bathroom, doing dishes and laundry, they did them only sporadically when their wives asked them to or were sick. No husbands cooked, except one who lived a long time as a bachelor in the U.S. Given this, cooking was the most feminized household task that was not shared by homemakers' husbands. The one task that most husbands and wives did together was grocery shopping. Many couples saw it as a good chance for the family to spend time together on weekends. Interestingly, homemakers' husbands were more actively participating in childcare on a regular basis than other housework. However, their contribution was limited to more joyful tasks such as playing with a baby when wives were cooking or doing dishes, bathing with babies, and going to gym with children. Few husbands changed diapers.

What are the factors that led to full-time homemakers performing such an exceptionally large share of housework after migration? First, their husbands often employed "gender strategies" (Pesquera 1993: 183): they utilized the structural constraints placed on their wives to effectively force their wives to do the majority of the domestic work while avoiding it themselves. In particular, as wives' statuses shifted from career women to full-time homemakers, many student husbands justifiably asked their wives to take on the overwhelming majority of the housework. Sukkyu, whose wife had been a teacher in Korea but became a full-time homemaker after migration, said,

> Because I now work [study] outside and my wife stays at home, she should accept the position of housewife as her occupation and perform it professionally. Of course, I do not say the housework is easy [to perform alone]. However, since she does not work, it is her responsibility to perform housework as well

as provide good care of a baby. If we both worked outside, I would be willing to share household labor with her.

Second, student husbands used their study as an excuse for not sharing the household labor. For those Korean ISWs who adopted "household strategies" (Kibria 1994; Espiritu 2008; Glenn 1983; Grahame 2003; Pessar 1995; Willis and Yeoh 2000) to maximize the overall well-being of their family while sacrificing their successful careers and social lives in Korea, the completion of the husband's studies was regarded as the family's only goal in the U.S. Hence, when their husbands argued that they could not contribute to the household labor because they needed to concentrate on their studies, homemakers accepted this as a legitimate reason. The account of a full-time homemaker, Mina's husband, Jaemin, exemplifies it: "I have to spend more time in study than other students since I want to finish my study quickly. I also have language barrier, so I have to make more effort than others [who don't have such barrier]."

Mina accepted her husband's argument as a valid reason for his coming home late and not sharing the housework and childcare. Mina said, "Since I know how hard my husband studies, I am even sorry for him. Although doing housework alone is strenuous, I cannot complain because he can catch up with study only when he does his best. Thus, I decide to tolerate the current division of household labor."

Another full-time homemaker, Joori, also accepted her overwhelmingly large share of housework on the basis that her husband had to concentrate on studying. Joori said,

> I did my best not to ask my husband to share housework with me. For example, it takes lots of time to meet a pediatrician, attend a parent-teacher conference, or give children a ride. If I asked my husband to do such works, there would be no reason for my husband's coming here. If he did such housework, it would be like he came to the U.S. to take care of children. Moreover, he would have no time for studying. Thus, I do all the housework and childcare. Only when I really cannot perform it alone, I ask my husband to help me.

In sum, for Korean homemakers who came to the U.S. for the sake of their families, the husband's need for study is a very persuasive reason for him to be relieved of the obligation to perform an equal share of housework.

Third, homemakers' paid employment did not enhance their bargaining power at home. Homemakers did not request that their husbands share household labor more equitably simply because they had paid employment. For some student families, the wives' income was desperately needed for family survival or for their children's education. Nevertheless, neither wives nor husbands viewed wives' paid employment as valued enough to renegotiate the current power relations between them. In addition, wives' under-the-table jobs lacked prestige and respect, and provided a much smaller income than their professions in Korea. Accordingly, wives' illegal jobs served solely as temporary means of making a living, rather than a source of power for women to ask for an egalitarian division of household labor.

Fourth, the traditional gender ideology, which frames housework as women's work and men as helpers, exempted many husbands from doing housework. Further, most homemakers' husbands never helped their wives until they were asked. Accordingly, only a small number of wives who incessantly asked their husbands to share household duties (often via confrontation and conflict) increased their husbands' involvement in the household labor, and even then only to a small extent. Hyomin, wife of a doctoral student, explained,

> After we came to the U.S., my husband expected me to do all the housework as well as childcare. Thus, we had many conflicts about how to divide domestic work in the beginning. Through confrontations, we have been seeking a balancing point that we both can compromise. He now does some housework such as bathing the baby and vacuuming on the weekend....However, he really hates to do it. He is the type of man who performs housework only when I ask. His participation is not voluntary but forced.

Thus, most homemakers, who were tired of continuously asking their resistant husbands to share the workload, simply gave up and did the overwhelming majority of housework alone.

Constrained by various structural and ideological pressures, many full-time homemakers accepted the traditional division of household labor rather than confronting it. These wives even felt grateful to their husbands for the small amount of physical or emotional support they did offer, because wives expected very little from their student husbands. In this way, the unequal gendered division of household labor was reinforced within the households of full-time homemakers after their migration to the U.S.

Division of Household Labor: Female Students

In contrast to homemakers, all seven female students in the study reported that they enjoyed an egalitarian division of household labor. Three of them even stated that their husbands did more of the housework than they did. Among three husbands of female students, two said that they equally shared household labor with wives and the other reported that he did 60% of housework. In contrast to full-time homemakers and their husbands, who viewed men as only helpers, all female student and their husband interviewers indicated that both spouses were responsible for housework. They also considered men's involvement in household tasks as a part of men's responsibility. In addition, unlike the husbands of full-time homemakers, most husbands of female students did housework voluntarily, without their wives' asking; only one husband did not do any housework until his wife initiated it.

Further, there was no gendered division of housework in the households of female students. In contrast to homemakers who did the overwhelming majority of household labor and childcare, female students and their husbands shared housework equally, which included cooking as well as doing dishes, cleaning, laundry, and taking out the trash. Female students also went grocery shopping with their husbands.

Such an egalitarian division of household labor was well demonstrated by the comments of female students in the study. According to Jisuk, a female doctoral student, there was no principal person doing the housework; rather, she and her husband shared it equally. Minyoung, a female doctoral student, provided a similar account: "I always do housework with my husband. When one person does housework, the other never takes a rest....We do housework together." Two other female students and their husbands also said that housework, including cooking, was done by whichever spouse was less busy on that day. Some husbands of female students even performed more of the routine housework, such as cooking and doing dishes, than their wives. In particular, cooking, which was exclusively done by wives in the households of homemakers, was not a feminized task in the households of female students. Six of the seven female students reported that their husbands shared cooking duties with them, and three female students even said that their husbands were the principal cooks in their households.

Interestingly, in contrast to homemakers, there were not many current issues related to the division of childcare in the households of female students. It is mainly because only two out of the seven female students in the sample were mothers, and these two women did not raise their children by themselves.

Female students adopted various gender strategies to reduce the total amount of housework to reconcile the conflicting demands of work and family. For example, female students ate out more often than full-time homemakers who prepared almost every meal at home. Female students also justified having a lower standard of household cleanliness than full-time homemakers. Accordingly, female students and their husbands cleaned their houses less frequently than full-time homemakers and their husbands.

What explains this more egalitarian division of household labor in the families of female students? First, unlike full-time homemakers who lacked formal legal status in the U.S., female students held the same legal status as their husbands: F1 students. With the confidence and power that resulted from their independent legal and social status, female students could make stronger demands on their husbands to share household labor equitably. Indeed, many husbands admitted that their wives' F1 student status was critical for their view of housework as husbands' work and their willingness to share it equitably. Sukkyu, who had been a successful businessman in Korea and was studying in a master's program at the time of interview, said,

> Housework is my work as well... It seems that I have a different idea on the housework now, as my status has changed from a businessman to a student. We are now equal international students... When I was a businessman in Korea, I took the responsibility of supporting my family economically. Thus, I thought that I was "helping" with my wife's work, when I was doing housework. How-

ever, we are now both international students with the similar amount of free time. As my status has changed [from a businessman to a student], my perspective on the housework has changed [from helping with my wife's work to doing my own work].

Jaekyun, whose wife was a doctoral student, also pointed out that he contributed equally to the housework mainly because his wife was a student like him: "If my wife were a full-time homemaker, I would do less housework... because she could have done all the housework before I paid attention to it."

Second, unlike the husbands of full-time homemakers, neither studying nor having F1 student status was an effective gender strategy for the husbands of female students to pass domestic responsibilities to their student wives. In these families, both husbands and their wives came to the U.S. to pursue their degrees. Therefore, husbands' claims that they could not participate in housework because they needed to concentrate on their studies were not accepted as legitimate by their wives. Further, because female students were just as busy as their student husbands, the husbands could not argue that they could not share household labor because of a lack of time.

Third, most student husbands in the sample could not perform the traditional gender role as the breadwinner because of their limited economic power. On the contrary, most female students made the same level of economic contribution to the family economy as their student husbands did. For student couples with limited economic resources, wives' income was particularly critical for the survival of the family. Minyoung, a female doctoral student, confidently reported, "I am studying to make a living. If I stop studying [and no longer earn money from my assistantship], we cannot survive with my husband's earnings."

While many scholars have argued that earning power increases migrant women's power at home (Blumberg 1991; Hertz 1986; Hondagneu-Sotelo 1994; Kibria 1994; Lim 1997; Min 2001; Pessar 1984), this was not generally the case in my sample. Instead, for middle-class Korean international student couples, a more important factor determining wives' leverage at home was whether their jobs were as prestigious as their husbands' jobs. Full-time homemakers' under-the-table paid jobs did not enhance their status at home despite their student husbands' limited economic power. While homemakers were concerned about losing face in the Korean community and about possible deportation because of their illegal dead-end jobs, the academic jobs of female students were valued just as much as their husbands' jobs. Hence, homemakers were unable to use their income from dead-end jobs as leverage to contest the gendered division of household labor, while female students with legal jobs were able to maintain an equal distribution of household labor.

Finally, different living arrangements led to different paths among the husbands. Most full-time homemakers in the sample came to the U.S. with their student husbands, and did not experience separation during their stay in the U.S. In contrast, half of the female students and their husbands came to the U.S. before they were married and therefore lived alone for years. Although the other half of the female students in the sample came to the U.S. with their husbands, all these couples lived apart for years to pursue degrees at different academic institutions. Interestingly, this difference in living arrangements accounted for differing levels of husbands' participation in domestic work. Student husbands who had lived as bachelors in the U.S. shared housework with their student wives more equally than those who came to the U.S. with their homemaker wives. Like the Mexican immigrants in Hondagneu-Sotelo's (1994) study, husbands of female students, through their earlier single lives in the U.S., obtained housework skills, which they would never have learned in Korea. Similarly, husbands who had lived separately from their student wives for years after marriage were also impelled to do traditional women's work as a result of the absence of women who could do chores for them. Consequently, even after marriage or reunion with their wives, these husbands did more housework than the husbands who had always been cared for by their homemaker wives. This is nicely illustrated by Jongmin's account of being a student in the U.S., who reunited with his student wife after two years of separation.

> After I lived alone in Ohio, I started to cook because I wanted to eat Korean food. Since then my disaster has begun. If we had continued to live together after we first came to the U.S., my wife would have continued to cook as well as do most housework, while I wouldn't have done much, because I would not know how to do it...When we lived in Korea, I did not know how to cook and thus I did not cook. If we had lived together in the U.S., I would have lived in that way. However, as I lived apart from my wife, I started to cook and I now cook more than my wife.

In sum, the husbands of female students who had lived without the presence and care of their wives for significant amounts of time were compelled to do domestic tasks that they did not typically do in Korea, and they continued to do housework even after they were married or reunited with their student wives because they had already obtained the skills to do so. In contrast, the husbands of full-time homemakers who had always lived with their wives during their stay in the U.S. did not need to learn domestic work, and thus effectively and justifiably avoided doing household labor. Confronted by their husbands' consistent resistance, homemaker wives did most of the housework, and tried to relieve their frustration by resorting to gendered arguments such as "men are less skilled at housework" or "men have a lower standard of hygiene."

Conclusion

In this paper, I explored the ways in which the spousal power relations and the division of household labor changed for Korean ISWs after migration to the U.S. In contrast to previous studies on ISWs that unanimously reported that the status of wives lowered after migration, I found that the spousal relations of Korean

ISWs were bifurcated between homemakers and female students. While homemakers became subordinate to their student husbands after migration, female students maintained egalitarian spousal relationships. In addition, homemakers' share of household labor and childcare responsibilities increased abruptly after migration, whereas female students enjoyed a much more equal division of household labor.

I discussed various factors that led to these divergent paths: the goals of migration, legal/social statuses and dependence on husbands, wives' paid employment, the extent of wives' social networks, and the living arrangements after migration. Wives had more leverage within their spousal relationships and enjoyed more equitable division of household labor in the following situations: (1) when they migrated to pursue their own career goals; (2) when they held an independent legal/social status as F1 students; (3) when their paid employment had the same level of prestige as their husbands' jobs; (4) when their social networks were independent from their husbands and were built via diverse routes; and (5) when they had lived apart from their husbands.

The implications of wives' paid employment merit further discussion. Previous studies of families have regarded social capital, such as paid employment and a high level of education, as a critical resource wives could leverage to obtain a more egalitarian division of household labor (Bianchi et al. 2000; England 2000; Hochschild 1989; Risman and Johnson-Sumerford 1998; South and Spitze 1994). Moreover, previous studies of working-class migrant women have often emphasized wives' income as a critical source of power that could be used to contest male dominance at home (Blumberg 1991; Hertz 1986; Hondagneu-Sotelo 1994; Kibria 1994; Pessar 1984; Pesquera 1993). However, my study demonstrated that wives' contributions to the family economy did not always empower Korean ISWs, particularly if their principal identity was full-time homemakers and their jobs were illegal and devalued. Only those wives who held the same F1 student status as their husbands were able to utilize paid employment and a high level of education as useful resources to demand egalitarian gender relations. Therefore, legal independence and job prestige were more important than economic power for middle-class temporary migrant women seeking to maintain an egalitarian division of household labor.

This study makes four major contributions to the fields of gender and immigration studies. First, I construct a more comprehensive picture of the gender relations within Korean international student couples by interviewing both wives and husbands, which has hardly been done by previous studies of temporary middle-class migrant women. In particular, by exploring various gender strategies adopted by Korean international student couples, my study enhances the understanding of the ways in which middle-class temporary migrant couples experience gender conflict and renegotiate power relations after migration. Second, by showing the bifurcated gender relations between two groups of Korean ISWs (i.e., homemakers and female students), my study demonstrates that legal and social independence from their student husbands is more critical for ISWs to achieve egalitarian gender relations rather than their income. Third, different paths of Korean ISWs after migration confront a monolithic picture of ISWs as "trailing spouses" or "tied migrants" who passively accompany their husbands. Rather, many ISWs have their own interests and goals of migration. Finally, although the current study is based on the experiences of Korean ISWs, the findings can provide insights into the lives of other ISWs and highly skilled migrants' wives in the U.S, because they may experience the same gender dynamics as middle-class temporary migrant women who have similar types of dependent visas, and thus often sacrifice their jobs to come to the U.S. and are not allowed to work after migrating.

Notes

1. An earlier version of this paper was presented at the annual meetings of the American Sociological Association, Las Vegas, August 2011 and the Eastern Sociological Society, Philadelphia, February 2011. I would like to acknowledge that the work reported here was supported by the Initiatives for Women Award of State University of New York at Albany, 2010.

References

Baldwin, Nancy Toman. 1970. "Cultural Adaptations of International Student Wives at the University of Florida." Ph.D. Dissertation. The University of Florida.
Bianchi, Suzanne M., Melissa A. Milkie, Liana C. Sayer, and John P. Robinson. 2000. "Is Anyone Doing the Housework? Trends in the Gender Division of Household Labor." *Social Forces* 79: 191-228.
Blumberg, Rae Lesser, ed. 1991. *Gender, Family, and Economy: The Triple Overlap.* Newbury Park, CA: Sage Publications.
Darvishpour, Mehrdad. 2002. "Immigrant Women Challenge the Role of Men: How the Changing Power Relationship within Iranian Families in Sweden Intensified Family Conflicts after Immigration." *Journal of Comparative Family Studies* 33 (2): 271-296.
England, Paula. 2000. "Marriage, the Costs of Children, and Gender Inequality." In *The Ties That Bind,* edited by L. Waite, 320-342. New York: Aldine de Gruyter.
Espiritu, Yen Le. 1995. *Filipino American Lives.* Philadelphia: Temple University Press.
Espiritu, Yen Le. 2008. *Asian American Women and Men: Labor, Laws, and Love,* Second Edition. Thousand Oaks, CA: Sage Publications.
George, Sheba Mariam. 2001. "When Women Come First: Gender and Class and Transnational Ties among Indian Immigrants in the United States." Ph.D. Thesis. UC Berkeley.
Glenn, Evelyn Nakano. 1983. "Split Household, Small Producer and Dual Wage-Earner: An Analysis of Chinese American Family Strategies." *Journal of Marriage and Family* 45 (1): 35-46.
Glenn, Evelyn Nakano. 1986. *Issei, Nisei, War Bride: Three Generations of Japanese American Women in Domestic Service.* Philadelphia: Temple University Press.
Grahame, Kamini Maraj. 2003. "For the Family: Asian Immigrant Women's Triple Day." *Journal of Sociology & Social Welfare* 30 (1): 65-90.
Hertz, R. 1986. *More Equal than Others: Men and Women in Dual-career Marriages.* Berkeley: University of California Press.
Hertzog, Esther. 2001. "Gender and Power Relations in a Bureaucratic Context: Female Immigrants from Ethiopia in an Absorption Centre in Israel." *Gender and Development* 9 (3): 60-69.
Hochschild, Arlie. 1989. *The Second Shift.* New York: Penguin Books.
Hondagneu-Sotelo, Pierrette. 1994. *Gendered Transition: Mexican Experiences in Immigration.* Berkeley: University of California Press.
Institute of International Education. 2010. *Open Doors Report on International Educational Exchange.* Retrieved from http://www.iie.org/opendoors.
Kanjananpan, Wilawan. 1995. "The Immigration of Asian Professionals to the United States: 1988-1990." *International Migration Review* 29 (1): 7-32.
Kibria, Nazli. 1993. *Family Tightrope: The Changing Lives of Vietnamese Americans.* Princeton, NJ: Princeton University Press.
Kibria, Nazli. 1994. "Migration and Vietnamese American Women: Remaking Ethnicity." In *Women of Color in US Society,* edited by M. B. Zinn and B. T. Dill, 247-264. Philadelphia: Temple University Press.
Kim, Minjeong. 2006. "'Forced' into Unpaid Carework: International Students' Wives in the United States." In *Global Dimensions of Gender and Carework,* edited by M. K. Zimmerman, J. Litt, and C. E. Bose, 162-175. Stanford, CA: Stanford University Press, 2006.

Lim, In-Sook. 1997. "Korean Immigrant Women's Challenge to Gender Inequality at Home: The Interplay of Economic Resources, Gender, and Family." *Gender & Society* 11 (1): 31-51.
Liu, Haidong. 1992. "Lives of Chinese Students' Wives in an American University Setting." Ph. D. Dissertation. The Pennsylvania State University.
Man, Guida. 2001. "From Hong Kong to Canada: Immigration and the Changing Family Lives of Middle-Class Women from Hong Kong." In *Family Patterns, Gender Relations,* edited by B. J. Fox, 420-440. New York: Oxford University Press.
Menjívar, Cecilia. 2006. "Family Reorganization in a Context of Legal Uncertainty: Guatemalan and Salvadoran Immigrants in the United States." *International Journal of Sociology of the Family* 32 (2): 223-245.
Min, Pyong Gap. 1997. "Korean Immigrant Wives' Labor Force Participation, Marital Power, and Status." In *Women and Work: Exploring Race, Ethnicity, and Class*, edited by E. Higginbotham and M. Romero, 176-191. Thousand Oaks, CA: Sage Publications.
Min, Pyong Gap. 2001. "Changes in Korean Immigrants' Gender Role and Social Status, and Their Marital Conflicts." *Sociological Forum* 16 (2): 301-320.
Moon, Seungsook. 2003. "Immigration and Mothering: Case Studies from Two Generations of Korean Immigrant Women." *Gender & Society* 17 (6): 840-860.
National Science Board. 2012. *Science and Engineering Indicators 2012*. Arlington, VA: National Science Foundation.
Ong, Aihwa. 2003. *Buddha is Hiding: Refugees, Citizenship, the New America*. Berkeley, CA: University of California Press.
Ong, Paul, and Tania Azores. 1994. "The Migration and Incorporation of Filipino Nurses." In *The New Asian Immigration in Los Angeles and Global Restructuring,* edited by P. Ong, E. Bonacich and L. Cheng, 164-195. Philadelphia: Temple University Press.
Parreñas, Rhacel Salazar. 2001. "The Transnational Family: A Postindustrial Household Structure with Preindustrial Values." In *Servants of Globalization: Women, Migration and Domestic Work,* edited by R. S. Parreñas, 80-115. Stanford, CA: Stanford University Press.
Perista, Heloísa. 2000. "EU Migrant Women: Migration, Family Life and Professional Trajectories." *Papers: Revista de Sociologia* 60: 153-166.
Pesquera, Beatríz. M. 1993. "In the Beginning He Wouldn't Even Lift a Spoon: The Division of Household Labor." In *Building with Our Hands: New Directions in Chicana Studies*, edited by A. Torre and B.M. Pesquera, 181-195. Berkeley, CA: University of California Press.
Pessar, Patricia R. 1984. "The Linkage between the Household and Workplace in the Experience of Dominican Immigrant Women in the United States." *International Migration Review* 18: 1188-1211.
Pessar, Patricia R. 1995. "On the Homefront and in the Workplace: Integrating Women into Feminist Discourse." *Anthropological Quarterly* 68 (1): 37-47.
Risman, Barbara J., and Danette Johnson-Sumerford. 1998. "Doing it Fairly: A Study of Postgender Marriages." *Journal of Marriage and the Family* 60: 23-40.
South, Scott, and Glenna Spitze. 1994. "Housework in Marital and Non-marital Households." *American Sociological Review* 59: 327-347.
Stone, Pamela. 2007. *Opting Out? Why Women Really Quit Careers and Head Home.* Berkeley, CA: University of California Press.
Weeks, Kerri A. 2000. "The Berkeley Wives: Identity Revision and Development among Temporary Immigrant Women." *Asian Journal of Women's Studies* 6 (2): 78-105.

Willis, Katie, and Brenda Yeoh. 2000. "Gender and Transnational Household Strategies: Singaporean Migration to China." *Regional Studies* 34 (3): 253-264.

Willis, Katie, and Brenda Yeoh. 2003. "Gender, Marriage, and Skilled Migration: The Case of Singaporeans in China." In *Wife or Worker?: Asian Women and Migration*, edited by N. Piper and M. Roces, 101-119. Lanham, MD: Rowman and Littlefield.

Wong, Madeleine. 2000. "Ghanaian Women in Toronto's Labour Market: Negotiating Gendered Roles and Transnational Household Strategies." *Canadian Ethnic Studies/Études ethniques au Canada* 32(2): 45-74.

Yeoh, Brenda S.A., and Louisa-May Khoo. 1998. "Home, Work and Community: Skilled International Migration and Expatriate Women in Singapore." *International Migration* 36 (2): 159-84.

Zentgraf, Kristine M. 2002. "Immigration and Women's Empowerment: Salvadorans in Los Angeles." *Gender & Society* 16 (5): 625-646.

Zhou, Yu. 2000. "The Fall of 'The Other Half of the Sky'? Chinese Immigrant Women in the New York Area." *Women's Studies International Forum* 23 (4): 445-459.

Chapter 9
Transnationalism and "Third Culture Kids": A Comparative Analysis of Korean American and Korean Chinese Identity Construction

by Helene K. Lee

Introduction

> I think that it's difficult to come to Korea to try to find out who you are, so to speak, understand your identity. Identity is not fixed, it changes depending on what kind of environment you are in, who you're with, a whole bunch of other things. [...] In Korea, my Americanness is so salient [...] but at home, my Koreanness is so salient.
>
> Eun Mi, 25-year-old Korean American

Identities in ethnic diasporas are shaped by competing allegiances that highlight the everyday realities and consequences of living in what Stuart Hall (1990) calls the liminal space "betwixt and between." These feelings of being rooted neither here nor there, or more accurately, both here and there, lead to what Yen Le Espiritu (2003) refers to as *"home making*—the processes by which diverse subjects imagine and make themselves at home in various geographic locations" (2). In this chapter, I trace the complications and contradictions of "home making," through a comparative analysis of the experiences of Korean American and Joseonjok actors who engage in return migration projects to their homeland, South Korea.

Both of these communities arrive in Seoul subscribing to certain notions of ethnicity established in the countries they consider "home"—China for Joseonjok and the U.S. for Korean Americans. Growing up immersed in Korean immigrant communities and families that maintained Korean customs, language and values, 1.5- and second-generation Korean Americans and second-, third- and fourth-generation Joseonjok have the added advantage of technological advances that keep immigrant Koreans around the world connected to the latest political, economic and cultural developments in South Korea. The benefits of globalization allow ethnicity to remain one of the most salient identity markers for later generation Korean Americans and Joseonjok, many of whom have had limited direct contact with South Korea itself. But this ethnic attachment operates as a double-edged sword with certain advantages and disadvantages in multiple national contexts.

Social Construction of Ethnicity

Cornell and Hartmann (1998) define an ethnic group as a "group of persons distinguished largely by common culture, typically including language, religion, or other patterns of behavior and belief" (17). Assimilationist theories of ethnicity predicted the decreasing significance of ethnic markers as immigrants slowly acculturated and assimilated into mainstream society (Park 1950; Gordon 1962). While this linear trajectory was possible for early European immigrants in the U.S. context whose whiteness facilitated their entry into the dominant racial group, the growing presence of immigrants from Africa, the Caribbean, Asia and Latin America necessitated new understandings of ethnicity.

As researchers shifted focus to the cultural traditions and historical contexts from which ethnic identities were constructed, three dominant perspectives on ethnicity characterize the majority of sociological work that followed—primordial, structural, and social construction. For this chapter, I utilize the last approach that emphasizes the fluid nature of ethnic attachments and the importance of context as the opening quote by Eun Mi illustrates in which Korean identity varies according to one's context. Gans (1979) and Waters (1994) argued that ethnicity was more voluntary in nature, with individuals exercising their "ethnic options" by personalizing ethnic attachments to their own needs. Symbolic aspects retain meaning and are asserted at certain moments while other aspects could be discarded or drawn on at specific moments such as ethnic holidays. Within the social constructionist approach, meanings of ethnicity are shaped through interactions with others and actively negotiated, challenged and resisted in relation to multiple salient identities such as gender and nationality. In this chapter, I emphasize the dynamic nature of Korean identities and how meanings of Koreanness constructed at home in the U.S. and China are challenged by South Korean ideas of ethnic authenticity.

To do this, I first briefly explore the context of Korean ethnic identity construction at home. In the case of Korean Americans in the U.S. and Joseonjok in China, many of the meanings attached to being Korean emerged from a combination of primordial characteristics, such as blood and ancestry, but also maintained and expressed through language, food and other cultural practices upheld by immigrant Korean parents and grandparents. I begin with a basic overview of Korean ethnic identities in the U.S. and then move to the Chinese context, outlining key similarities and differences within these two diasporic Korean communities.

Korean Ethnic Identities at "Home" in the U.S. and China

Although much research has documented the experiences of Asian immigrants with linguistic and cultural barriers in the U.S. as well as historically restrictive immigration policies, this chapter engages with ethnic and racial struggles within the "new second generation," referring to the children of immigrants entering after the passage of the Immigration and Nationality Act of 1965 (Waters 1994; Kibria 2002a; Louie 2002). For 1.5- and second-generation Korean Americans, straddling two separate and at times incompatible Korean and American worlds required constant negotiation. In the home, Korean often was the primary language, the family ate Korean food and observed Korean holidays and customs such as taking their shoes off as they entered the home, bowing greetings to family friends and relatives and stressing the importance of the family. Some (begrudgingly) attended weekly Saturday school to improve their Korean reading and writing skills at a Korean church with other second-generation Korean Americans. At the same time, many were encouraged outside of the home to be more "American." As a result, many second-generation Korean Americans became adept at what Maira (2002) referred to as "switching of cultural codes" between their Korean and American lives by adapting language, physical appearance and behaviors to the context they were in. The educational and socioeconomic success of second-generation Asian Americans has been used to uphold their status as "model minorities" that places them in the precarious position between whites and non-whites in U.S. racial logics while denying them acceptance in either group.

Despite their publicly lauded achievements, second-generation Korean Americans continued to be defined by their racial otherness. They did not fit the blond hair/blue eyes combination of the typical image of an "American" that dominated toys, media and the "popular" cliques in school. Their racialization as Asians marked them as foreigners, even if they were born in or spent most of their formative years in the U.S. (Min 2002). The question, "Where are you from?" and the inevitable follow up, "No, where are you *really* from?" or even the more directly racist "Go back to where you came from," reinforced perceptions of Asians as "perpetual foreigners" regardless of their citizenship status or length of settlement in the U.S. (Min and Kim 1999; Tuan 1999; Kibria 2002a). Their racial minority status was the salient factor in how others saw them, and in turn, how they came to see themselves. While second-generation Korean Americans grew up in the context of multiculturalism and cultural pluralism that celebrated ethnic and racial diversity, this did not ease their experiences of alienation, outright racism and discrimination, or lessen the feeling that they would never be "real" Americans in a dominant culture marked by whiteness.

Despite longer immigration histories in China, Joseonjok also navigated between ethnic and mainstream worlds. While shared physical appearance, similar Confucian values, and favorable state policies towards national minorities allowed them to integrate into a Chinese society that was predominantly Han, Joseonjok also retained a strong sense of pride in their Korean ethnic origins. Like second-generation Korean Americans, many Joseonjok, despite being second-, third- or even fourth-generation Koreans, were familiar with Korean holidays and customs and often spoke Korean as the dominant language at home. In a marked difference from Korean Americans, a majority of Joseonjok reside in Yanbian Korean Autonomous Prefecture in the northeastern region of China bordering North Korea. In this area, Korean and Chinese are officially recognized languages with established Joseonjok schools that are considered one of the best educational systems among minority groups in China (Choi 2001; He 1990; Jin 1990). Joseonjok are also seen as one of the most "modern" national minorities because of their high socioeconomic status, high levels of literacy and educational attainment, mirroring the "model minority" status of Korean Americans in the U.S.

The context of ethnic Korean migration into China, which began in the 1880s but accelerated under Japanese colonization, is also an important factor in the strength of ethnic attachment. Japanese attempts to colonize Manchukuo strengthened the desire of Joseonjok to preserve Korean culture and language as well as encouraged their solidarity with China in the fight against the Japanese. As a result, second-, third- and fourth- generation Joseonjok have developed a strong allegiance to China alongside a strong sense of ethnic pride.

In both Korean American and Joseonjok communities, ethnicity is expressed through cultural practices such as language and customs, but also through a strong emotional attachment to the homeland as the root of their ethnic origins. However, there are key differences between the two contexts that are important to note. First are the histories of out-migration for Korean Americans and Joseonjok. Because of their more recent immigration histories, Korean Americans in the present study were exclusively 1.5- and second generation ethnics, while Joseonjok were spread across the second- through fourth-generation. A second key difference is the existence of Yanbian Prefecture that allows for strong, geographically concentrated ethnic Korean communities and political, social and economic protections by the state, something Korean Americans lack. However, in both cases, exclusion from full social citizenship at "home" lead many to think of the homeland as a place in which ethnic difference would no longer characterize them and offers the chance for acceptance and belonging. As will be explored in the narratives themselves, return migration projects further complicate meanings of ethnicity rather than resolve their identity crises.

Ethnic Identity, Diasporas and Return Migration

As this is a story of homecomings, I expand this discussion of ethnicity in the context of the growing field of transnationalism and diaspora studies, particularly current research on homeland trips. Despite displacement due to economic hardships, political or religious persecution, diasporas remain connected to the homeland through sustained exchanges of ideas, communication, goods and even migrating bodies across national borders (Levitt 2001; Safran 1991; Glick Schiller et al. 1992). In their work on diasporas in the Asian context, Kibria (2002b) and Louie (2002) examined the ways second-generation Korean and Chinese Americans and second-generation Chinese Americans respectively, undertook trips to China and South Korea to discover and strengthen cultural, linguistic and familial ties to the homeland. The findings of these two studies suggested that homeland trips had the contradictory effects of both affirming and marginalizing their positions in relation to questions of true authenticity.

Roth (2002) and Tsuda (2003) explored similar questions in their ethnographic work on the return migration of Brazilian *nikkeijin*, or ethnic Japanese living abroad, who were recruited in large numbers by Japanese companies in the 1980s and 1990s. While Brazilian *nikkeijin* exhibited strong Japanese identities at home in Brazil, the reactions of their Japanese co-workers and larger Japanese society challenged the "authenticity" of their Japaneseness, demonstrating how "[t]ransnational migration can be destabilizing and disorienting as much as it can be enabling and emancipatory" (Tsuda 2003: 140). These two studies found that their marginalization in Japan as not "real" Japanese strengthened national identities as Brazilians who have created their own unique hybridized Japanese culture.

As diasporas produce new cultural forms with migration back and forth between home and homeland countries, they offer important areas of new research. The current project brings together research on ethnicity with diaspora studies to analyze the context of South Korea, which has adopted immigration policies in the past few decades specifically targeted at *dongpo*, or ethnic Koreans living abroad. For Korean Americans and Joseonjok, their ethnic authenticity as Koreans is never questioned at home in the U.S. and China on the basis of primordial concepts of blood and ancestry as well as culture as evidenced in language, food and larger values and customs. Yet the legitimacy of these hybrid forms of Koreanness comes into question when these diasporic individuals return to the homeland and are not seen as "Korean" enough. In the context of this chapter, I explore the fluidity of ethnic identity construction among Korean Americans and Joseonjok by tracing the impact of direct experiences in the homeland on their ethnic identities. When competing meanings of Koreanness collide, how do individuals negotiate what it means to be Korean within a South Korean context that denies them "real" and authentic Koreanness? How are new meanings of Koreanness actively reasserted as diasporic Koreans negotiate social interactions with South Korean co-workers, family members and friends?

Data Sources

A total of sixty-three semi-structured interviews were conducted during the fieldwork period between August 2004 and December 2005 in Seoul, South Korea. The sample included thirty-three semi-structured interviews with Joseonjok, eighteen women and fifteen men, and an age range that spanned from early twenties to late sixties, with a concentration of second- and third-generation ethnics. The community was evenly split between educational migrants pursuing graduate work in Masters and Ph.D. programs and labor migrants largely employed in manufacturing and service industries. In total, thirty interviews were conducted with 1.5- and second-generation Korean Americans, eighteen women and twelve men. The population was concentrated in their early to late twenties and all had legal status in South Korea. Most were engaged in some form of labor in the English teaching industry, college preparation industry or professional positions dependent on their native English fluency and knowledge of U.S. business practices.

All interviewees, Korean American and Joseonjok, had been in South Korea for at least three months, and the average length of stay was 2.1 years. This was intended to cull out those in South Korea for short-term family visits or as tourists and focus on those who had uprooted their lives to relocate in Seoul for a longer length of time.

Complications of Transnationalism

Strengthening Ethnic Identities: "I am you..."

> But in my heart, I felt that I would go to South Korea because it is the land of my ancestors. I thought I would hear Korean whether I was awake or asleep and I would feel more comfortable and this was true.
>
> Kwang Soo, Joseonjok male

I begin with the ambivalence both groups of diasporic Koreans struggled with in South Korea because of the clash between their ethnic Korean ties and their foreignness as non-South Koreans. Maya, a Korean American woman, described her feelings about South Koreans in this way, "I am you but I'm not you." She voiced an indecisiveness that was a common theme across all the interviews with Korean Americans and Joseonjok. The first part of her quote spoke to the strengthening of ethnic identity as they immersed themselves in a completely Korean environment. As Adam, a Korean American man, explained, "There's some sort of cosmic one-ness with [South Korea]. My parents came from here, my sister was born here. My god, there are Koreans everywhere, it's amazing!" Despite being two or three generations removed from the migration out of the Korean peninsula, emotional connections to South Korea also remained strong for most Joseonjok. As one second-generation Joseonjok man said emphatically during our interview, "Before I die, I must see my hometown, not just to earn money. [..] I came because it's my homeland. Joseon is our homeland." As diasporic Koreans, they could see themselves as part of a larger Korean family because of their physical and emotional ties.

While these aspects of homecoming were present in the interviews with both Joseonjok and Korean Americans, the conflicted nature of transnationality also included strong critiques of South Korean society as the initial warm feelings of belonging faded and social interactions with South Koreans proved to be less welcoming.

Disenchantment with contemporary South Korea: "... but I'm not you."

> In America, I thought I was more Korean than I was because people would make me out to be like that. When I came to Korea, in the first couple months, I realized how very unKorean I was. And the longer I stay here, the more I say I've become less Korean, identity runs far deeper than blood.
> Craig, Korean American male

Alongside the increased awareness of what it meant to be Korean, Joseonjok and Korean Americans also talked about the deep cultural divide that contributed to a decrease in ethnic attachment. Many interviewees who felt more Chinese or American rather than Korean the longer they lived in Seoul echoed Craig's comment. The critiques of Koreanness by Korean Americans and Joseonjok were largely rooted in a negative assessment of contemporary South Korean society.

Coming from the comparatively diverse American population, Korean Americans talked disparagingly about the level of uniformity in Seoul. As John explained, "In America you have so many points of view. In Korea there are no opposing points of views. Everyone is the same, dress[es] the same, thinks the same... Korea is very homogeneous." This critique ran counter to the high expectations of many Korean Americans like Lane who said about her decision to move to Seoul, "I thought that I would fall in love with Korea, and Korean people and Korean culture." Instead, they confronted a contemporary South Korea, particularly in Seoul, obsessed with Western ideas, products, language and culture. In addition to the homogeneity, Korean Americans were very critical of high levels of materialism they perceived in South Korea. As Eun Mi, a Korean American woman, explained, "There's something that rubs me the wrong way about the way Koreans like to flaunt wealth even when they don't have it."

Rather than increased pride in their Korean roots, some respondents felt disappointment, even disgust, at the changed Westernized landscape of Seoul and the perceived erosion of traditional Korean culture. Maya, a Korean American woman, explained her thoughts in this way:

Shil mang (disappointment), everything is so *shilmangseoro*[1] (disappointing). I can't believe my parents came from this filth, I was living in Sincheon, you know. [...] I felt embarrassed that my family comes from here. I think the Korean culture has changed a lot right now. I think right now, they're at this void, they have no culture, type of thing. The culture is money here. That's all it is.

Maya, Korean American woman

Chang hae, a Joseonjok male, echoed a similar resistance to identifying with South Koreans. As he explained, "Ever since coming here, I've felt the fact that I'm Chinese more keenly," especially given the social discrimination that he and other Joseonjok in Seoul have faced. This was largely rooted in the perception that compared to South Korea, China was seen as less developed and poor. As Chinese citizens, Joseonjok were dismissed as uneducated, low-class, and manual laborers. One Joseonjok woman, Yeon Hwa, shared stories of how badly informed South Koreans were about China, including an encounter with a South Korean woman who held up a strawberry close to her face and asked if she had ever seen one before. As she explained, "It's not out of curiosity, it's just that kind of feeling that they are looking down on us." Despite their comparatively lower educational levels and the "Third World" status of their home country, Joseonjok felt that South Koreans were more parochial in their way of thinking. As Yeon Hwa stated, "South Korea might be advanced, but they don't seem to know much. We may live in China, but we are aware of what's going on in the world, advances in the world."

Many Joseonjok also critiqued South Koreans for discarding Korea's rich cultural traditions, choosing instead to align themselves closer to the U.S. and Western ways. As Hye Soon, a Joseonjok woman, explained, "I'm 57, but I found out there are a lot of [South Koreans] my age who don't know their Chinese characters. [...] But they think that we're uneducated and, how should I say this, are kind of dumb or less than them." While contemporary South Koreans have incorporated more English terminology and moved away from Korean words derived from Chinese characters, Joseonjok continue to use what they see as the purer, more authentic version of Korean, untouched by Westernization. Joseonjok resented that their preservation of traditional language and customs contributed to their marginalization in South Korea as "backwards," inferior Koreans locked in the past.

"Bubbles:" Diasporic Ethnic Enclaves

At some point, I stopped integrating myself into Korea. I got stuck in a Korean American bubble, but I didn't change it. I am most comfortable with Korean Americans and ... that was disappointing. I am happy enough to be with my foreigner friends and speak English.

Linda, Korean American woman

> Meeting Joseonjok is more comfortable. When I meet South Koreans, I must be careful especially of what I say. There is a cultural difference. [...] I must be cautious and on guard whereas if I am with Joseonjok, I can talk comfortably. With South Koreans, that doesn't happen. It is stressful and uncomfortable.
>
> Kyeong Won, Joseonjok woman

The formation of diasporic sub-ethnic enclaves was a transnational practice that expressed the ambivalence of Korean Americans and Joseonjok towards a Koreanness that simultaneously included and excluded them. By building social networks that included other diasporic Koreans like themselves, Korean Americans and Joseonjok formed self-segregated communities, or "bubbles," that insulated them from South Koreans but also each other. Across all the interviewees, the majority of Joseonjok felt more comfortable around other Joseonjok, just as Korean Americans found themselves increasingly in all-Korean American cliques the longer they stayed in Seoul. Familiarity of language, cultural contexts and similar backgrounds reinforced the line drawn between South Koreans and these two diasporic communities despite their ethnic ties.

The paradox, particularly for Korean Americans, is that by doing so, many of them were moving farther away from their original desires of finding a sense of belonging in the homeland. Language proficiency provides an illustrative way of considering this issue. Unlike Joseonjok who were largely native or advanced Korean speakers, a majority of Korean American research participants had some degree of oral comprehension but were unable to write, read or speak proficiently. Since many found employment in English-teaching or college prep fields, Korean Americans ended up using English everyday and their co-workers were often also Korean American or native English speakers. What initially may have been inadvertent—existing in a Korean American bubble—often became a more deliberate choice. Comments like, "I rarely meet with Korean Koreans, it seems harder in Korea," and "I haven't met too many Korean Koreans," or "I don't think that I can ever hang out with Korean Koreans all the time," were very common within my Korean American sample. These statements are ironic considering they were living in the capital city with a population of over ten million South Koreans, but they also illustrate the impermeability of these tightly-knit, insular Korean American communities.

The Joseonjok bubble was also isolated, but more complicated given the issue around legal documentation as well as the split in my sample between labor migrants and educational migrants. Many Joseonjok deliberately came to the church where I met them not simply for religious reasons but also because they were in search of a community of other Joseonjok who struggle with similar issues as themselves. Given fears of detection and deportation among undocumented labor migrants in my sample, their "bubbles" were defined by vulnerability and suspicion. These Joseonjok monitored their own behaviors very carefully and were cautious in building their social networks to avoid anyone who could endanger their abilities to live and work in Seoul.

Unlike labor migrants, educational migrants, who were on the whole, third- and fourth-generation Joseonjok, had the advantage of legal status in South Korea. But this did not prevent them from discrimination as many shared stories of being ridiculed by professors and classmates because of their Joseonjok identities. To provide networking, support and social opportunities, many research participants were highly active in a Joseonjok graduate student organization that allowed them to create "bubbles" within the South Korean academic community.

The "bubbles" illustrate the internal divisions within diasporic communities in South Korea. Rather than a shared sense of identity as members of the larger Korean diaspora, Korean Americans and Joseonjok rarely occupied the same neighborhoods and their social networks never intersected. Joseonjok I met had very few interactions with Korean Americans though they were very much aware of their elevated status in South Korea compared to their own. Likewise, Korean Americans in my sample had little to no contact with Joseonjok, and had limited awareness of the presence of Joseonjok in Seoul.

The "bubbles" illustrate how return migrant communities navigated Seoul within constructed pockets of transnationalized space with a unique cultural hybridity, including language, food and music that reflected their own emergent sensibilities as Korean Americans and Joseonjok. The next section examines how these bubbles also illuminate the salience of nationality in the context of ethnic identities.

The Realities of Citizenship within Ethnic Identities

While fluidity of ethnicity allows Joseonjok and Korean Americans to construct themselves as both Korean and not-Korean depending on the context, they also struggle to pinpoint where they belong in the space between ethnic identification and nationality. What does it mean to be Korean American and Joseonjok if one feels excluded in the U.S. and China as well as in South Korea? One consequence to the "in-between" state of hybridity is that many interviewees felt they didn't fit in anywhere. A common statement was expressed in this way by Catherine, a Korean American woman, "When I'm in Korea, I feel very American and when I'm in America, I feel very Korean. So it is kind of like, what the hell am I?" Chul Mu is a Joseonjok man who has been in South Korea for ten years and is married to a South Korean woman with whom he has two children. Even after a decade, he explained the constant pressure as follows, "People always ask us, 'Are you Korean or Chinese?' But we're not Korean, and we're not Chinese. While in China, Joseonjok may be seen as Korean, but in South Korea, Joseonjok are seen as Chinese."

The narratives revealed hierarchies of nationality within diasporic communities that privileged U.S. citizens while marginalizing Chinese citizens despite their shared Korean ancestry. A recurring theme in the Joseonjok interviews was the ways Chinese citizenship created both structural and social disadvantages for them in Seoul. The biased visa system enforced by the South Korean state offered preferential status to Korean ethnics largely from First World nations like the U.S. and Japan, but excluded co-ethnics from developing countries like China and Russia. This emphasized the status of Joseonjok as foreigners, rather than *dongpo*. As Kwang Soo, a Joseonjok man explained, "The conclusion is that South Koreans call Joseonjok 'brother' only by name, [but] they don't acknowledge us with their hearts." With out-migration histories before the establishment of North and South Korea, most Joseonjok were exempt from special status accorded to *gyopo* and had limited legal paths to enter to South Korea.

In contrast, favorable visa policies as well as economic opportunities related to their U.S. citizenship and cultural capital attached to being Americans worked to the advantage of Korean Americans on the whole. This did not go unnoticed by many interviewees who realized that being *jemi gyopo* allowed them to couple American citizenship with their Korean ancestry to their economic and social benefit in South Korea. As Matt explained:

> I'm definitely aware that I have a privileged status in Korea simply due to the economic and political power of America. [...] I don't really place that much emphasis [on] whether I'm Korean or American or Korean American, perhaps because all the choices are open for me because of the fact that I'm Korean American.

Rethinking the "Korean" in Korean American

Return migration projects allowed Korean Americans to reframe their identities in a positive light as transnational Americans with roots both inside and outside of the U.S. As Catherine put it, "my *shiminkwon* (citizenship) is American but my parents are Korean. My ethnicity is Korean, right. Well I kind of think of myself as both. Isn't that the whole point of *jemi gyopo* (Korean American)?[2]" Some interviewees felt that being Korean American also made them "better" Americans in part because of the increasingly larger role immigrant communities play in the U.S. Jessica explained her logic in this way, "Immigrant culture is a core part of American identity. [...] I'm more American because I'm Korean American. I make that the root of why I'm American."

Changing Perceptions of Koreanness as Joseonjok

Despite their shared Korean ancestry, the Joseonjok in my sample held less stable relationships to South Korea in large part because of their nationality as Chinese as well as their migration histories. The defining difference between Korean Americans and Joseonjok is how the latter tie Koreanness to a historical period predating the establishment of North and South Korea. Joseonjok often spoke about the Korean peninsula itself as their homeland, using historical terms like *Goryeo* (918-1392) or *Joseon* (1392-1910). As explained by Kyeong Won, a Joseonjok woman, "Well, South Korea and North Korea are Joseon, right? We think they used to be one country. [...] We are all Joseon people." Both North and South Korea figured prominently in Joseonjok identities, unlike Korean Americans who were all descended from former South Korean citizens. As a result, most Joseonjok framed their identities as Korean in a broader traditional and historical sense that encompassed the entire Korean peninsula. As many pointed out, the name itself, Joseonjok referred to Joseon, an undivided Korean dynasty, not nation. In fact, many considered Joseonjok culture as more "authentically" Korean than contemporary South Korean culture because they were truer to traditional ways. As Hye Soon pointed out, "Blood is more important than citizenship," and the purity and legitimacy of their Korean blood should be grounds for inclusion rather than exclusion in South Korea.

"Be the Reds"[3]: Red Devils and Korean Pride

Despite the disparities in experience within the two communities, there remained an emotional connection to South Korea that was not rooted in political or economic factors but came up most frequently in discussions about international sporting events such as the World Cup soccer tournament or the Olympics. However, there were differences between Joseonjok and Korean Americans, despite a general support of South Korea in international competition. As Jim, a Korean American, explained, "If you watch sports, in general, as a Korean, obviously you are going to root for Korea. Even during the [World Cup soccer] game against U.S., most Korean Americans would root for Korea. It was the more national closeness everyone was accepting of each other because you're from that country. Everyone was united." For many Korean Americans I spoke with, international sporting events like the World Cup in 2002 in which the South Korean team and co-hosts defied expectations to reach the semi-final round evoked a "national closeness" grounded in shared ethnic ties.

For Joseonjok, this sense of Korean pride was still evident, but with a distinction between North and South Korea, as explained by Kyeong Won, a Joseonjok woman, "If you ask anyone about this, in competition, Korea and China were to compete in a soccer match, we would want China to win. Next to that, if North Korea and South Korea were to compete... I might want North Korea to win. If South Korea is playing any other country, then we would root for South Korea." Hee Sook, another Joseonjok woman, echoed these thoughts, "The thing people asked most, 'if perchance, in soccer, a Chinese and South Korean team were to play each other, which one would you root for?' Without any thought, I would say China. Not just me, but most all Joseonjok would say that. But if it was South Korea vs. any other team in the world, we would root for South Korea. That is something unavoidable."

Conclusion: Living in Liminality

> I want to say that I'm a third culture kid, right. You're a new type of nationality, where there's a mix of outside cultures coming together. And for me, being Korean American, that's basically what it is, it's mixing two different cultures and putting them together and make who I am.
>
> Gloria, 26-year-old Korean American

Despite blood ties, physical, and emotional connections to South Korea, the narratives of these return migrants illustrate the ways in which home and belonging cannot easily be untangled from the larger story of ethnicity, nationality, blood and history. In this paper, I highlighted the strategies that Korean Americans and Joseonjok took as they navigated the global and local intricacies of Korean ethnic identity in contemporary South Korea.

The comparative analysis of two diasporic return migrants reveals internal hierarchies within Korean transnational identities that mirror global political and economic inequalities. The privileging of Western cultural capital in terms of desired characteristics for remaking South Korea from its underdeveloped, war-torn past to a cosmopolitan global force also translated into material privileges for Korean Americans in Seoul. While Joseonjok were integral actors that provided much of the labor behind South Korea's industrialization in the 1970s to the present, they are excluded from the South Korean family because of their Third World citizenship.

The return migration project provided an essential piece of ethnic identity construction—a decentering of the homeland and the construction of a hybridized, transnational Korean identity. For Joseonjok and Korean Americans, their experiences in South Korea helped them discover their status as "third culture kids" who actively challenge the notion that Koreanness can be defined by South Korea alone. In the search for ethnic identities between the home and homeland, the findings of the present study hint that the centrality of the homeland may erode in future generation of diasporic Koreans who will negotiate new ethnic identities and meanings as "third culture kids."

Notes

1. Korean words in quotes are from the original.
2. Korean words are from the original quote.
3. This was the slogan for the South Korean soccer team, the Red Devils, during the World Cup.

References

Choi, Woo-Gil. 2001. "The Korean Minority in China: The Change of its Identity." *Development and Society* 30 (1):119-141.

Cornell, Stephen, and Douglas Hartmann. 1998. *Ethnicity and Race: Making Identities in a Changing World*. Thousand Oaks, CA: Pine Forge Press.

Espiritu, Yen Le. 2003. *Home Bound: Filipino American Lives Across Cultures, Communities, and Countries*. Berkeley: University of California Press.

Gans, Herbert. 1979. "Symbolic Ethnicity: The Future of Ethnic Groups and Cultures in America." In *On the Making of Americans*, edited by Herbert Gans, Nathan Glazer, Joseph Guofield, and Christopher Jencks. Philadelphia: University of Pennsylvania Press.

Glick Schiller, Nina, Linda Basch, and Cristina Blanc-Szanton. 1992. "Transnationalism: A New Analytic Framework for Understanding Migration." In *Towards a Transnational Perspective on Migration: Race, Class, Ethnicity, and Nationalism Reconsidered*, edited by Nina Glick Schiller, Linda Basch, and Cristina Blanc-Szanton, 1-24. New York: New York Academy of Sciences.

Gordon, Milton. 1962. *Assimilation in American Life: The Role of Race, Religion and National Origins*. Oxford: Oxford University Press.

Hall, Stuart. 1990. "Cultural Identity and Diaspora." In *Identity: Community, Culture, Difference*, edited by Jonathan Rutherford, 222-237. London: Lawrence and Wishart.

He, Jiancheng. 1990. "China's Policy on Nationalities." In *Koreans in China*, edited by Dae-Sook Suh and Edward Shultz, 1-20. Papers of the Center for Korean Studies No. 16.

Jin, Shangzhen. 1990. "The Rights of Minority Nationalities in China: The Case of the Yanbian Korean Autonomous Prefecture." In *Koreans in China*, edited by Dae-Sook Suh and Edward Shultz, 31-43. 1990. Papers of the Center for Korean Studies No. 16.

Kibria, Nazli. 2002a. *Becoming Asian American: Second-Generation Chinese and Korean American Identities*. Baltimore: Johns Hopkins University Press.

_____. 2002b. "Of Blood, Belonging, and Homeland Trips: Transnationalism and Identity among Second-Generation Chinese and Korean Americans." In *The Changing Face of Home: The Transnational Lives of the Second Generation*, edited by Peggy Levitt and Mary C. Waters. New York: Russell Sage Foundation.

Levitt, Peggy. 2001. "Transnational Migration: Taking Stock and Future Directions." *Global Networks* 1 (3): 195-216.

Louie, Andrea. 2002. "Creating Histories for the Present: Second-Generation (Re)definitions of Chinese American Culture." In *The Changing Face of Home: The Transnational Lives of the Second Generation*, edited by Peggy Levitt and Mary C. Waters. New York: Russell Sage Foundation.

Maira, Sunaina Marr. 2002. *Desis in the House: Indian American Youth Culture in New York City*. Philadelphia: Temple University Press.

Min, Pyong Gap, ed. 2002. *Second Generation: Ethnic Identity among Asian Americans*. Walnut Creek: Altamira Press.

Min, Pyong Gap and Rose Kim, eds. 1999. *Struggle for Ethnic Identity: Narratives by Asian American Professionals*. Walnut Creek: Altamira Press.

Park, Robert. 1950. *Race and Culture*. Glencoe, IL: The Free Press.

Roth, Joshua Hotaka. 2002. *Brokered Homeland: Japanese Brazilian Migrants in Japan.* Ithaca: Cornell University Press.

Safran, William. 1991. "Diasporas in Modern Societies: Myths of Homeland and Return." *Diaspora* 1: 83-99.

Tsuda, Takeyuki. 2003. *Strangers in the Ethnic Homeland.* New York: Columbia University Press.

Tuan, Mia. 1999. *Forever Foreigners or Honorary Whites?: The Asian Ethnic Experience Today.* New Brunswick: Rutgers University Press.

Waters, Mary C. 1994. "Ethnic and Racial Identities of Second-Generation Black Immigrants in New York City." *International Migration Review* 28 (4): 795-820.

Chapter 10
Authenticity Dilemma among Pre-1965 Native-Born Koreans

by Linda S. Park

The American-born second generation of immigrant families often struggle with questions of authenticity and fitting into their own ethnic communities within the U.S. This struggle is part of a larger question on who defines an individual's inclusion in a group. American-born Asians, in particular, struggle with authenticity in a unique way as they are often seen as "foreigners" in America because of their race (Tuan 1998) and as "cultural foreigners" in the home country of their parents because of their unfamiliarity with cultural markers defining that society (N. Kim 2009). Questions of authenticity arise when there is a conflict between your self-identification and how others identify you. Ethnic identity, an important element of self-identity, is established internally by the individual and is externally imposed by others.

Nadia Kim (2009) used the term "authenticity dilemma" for Korean Americans who experienced "cultural foreignness" in Korea. However, her focus was on the Korean American experience in Korea. This chapter explores how participants in this study struggled with issues of "authenticity" as a Korean, and how being a "cultural foreigner" within the Korean community created difficulty in connecting with and being accepted by the immigrant Korean communities that have emerged since the 1970s. One possible explanation for this authenticity dilemma faced by the pre-1965 native-born Korean Americans arises from a conflict between a strong assimilation ideology, which led participants in this study to have heritage, language and cultural barriers, and the deep-rooted sense of ethnic nationalism (known as *danil minjok*) of Korean people which create strong in-group/out-group boundaries. This conflict stems from how differences in the social construction of race in two different countries have created different definitions of "who" or "what" is Korean.

Immigration scholars tend to focus on adaptation and incorporation into the dominant host society in the form of acculturation and assimilation (Alba and Nee 1997, 2003; Berry 2003), while ethnic identity scholars tend to focus on ethnicity and heritage retention (Chong 1998; Min and Kim 2002). However, not much attention has been given to the issue of how assimilated individuals fit into their own ethnic communities. The data in this chapter calls attention to how the consequences of assimilation influence ethnic identity and this issue of authenticity with one's own ethnic community rather than the dominant society. I shift emphasis to how individuals found meaning in or defined being Korean in a Korean community and not as assimilated Americans in the dominant society at large. Having spent most of their critical developmental years of childhood and adolescence in predominantly white communities created challenges when trying to associate with co-ethnic peers and the immigrant Korean community.

Data for this chapter comes from my dissertation which focused on how a particular cohort of Korean Americans negotiated and defined the meaning of their ethnicity as adults in midlife. This cohort is made up of descendants of Korean students who emigrated to the U.S. between 1950 and 1965, a very small group for which very little information is known (Hurh 1980, Kitano and Daniels 1995; Yu and Choe 2003-2004). Although there are a few studies that examined ethnic identity among children of the pre-1965 Asian immigrants (Min and Kim 1999; Tuan 1999), most studies of second-generation ethnic identity focus on children of the post-1965 immigrants. My study specifically focused on children of the pre-1965 Asian immigrants—during a time when there were not many Korean and other Asian Americans, and when the U.S. government enforced a strong assimilation policy.

Background

The complexity of the Korean American experience warrants some background information to situate the participants in this study. This section situates their parents' immigration experience and the ideology of assimilation within a social and historical context. The last part briefly describes differences in the social construction of race between two countries.

Korean immigrants to the U.S. arrived in three distinct waves. The first wave of 8,000 arrived in Hawaii between 1903 and 1924 (Hurh 1980; Min 1998; Takaki 1998). Although Asian immigration was banned between 1924 and 1965, certain circumstances allowed for entry into the U.S. (Okihiro 2001; Takaki 1998). The second wave of about 14,000 arrived between 1950 and 1965 under three categories: Korean adoptee children (5,300), Korean War brides (6,400), and South Korean students (2,300) seeking post-baccalaureate degrees (Hurh

1980). The third and current wave of Korean immigrants arrived after the passage of a landmark immigration act in 1965, which ended discriminatory quotas and lifted the Asian Exclusion Act (Suarez-Orozco 2001). For fifteen years (1972 to 1987), a mass emigration of Koreans, approximately 30,000 per year, entered the U.S. By the year 2000, the Korean population in the U.S. had reached over a million (Yu and Choe 2003-2004). Much of the research has focused on Korean immigrant families arriving after 1965. However, this study focused on the families of a small group of students who were first scattered across the U.S. at different universities during the 1950s and 1960s, and later scattered in the suburbs of predominantly white homogeneous neighborhoods as the lone Korean (or Asian) family.

For over a century and a half prior to 1965, many immigrants had to establish their own communities while also feeling that assimilation for their children was a necessary process and outcome to survive in the U.S. (Eckstein and Barberia 2002). For decades, assimilation in the U.S. meant relinquishing one's cultural heritage and moving towards the dominant American culture, most commonly associated with middle-class white Anglo-Saxon Protestants (WASPs). Until the civil rights and affirmative action movements of the late 1960s, America's national identity was rooted in this ideology. As long as the U.S. remained predominantly white, it was not problematic to expect immigrants to change. A strong command of the English language was prerequisite for assimilation and establishing an American identity (Portes and Rumbaut 1996). Participants in this study were born during this time where laws severely restricted Asian immigration to U.S. and when an assimilation ideology insisted on a strong command of the English language. This was the context immigrant families faced, and it influenced how immigrant parents socialized their children.

The crux of the authenticity dilemma that second-generation Korean Americans face within the Korean community seems to stem from differences in how race is socially constructed within the U.S. and in Korea. Recognizing these differences enlightens us on how South Koreans view Korean Americans and vice versa. Although there is no biological basis to race, in the U.S., race continues to be based on phenotypical (or physical) features and is frequently used to categorize people and establish identity (Yanow 2003). Race is also one element of ethnicity—referring to one's culture and ancestry (Omi and Winant 1994). American citizenship does not lend itself to a national identity as it does in many other countries. As a nation, the U.S. is not defined "by blood or ancestry, but by a set of shared ideas [e.g., freedom, democracy, and the Constitution]" (Jacoby 2004). For Asian Americans, their race, ethnicity, and citizenship are fairly independent (e.g., race is Asian, ethnicity is Korean, and citizenship is American).

However, this is not the case in a country like South Korea, where nationality is conflated with race, ethnicity and national identity (N. Kim 2008; Shin 2006b). South Korea is considered to be one of the few ethnically homogeneous nation-states in the world (H. Kim 2009; Min 1991).[1] According to Shin (2006a), "Koreans believe that they belong to a 'unitary nation' (*danil minjok*), one that is ethnically homogeneous and racially distinctive" (1). This point is reiterated in

H. Kim's (2009) observation of Korea as "a country notorious for its strong ethno-cultural definition of nationhood and its obsession with purity of blood... the unspoken and unquestioned yardstick for membership in the Korean national community" (1). The ideology of modern *danil minjok* emerged during the Japanese colonial rule of Korea as a strategy to resist Japanese nationalism (Shin 2006a). To counteract Japanese assimilation policies, Korean intellectuals and historians used the legend of Tan'gun[2] as the foundation to their ethnic homogeneity to create a strong blood-based ethnic national identity. Since its independence from Japan in 1945, Korea promoted this version of Korean nationalism for the next thirty-five years[3] (H. Kim 2009; Shin 2006b). This deep-rooted sense of ethnic nationalism remains in Koreans' consciousness even when emigrating. Knowing this part of Korean culture and history helps to frame the experiences of Korean immigrants and Korean Americans.

Methods

Participants in this study were born in the U.S. between 1953 and 1965. Due to difficulties in locating this particular cohort,[4] convenience and snowball sampling techniques were used (the internet, books on Asian Americans, newspaper articles, and conversations with other people). Of the thirty-eight people found, sixteen people consented to an interview.[5] Demographics are presented in Table 10.1.

Table 10.1: Demographic Data (N=16)

Gender	Male= 6	Female= 10	
Education Level	College = 7	Post-College = 9	
Dominant Language	English = 16	Korean = 0	
Age at time of interview	40-45 yrs = 7	46-50 yrs = 5	51-55 yrs = 3
Marital Status	Single = 6	Married = 9	Divorced = 1
Ethnicity of Partner (n =9)	Korean = 1	White = 5	Other Asian = 3
Current Regional Residence	East Coast = 9	West Coast = 6	Midwest = 1

One-time face-to-face interviews, averaging one to two hours, were conducted in seven metropolitan areas.[6] Participants' stories were mostly retrospective. They recounted past events but reported through present reactions, meaning their reflections represented their understanding of past events now as adults rather than when they were young (Scott and Alwin 1998). All the participants' stories together present valuable "oral sources" historically documenting a comprehensive portrayal of that social and historical time period (Portelli 1991: 26).

Results

The findings on cultural foreignness are reported here in two broad sections. The first section illustrates how participants experienced being a "racial foreigner" as they attempted to blend in with their white peers. However, as participants struggled to blend in, they simultaneously understood how different they were. It is because of these experiences that participants sought out co-ethnic peers as the Korean immigrant communities grew around them. The second section focuses on participants' experience with "othering" and exclusion from their co-ethnic community and peers. The combination of these experiences resulted in participants questioning their authenticity as Koreans.

Racial Foreigner: Attempts to "Blend in" with White Communities

The 1940 U.S. Census listed less than 2,000 Koreans outside of Hawaii in the mainland U.S., signifying the virtually non-existent Korean communities outside of Los Angeles and Hawaii (Patterson 2000; Segal 2002). Also, because that small number of Koreans came to the United States to study, their points of entry were scattered across the U.S. at different universities during the 1950s and 1960s. Upon graduation, these families continued to be scattered mostly at different universities for employment (e.g., Massachusetts, Louisiana, Kansas, Virginia, Minnesota, and Ohio). Consequently, most participants in this study spent much of their developmental years growing up in predominantly white communities where often times, participants recalled that they were the only "Asian kid" around in their schools or neighborhoods. Growing up in this type of environment left the children no choice in who their peers were. Jessica aptly summed up many participants experiences during their early school years: "I think part of it was growing up in such an overwhelmingly white suburban neighborhood as I did in Ohio, I had no choice but to hang out with white people." Time and time again, almost all participants stated similar scenarios about growing up in predominantly white neighborhoods and learning to "blend in" with the communities around them. "Blending in" was a term used by many participants to describe how they attempted to fit into their surroundings with their white friends. As Kathy reflected:

> Between the time I was born and middle school, we grew up I guess like a typical "American" suburban family with a house. We went to the local elementary school, got involved in some sports and played with our friends, hung out and did the usual, I guess, *Leave it to Beaver* type of thing. I think it seems like we were very blended in with every other "American" type family.

And as Mina reflected:

> Did I think much about being Korean? When I was young, I think I really didn't. You know, actually it probably wasn't until college when I was really actively sort of thinking about my identity because I think that whole time until I went to college, I probably just tried to blend in.

During the 1970s, as Korean communities began to flourish in certain regions of the U.S. with the mass influx of Korean immigrants, participants continued blending in with the white community around them. In fact, blending in was so important that several participants told stories of how they distanced themselves from new Korean immigrant youth for fear that they would be mistaken as "one of them." Kathy remembered:

> But then I could always tell the [new Korean immigrants] that just came because they couldn't mingle in with me or my other friends. We still hung out but you could tell that they were the weird ones and I guess there was that term called FOB, "fresh off the boat." I didn't want to look like that. I wanted to look like my blond-headed American friends and do what they do.

Michelle recalled how blending in with the majority group (white peers) was more important than connecting with the newer Korean students that entered her school:

> Yeah, I mean growing up through high school, it was mostly white friends because again, there were very few Koreans and Asians where I lived. And I think that the few that were around tended to be, you know, more recent Korean immigrants. And, you know, again, you're just trying to fit in. And I think there was one woman in my high school that came from Korea. I didn't reach out to her and I felt that I had very little in common with her.

While participants were aware that being Korean was different, they continued to make efforts to blend in as Jessica comments reflected:

> I just became like everybody else even though I wasn't. For the most part I behaved like they did. You know, I dated the same kids that everyone else dated. I did the same, you know, [...] went to the football game every Friday night. I didn't stand out in that many ways.

The consequence of growing up in predominantly white environments was that this was what they became the most familiar with. Unfortunately, this had consequences for many participants later in life as they tried to enter Korean communities during their college years and beyond. As participants grew older and the Korean immigrant communities grew around them, they soon felt the exclusion and realized they were outsiders in the Korean communities. This left them little choice but to continue surviving within the white communities around them, or for some, finding an Asian American community to associate with.

However, this does not mean that participants were not conscious that they were Korean. When participants were young, their ethnic identity was ascribed to them by outside forces such as their parents and the dominant white society at large. They remembered being told by their parents that they were Korean. Although they wanted their children to assimilate, immigrant parents were proud of their Korean heritage (*danil minjok*) and so they taught their children that they were different from the majority community around them. Participants recalled these memories: "Haha, because we were told [that we are Korean] as we were growing up" (Wilson). "They [his parents] would talk about it when I was at a very early age 'We're Korean'" (Derek). "I think when I was really young my parents told me I was Korean and so that had a big influence" (Mina).

A common theme for many was the feeling of being different from everyone else around them. They were conscious of being racially different and yet wanting to fit in with their white peers. Patrick remembered when he started kindergarten in Kansas: "I noticed that none of my friends looked like me." And his awareness of being Korean became a negative reaction "because I didn't look like my friends so I didn't like being different from my friends." Elena had already graduated from high school and was in college by the time the Korean immigrant communities began to grow. As such, she hardly had any contact with Korean communities and has always been quite comfortable within the dominant white society. And yet, she remembered feeling different from her peers when she was young and going to school: "I wasn't in a place where there were a lot of minority students and so it was clear that I was different." Wilson's comment illustrates the complicated nature native-born Koreans lived in:

> Oh early on, I think, I've always felt like I was the minority. We grew up in mostly white neighborhoods and the only Korean access was at church and it seemed like I was always surrounded by non-Koreans from early times. I thought ok, I'm different. I don't know why exactly but I have differences in everything—what we eat and what we talked about and the language […] very early […] as early as I can remember.

Some comments were based clearly on their phenotypic features. Kathy recounts, "I would consider myself Korean American because I still have the Korean look." Elena recalls, "I consider it's more accurate because obviously I don't look Euro-American so I guess I always kind of knew, even as a child that 'oh we're Korean.'" It could be argued that any racism participants faced was based on the fact that Asians are not phenotypically white. This could explain the constant need of wanting to blend in because, for many, there was lack of "full" acceptance into the dominant society.

Nativist attitudes have endured in the U.S. for over two centuries. The racial divide between whites and the African American communities has remained long after the Civil Rights movement. Many scholars (e.g., Takaki, Tuan, and Kim) have noted the challenges that Asian/Asian Americans pose in the racial constructions in America. There are two common ways this occurs: constantly being mistaken for another Asian group (because all Asians look alike) or constantly being perceived as a foreigner in the U.S. As the data reflected in the previous section, this cohort of second-generation Korean Americans did culturally assimilate to the dominant white society around them because that is all they could do. Interestingly, participants were somewhat divided in their responses regarding their experiences with racism. Some participants recalled their experiences with racism vividly as racial slurs. Yoona painstakingly remembered and bitterly related this account, "It was very blatant. First of all, I can't date the white people. This is a small city in Texas. I was always considered 'Oriental' so it wasn't considered that I could date the white people. It's hard to explain. It's just, that's just the way it was." In this instance, the geographical location of where participants grew up had an impact on how much racism they experienced. Growing up in the South or the Midwest was different compared to growing up on either the West or East coasts. Some participants realized that they posed no threat to their white peers since they were the only Asian in their schools. However, for others, being the only Asian brought on more opportunities for racism. Yoona recognized how this experience can be exponential as she said:

> I mean, you know, because there's not that many of us [second generation] [...] so the amount of racism when there's only one or maybe two is a lot! Because you're the only one and so they pick one; you're like a circus show to them. If they've never seen an Asian before and you're the only one that's like not a good situation, you know.

Jessica grew up in the Midwest and was able to blend in with her white peers but that was also during a time before Korean and other Asian communities began to grow. Her younger sister, on the other hand, had some different experiences. Jessica recalled this particular incident:

> I remember when my sister ran for student council in Ohio and she was like class president and all that, but someone scrawled on her campaign posters 'Remember Pearl Harbor.' I don't think the community viewed itself as racist even though I think it probably was extremely so.

Jessica continued to speculate as to whether an incident such as this would be tolerated today. It seemed like nobody was punished for this reference to Pearl Harbor back then. Abby, a Los Angeles native, described her childhood neighborhood as being more diverse with Latino and African American communities. And she remembered this:

> All through your life you encounter these incidents where people make fun of how you're looking, make fun of your speech [...] [references to] the "ching chong, China man" as a child [...] and then as you get older, it's different because it becomes more subtle [...] Just realizing that in a place like LA, where

it's diverse, the diversity still causes more tension and sometimes there's a clash because people have biases.

Both the reference to Pearl Harbor and the reflection from the Los Angeles native represent lingering negative attitudes associated with Asians. In this case, the first negative association is with the Japanese during WWII. The second negative association revolves around the tumultuous race relations between the African American and Korean communities during the LA riots on April 29, 1992.

It seemed that for many participants, subtle examples of racism were more common than incidents of blatant racism. It was difficult for Dylan to remember any incidents of racism in his life, but he did recall this incident when he was young and living in the suburbs of Maryland:

> I think that most of the time, it's subtle. It's more, if it's related to being Korean but just being Asian probably. I don't have any recollections of anything blatant. But I do feel there subtle ways that are always there. I mean when I was in fourth grade, there were clearly very few Asians and I can remember kids, you know, name calling. I honestly don't remember what the terms were but I do remember that it existed and that it was always, you know, there was always some reference to what your race was.

Others felt the racism was fairly minimal and attributed ignorance to the name calling. Since the U.S. is a country that has been predominantly white (until more recent years), there is a strong tendency and connection that "American" means white. Often times the term "American" is a loose reference to a white person, just as Josie stated: "Because when I think American, I think of, you know, sort of Caucasian, sort of classic, although that's not really." So while European immigrants and their children are able to blend into the dominant white society over time, Koreans have a tougher time because they are not white. These participants were asked constantly "what they were," implying the lack of recognition as Americans, even though they were U.S. citizens by birth.

By 1924 when the Asian Exclusion laws took effect, it was estimated that there were already 225,000 Chinese and 72,000 Japanese living in the U.S. compared to 8,000 Koreans (Segal 2002). And because the Chinese and Japanese communities in the U.S. have longer histories and exist in greater numbers, participants were often mistaken for being Chinese or Japanese.[7] As such, many people in the U.S. did not know where Korea was or who Korean people were. Many participants were mistaken to be Chinese, as reflected in the racial slurs they encountered. Several participants shared memories of being called "chink," but not many remembered being attacked physically, except Wilson, who remembered as a child, "being called 'chink' or something and maybe it would get physical, there would be a fight [...] there would be one or two."

Devin recalled a very familiar incident that resonates with many Asian Americans: "I get that all the time too, haha [...] 'What are you?' 'American.' 'What?! No, no I mean what ARE you?' Yeah yeah, I get that [...] hahaha."

Participants in this study also experienced the perception from others that they were foreigners in the U.S. even though they were born with U.S. citizenship. For instance, participants were constantly asked what they were, where they were from, that they spoke "really good English" and inquiries to when they were going back to their homelands. For instance, Elena, who spent parts of her childhood between the East coast and the Midwest said:

> Oh clearly there were a lot of questions like 'what are you?' I'm not sure if that was being discriminating against [...] I've been told I speak English very well and asked 'when are you going to go back?' [...] More people were just ignorant and I came to appreciate that later. Obviously it was becoming burdensome to have to continually explain who you were.

Many felt these remarks were often subtle and stemmed from ignorance. Wilson had friends who accepted him, but at the same time there were others around him who did not:

> Some were cruel [...] they reminded me all the time [...] new people, new situations. That first time, if they didn't know me but the first time they'd see me, I think it was pretty obvious I was different. Oh Chinese, Japanese, what are you? Then I felt that I was Korean. But most of the time I didn't.

For some participants, it was during these types of experiences of feeling like a racial foreigner that participants had no confusion that they were Korean. They were sent clear messages from their white peers that they were not white or even American. Min and Kim (1999) state that even later-generation Asian Americans cannot help but accept their ethnic identity because they are not accepted by "real Americans." Thus, while Asian Americans may want to assimilate (and have succeeded culturally) and identify with the dominant group (American), they are never completely accepted as American as the European Americans are. In this way, by the time many participants reached college age in the late 1970s and into the 1980s, they welcomed the opportunity to meet co-ethnic peers. However, their place as a cultural foreigner soon became evident.

Cultural Foreigner: "Othering" and Exclusion from Co-Ethnic Community and Peers

The previous section explained how the efforts of native-born Korean Americans to assimilate and blend in to the dominant white community around them still left them knowing that they were different but affirmed that they were Korean. This section describes how, as opportunities arose, participants tried to engage with the Korean immigrant communities only to experience cultural foreignness. This section is divided into three parts. The first subsection illustrates how the deep rooted consciousness of *danil minjok* affected the interactions between this small cohort of native-born Korean Americans with a significantly much larger cohort of 1.5-generation Korean immigrants. The second subsection explains how the influences of assimilation put participants at a disadvantage within a community that strongly values language and culture. The third subsection summarizes the end result of both the attempted assimilation efforts and the exclusion from the Korean community.

Danil Minjok and Strong In-group/Out-group Boundaries.

Nadia Kim (2009) defines the idea of being a cultural foreigner in one's home country to individuals who have a Korean face but lack knowledge around Confucian norms, style of dress, sense of history, and most important, Korean language skills. She goes further to say, "They [Korean Americans] are especially foreign in a nationalistic society that conflates race and culture (e.g., Korean blood explains our diligence; Koreans naturally love kimchi). In this way, children of immigrants completely disrupt South Koreans' sense of identity (N. Kim 2009: 3). In this sense, a cultural foreigner differs from a racial foreigner because it is more about cultural norms than race. Thus language (a cultural marker) becomes an integral part of Korean national identity. While phenotype is commonly associated with race for white people in the U.S., for Koreans (nationals and first-generation immigrants), it is culture that defines who is Korean. In this way, emphasis on language was a recurring theme. Participants noted the pride in ethnic nationalism. Jessica plainly summed up: "But you know, that to me was always this very Korean attribute also. This like pride and, you know their language and their culture and sort of, you know, screw everybody else who didn't understand." Mina remembered a particular conversation her mother had with a friend when Mina was in elementary school. This friend was a second-generation Korean born in Hawaii, but similar in age to Mina's mother. Mina recalled that they were arguing about whether Mina was a Korean or an American:

> Well, they're not Korean, they're American. They are born in this country. And my mother was like "No! Mina, come here! What are you? Just say, what are you?" I said "I'm Korean" because that's all I knew. So I don't know if I started thinking about it more, but clearly that was a debate that existed.

This debate Mina was referring to also exemplifies how strongly the ideology of *danil minjok* continues to influence Koreans' perceptions of outsiders. In this case, whether Mina was a Korean or not was based on citizenship.

However, this type of not fitting into Korean communities existed not only here in the U.S., but also when they visited their ancestral homeland, Korea. Many participants recalled how they were made to feel ashamed for not knowing their heritage language. Dylan remembered: "We were constantly berated by people who lived there [Korea] that we didn't speak Korean." Several participants' memories of visits to Korea involved stories of taxi cab drivers. For instance, two different women related these scenarios: Jessica recounts, "Oh yeah!

And there are the taxi cab drivers [who] yell at you for your Korean being so bad!" Josie says, "I remember once when we went to Korea, it was post-college and I remember a taxi cab driver was lecturing me because I couldn't speak Korean and it was like, he has a point—I look Korean, why can't I speak?" In Josie's case, her questioning of her authenticity as a Korean is very real. Her understanding of her Koreanness is based on how race and ethnicity are defined in the U.S. She does not understand what defines being a Korean aside from her looks. In a very different scenario, Wilson related an incident that occurred while he was in a summer language program during college in the early 1980s:

> Actually in Korea, in summer school walking back one night, I was with one of the Korean American girls speaking English down an alleyway when a drunk Korean man came out. And he was like "Why are you not speaking Korean?!" and then he attacked me and we fought too. I tried not to fight but it ended up that he was very aggressive. It was a short battle pretty much. She dragged me away and he was throwing bottles around. Yeah, it was crazy!

In each of these examples, language was one of the key factors attributed to being Korean. And yet, it was their parents who did not teach their children how to speak Korean. Although not having heritage language skills put participants at a disadvantage, this represents how immigrant parents get caught in the middle between wanting their children to succeed in America and how much culture to preserve. However, we see here how Mina aptly summed up her impression regarding Koreans:

> I think Korea is very unique. It's actually, I think, one of the most homogeneous, racially homogeneous and ethnically homogeneous, countries and there probably isn't a whole lot of mixed kids in Korea and so I DO think there is an emphasis of racial purity in Korea. Their [Korean people] identity is based on who they are—has to do with blood lines or whatever ethnic purity. But I think it's really extreme with Koreans. And a lot of other countries there's so more much diversity that I don't think you can just narrow it down like that.

Many participants acknowledged that the strong sense of ethnic nationalism Koreans possess result in strong xenophobic (or ethnocentric) attitudes towards outsiders (Cummings 1997). This creates a very strong sense of in-group solidarity (Chong 1998; Shim et al. 2008). Korean immigrants retain this strong sense of ethnic nationalism, especially when confronted with other people outside "their" group.

With the massive influx of new Korean immigrants to the U.S. beginning in the early 1970s, the proportion of immigrant youth (the 1.5 generation) proliferated and soon outnumbered the very small population of American-born second-generation Koreans already living in the U.S. Zhou (1997) notes that the differences between the 1.5 generation and second generation are worth paying attention to "particularly in their physical and psychological developmental stages, in their socialization processes in the family, the school, and the society at large, as well as in their orientation toward their homeland" (64). In particular, because the 1.5 are foreign-born, they generally do not have concerns about their ethnic identity in the same way that the second generation does, although they may feel challenged in how to balance their ethnic identity with American identity (Phinney 2003). This difference may have a conscious effect on identity and may influence the experiences that each group has in relationship to their place in American society (Danico 2004).

As Korean communities began to grow, the likelihood for participants in this study to encounter other Koreans increased, especially in college. As the data showed earlier, after years of being the "only" (or almost only) Asian person in their neighborhoods or schools, participants in this study had learned to blend in with the community around them. And yet, because of experiences with racism from the dominant white society around, participants were well aware of the differences between themselves and their white peers. Thus, during their college years, when opportunities arose to meet other Koreans, participants were enthralled by the idea of meeting co-ethnic peers. However, it did not take long before they felt the exclusion that was indirectly communicated to them as "outsiders" by the 1.5-generation Korean immigrants. Disappointingly, participants realized they did not fit in with their co-ethnic peers. This is clearly depicted by these participants' statements regarding their experiences with Korean student organizations in college. For instance Dylan's reflection:

> There was a group of Korean students at Harvard, and it was nice to meet people, but it was clear that people were really actively seeking out, you know, really a Korean bond and Korean identity and wanting to just seek a connection with a lot of other Koreans. And I think that didn't seem as important to me at that time.

Josie also recalled:

> I did do a little bit with a Korean club. But a lot of the folks in that were actually from Korea [1.5-generation immigrant youth]. So I didn't totally identify with them because they all had grown up in Korea, at least through some significant period of time. Korean was their first language and I didn't speak Korean and I didn't feel like I fit in with that group. And so I did a little bit with them but not a lot. It didn't really feel quite comfortable to me. And for the most part I ended up assimilating more with sort of more American Americans.

Again, both participants expressed feelings of not fitting in primarily because of the in-group solidarity of the immigrant population and language barriers. What is interesting about both of these participants is that they are siblings who grew up in Hawaii. So as multicultural and diverse as Hawaii is, both participants felt more comfortable socializing with their white peers and more distanced from co-ethnic peers. Wilson also related his experience from college:

> There was a Korean American group at UVA. You know they didn't talk to me. I didn't talk to them. It was the language barrier and cultural barrier, you could tell. They hung out themselves, by themselves, and I just blended in with everybody else because that's what I've always done.

Again as Jessica noted:

> You know there was a Korean student organization and there was an Asian student organization. I joined both of them but you know the Korean student organization, like [...] they would speak Korean at the meetings which made those of who didn't speak Korean feel excluded.

During the 1970s and 1980s, the new Korean immigrant population grew to be so large that they treated the American-born Koreans in a similar manner to how Nadia Kim's recent study of young second-generation Korean Americans were treated when they went to Korea. For this small cohort of American-born Korean Americans, not having heritage language skills in Korean created feelings of exclusion from the 1.5-generation Korean immigrant youth and the larger Korean community around them. These accounts of being excluded stem from the in-group solidarity that Koreans strongly adhere to. This also indicates that the 1.5-generation Koreans considered the second-generation Korean Americans to be outsiders. At that time, the difference in immigrant generational status (1.5 versus second) was the driving force behind this intra-group difference. It is important to note that the differences between the 1.5 generation and second generation were more blatant thirty years ago (compared to today) as the foreign-born Korean population was significantly larger than the U.S. born Koreans at that time. However, as recent immigrants, the 1.5 generation were not being consciously malicious by their actions of exclusion towards the second generation, they were just behaving as they would have in Korea. In essence, it was more like a misunderstanding between two cultures.

Korean Language versus English-only

Prior to 1970, there were strong social forces supporting assimilation—scientific research that genetically linked intelligence to language and claimed children learning more than one language would be confused and be cognitively slower (Portes and Rumbaut 1996). This basis justified the English language as the means for social acceptance and integration into American society (assimilation). Looking back on their childhood years, participants in this study were conscious of this assimilation that their parents desired for them. Yoona remembered her parents being told by their pediatrician to not teach their children Korean because it would lead to confusion, and their children would be made fun of by other children. She also said: "So [my parents] didn't know better. At the time, they didn't know that bilingual children actually had better brains [...] They didn't know stuff like that and they just wanted us to do as well as possible in this country." Devin, whose mother was a physician, clearly remembered:

"My parents were really very conscious not to speak Korean around me. They explained it to me later that they thought if they had exposed me to two languages, it would be confusing for me and I wouldn't really have the mastery of one over the other." This was the social and historical context that the second-wave Korean immigrant families faced, where the "English only" emphasis from the 1950s to the 1970s affected immigrant parents' perception and manner of how they socialized their children (emphasizing English over bilingual English and Korean).

In general, many Korean parents struggled with wanting to maintain the Korean culture within the family but simultaneously wanting their children to succeed in American culture. However, because the Korean community around this cohort was virtually non-existent, no one could foresee any future benefit of maintaining heritage language skills, which is strongly associated with ethnic identity (Min and Kim 1999; Portes and Hao 2002; Portes and Schauffler 1994, J. S. Lee 2002). Instead, these Korean parents (of the second immigration wave) encouraged their children to assimilate through English usage and to experience American culture in everyday living. Many participants expressed similar sentiments. Caterina says, "I didn't speak Korean. My parents didn't teach me any Korean." Patrick recalls, "I think my parents didn't push us to learn the Korean language. They spoke to us in English. They wanted us to assimilate." All the participants were keenly aware that their parents were conscious not to speak Korean around them, and some felt that as children they were blocked from learning their own heritage language: Korean. Mina remembered:

> My parents did not try very hard to teach us Korean. We were not raised to be bilingual. They pretty much always talked to us in English. They would often talk to themselves in Korean. That was a decision that they made. But I do know that she [mother] really wanted us to master English and she felt that if she tried to teach us both languages that it would hinder our ability to grasp English.

There was notable frustration as Jessica commented: "It's not that I didn't want to learn Korean. I mean, you know, I was a baby and was not taught it. I had no choice!" In looking back, some participants expressed regret over how they were raised. Randy lamented: "I have regrets about this looking back on this. Great efforts were made to assimilate us and therefore essentially limit our exposure to Korean language growing up." Interestingly, because education was the driving force that brought this second wave of Korean immigrants to America, these parents were in a unique position to facilitate the assimilation process for their children by speaking English to them. The experiences early in their developmental years had a significant impact on participants as they got older because language barriers to their heritage language continued to impede their inclusion into the Korean community. These reflections from participants also illustrate the tremendous pressure on the immigrant parents to teach their children English, especially if they wanted their American-born children to succeed in the U.S.

"I'm not really Korean"

The encounters participants had with the 1.5 generation and on visits to South Korea brought them to an unsettling conclusion. There were several poignant moments during the various interviews where participants articulated their feelings on not being accepted as Korean or not really considering themselves as being Korean. Caterina displayed mixed emotions as she related to me her move to South Korea and the reception she received from the Korean community:

> And then the first shocker came when I was nine years and moved to Korea. And then I realized that they didn't look at me as Korean at all. They called me the "American kid" even though I was from Canada. I was the "American kid." They all thought I was half Asian! None of them thought I looked Korean. So my identity there was as an outsider, of somebody with an accent who was viewed as half Korean [...] I did not view myself as American. But when I was in Korea, I did not view myself as Korean either. In Korea, I realized that I'm not fully Korean. And that Koreans don't view me as Korean at all.

This is a clear example of how Koreans conflate race, ethnicity, and citizenship. To the South Koreans, Caterina was an "American" citizen entering Korea. This is also a clear example of how Koreans perceive others who were born outside of South Korea. What a shock to be perceived as "half Asian." Both of her parents were full-blooded Koreans, born and raised in Korea, but who happened to emigrate to the U.S. for graduate studies and eventually return to their South Korean homeland. It may have been that her parents had not anticipated a return to their native homeland and as such, did not teach their daughter how to speak Korean or practice cultural mannerisms. Along these same lines, Josie ruefully stated: "I mean, I'm not Korean, really. I mean 'Korean-Korean.' I mean I don't speak the language, right?" Many other participants also felt marginalized from their ethnic communities because of this language barrier. They expressed regret or confusion just as Jessica articulated:

> I did not grow up speaking Korean. I understand quite a lot of it but at some point very early on my parents stopped teaching me Korean, which was a big mistake [...] I think if there weren't as much a language barrier and I could operate more freely like in, you know, what is a very large Korean community here and in Flushing and various other places. I probably wouldn't have the same issues, but like I don't even feel comfortable.

Or as Derek exclaimed: "Yeah it's a head trip and you can't speak to them and you really want to. You're aching to engage with them and you can't because you can't speak the language!" Derek also observed that:

> I think being Korean or being of any ethnic identity is governed by language and you access culture through language. If you do not speak that language, then you have a very limited ability to access that culture. I don't speak Korean so I am fully aware of the fact that I can never be "fully" Korean.

This last comment was so eloquent in connecting language to culture and how that connection is used to define who is Korean. The participants in this study tried so diligently to learn English and to assimilate into American culture that it created a language barrier to their own heritage language. This language barrier, in turn, was the prominent obstacle for participants to fully accept themselves as Korean or be accepted as being a "real Korean" by other Koreans. The effect of not knowing the Korean language continues to have an impact on participants today. As summed up by Nadia Kim (2009), it is the "Korean American's inability to gain acceptance from people who look just like them proves rather disappointing and disheartening" (409).

Discussion

This chapter focused on authenticity issues as a "Korean" that this group of second-generation Korean Americans faced as they were caught between two cultural worlds that are so prominent in their lives. There are some important implications found in the data. The first is that even at an early age, participants had to negotiate their identity between trying to be white and comprehending their Koreanness. Participants' experiences with racial foreignness from their white peers only reinforced to them their Koreanness. These experiences helped participants to realize their Korean identity. Also, having two Korean parents, participants know they are genetically and ethnically Korean. However, though they understood that their phenotypical features were Korean, they were more knowledgeable about and culturally more comfortable to behave like their white peers rather than their co-ethnic peers.

For these participants, the issue of authenticity as Koreans arose primarily from not being accepted by their co-ethnic peers and community. In the company of other Koreans, mainly from the immigrant community, the "authenticity" of their Koreanness would come into question. Whenever participants were in a Korean community setting (whether in the U.S. or in Korea), their co-ethnic peers identified them as cultural foreigners, and the message was that they were not really "Korean." It seems like there was confusion from being told by their parents they are Korean but also being told by their co-ethnic peers they are not. There was confusion from differing sets of expectations, without explanations from either side as to why they were not accepted as a Korean.

Another part of the issue surrounding this idea of authenticity stems from differences in how identity is defined. In a country such as the U.S. that was founded on diverse immigrant groups, ethnicity is a strong marker for ethnic identity. Ethnic identity is also often associated with racial identity. However, the critiques around that association are better left for another conversation. Nonetheless, the racial divide between whites and blacks in the U.S. seems to be resistant to time. Today, the unresolvable question is where Asians/Asian Americans (who are neither white nor black) fit into this schema. Tuan (1999) states that the debate surrounding the authenticity dilemma for Asian Americans in the U.S. is that they are considered neither real "Americans" nor real "Asians." In this way, we can see how the U.S. tends to categorize and group people by their race or phenotypical features. However, in Korea, race is defined differently. In Korea, a country that is obsessed with purity of blood and views themselves as ethnically homogeneous, every other Asian group is considered another race. This definition of race does not focus solely on phenotypical features as it does in the U.S., but rather, it is a proxy for ethnicity and culture. Consequently, this is how race and culture plus citizenship define a national identity in Korea.

On a concluding note, there are additional thoughts to consider. One is that for many immigrants, their heritage culture seems to get "frozen" in time, meaning they bring with them the prevailing culture at the time of emigration. However, culture does not stand still and is continuously changing (i.e. in South Korea, as well as in the U.S.). Over the last several decades, South Korea has undergone dramatic changes as they moved from a military dictatorship to a democratic nation, plus the rapid economic boom. Recent liberalized immigration laws have started to change Korea into a more multicultural nation. Although the deep-rooted ideology from the early twentieth century until the late 1980s was *danil minjok*, there has recently been a shift to another discourse, moving away from the ethnic blood-based ideas of nationhood to one focusing on a democratic Korea called *minjung* (the masses) (H. Kim 2009; Shin 2006b). All these changes lead to a change in how Koreans begin to understand Koreans in the diaspora. Participants in this study might find that "newer" Korean immigrants are different compared to the Korean immigrants of the 1970s and 1980s. This is another area of future research in how these changes in South Korea are affecting the immigrant communities in the U.S. And a final note is that in recent years, there has been a growing Korean American community within the U.S. Two excellent examples are the website titled "I am Korean American," and the KYOPO Project (2011) by Cindy Hwang (CYJO), which is both a book and a photography exhibit. All the 200+ photographs from the book are on display at the Smithsonian National Portrait Gallery in Washington, D.C. until October 2012. This is also noteworthy of more research into the meaning and culture behind the Korean American community.

Notes

1. Although the influx of migrant workers and intermarried brides from many Asian countries over the last two decades has made South Korea far more diverse than before.

2. Tan'gun is the mythical founder of the Korean people (N. Kim 2008; Shin 2006b).

3. *Danil Minjok* was firmly established during the regimes of Rhee Syngman (1956-1960) and Park Chung Hee (1971-1979). This form of Korean nationalism was later replaced with *minjung* as Korea transitioned from a military dictatorship to a democratic nation.

4. Census information and/or other datasets do not identify them and this cohort is not connected with Korean communities.

5. Excluded from this study were immigrant children (the 1.5 generation), Korean adoptees, and children of inter-racial marriages.

6. Boston, New York, Washington D.C., Los Angeles, San Francisco, Seattle, and Chicago.

7. Remember that most of the Korean community lived either in Hawaii or California.

References

Alba, Richard, and Victor Nee. 1997. "Rethinking Assimilation Theory for a New Era of Immigration." *The International Migration Review* 31 (4), 826-875.

Alba, Richard, and Victor Nee. 2003. *Remaking American Mainstream: Assimilation and Contemporary Immigration.* Cambridge: Harvard University Press.

Berry, John. 2003. "Conceptual Approaches to Acculturation." In *Acculturation: Advances in Theory, Measurement, and Applied Research*, edited by Kevin M. Chun, Pamela Balls Organista, and Gerado Marin, 17-37. Washington, DC: American Psychological Association.

Chong, Kelly H. 1998. "What it Means to be Christian: The Role of Religion in the Construction of Ethnic Identity and Boundary among Second-Generation Korean Americans." *Sociology of Religion* 59 (3), 259-267.

Cummings, Bruce. 1997. *Korea's Place in the Sun: A Modern History.* New York: W.W. Norton and Company.

Danico, Mary Yu. 2004. *The 1.5 Generation: Becoming Korean American in Hawaii.* Honolulu, HI: University of Hawaii Press.

Eckstein, Susan, and Lorena Barberia. 2002. "Grounding Immigrant Generations in History: Cuban Americans and their Transnational Ties." *The International Migration Review* 36 (3), 799-838.

Hurh, W. M. 1980. "Towards a Korean American Ethnicity: Some Theoretical Models. *Ethnic and Racial Studies* 3 (4).

Jacoby, T. 2004. "What it Means to be American in the 21st Century." In *Reinventing the Melting Pot: The New Immigrants and What It Means To Be American*, edited by Tamar Jacoby. New York: Basic Books.

Kim, H. J. 2009. *Immigration Challenges and 'Multicultural' Responses: The State, The Dominant Ethnie and Immigrants in South Korea.* Unpublished dissertation (sociology). University of Wisconsin-Madison.

Kim, Nadia Y. 2008. *Imperial Citizens. Koreans and Race from Seoul to LA.* Stanford, CA: Stanford University Press.

Kim, Nadia Y. 2009. "Finding Our Way Home: Korean Americans, 'Homeland' Trips, and Cultural Foreignness." In *Diasporic Homecomings: Ethnic Return Migration in Comparative Perspective*, edited by Takeyuki Tsuda, 409-430. Stanford University Press.

Kitano, H., and R. Daniels. 1995. *Asian Americans: Emerging Minorities.* Englewood Cliffs, NJ: Prentice Hall.

Lee, J. S. 2002. "The Korean Language in America: The Role of Cultural Identity in Heritage Language Learning." *Language, Culture and Curriculum* 15 (2), 117-133.

Min, Pyong Gap. 1998. *Changes and Conflicts: Korean Immigrant Families in New York.* Boston: Allyn and Bacon.

Min, Pyong Gap, and Rose Kim (eds.). 1999. *Struggle for Ethnic Identity: Nar-*

ratives by Asian American Professionals. Walnut Creek, CA: Altamira Press.
Min, Pyong Gap, and Rose Kim. 2002. "Formation of Ethnic and Racial Identities: Narratives by Asian American Professionals." In *The Second Generation: Ethnic Identity among Asian Americans*, edited by Pyong Gap Min, 153-181. Walnut Creek, CA: Altamira Press.
Okihiro, G. Y. 2001. *The Columbia Guide to Asian American History*. New York: Columbia University Press.
Omi, M., and H. Winant. 1994. *Racial Formation in the United States* 2nd Edition. New York: Routledge.
Patterson, W. 2000. *The Ilse: 1st Generation Korean Immigrants in Hawaii, 1903-1973* (Hawaiian Studies on Korea). Honolulu, HI: University of Hawaii Press.
Phinney, J. 2003. "Ethnic Identity and Acculturation." In *Acculturation Advances in Theory, Measurement, and Applied Research*, edited by Kevin M. Chun, Pamela Balls Organista, and Gerado Marin, 63-81. Washington, DC: American Psychological Association.
Portelli, A. 1991. *Death of Luigi Trastulli, and Other Stories: Form and Meaning in Oral History*. Albany, NY: State University of New York Press.
Portes, A., and L. Hao. 2002. "The Price of Uniformity: Language, Family, and Personality Adjustment in the Immigrant Second Generation." *Ethnic and Racial Studies* 25 (6): 889-912.
Portes, A., and R. G. Rumbaut. 1996. *Immigrant America: A Portrait*. Berkeley, CA: University of California Press.
Portes, A., and R. G. Rumbaut. 2001. *Legacies: The Story of the Immigrant Second Generation*. Berkeley, CA: University of California Press.
Portes, A., and R. Schauffler. 1994. "Language and the Second Generation: Bilingualism Yesterday and Today." *The International Migration Review* 28 (4): 640-658.
Scott, J., and D. Alwin. 1998. "Retrospective vs. Prospective Measurement of Life Histories in Longitudinal Research." In *Crafting Life Studies: Intersection of Personal and Social History*, edited by J. Z. Geile and G. H. Elder, Jr. Thousand Oaks, CA: Sage Publications.
Segal, U. A. 2002. *Framework for Immigration: Asians in the United States*. New York: Columbia University Press
Shim, T. Y., M. S. Kim, and J. N. Martin. 2008. *Changing Korea: Understanding Culture and Communication*. New York: Peter Lang Publishing, Inc.
Shin, G. W. 2006a. "Ethnic Pride Source of Prejudice, Discrimination." *Korea Herald*. August 2, 2006.
Shin, G. W. 2006b. *Ethnic Nationalism in Korea: Genealogy, Politics, and Legacy*. California: Stanford University Press.
Suárez-Orozco, C., and M.M. Suárez-Orozco. 2001. *Children of Immigration*. Cambridge, MA: Harvard University Press.
Takaki, R. 1998. *Strangers from a Different Shore: A History of Asian Americans*. Boston: Back Bay Books: Little, Brown, and Company.
Tuan, M. 1998. *Forever Foreigners or Honorary Whites?: The Asian Ethnic*

Experience Today. New Brunswick, NJ: Rutgers University Press.

Tuan, M. 1999. "Neither Real Americans nor Real Asians?: Multigenerational Asian Ethnics Navigating the Terrain of Authenticity." *Qualitative Sociology* 22 (2): 105-125.

Yanow, D. 2003. *Constructing "Race" and "Ethnicity" in America: Category-Making in Public Policy and Administration.* New York: M.E. Sharpe, Inc.

Yu, E. Y., and P. Choe. 2003-2004. "Korean Population in the United States as Reflected in the Year 2000 U.S. Census." *Amerasia Journal* 29 (3): 2-21.

Zhou, M. 1997. "Growing up American: The Challenge Confronting Immigrant Children and Children of Immigrants." *Annual Review of Sociology* 23: 63-95.

Chapter 11
A Four-Decade Literature on Korean Americans: A Review and a Comprehensive Bibliography

by Pyong Gap Min

Introduction

Approximately 7,200 Korean workers who moved to sugar plantations in Hawaii between 1903 and 1905 comprised the first wave of Korean immigrants to the United States. However, this pioneering Korean immigration came to a sudden end in 1905 when Korea became a protectorate of Japan in 1905. Only about 2,000 more Koreans, mostly consisting of "picture brides" of the pioneer bachelor immigrants and political refugees/students during the Japanese annexation period, moved to the United States before Congress completely barred immigration from Korea and other Asian countries with the passage of the so-called national-origin quota system (National Origins Formula) in 1924. The military, political, and economic linkages between the United States and South Korea with the start of the Korean War in 1950 contributed to a resumption of Korean immigration to the United States. But the total number of Korean immigrants who immigrated to the United States between 1950 and 1964 was only about 15,000.

It was the liberalized Immigration and Nationality Act of 1965 that ignited the mass migration of Koreans to the United States. Between 1976 and 1990, South Korea sent more than 30,000 immigrants annually to the United States, emerging as the third largest source country of immigrants to this country. The improvements in economic, political, and social conditions in South Korea has contributed to a moderation of the Korean immigration flow to the United States since the early 1990s, but South Korea still remains as one of the top ten source countries of immigrants. The influx of Korean immigrants to the United States since the late 1960s has led to the increase in the Korean American population from less than 70,000 in 1970 to nearly 1.4 million (including multiracial Koreans) in 2005.

One of the major results of the mass migration of Koreans to the United States in the last four decades is a phenomenal increase in numbers of both scholars studying Korean Americans and scholarly publications on Korean Americans. As listed in the attached bibliography, more than one hundred books and several hundred journal articles and book chapters focusing on or covering Korean Americans have been published. Topics covered in these publications are diverse, but some topics have received far more attention than others. There have been changes over time in the authors' gender and generation compositions.

Providing a comprehensive review of the four-decade literature on Korean Americans should be of great help to doctoral students and scholars who conduct research on Korean Americans. In order to facilitate the research of others, I intend to do two interrelated things in this chapter regarding the literature on Korean Americans. First, I will provide a systematic review of studies of Korean Americans. By "systematic review," I am referring to reviewing studies and their authors both chronologically and topically. A chronological analysis of Korean American studies includes examining changes in research trends in terms of the authors' gender, generation, and age. My topical review includes making complimentary comments on significant books and journal articles related to particular research topics and suggesting research issues of importance that have been neglected by researchers. Second, I will provide a comprehensive list of books, journal articles, and book chapters focusing on or covering Korean Americans. I will list books and edited anthologies first, and then journal articles and book chapters divided into major topics. I believe that a comprehensive bibliography will be very useful to those researchers who need to conduct library research for the literature review on a chosen topic. Moreover, my informed review of the literature on Korean Americans is expected to help researchers to choose topics of importance on Korean Americans. In addition, I hope this review article will give researchers general ideas about the past and current status of Korean American studies and its future direction.

In the remainder of the introductory section, I need to give criteria for selecting scholarly works focusing on Korean Americans in the bibliography. Scholarly publications include books, edited anthologies, peer-reviewed journal articles, book chapters, working papers, research reports, dissertations, and other forms. But not all can be included in this bibliography. I have selected those works that have been recognized as important works through peer reviews or considered to be important for Korean American experiences. First, I have selected books, including edited anthologies, focusing on or related to Korean American experiences. Many good academic books about particular aspects of

Korean American experiences have been published through university presses or commercial publishers over the past forty years. I have tried to include all these books. Some books cover Korean Americans as one of several major Asian ethnic groups without focusing on them, but provide very useful information about them. For example, Ronald Takaki's *Strangers from a Different Shore* (1989) is a popular textbook for Asian American history classes. It devotes one separate chapter to Korean immigration history and another chapter to the discussion of Korean and other Asian immigrants' adjustments. I have included this and other similar books.

University research centers and professional organizations have published many edited books focusing on Korean immigrants, especially in the 1970s and early 1980s. Although some of these earlier publications are based on papers presented at conferences, the quality of many of them is dubious. Some of these books have reprinted articles that were already published in journals. Nevertheless, I have tried to include most of these edited books. Some edited books cover Korean Americans as one of several major Asian American groups in particular chapters. I have included these edited books because they too can serve as good guides for research on Korean Americans.

I have tried to select almost all articles published in major academic journals and book chapters that focus on Korean Americans or treat the Korean group as one of the major Asian groups. However, I have not included articles published in marginal Korean American journals. Also, I have not separately listed those book chapters included in the edited anthologies focusing on Korean Americans already listed in the book section. The main reason I have not included these book chapters separately is that, as already pointed out above, most of these edited books include low-quality pieces. In some cases, the edited books have used already-published journal articles. The exceptions to this rule are two books, *Korean Americans and Their Religion: Pilgrims and Missionaries from a Different Shore*, edited by Ho-Youn Kwon, Kwang Chung Kim, and Stephen Warner (2001), and *Korean Economy and Community in the 21st Century*, edited by Eui-Young Yu, Houjoung Kim, Kyeyoung Park, and Moonsong David Oh (2009). Most chapters in these two anthologies are high-quality pieces based on newly collected data. Thus, I have decided to include most chapters of these two books in the separate article/book chapter category.

I have included book chapters that cover Korean Americans that are included in edited books focusing on Asian Americans or other minority groups. For many working papers and research reports that cover Korean American experiences, I have selected only those that I consider very important for research on Korean Americans. A large number of dissertations focusing on Korean Americans are available, but I have not included any of them in this bibliography unless they have been published as monographs by publishers.

The vast majority of works included in this bibliography were written by sociologists or other social scientists. The other reference entries belong mostly to historical or cultural studies. But I have not included any literary works about Korean American experiences. I may have failed to include many social science studies in such fields as education, social services, and health science, mainly because I have little connection with Korean American faculty members in these fields.

I. Review of the Literature on Korean Americans

As shown in Table 11.1, all together, I have located 122 books focusing on or covering Korean Americans. Even after eliminating books that cover Korean Americans along with other Asian American groups (16), there are more than 100 published books and edited anthologies that focus only on Korean American experiences. Thirty-one of them, which are edited books, are generally based on papers presented at conferences or rehashes of already-published materials. They were published by university centers, professional organizations, or university publishers in Korea. These are academically low-quality books. The remaining seventy-seven books are important scholarly works based on solid research and published by university presses or major commercial publishers.

Table 11.1: Number of Books and Edited Anthologies Focusing on or Covering Korean Americans

Books Focusing on Korean Americans	Edited Anthologies Focusing on Korean Americans	Books or Edited Books that Cover Korean Americans in Two or More Chapters	**Total**
77	31	16	**124**

I have gathered 462 journal articles and book chapters (see Table 11.2). Due to my unfamiliarity with other fields of studies, I may have failed to locate many journal articles and book chapters that focus on Korean immigrants or Korean Americans. Given that, I suggest that the actual number of published journal articles and book chapters that cover Korean immigrants and/or Korean Americans may be close to 600 as of November 2009.

Considering that research on Korean immigrants and Korean Americans only started in the 1970s, we can say that Korean Americans have been actively researched over the last thirty or forty years. Korean Americans have received more scholarly attention than any other Asian group, with the exception of Chinese Americans. One reason that Korean Americans have been studied so much is the presence of many Korean American social scientists who have shown great interest in conducting research on their own group. As we can see from the bibliography, the vast majority of the authors of books, book chapters, and journal articles have Korean surnames. Both the Filipino and Indian communities have much larger populations than the Korean community and have advantages in English, yet they have much fewer scholars studying their own ethnic groups.

Table 11.2: Number of Articles and Book Chapters by Topic

Businesses and Business-Related Inter-group Conflicts	102	22%
Family Relations, Women, the Elderly, and Social Services	81	18%
Religious Practices and Religious Organizations	47	10%
Children, Education, and Psychology	54	12%
Socioeconomic Attainments and Assimilation	38	8%
Adoptees, War Brides, and Others	37	8%
Other Categories*	103	22%
Total	**462**	**100%**

*Other categories include (1) History, (2) Immigration and Settlement Patterns, (3) Ethnicity and Transnationalism, (4) Korean Community, Ethnic Organizations and Political Development, (4) Children, Education and Psychology, and (5) Korean Americans in General

II. Review by Chronological Order

In the 1970s and 1980s, several Korean immigrant scholars, predominantly sociologists, played a key role in conducting research on Korean immigrants, laying the groundwork for Korean American studies. They include Hyung Chan Kim, Won Moo Hurh, Kwang Chung Kim, Eui-Young Yu, Eui Hang Shin, and Pyong Gap Min. These social scientists have published a large number of books and journal articles focusing on Korean immigrants. All these Korean pioneering scholars, with the exception of Eui Hang Shin and Pyong Gap Min, are now retired from their universities. Nevertheless Kwang Chung Kim and Eui-Young Yu are still actively engaged in research after retirement. I should also point out that Alice Chai and Bok Lim Kim, as Korean immigrant women scholars, greatly contributed to research on Korean immigrants in the earlier period. Finally, Illsoo Kim is another pioneering immigrant scholar, although he stayed in academia only for a short period of time. His 1981 book focusing on the Korean immigrant community in New York, *New Urban Immigrants: The Korean Community in New York,* still remains as a classic in the field of research on new immigrants.

Young In Song, Ailee Moon, and Kyeyoung Park comprise the second group of Korean immigrant scholars who have emerged since the late 1980s.

Kyeyoung Park is an anthropologist while the other two scholars specialize in social work. As a fierce feminist, Young In Song did extensive research on women's issues from a feminist perspective. But sadly, I learned that she passed away four years ago at a young age. Ailee Moon has made a major contribution to research on the Korean elderly. Including the articles cited here, she has published over thirty single-authored or co-authored articles on Korean and other ethnic elderly people. Still young, she is expected to publish more in the coming years.

The establishment of Asian American studies programs in many colleges and universities over the past two decades has helped many young 1.5- and second-generation Korean social scientists and Asian American specialists find academic positions. Many of them have joint appointments with Asian American studies programs and social science departments. The gradual increase in the number of younger-generation Korean American professors in ethnic studies, sociology, anthropology, education, and other social science fields has contributed to the expansion of Korean American studies over the last two decades. Edward Chang and Edward Park, both 1.5-generation Korean Americans, are older members of this newly emerging younger-generation group of Korean American specialists. In-Jin Yoon is not a product of Asian American studies, but belongs to the same cohort as Edward Chang and had some teaching experience in the Asian American Studies Department at University of California-Santa Barbara before he moved to Korea University. Many younger 1.5- and second-generation Korean Americans have followed their footsteps and have been conducting research on Korean Americans since the mid-1990s. The list of these younger-generation scholars includes David Yoo, Karen Chai, Kelly Chong, Angie Chung, Ruth Chung, Miliann Kang, Dae Young Kim, Nadia Kim, Rebecca Kim, Jennifer Lee, Jamie Lew, and Eleana Kim. As many younger-generation Korean Americans are currently writing Ph.D. dissertations focusing on Korean Americans, the list of these young scholars will continue to expand, which means that the social science literature on Korean Americans will also continue to grow.

Like the pioneering Korean immigrant scholars, most of these younger-generation scholars are sociologists. But while the immigrant scholars are overwhelmingly men, almost all of the above-mentioned younger-generation scholars are women. This radical gender reversal over generations partly reflects the general pattern in social science disciplines in the United States. Whereas the predominant majority of Ph.D. students in sociology and other social science disciplines in the 1960s and early 1970s were men, the majority of recipients of Ph.D. degrees during recent years have been women. For example, approximately 70% of current Ph.D. students in my sociology classes at the CUNY Graduate Center are women. But women seem to be overrepresented among younger-generation Korean American scholars studying Korean Americans to a greater extent than young social scientists in the United States in general. The numerical dominance of women in Korean American studies may be due partly to the nature of ethnic studies, which Korean American studies is a part of. Ethnic studies, with more humanistic and post-modernist approaches, may be more popular to women than to men.

The drastic change in the gender composition between immigrant-generation and younger-generation scholars has also led to major changes in research methods used. The pioneering immigrant sociologists mainly used quantitative data, especially survey and census data, for research on Korean immigrants, although Illsoo Kim and Pyong Gap Min usually combined both quantitative and qualitative data. In sharp contrast to the immigrant sociologists, 1.5- and second-generation Korean American sociologists and other social scientists exclusively use qualitative methods involving participant observations and in-depth personal interviews. Many of them also take the post-modernist approach, using discursive analysis. The radical transformation in research methods and approaches can be attributed to their age and gender. Young female social scientists have a greater tendency to utilize qualitative research methods and the post-modernist approach than other social scientists. The major methodological difference between Korean immigrant and younger-generational sociologists is also due to the effect of time. Sociologists today use qualitative data and take the post-modernist approach far more frequently than they did twenty or thirty years ago.

Younger-generation Korean American scholars' utilization of qualitative data, combined with their good writing skills, gives them advantages in publishing books through major publishers. Several younger-generation Korean social scientists have turned their dissertations into significant books during recent years. For example, Nadia Kim, a second-generation Korean American rising star in sociology, typically uses the qualitative method. Her 2008 dissertation-turned-book, *Imperial Citizens: Koreans and Race from Seoul to LA*, received national book awards from two sections of the American Sociological Association in 2009. For this book, she used tape-recorded personal interviews and ethnographic observations of Korean immigrants in Los Angeles. She argued that Korean immigrants' views of the white-black racial hierarchies in America was shaped in Korea under the impact of American state power, media, and consuming markets there, with some views transformed while others consolidated in Los Angeles. I will have a chance to introduce other prominent books by second-generation Korean scholars later in connection with particular topics of research.

III. Review by Topic

There are not many historical studies of Korean Americans because Korean immigration history is relatively short, much shorter than Chinese, Japanese, and Filipino histories in the United States. I have counted only two dozen journal articles and book chapters that I can put into the category of history. However, I have found twenty-three books that focus on Korean immigration history, which is a significantly higher number than I had originally anticipated. Wayne Patterson and Hyung Chan Kim, two historians, are responsible for seven of these books. Without these two dedicated historians, we would suffer from a lack of historical information about the Korean American community. In particular, Wayne Patterson's books are based on solid historical research involving documents in Korea, Hawaii, and the U.S. mainland. Bong-Youn Choi's book, *Koreans in America,* published in 1979, is also a useful book to researchers of Korean American history. Korean immigrant sociologists who have conducted research on Korean immigrants, including myself, have immensely benefited from it.

David Yoo is a well-known second-generation Korean historian. He has conducted historical research mainly on Japanese Americans, but recently he completed a very important book, *Contentious Spirits: A Religious History of Korean Americans* (2010). The book highlights the role of Korean immigrant churches in the West Coast in the transnational Korean independence movement during the colonization period. Published in 2010, this book has already attracted a lot of attention. Ji-Yeon Yuh, another younger-generation historian, published *Beyond the Shadow of Camptown: Korean Military Brides in America* (2002). This book, based on oral history of many former camptown women, is both historical and sociological.

The following three sources should be greatly useful to researchers who want to explain the influx of Korean immigrants to the United States in the post-1965 period: (1) Illsoo Kim's 1981 book *New Urban Immigrants: The Korean Community in New York,* (2) In-Jin Yoon's 1993 paper "The Social Origins of Korean Immigration to the United States from 1965 to the Present," which was published by the Population Institute, East-West Center, and (3) Pyong Gap Min's 2006 book chapter "Asian Immigration: History and Contemporary Trends." Researchers who want know about changes in Korean immigrant patterns during recent years should consult Eui-Young Yu's chapter (Chapter 1) included in his 2009 co-edited book *Korean Economy and Community in the 21st Century* and Pyong Gap Min's 2006 book chapter on Asian immigration history in his edited book *Asian Americans: Contemporary Trends and Issues.*

Researchers interested in Korean Americans' overall settlement patterns should read Pyong Gap Min's 2006 book chapter "Settlement Patterns and Diversity" and Eui-Young Yu's 2003-2004 co-edited article "Korean Population as Reflected in the Year 2000 U.S. Census." Los Angeles's Koreatown has several sociologically interesting dimensions of an immigrant enclave. With the exception of Katherine Yungmee Kim's *Los Angeles's Koreatown* (2011), which has a more journalistic and historical style and approach, no one has written a book focusing on Koreatown. Considering that there are a dozen books about Chinatowns, someone should start a book project on Koreatown in Los Angeles. He/she will find enough sources for such a book: (1) Eui-Young Yu's two articles on Koreatown (1985 and 2004), (2) Angie Chung's 2007 book, *Legacies of Struggles,* and (3) two book chapters focusing on Koreatown, one by David Lee and the other by Kyonghwan Park and Youngmin Lee, included in *Korean*

American Economy and Community in the 21st Century (2009), and (4) Katherine Yungmee Kim's aforementioned book (2011).

Korean immigrants' business activities and their business-related intergroup conflicts have received more scholarly attention than any other topic. Twenty-two (18%) of the 120 books and 102 (about 22%) of the 462 articles/book chapters are related to Korean immigrants' commercial activities and business-related conflicts with other ethnic groups. Considering that nearly half of Korean immigrant families were engaged in small businesses in the 1980s and 1990s, and that Korean immigrant merchants encountered severe conflicts with black customers, white suppliers, Latino employees, and government agencies during these time periods, it is not surprising that this topic received a great deal of scholarly attention.

These business-related inter-group tensions include Korean-black conflicts in the forms of black boycotts of Korean stores in New York City and Los Angeles and the victimization of many Korean merchants during the 1992 Los Angeles riots. These occurrences can be considered among the most significant historical events in Korean American history. Fifteen books and about forty journal articles/book chapters cover Korean-black conflicts during the fifteen-year period between 1980 and 1995. This topic drew the attention of many researchers, whose books in turn were well received in academia. Clair Jean Kim's *Bitter Fruits* (2000) and Pyong Gap Min's *Caught in the Middle* (1996) each received two national book awards. Other books focusing on Korean-black conflicts that have received a great deal of attention are Nancy Abelmann and John Lie's *Blue Dreams* (1995), Jennifer Lee's *Civility in the City* (2002), and In-Jin Yoon's *On My Own* (1997). In 2002, Jennifer Lee's article "From Civil Relations to Racial Conflict: Merchant-Customer Interactions in Urban America" was published in the *American Journal of Sociology*, the most prestigious sociology journal. Several years earlier, in 1996, Kyeyoung Park published her article, "Use and Abuse of Race and Culture: Black-Korean Tension in America," in *American Anthropologist*, probably the most important anthropological journal.

A review of Korean ethnic dailies reveals that black boycotts of Korean stores, which were prevalent in the 1980s and early 1990s, have disappeared with the two last boycotts in New York City and Los Angeles in 1995. Researchers had long kept silent about whether black boycotts of Korean stores came to an end, and if so why. Pyong Gap Min finally broke this silence with publication of his book, *Ethnic Solidarity for Economic Survival: Korean Greengrocers in New York City*, in 2008. In this book, he explains that due to changes in the structure of lower-income black neighborhoods, Korean merchants there no longer play the typical middleman minority role. The changes in structure of black neighborhoods are characterized by a phenomenal increase in retail mega-stores under the impact of urban renovations, and the racial and ethnic diversity of both business owners and residents there influenced by the diversity of the contemporary immigration flows. This means that Korean-black conflict is no longer an important research topic.

In his two major books (1996 and 2008) and many other publications, Pyong Gap Min has also examined the positive effect of Korean immigrants' business-related inter-group conflicts on ethnic solidarity. Theoretically, this direction of research is almost the opposite of the ethnic resources theory in conventional studies of immigrant entrepreneurship, the theory that ethnic ties and resources contribute to the development and operation of immigrant businesses. His immigrant business-ethnic solidarity hypothesis is considered a unique and very significant theoretical contribution to the field of immigrant entrepreneurship.

The articles and book chapters focusing on family relations, women, the elderly, and social services comprise the second largest category with eighty-one. Given the importance of family life and different components of the family, it is quite natural that these family-related topics have been popular among researchers. As previously pointed out, Ailee Moon has published a large number of articles and book chapters focusing on the Korean elderly, which comprise a significant portion of the publications included in this category. When we set aside her work, we find that most of the other articles and book chapters included in this category focus on Korean immigrant families and Korean immigrant women. Kwang Chung Kim and Pyong Gap Min are responsible for a large number of these publications. Kim and Min, both male sociologists, have shown that Korean immigrant women suffer from double burdens as housewives and participants in paid work. *Changes and Conflicts: Korean Immigrant Families in New York* (1998), a shorter book by Min, has been widely used as a reader in many Asian American and sociology courses. It is somewhat surprising that no female sociologist has conducted extensive research on Korean immigrant families. Also, there is currently no study available that sheds light on second-generation Korean American families. Younger-generation Korean American scholars are strongly encouraged to conduct research on their own families.

There are a few scholars who deserve to be mentioned in connection with their contribution to Korean immigrant women's issues. As noted earlier, feminist scholar Young In Song, who passed away a few years ago, had conducted extensive research on important women's issues, including the issue of family violence. In the book section, we can find a book authored by her, *Silent Victims: Battered Women in Korean Immigrant Families* (1996), and two co-edited books focusing on women's issues. Social workers and graduate students who are interested in Korean immigrant women should consult these books. Although the book chapters in the two edited books are not all excellent, they provide valuable data sources for beginning researchers. Miliann Kang has four articles/book chapters and a forthcoming book focusing on Korean nail salons in New York City. She has analyzed Korean nail salon workers from a feminist perspective. Her 2003 article, entitled "The Managed Hand: The Commercialization of Bodies and Emotions in Korean Immigrant-Owned Nail Salons," published in *Gender and Society*, has been reprinted in several other books.

Won Moo Hurh and Kwang Chung Kim received a few major grants from the National Institute of Mental Health to conduct research on Korean immigrants in Los Angeles and Chicago in the 1980s. Their surveys examined Korean immigrants' cultural and social assimilation, and socioeconomic adaptations. Based on survey data collected in Chicago, the two Korean immigrant sociologists published many articles and a major book, *Korean Immigrants in America: A Structural Analysis of Ethnic Confinement and Adhesive Adaptation* (1985). The main findings of the book are that Korean immigrants achieve cultural and limited social assimilation in proportion to their length of residence, but that the latter does not reduce their ethnic attachment. They thus argue that assimilation and ethnic attachment do not maintain the zero-sum relationship. Hurh and Kim have co-authored so many publications that they have become household names, not only to most Korean American sociologists, but also to many other Asian American sociologists. They made an important scholarly contribution to research on immigrants through major survey studies.

Researchers usually use publicly available census data, like Public Use Microdata Sample (PUMS), to examine the socioeconomic attainments of minority groups. When Asian American scholars analyze PUMS to examine Asian Americans' socioeconomic attainments and intergenerational mobility, they usually treat major Asian ethnic groups separately. The 1980 and 1990 U.S. Censuses did not have a native-born Korean sample large enough for data analyses. But the 2000 Census and the American Community Surveys conducted since 2001 have included a native-born Korean sample large enough for data analyses. Arthur Sakamoto and his associates have published numerous articles that examined major Asian ethnic groups' socioeconomic attainments separately. I have included in the bibliography several studies by Sakamoto and his associates, in addition to studies by Yoon that examine native-born Korean Americans' socioeconomic attainments in comparison to other Asian groups.

These studies show that native-born Korean Americans have a substantially higher educational level than Korean immigrants. In addition, the majority of second-generation Korean Americans hold professional and managerial jobs in the mainstream economy, which is in sharp contrast to the prevalence of small-business owners among their parent generation. Results of Dae Young Kim's survey of more than two-hundred 1.5- and second-generation Koreans confirm the major findings from census data about the overwhelming majority of native-born Koreans participating in the mainstream economy (see Kim's 2004 book chapter "Leaving the Ethnic Economy: The Rapid Integration of Second-Generation Korean Americans in New York," and 2006 article "Stepping Stone to Intergenerational Mobility?: The Springboard, Safety Net, or Mobility Trap Functions of Korean Immigrant Entrepreneurship for the Second Generation").

Intermarriage is an important indicator of assimilation. Researchers have frequently used census data to analyze intermarriage patterns. I have listed several studies that examined Asian Americans' intermarriage rates and patterns. Previous studies overestimated the intermarriage rate of native-born Koreans by including all married people in the sample because older native-born Koreans who grew up with little interaction with other Koreans before 1950 had a much higher intermarriage rate. In order to assess the intermarriage rates and patterns among children of recent Asian immigrants, Pyong Gap Min and Chigon Kim (2009) selected only native-born Asian Americans born in 1965 and after from the 2001-2005 American Community Surveys. Their analyses show that native-born Korean Americans' intermarriage rate is 54%, close to the Asian American average of 55%. They also show that another 23% of native-born Koreans are married to 1.5- or first-generation Korean immigrants. This means that only 23% of native-born Koreans have other native-born co-ethnic partners. Previous intermarriage studies, whether focusing on Asian Americans or other minority groups, have usually used marriage as a dichotomous variable involving inter-marriage and in-marriage. But Min and Kim's study (2009) has shown that about half of native-born Korean and other Asian Americans with co-ethnic partners engage in what is called "cross-generational in-marriage." Separating different types of in-marriage has an important implication for research on the adaptation of native-born Korean Americans because those married to co-ethnic immigrant partners are far more likely to use mother tongue at home and maintain much stronger transnational ties with their homeland than those married to native-born co-ethnic partners (see Kim and Min's 2010 article "Marital Patterns and Use of Mother Tongue at Home among Native-Born Asian Americans").

Since the majority of native-born Koreans engage in intermarriage, it is important to include intermarried couples in studies of second-generation families. Findings from studies of Korean-white and Korean-other minority families are also likely to be useful for understanding Korean-other Asian intermarried families in Korea, a very hot topic at present. Given that about half of in-married native-born Koreans have 1.5- or first-generation immigrant partners, it is also important to examine the differentials in ethnic retention among three different native-born in-married groups. Second-generation Korean women scholars are in a good position to study their own families. I would like to challenge them to study different types of intermarriage and in-marriage using in-depth personal interviews.

When Won Moo Hurh and Kwang Chung Kim were conducting survey research in the 1980s, assimilation was considered a sociologically important issue. However, under the impact of multiculturalism and the post-modernist orientation, assimilation has a very negative connotation at present. Thus younger-generation Korean American sociologists and other social scientists are not that interested in assimilation. Instead, they are greatly interested in ethnicity (ethnic attachment, ethnic identity, ethnic solidarity, etc.), transnationalism, and religious practices.

Almost all articles and book chapters included in the section on "Ethnicity and Transnationalism" examine ethnicity issues, mostly focusing on ethnic identity among 1.5- and second-generation Korean Americans. Ethnic identity is a very popular research topic to younger-generation Korean American scholars as well as to other ethnic studies scholars because of their emphasis on multiculturalism and identity politics. Two books, one by Mary Yu Danico and the other by Nazli Kibria, also focus on ethnic identity among 1.5- and/or second-generation Korean American young adults. In addition, Pyong Gap Min's two edited books on Asian Americans' ethnic identity (1999 and 2002) also focus on 1.5- and second-generation Korean and other Asian American young adults.

Due to their heavy dependency upon 1.5- and second-generation young adults as subjects of their studies, predominantly children of post-1965 Asian immigrants, recent studies of ethnic identity have limitations in the findings. As a result of the subjects' similar experiences with American multiculturalism and large Korean and Asian communities, the findings of most of these studies reflect younger-generation Korean Americans' positive experiences. The life experiences of the post-1950 native-born Korean Americans now in the middle years, who grew up with little contact with other Korean and Asian Americans, must have had very different experiences from the post-1965 native-born second-generation young adults. But to my knowledge there is no journal article or book chapter, let alone a book, which sheds light on life experiences and ethnic identity among these middle-aged native-born Korean Americans. The only unpublished study I know at present is Linda Suzanne Park's dissertation (University of Wisconsin at Madison) entitled "Ethnic Identity in Midlife: Exploring Socio-Historical Context, Identity and Parenting." We are waiting to read her scholarly publications with great interest. And we need one or more additional studies that examine the life experiences of native-born Koreans in the pre-1950 era.

Only two articles—one by Nazli Kibria and the other by Nadia Kim—included in the subsection on "Ethnicity and Transnationalism" cover transnationalism. To my knowledge, there is no book that examines contemporary Korean immigrants' transnational ties systematically. But there are several studies that have transnational components. As shown in the section on "Adoptees, War Brides, and Others," Eleana Kim has published several journal articles and book chapters focusing on Korean adoptees' life experiences in their homeland, South Korea. Since she interviewed Korean adoptees staying in Korea, her works captured their transnational lives. The title of her forthcoming book (*Adopted Territories*: *Transnational Korean Adoptees Remapping Kinship and Rewriting Citizenship*) reflects the transnational component. Nadia Kim's *Imperial Citizens: Koreans and Race from Seoul to Los Angeles* (2008) also covers enough transnational aspects by showing how Korean immigrants learned ideas about American racial hierarchies in Korea. David Yoo's historical book, *Contentious Spirits*: *A Religious History of Korean Americans*, which we mentioned earlier focuses on Korean Protestant immigrants' transnational independence movement connecting the United States, Korea, and China before World War II. This book is expected to make an important contribution to the transnational literature too. Pyong Gap Min's 1998 book on Korean immigrant families in New York includes a chapter focusing on Korean transnational families consisting of husbands working in Korea and wives and children living in the United States for the children's education.

The Korean community is characterized by an exceptionally large number of ethnic organizations. For example, there are more than 1,300 ethnic organizations, including about 600 Korean Protestant churches, in the New York-New

Jersey Korean community. It is thus important to examine ethnic-based organizations and community politics in the Korean community. But the literature on Korean ethnic organizations and community politics is thin. Angie Chung's *Legacies of Struggle: Conflict and Cooperation in Korean American Politics* (2007) is the only book that focuses on ethnic politics and ethnic organizations in the Korean community. The book focuses on two major 1.5- and second-generation social service organizations in Los Angeles. A positive element of the book is its coverage of inter-group and intra-group conflicts and cooperation related to the younger-generation organizations' service delivery. Pyong Gap Min's two books (1996 and 2008) highlighted Korean immigrant business associations' solidarity in reactions to external interest groups and government agencies in New York and Los Angeles. Edward Park examined conflicts in community politics in the Los Angeles Korean community along the generational and ideological divisions in a few publications. We need more books that shed light on conflicts and coordination among ethnic organizations in the Korean community.

I have counted seventeen books and forty-seven articles/book chapters focusing on Korean Americans' religious practices. Almost all of these publications focus on Korean Protestant immigrants and second-generation adults, and their congregations. Compared to other Asian groups' religious practices, first- and second-generation Korean Protestants' religious practices have been well studied. Seven books that analyze religious practices in 1.5- and second-generation Korean English-language congregations have been published or are in the process of being published. I suggest that active research on Korean churches in the United States has been possible mainly because there are enough Korean immigrant and second-generation Protestant sociologists who are highly motivated to study their own ethnic-religious group. For example, Kwang Chung Kim, Eui-Young Yu, Shin Kim, and Eui-Hang Shin, who have undertaken research on Korean immigrant churches, have all served as elders in their churches for many years. Pyong Gap Min has a much weaker religious background than these Korean Protestant scholars, but even he attended Korean immigrant churches long enough to understand them. Second-generation Korean scholars, such as Rebecca Kim, Karen Chai, and David Yoo, who have conducted research on second-generation Korean congregations, also grew up in very religious Christian families.

While Korean Protestant churches in the United States have been actively researched, there is no single study focusing on Korean Catholic churches. We are in need of a study of Korean Catholic parishes or communities. Buddhists comprise a smaller proportion of Korean immigrants (about 8%) than Catholics (14%) (see Min's 2009 article or Chapter 5 in this book, which compares Korean Protestant, Catholic, and Buddhist institutions in the United States). However, there are several scholarly works focusing on Korean Buddhist temples in the United States. They include Sharon Suh's 2004 book, *Being Buddhist in a Christian World: Gender and Community in a Korean-American Temple.*

Researchers who are interested in getting statistical data on Korean immigrant churches should read *Korean Americans and Their Religions: Pilgrims and Missionaries from a Different Shore* (2001), edited by Ho-Youn Kwon, Kwang Chung Kim, and R. Stephen Warner, and Pyong Gap Min's 2010 book, *Preserving Ethnicity through Religion: Korean Protestants and Indian Hindus across Generations*. In particular, Chapter 4 of *Korean Americans and Their Religions*, "Ethnic Roles of Korean Immigrant Churches in the United States," by Kwang Chung Kim and Shin Kim, provide important statistical data about Korean Presbyterian immigrants' religious participation and other aspects of their religious practices, compared to black, Latino, and white Presbyterians.

Ai Ra Kim, a Korean immigrant feminist, and Jung Ha Kim, a 1.5-generation Korean feminist, both trained in theological schools, published their books in the mid-1990s, Ai Ra in 1996 (*Women Struggling for New Life*) and Jung Ha Kim in 1997 (*Bridge Makers and Cross-Bearers*). Both books focus on women's loss of power in Korean immigrant churches. While Ai Ra Kim mostly holds Korean Confucian cultural traditions accountable for women's powerlessness in Korean immigrant churches, Jung Ha Kim considers Christian theology as the main culprit of the sexist organization of Korean immigrant churches. For information about second-generation Korean English-language congregations, the following two books are very useful: Rebecca Kim's *God's New Whiz Kids* (2006) and Pyong Gap Min's *Preserving Ethnicity through Religion* (2010).

Rebecca Kim's and Min's books and other journal articles (see Chai 1998; Min and Kim 2005; Park 2001) have consistently shown that most second-generation Korean Protestant adults accept their being Christian as their primary identity and being Korean as their secondary identity. This finding suggests that when studying second-generation Koreans' ethnic identity, we need to consider the role of their religion as well as other factors. However, none of the ethnic identity studies cited in the subsection of "Ethnicity and Transnationalism" has paid attention to the role of religion in second-generation Koreans' identity formation. Future studies of ethnic identity among second-generation Koreans should consider it.

The section on "Children, Education, and Psychology" includes fifty-four pieces of published work, accounting for 12% of all articles and book chapters. Since education covers a variety of majors, such educational counseling, educational psychology, curriculum and instruction, and bilingual education, there must be many Korean professors who teach in various schools of education. Given this, with more systematic search we are likely to find far more sources in this category. The list shows that Jamie Lew is the author of multiple articles and book chapters, and a major book focusing on Korean children's educational issues.

Many doctoral students have written dissertations about Korean adoptees in the United States, but until recently none of them had published articles in major journals or books based on their data sets. But, as noted above, Eleana Kim, a Korean anthropologist, has published several articles and book chapters over the last ten years based on her interviews with adoptees living in Korea. In the section on "Adoptees, War Brides, and Others" I have listed another set of articles and book chapters about Korean adoptees conducted by Jiannbin Lee Shiao and Mia Tuan, both Chinese American sociologists. Their study yielded several articles and book chapters. One of their articles was published in *American Journal of Sociology* in 2008. Interestingly, while Kim's study emphasizes Korean adoptees' sense of rejection in their birth country, Shiao and Tuan's studies highlight their experiences with racism in their white adoptive families and American society.

A Comprehensive Bibliography

Books and Edited Anthologies

Abelmann, Nancy. 2009. *The Intimate University: Korean American Students and the Problems of Segregation.* Durham, NC: Duke University Press.

Abelmann, Nancy, and John Lie. 1995. *Blue Dreams: Korean Americans and Los Angeles Riots.* Cambridge, MA: Harvard University Press.

Aguilar-San Juan, Karen (ed.). 1994. *The State of Asian America: Activism and Resistance in the 1990s.* Boston: South End Press.

Alumkal, Antony. 2003. *Asian American Evangelical Churches: Race, Ethnicity, and Assimilation in the Second Generation.* New York: LFB Scholarly Publishing LLC.

Amerasia Journal. 2012. *Los Angeles Since 1992: Commemorating the 20th Anniversary of the Uprisings*: A Special Issue (38): 1. Los Angeles: UCLA Asian American Studies Center Press.

Baldassare, Mark (ed.). 1994. *The Los Angeles Riot: Lessons for the Urban Future.* Boulder, CO: Westview Press.

Bergsten, Fred, and Inbom Choi. 2003. *The Korean Diaspora in the World Economy.* Washington, D.C.: Institute for International Economics.

Bonacich, Edna, and Ivan Light. 1988. *Immigrant Entrepreneurs: Koreans in Los Angeles, 1965-1982.* Berkeley: University of California Press.

Centennial Committee of Korean Immigration to the United States. 2003. *The Independence Movement and Its Outgrowth by Korean Americans.* Los Angeles: Centennial Committee of Korean Immigration to the United States.

Cha, Marn J. 2010. *Koreans in Central California, 1903-1957.* Lanham. MD: University Press of America.

Chan, Sucheng. 1991. *Asian Americans: An Interpretive History.* Boston: Twayne Publishers.

Chang, Edward, and Jeannette Diaz-Veizades. 1999. *Ethnic Peace in the American City: Building Community in Los Angeles and Beyond.* New York: New York University Press.

Chang, Edward, and Russell C. Leong (eds.). 1994. *Los Angeles-Struggles toward Multiethnic Community: Asian American, African American, & Latino Perspectives.* Seattle: University of Washington Press.

Chin, Soo-Young. 1999. *Doing What Had to Be Done: The Life Narrative of Dora Yum Kim.* Philadelphia: Temple University Press.

Cho, Myung Ji, Jung Ha Kim, Unzu Lee, and Su Yon Park. 2005. *Singing the Lord's Song in a New Land: Korean American Practice of Faith.* Louisville, KY: Westminster John Knox.

Ch'oe, Yong-ho (ed.). 2007. *From the Land of Hibiscus: Koreans in Hawaii.* Honolulu: University of Hawaii Press.

Choy, Bong-Youn. 1979. *Koreans in America.* Chicago: Nelson Hall.

Chun, Hyuk, Kwang Chung Kim, and Shin Kim (eds.). *The Koreans in the Windy City*. New Haven, CT: East Rock Institute.

Chung, Angie Y. 2007. *Legacies of Struggle: Conflict and Cooperation in Korean American Politics*. Stanford, CA: Stanford University Press.

Danico, Mary Yu. 2004. *The 1.5 Generation: Becoming Korean American in Hawaii*. Honolulu: University of Hawaii Press.

Ecklund, Elaine Howard. 2006. *Korean American Evangelicals: New Models for Civic Life*. New York: Oxford University Press.

Gooding-Williams, Robert (ed.). 1993. *Reading Rodney King/Reading Urban Uprising*. New York: Routledge.

Harvey, Y.S., and S. H. Chung. 1980. *The Koreans*. Honolulu: University of Hawaii Press.

Hahn, Cora. 1978. *A Case Study, How Twenty-One Koreans Perceive America* (World Education Monograph Series, 4). Storrs, CT: World Education Project, University of Connecticut.

Hazen, Don. 1993. *Inside the Los Angeles Riots: What Really Happened and Why It Will Happen Again*. New York: Institute for Alternative Journalism.

Hertic, Young Lee. 2001. *Cultural Tug of War: The Korean Immigrant Family and Church in Transition*. Nashville: Abington.

Hurh, Won Moo. 1977. *Comparative Study of Korean Immigrants in the United States: A Typological Approach*. San Francisco: R & R Research Associates.

_____. 1998. *The Korean Americans*. Westport, CT: Greenwood Press.

Hurh, Won Moo, and Kwang Chung Kim. 1984. *Korean Immigrants in America: A Structural Analysis of Ethnic Confinement and Adhesive Adaptation*. Madison: Fairleigh Dickinson University Press.

Hurh, Won Moo, Kwang Chung Kim, and Hei Chu Kim. 1979. *Assimilation Patterns of Immigrants in the United States: A Case Study of Korean Immigrants in the Chicago-Area*. Washington, D.C.: University Press of America.

Hyun, Peter. 1995. *In the New World: The Making of a Korean American*. Honolulu: University of Hawaii Press.

Jo, Moon H. 1999. *Korean Immigrants and the Challenge of Adjustment*. Westport, Connecticut: Greenwood Press.

Joyce, Patrick D. 2003. *No Fire Next Time: Black-Korean Conflicts and the Future of America's Cities*. Ithaca, NY: Cornell University Press.

Kang, K. Connie. 1995. *Home Was the Land of Morning Calm: A Saga of a Korean American Family*. Reading, MA: Addison-Wesley.

Kang, Miliann. 2010. *The Managed Hand: Race, Gender and the Body in Beauty Service Work*. Berkeley: University of California Press.

Kibria, Nazli. 2002. *Becoming Asian Americans: Second Generation Chinese and Korean American Identities*. Baltimore, MD: The Johns Hopkins University Press.

Kim, Ai Ra. 1996. *Women Struggling for a New Life: The Role of Religion in the Cultural Passage from Korea to America.* Albany, NY: State University of New York Press.

Kim, Bok-Lim. 1978. *The Asian Americans: Changing Patterns, Changing Needs.* Montclair, NJ: The Association of Korean Christian Scholars in North America.

Kim, Byong-Suh, and Sang Hyun Lee (eds.). 1980. *The Korean Immigrants in America.* Montclair, NJ: The Association of Korean Christian Scholars in North America.

Kim, Claire Jean. 2000. *Bitter Fruit: The Politics of Black-Korean Conflict in New York City.* New Haven, CT.: Yale University Press.

Kim, Elaine H., and Eui-Young Yu. 1996. *East to America: Korean American Life Stories.* New York: The New Press.

Kim, Eleana. 2010. *Adopted Territories: Transnational Korean Adoptees Remapping Kinship and Rewriting Citizenship.* Durham, NC: Duke University Press.

Kim, Elizabeth. 2000. *Ten Thousand Sorrows: The Extraordinary Journey of a Korean War Orphan.* New York: Doubleday.

Kim, Hyojung (ed.). 2005. *Korean Americans Identities: A Look Forward.* Seattle: The Seattle-Washington State Korean American Association.

Kim, Hyung-Chan. 1971. *Korean Diaspora.* Santa Barbara, CA: ABC-Clio Press.

_____. 1974. *The Koreans in America, 1882-1974: A Chronology and Fact Book.* Dobbs Ferry, New York: Oceana Publication, Inc.

_____ (ed.). 1977. *East across the Pacific: Historical and Sociological Studies of Korean Immigration and Assimilation.* Santa Barbara: ABC Clio Press.

Kim, Ilpyong (ed.). 2004. *Korean Americans: Past, Present, and Future.* Elizabeth, NJ: HollymInternational.

Kim, Illsoo. 1981. *New Urban Immigrants: The Korean Community in New York.* Princeton, New Jersey: Princeton University Press.

Kim, Jung Ha. 1997. *Bridge-makers and Cross-bearers: Korean-American Women and the Church.* Atlanta: Scholars Press.

Kim, Katherine Yungmee. 2011. *Los Angeles's Koreatown* (Images of America Series). Mount Pleasant, SC: Arcadia Publishing.

Kim, Kenneth, Kapson Lee, and Tai-Yul Kim. 1981. *Korean-Americans in Los Angeles: Their Concerns and Language Maintenance.* Los Angeles: National Center for Bilingual Research.

Kim, Kwang Chung (ed.). 1999. *Koreans in the Hood: Conflict with African Americans.* Baltimore, MD.: The Johns Hopkins University Press.

Kim, Nadia. 2008. *Imperial Citizens: Koreans and Race from Seoul to LA.* Stanford, CA: Stanford University Press.

Kim, Rebecca Y. 2006. *God's New Whiz Kids? Korean American Evangelicals on Campus.* New York: New York University Press.

Kim, Won Yong. 1971. *Koreans in America.* Seoul, Korea: Po Chin Chai.

Kwak, Tae-Hwan, and Seong Hyong Lee (eds.). 1990. *The Korean-American Community: Present and Future*. Masan, Korea: Kyung Nam University Press

Kwon, Brenda L. 1999. *Beyond Ke'eamoku Street: Koreans, Nationalism, and Local Culture in Hawaii*. New York: Garland Publishing.

Kwon, Ho-Youn (ed.). 1994. *Korean Americans: Conflict and Harmony*. Chicago: North Park College and Theological Seminary.

Kwon, Ho-Youn, Kwang Chung Kim, and Stephen R. Warner (eds.). 2001. *Korean Americans and Their Religions: Pilgrims and Missionaries from a Different Shore*. University Park, PA: Pennsylvania State University Press.

Kwon, Ho-Youn, and Shin Kim (eds.). 1993. *The Emerging Generation of Korean Americans*. Seoul, Korea: Kyung Hee University Press.

Kwon, Okyun. 2003. *Buddhist and Protestant Korean Immigrants: Religious Beliefs and Socioeconomic Aspects of Life*. New York: LFB Scholarly Publishing LLC.

Kwon, Victoria Hyonchu. 1997. *Entrepreneurship and Religion: Korean Immigrants in Houston, Texas*. New York: Garland Publishing, Inc.

Lee, Ellen. 1995. *The Planted Seed: History of the English Language Ministry of the Korean Methodist Church and Institute*. New York: Korean Methodist Church and Institute.

Lee, Hwain Chang. 2000. *The Korean American YWCA and the Church: Dialogue Face-to-Face, Partnership Hand-in-Hand*. Lanham, MD: University Press of America.

Lee, In Sook (ed.). 1985. *Korean-American Women: Toward Self-Realization*. Mansfield, OH: Association of Korean Christian Scholars in North America.

Lee, Jae-Hyup. 1998. *Dynamics of Ethnic Identity: Three Asian American Communities in Philadelphia*. New York: Garland Publishing.

Lee, Jennifer. 2002. *Civility in the City: Blacks, Jews, and Koreans in Urban America*. Cambridge, MA: Harvard University Press.

Lee, Jennifer, and Min Zhou (eds.). 2004. *Asian American Youth: Culture, Identity, and Ethnicity*. New York: Routledge.

Lee, Mary Paik. 1990. *Quiet Odyssey: A Pioneer Korean Woman in America*, edited by Sucheng Chan. Seattle: University of Washington Press

Lee, Sang Hyun, and John V. Moore (eds.). 1993. *Korean American Ministry*. Louisville, KY: Presbyterian Church.

Lee, Stacey. 1996. *Unraveling the "Model Minority" Stereotype: Listening to Asian American Youth*. New York: Teachers College Press.

Lee, Seung Hyong (ed.). 1988. *Koreans in North America*. Masan, Korea: Kyungnam University Press.

Lee, Yoon Mo. 1993. Inter-Organizational Context of the Korean Community for the Participation of the Emerging Generation of Korean-Americans. Seoul: Kyung Hee University Press.

Lew, Jamie. 2006. *Asian Americans in Class: Charting the Achievement Gap among Korean American Youth*. New York: Teachers College Press.

Lewis, Cherie S. 1994. *Koreans and Jews*. New York: Institute of Race Relations, American Jewish Congress.
Light, Ivan, and Edna Bonacich. 1988. *Immigrant Entrepreneurs: Koreans in Los Angeles 1965-1982*. Berkeley: University of California Press.
Mangiafico, Luciano. 1988. *Contemporary American Immigrants: Patterns of Filipino, Korean, Chinese Settlement in the United States*. New York: Praeger.
Melendy, H. Brett. 1977. *Asians in America: Filipinos, Koreans, and East Indians*. Boston: G.K.Hall.
Min, Pyong Gap. 1988. *Ethnic Business Enterprises: Korean Small Business in Atlanta*. New York: Center for Migration Studies.
_____ (ed.). 1995. *Asian Americans: Contemporary Trends and Issues*. Thousand Oaks, CA: Sage Publication.
_____. 1996. *Caught in the Middle: Korean Communities in New York and Los Angeles*. Berkley, CA: University of California Press.
_____. 1998. *Changes and Conflicts: Korean Immigrant Families in New York*. Boston: Allyn & Bacon.
_____ (ed.). 2002. *The Second Generation: Ethnic Identity among Asian Americans*. Walnut Creek, CA: Altamira Press.
_____ (ed.). 2006. *Asian Americans: Contemporary Trends and Issues*, Second Edition. Thousand Oaks, CA: Pine Forge Press.
_____. 2008. *Ethnic Solidarity for Economic Survival: Korean Greengroceries in New York City*. New York: Russell Sage Foundation.
_____. 2010. *Preserving Ethnicity through Religion in America: Korean Protestants and Indian Hindus across Generations*. New York: New York University Press.
_____. 2012 (ed.). *Koreans in North America: Their Twenty-First Century Experiences*. Lanham, Maryland: Lexington Books.
Min, Pyong Gap, and Jung Ha Kim (eds.). 2002. *Religions in Asian America: Building Faith Communities*. Walnut Creek, CA: Altamira Press.
Min, Pyong Gap, and Rose Kim (eds.). 1999. *Struggle for Ethnic Identity: Narratives by Asian American Professionals*. Walnut Creek, CA: Altamira Press.
Pang, Keum-Young Chung. 1991. *Korean Elderly Women in America: Everyday Life, Health, and Illness*. New York: AMS Press.
_____. 2000. *Virtuous Transcendence: Holistic Self-Cultivation and Self-Healing in Elderly Korean Immigrants*. New York: Haworth Press.
Park, Kyeyoung. 1997. *The Korean American Dream: Immigrants and Small Business in New York City*. Ithaca, NY: Cornell University Press.
Park, Lisa Sun-Hee. 2005. *Consuming Citizenship: Children of Asian Immigrant Entrepreneurs*. Stanford, CA: Stanford University Press.
Patterson, Wayne. 1988. *The Korean Frontier in America: Immigration to Hawaii, 1896-1910*. Honolulu: University of Hawaii Press.
_____. 1992. *Koreans in America*. Minneapolis, MN: Lerner Publications Company.

_____. 2000. *Ilse: First Generation Korean Immigrants in Hawaii, 1903-1973.* Honolulu: University of Hawaii Press.
Patterson, Wayne, and Hyung-Chan Kim (eds.). 1977. *The Koreans in America.* Minneapolis: Lerner Publications.
Robinson, Kay. 2002. *A Single Square Picture: A Korean Adoptee's Search for Her Roots.* New York: Berkeley Books.
Song, Min Hyoung. 2005. *Strange Future: Pessimism and the 1992 Los Angeles Riots.* Durham, N.C.: Duke University Press.
Song, Young In. 1987. *Silent Victims: Battered Women in Korean Immigrant Families.* San Francisco: Oxford University Press.
_____. 1996. *Battered Women in Korean Immigrant Families: The Silent Scream.* New York: Garland Publications.
Song, Young In, and Ailee Moon Lee (eds.). 1997. *Korean American Women Living in Two Cultures.* Los Angeles: Keimyung-Baylo University Press.
_____ (eds.). 1998. *Korean American Women: From Tradition to Modern Feminism.* Westport, CT: Praeger.
Suh, Sharon. 2004. *Being Buddhist in a Christian World: Gender and Community in a Korean American Temple.* Seattle: University of Washington Press.
Sunoo, Harold Hakwon, and Dong Soo Kim (eds.). 1978. *Korean Women in a Struggle for Humanization.* Memphis, TN: The Association of Korean Christian Scholars in North America.
Sunoo, Sonia Shin. 1982. *Korea Kaleidoscope: Oral Histories Vol.1. Early Korean Pioneers in USA, 1903-1905.* Davis, CA: Korean Oral History Project.
Takaki, Ronald. 1989. *Strangers from a Different Shore: A History of Asian Americans.* Boston: Little, Brown and Company.
Um, Shin Ja. 1996. *Korean Immigrant Women in the Dallas-Area Apparel Industry.* New York: University Press of America.
Yoo, David K. 2010. *Contentious Spirits: Religion in Korean American History, 1903-1945.* Stanford, CA: Stanford University Press.
Yoo, David K., and Hyung-ju Ahn. 2004. *Faithful Witness: A Centennial History of the Los Angeles Korean United Methodist Church, 1904-2004.* Seoul: Doosan.
Yoo, David K., and Ruth H. Chung (eds.). 2008. *Spiritual Practices: Mapping Korean American Religions.* Champaign, IL: University of Illinois Press.
Yoo, Jin Kyung. 1998. *Korean Immigrant Entrepreneurs: Network and Ethnic Resources.* New York: Garland Publishing, Inc.
Yoon, In-Jin. 1997. *On My Own: Korean Businesses and Race Relations in America.* Chicago: University of Chicago Press.
Yu, Eui-Young. 1987. *Juvenile Delinquency in the Korean Community of Los Angeles.* Los Angeles: The Korea Times, Los Angeles.
_____ (ed.). 1994. *Black-Korean Encounter: Toward Understanding and Alliance.* Los Angeles: Institute for Asian American and Pacific Asian Studies, California State University.

_____ (ed.). 2002. *100 Year History of Korean Immigration to America*. Los Angeles: Korean American United Foundation.
Yu, Eui-Young, Hyojoung Kim, Kyeyoung Park, and Moonsong Oh (eds.). 2009. *Korean American Economy and Community in the 21st Century*. Los Angeles: The Korean American Economic Development Center.
Yu, Eui-Young, and Earl H. Phillips (eds.). 1987. *Korean Women in Transition: At Home and Abroad*. Los Angeles: Center for Korean-American and Korean Studies, California State University, Los Angeles.
Yu, Eui-Young, Earl H. Phillips, and Eun Sik Yang (eds.). 1982. *Koreans in Los Angeles: Prospects and Promises*. Los Angeles: Koryo Research Institute, Center for Korean-American and Korean Studies, California State University.
Yu, Diana. 1991. *Winds of Change: Korean Women in America*. Silver Spring, MD: Women's Institute Press.
Yu, Jin H. 1980. *The Korean Merchants in the Black Community: Their Relations and Strategies for Conflict Resolution and Prevention*. Elkins Park, PA: Philip Jaisohn Memorial Foundation.
Yuh, Ji-Yeon. 2002. *Beyond the Shadow of Camptown: Korean Military Brides in America*. New York: New York University Press.
Zhou, Min, and James Gatewood (eds.). 2000. *Contemporary Asian America: A Multidisciplinary Reader*. New York: New York University Press.

Journal Articles and Book Chapters

1. History

Chai, Alice Yun. 1981. "Korean Women in Hawaii, 1903-1945." In *Women in New Worlds*, edited by Hilah F. Thomas and Rosemary Skinner Keller, 328-344. Nashville, TN: Abingdon.
_____. 1987. "Freed from the Elders But Locked into Labor: Korean Immigrant Women in Hawaii." *Women's Studies* 13: 223-234.
_____. 1988. "Women's History in Public: 'Picture Brides' of Hawaii." *Women's Studies Quarterly* 1 and 2 (Spring/Summer): 51-62.
_____. 1992. "Picture Brides: Feminist Analysis of Life Histories of Hawaii's Early Immigrant Women from Japan, Okinawa, and Korea." In *Seeking Common Ground: Multidisciplinary Studies of Immigrant Women in the United States*, edited by Donna Gabaccia, 123-138. Westport, CT: Greenwood Press.
Choi, Anne Soon. 2003-2004. "'Are They Koreaned Enough?': Generation and the Korean Independence Movement before World War II." *Amerasia Journal* 29 (3): 57-78.
Choy, Peggy Myo-Young. 2000. "Anatomy of a Dancer: Place, Lineage and Liberation." *Amerasia Journal* 26 (2): 234-252.

Houchins, L., and Chang-Su Houchins. 1974. "The Korean Experience in America, 1903-1924." *Pacific Historical Review* 43: 548-575.

_____. 1976. "The Korean Experience in America, 1903-1924." In *The Asian American: The Historical Experience*, edited by Norris Hundley, Jr., 129-156 Santa Barbara, CA: ABC-Clio Press.

Ishi, Tomoji. 1988. "International Linkage and National Class Conflict: The Migration of Korean Nurses to the United States." *Amerasia Journal* 14 (1): 23-50.

Kim, Lili M. 2003-2004. "The Limit of Americanism and Democracy: Korean Americans, Transnational Allegiance, and the Question of Loyalty on the Homefront during World War II. *Amerasia Journal* 29 (3): 79-98.

Kim, Richard S. 2005. "A Conversation with Chol Soo Lee and K. W. Lee." *Amerasia Journal* 31 (3): 76-108.

Liem, Ramsay. 2003-2004. "History, Trauma, and Identity: The Legacy of the Korean War for Korean Americans." *Amerasia Journal* 19 (3): 111-132.

Louie, Miriam Ching Yoon. 2004. "Doing Durepae Duty: Korean American Radical Movement after Kwangju." *Amerasia Journal* 31 (1): 88-106.

Lyu, Kingsley K. 1977a. "Korean Nationalist Activities in Hawaii and the Continental United States, 1900-1945, Part I: 1900-1919." *Amerasia Journal* 4 (1): 23-90.

_____. 1977b. "Korean Nationalist Activities in Hawaii and the Continental United States. 1900-1945, Part II: 1919-1945." *Amerasia Journal* 4 (2): 53-100.

Parkman, Margaret, and Jack Sawyer. 1967. "Dimensions of Ethnic Intermarriage in Hawaii." *American Sociological Review* 32: 593-606.

Patterson, Wayne. 1979a. "Horace Allen and Korean Immigration to Hawaii." In *The United States and Korea: America-Korean Relations, 1866-1976*, edited by Andrew C. Nahm. Kalamazoo: Center for Korean Studies, Western Michigan University.

_____. 1979b. "Sugar-Coated Diplomacy: Horace Allen and Korean Immigration to Hawaii, 1902-1905." *Diplomatic History* 3: 19-38.

Shin, Linda. 1971. "Koreans in America, 1903-1945." In *Roots: An Asian American Reader*, edited by Amy Tachik, et al., 201-206. Los Angeles: Center for Asian American Studies, University of California, Los Angeles.

Sunoo, Sonia. 1978. "Korean Women Pioneers of the Pacific Northwest." *Oregon Historical Quarterly* 79: 51-64.

Yang, Eun Sik. 1984. "Korean Women in America: From Subordination to Partnership, 1903-1930." *Amerasia Journal* 11 (1): 1-28.

Yoo, David K. 2006. "Nurturing Religious Nationalism: Korean Americans in Hawaii." In *Practicing Protestants: Histories of the Christian Life in America*, edited by Laurie Maffly-Kipp, Leigh Schmidt, and Mark Valeri, 100-117, 314-317. Baltimore, MD: The Johns Hopkins University Press.

_____. 2009. "Japanese and Korean Migrations: Buddhist and Christian Communities in America, 1885-1945." In *Immigration and Religion in America: Comparative and Historical Perspectives*, edited by Richard Alba, Albert J.

Raboteau, and Josh DeWind, 106-134. New York: New York University Press.

2. Immigration and Settlement Patterns

Arnold, Fred, Benjamin V. Carino, James T. Fawcett, and Insook Han Park. 1989. "Estimating the Immigration Multiplier: An Analysis of Recent Korean and Filipino Immigration to the United States." *International Migration Review* 23: 813-838.
Chung, Angie Y. 2000. "The Impact of Neighborhood Structures on Korean American Youth in Koreatown." *Korean and Korean American Studies Bulletin* 11: 21-35.
Danico, Mary Y., and Linda Trinh Vo. 2004. "The Formation of Post-Suburban Communities: Koreatown and Little Saigon, Orange County." *International Journal of Sociology and Social Policy* 24 (7/8): 15-45.
Ishi, Tomoji. 1988. "International Linkage and National Class Conflict: The Migration of Korean Nurses to the United States." *Amerasia Journal* 14 (1): 23-50.
Kim, Anna Joo. 2009. "LA's Koreatown: Ethnicity, Entrepreneurship, and Entertainment." In *Korean Economy and Community in the 21st Century*, edited by Eui-Young Yu, Hyojoung Kim, Kyeyoung Park, and Moonsong Oh, 369-392. Los Angeles: Korean American Economic Development Center.
Kim, Dong Ok. 1995a. "Koreatown and Korean Small Firms in Los Angeles: Locating in the Ethnic Neighborhoods." *Professional Geographer* 47: 184-195.
_____. 1995b. "Response to Spatial Rigidity in Urban Transformation: Korean Business Experience in Los Angeles." *International Journal of Urban and Regional Research* 19: 40-54.
Kim, Hyun Sook, and Pyong Gap Min. 1992. "The Post-1965 Korean Immigrants: Their Characteristics and Settlement Patterns." *Korea Journal of Population and Development* 21: 121-143.
Kim, Illsoo. 1987. "Korea and East Asia: Pre-emigration Factors and U.S. Immigration Policy." In *Pacific Bridges: The New Immigration from Asia and the Pacific Islands*, edited by James T. Fawcett and Benjamin V. Carino, 327-345. Staten Island, NY: Center for Migration Studies.
Kitano, Harry L. 1981. "Asian Americans: The Chinese, Japanese, Koreans, Filipinos and Southeast Asians." *Annals of the American Academy of Political and Social Science* 454: 125-138.
Koo, Hagen, and Eui-Young Yu. 1981. "Korean Immigration to the United States: Its Demographic Pattern and Social Implications for Both Societies." Papers of the Population Institute, No.74. Honolulu: East-West Center.
Lee, David. 2009. "Changing Landscape: Locating Global and Local Factors in the Development of Los Angeles' Koreatown." In *Korean Economy and Community in the 21st Century*, edited by Eui-Young Yu, Hyojoung Kim,

Kyeyoung Park, and Moonsong Oh, 349-368. Los Angeles: Korean American Economic Development Center.

Min, Pyong Gap. 1993. "Korean Immigrants in Los Angeles." In *Immigration and Entrepreneurship: Culture, Capital, and Ethnic Networks*, edited by Ivan Light and Parminder Bhachu, 185-204. New York: Transaction Publishers.

———. 2006a. "Asian Immigration: History and Contemporary Trends." In *Asian Americans: Contemporary Trends and Issues*, Second Edition, edited by Pyong Gap Min, 7-31. Thousand Oaks, CA: Pine Forge Press

———. 2006b. "Settlement Patterns and Diversity." In *Asian Americans: Contemporary Trends and Issues*, Second Edition, edited by Pyong Gap Min, 32-53. Thousand Oaks, CA: Pine Forge Press.

———. 2011. "The Immigration of Koreans to the United States: A Review of 45 Year (1965-2009) Trends." *Development and Society* 40 (2): 195-224.

———. 2012. "Twice-Migrant Koreans in the U.S.: Their Countries of Origin, Socio-Economic Characteristics, and Attachment to Korea." *Journal of Diaspora Studies* 6.

Park, Insook Han, James T. Fawcett, Fred Arnold, and Robert W. Gardner. 1990. "Korean Immigrants and U.S. Immigration Policy: A Pre-departure Perspective." Papers of the Population Institute, No.114. Honolulu: East-West Center.

Park, Kyeyoung, and Jessica Kim. 2008. "The Contested Nexus of Los Angeles Koreatown: Capital Restructuring, Gentrification, and Displacement." *Amerasia Journal* 34 (3): 127-150.

Park, Kyonghwan, and Youngmin, Lee. 2009. "Thinking Koreatown as a Place of Lived Economy." In *Korean Economy and Community in the 21st Century*, edited by Eui-Young Yu, Hyojoung Kim, Kyeyoung Park, and Moonsong Oh, 409-544. Los Angeles: Korean American Economic Development Center.

Pomerantz, Linda. 1984. "The Background of Korean Emigration." In *Labor Immigration under Capitalism: Asian Workers in the United States before World War II*, edited by Lucie Cheng and Edna Bonacich, 277-315. Berkeley and Los Angeles: University of California Press.

Yoon, In-Jin. 1993. "The Social Origins of Korean Immigration to the United States from 1965 to the Present." Papers of the Population Institute, No. 114. Honolulu: East-West Center.

Yu, Eui-Young. 1985. "Koreatown, Los Angeles: Emergence of a New Inner-city Ethnic Community." *Bulletin of the Population and Development Studies Center* 60: 29-44.

———. 2009. "Korean Community in the United States: Socioeconomic Characteristics and Evolving Immigration Patterns." In *Korean Economy and Community in the 21st Century*, edited by Eui-Young Yu, Hyojoung Kim, Kyeyoung Park, and Moonsong Oh, 31-66. Los Angeles: Korean American Economic Development Center.

Yu, Eui-Young, and Peter Choe. 2003-2004. "Korean Population in the United States as Reflected in the Year 2000 U.S. Census." *Amerasia Journal* 29 (3): 23-29.
Yu, Eui-Young, Peter Choe, Sang Il Han, and Kimberly Yu. 2004. "Emerging Diversity: Los Angeles' Koreatown, 1900-2000." *Amerasia Journal* 30 (1): 25-52.
Yum, June Ock. 1985. "Social Networks of Korean Immigrants in Hawaii." *Journal of East and West Studies* 14: 115-126.

3. Socioeconomic Attainment and Assimilation

Choe, Sang T., Louis M. Capella, and Danny R. Arnold. 1993. "Acculturation, Ethnic Consumers, and Food Consumption Patterns." *Journal of Food Products Marketing* 1: 61-79.
Hurh, Won Moo. 1977. "Assimilation of the Korean Minority in the United States." Research Report, Elkins Park, PA: Philip Jaisohn Memorial Foundation.
_____. 1980. "Towards a Korean-American Ethnicity: Some Theoretical Models." *Ethnic and Racial Studies* 3: 444-463.
_____. 1993. "The '1.5 Generation': A Paragon of Korean-American Pluralism." *Korean Culture* 14: 17-27.
Hurh, Won Moo, and Kwang Chung Kim. 1980. "Social and Occupational Assimilation of Korean Immigrant Workers in the United States." *California Sociologist* 3: 125-142.
_____. 1984. "Adhesive Sociocultural Adaptation of Korean Immigrants in the U.S.: An Alternative Strategy of Minority Adaptation." *International Migration Review* 18: 188-216.
_____. 1989. "The 'Success' Image of Asian Americans: Its Validity and Its Practical and Theoretical Implications." *Ethnic and Racial Studies* 12: 512-538.
_____. 1991. "Adaptation Stages and Mental Health of Korean Male Immigrants in the U.S." *International Migration Review* 24: 456-479.
Hurh, Won Moo, Hei Chu Kim, and Kwang Chung Kim. 1980. "Cultural and Social Adjustment Patterns of Korean Immigrants in the Chicago Area." In *Sourcebook on the New Immigration: Implication for the United States and the International Community*, edited by R. Bryce-Laporte, 295-302. New Brunswick, NJ: Transaction Books.
Kang, Tai Shick. 1971. "Name Change and Acculturation." *Pacific Sociological Review* 14: 403-412.
Kim, Chigon, and Pyong Gap Min. 2010. "Marital Patterns and Use of Mother Tongue at Home among Native-Born Asian Americans." *Social Forces* 88: 233-256.
Kim, Dae Young. 2004. "Leaving the Ethnic Economy: The Rapid Integration of Second-Generation Korean Americans in New York." In *Becoming New*

Yorkers: Ethnographies of the New Second Generation, edited by Philip Kasinitz, John H. Mollenkopf, and Mary C. Waters, 154-188. New York: Russell Sage Foundation.

_____. 2006. "Stepping Stone to Intergenerational Mobility?: The Springboard, Safety Net, or Mobility Trap Functions of Korean Immigrant Entrepreneurship for the Second Generation." *International Migration Review* 40: 927-962.

_____. 2009. "Second-Generation Korean Americans in Professional Fields in New York." In *Korean Economy and Community in the 21st Century*, edited by Eui-Young Yu, Hyojoung Kim, Kyeyoung Park, and Moonsong Oh, 393-422. Los Angeles: Korean American Economic Development Center.

Kim, Kwang Chung, and Won Moo Hurh. 1983. "Korean Americans and the 'Success' Image: A Critique." *Amerasia Journal* 10 (2): 3-21.

_____. 1980. "Social and Occupational Assimilation of Korean Immigrants in the United States." *California Sociologist* 3: 125-142.

_____. 1993. "Beyond Assimilation and Pluralism: Syncretic Sociocultural Adaptation of Korean Immigrants in the U.S." *Ethnic and Racial Studies* 16: 696-713.

Kim, Kwang Chung, Hei Chu Kim, and Won Moo Hurh. 1981. "Job Information Deprivation in the United States: A Case Study of Korean Immigrants." *Ethnicity* 8: 161-232.

Kitano, Harry, and Lynn Kyung Chai. 1982. "Korean Interracial Marriage." *Marriage and Family Review* 5:75-89.

Kitano, Harry, Wai-Tsang Yeung, Lynn Kyung Chai, and Herbert Tanakana. 1984. "Asian-American Interracial Marriage." *Journal of Marriage and the Family* 46:179-190.

Lee, Dong Chang. 1975. "Acculturation of Korean Residents in Georgia." San Francisco: R and E Research Associates.

Lee, Sharon, and Marilyn Fernandez. 1998. "Trends in Asian American Racial/Ethnic Marriages: A Comparison of 1980 and 1990 Census Data." *Sociological Perspectives* 42: 323-342.

Lee, Sharon, and Monica Boyd. 2007. "Marrying Out: Comparing the Marital and Societal Integration of Asians in the U.S. and Canada." *Social Science Research* 37: 311-329.

Lee, Sun Kyong, J. Sobal, and E. A. Frongillo, Jr. 2003. "Comparison of Models of Acculturation: The Case of Korean Americans." *Journal of Cross-Cultural Psychology* 34: 282-296.

Liang, Zai, and Naomi Ito. 1999. "Intermarriage of Asian Americans in the New York City Region: Contemporary Patterns and Future Prospects." *International Migration Review* 33: 876-900.

Min, Pyong Gap, and Chigon Kim. 2009. "Patterns of Intermarriages and Cross-Generational In-marriages among Native-Born Asian Americans." *International Migration Review* 43: 447-470.

Okamoto, D. G. 2007. "Marrying Out: A Boundary Approach to Understanding the Marriage Integration of Asian Americans." *Social Science Research* 36: 1391-1414.

Park, Jin Heum. 1999. "The Earnings of Immigrants in the United States: The Effect of English-Speaking Ability." *American Journal of Economics & Sociology* 58: 43-56.

Ratliff, Bascom W., Harriett F. Moon, and Gwendolyn A. Bonacci. 1978. "Intercultural Marriage: The Korean American Experience." *The Social Casework* 59: 221-226.

Shinagawa, Larry, and Gin Y. Pang. 1996. "Asian American Panethnicity and Intermarriage." *Amerasia Journal* 22 (2): 127-152.

Sakamoto, Arthur, Changhwan Kim, and Isao Takei. Forthcoming. "Moving Out of the Margins and Into the Mainstream: The Demographics of Asian Americans in the New South." In *Asian Americans and the New South*, edited by Khyati Y. Joshi and Jigna Desai. Atlanta: University of Georgia Press.

Sakamoto, Arthur, Kimberly A. Goyette, and Chang Hwan Kim. 2009. "Socioeconomic Attainments of Asian Americans." *Annual Review of Sociology* 35: 255-276.

Sakamoto, Arthur, Hyeyoung Woo, and Keng-Loong Yap. 2006. "Are Native-Born Asian Americans Less Likely to be Managers? Further Evidence on the Glass-Ceiling Hypothesis." *AAPI Nexus: Asian Americans & Pacific Islanders, Policy, Practice & Community* 4: 13-37.

Sakamoto, Arthur, and Yu Xie. 2006. "The Socioeconomic Attainments of Asian Americans." In *Asian Americans: Contemporary Trends and Issues*, Second Edition, edited by Pyong Gap Min, 54-77. Thousand Oaks, CA: Pine Forge Press.

Shin, Eui Hang, and Kyung-Sup Chang. 1988. "Peripherization of Immigrant Professionals: Korean Physicians in the United States." *International Migration Review* 22: 609-626.

U.S. Commission on Civil Rights. 1975. "A Dream Unfulfilled: Korean and Philipino Health Professionals in L.A." Washington, D.C.: U.S. Commission on Civil Rights.

Won-Doornick, Myong Jin. 1988. "Television Viewing and Acculturation of Korean Immigrants." *Amerasia Journal* 14 (1): 79-92.

Yim, Sun Bin. 1978. "The Social Structure of Korean Communities in California, 1903-1920." In *Labor Immigration under Capitalism*, edited by Lucie Cheng and Edna Bonacich, 515-548. Berkeley: University of California Press.

Yoon, In-Jin. 2009. "The Intergenerational Transition in Occupation and Economic Status among Korean Americans." In *Korean Economy and Community in the 21st Century*, edited by Eui-Young Yu, Hyojoung Kim, Kyeyoung Park, and Moonsong Oh, 423-456. Los Angeles: Korean American Economic Development Center.

Yu, Eui-Young, Peter Choe, and Sang Il Han. 2002. "Korean Population in the United States, 2000: Demographic Characteristics and Socio-Economic Status." *International Journal of Korean Studies* 6: 71-108.

4. Business and Business-Related Inter-group Conflicts

Ahn, Hyeon-hyo. 2001. "The Development of Korean American Banks in the Context of Ethnic Banking in Southern California." *Journal of American Studies* 35: 111-138.

Ahn, Hyeon-hyo, and Jang-pyo Hong. 2001. "The Evolution of Korean Ethnic Banks in California." *Journal of Regional Studies* 7: 97-120.

Aubry, Larry. 1993. "Black-Korean American Relations: An Insider's Viewpoint." *Amerasia Journal* 19 (2): 149-156.

Bates, Timothy. 1994. "An Analysis of Korean Immigrant-Owned Small-Business Start-Ups with Comparisons to African American and Nonminority-Owned Firms." *Urban Affairs Quarterly* 30: 227-248.

———. 1997. "Financing Small Business Creation: The Case of Chinese and Korean Immigrant Entrepreneurs." *Journal of Business Venturing* 12: 109-124.

Bonacich, Edna. 1994. "Asians in the Los Angeles Garment Industry." In *The New Asian Immigration in Los Angeles and Global Restructuring*, edited by Paul Ong, Edna Bonacich, and Lucie Cheng, 137-163. Philadelphia: Temple University Press.

Bonacich, Edna, Ivan Light, and Charles Choy Wong. 1976. "Small Business among Koreans in Los Angeles." In *Counterpoint: Perspectives on Asian America*, edited by Emma Gee, 437-449. Los Angeles: Asian American Studies Center, University of California, Los Angeles.

———. 1980. "Korean Immigrants: Small Business in Los Angeles." In *Sourcebook on the New Immigration: Implications for the United States and the International Community*, edited by Roy Simon Bryce-Laporte, 167-184. New Brunswick, NJ: Transaction.

Chang, Edward Taehan. 1991. "New Urban Crisis: Intra-Third World Conflict." In *Asian Americans: Comparative and Global Perspectives*, edited by Shirley Hune, Hyung Chan Kim, Stephen Fugita, and Amy Ling. Pullman, WA: Washington State University Press.

———. 1992. "Building Minority Coalitions: A Case Study of Koreans and African Americans." *Korean Journal of Population and Development* 21: 37-56.

———. 1995. "Korean American Dilemma: Violence, Vengeance, Vision." In *Multiculturalism from the Margins: Non-Dominant Voices on Difference and Diversity*, edited by Dean A. Harris, 129-138. Westport, CT: Bergin & Garvey.

———. 1996. "Jewish and Korean Merchants in African American Neighborhoods: A Comparative Perspective." In *Los Angeles—Struggle toward Mul-*

tiethnic Community: Asian American, African American and Latino Perspectives, edited by Edward Chang and Russell Leong. Seattle: University of Washington Press.
_____. 2004. "Korean Swapmeets in Los Angeles: Economic and Racial Implications." *Amerasia Journal* 30 (1): 53-74.
_____. 2009. "From Informal to Mainstream Economy: Korean Indoor Swapmeets in Los Angeles and Beyond." In *Korean Economy and Community in the 21st Century*, edited by Eui-Young Yu, Hyojoung Kim, Kyeyoung Park, and Moonsong Oh, 457-484. Los Angeles: Korean American Economic Development Center.
Chang, Jeff. 1993. "Race, Class, Conflict and Empowerment: On Ice Cube's 'Black Korea.'" *Amerasia Journal* 19 (2): 87-108.
Cheng, Lucie, and Yen Le Espiritu. 1989. "Korean Businesses in Black and Hispanic Neighborhoods: A Study of Intergroup Relations." *Sociological Perspectives* 32: 521-34.
Chin, Ku-Sup, In-Jin Yoon, and David Smith. 1996. "Immigrant Small Business and International Economic Linkage: A Case of the Korean Wig Industry in Los Angeles, 1968-1977." *International Migration Review* 30: 485-510.
Cho, Namju. 1992. "Check Out, Not In: Koreana Wilshire/Hyatt Take-Over and the Los Angeles Korean Community." *Amerasia Journal* 18 (1): 131-139.
Cho, Sumi K. 1993. "Korean Americans vs. African Americans: Conflict and Construction." In *Reading Rodney King/Reading Urban Uprising*, edited by Robert Gooding-Williams. New York: Routledge.
Fawcett, James T., and Robert W. Gardner. 1994. "Asian Immigrant Entrepreneurs and Non-Entrepreneurs: A Comparative Study of Recent Korean and Filipino Immigrants." *Population and Environment* 15: 211-238.
Fernandez, Marilyn, and Kwang Chung Kim. 1998. "Self-employment Rates of Asian Immigrant Groups: An Analysis of Intra-group and Inter-group Differences." *International Migration Review* 32: 654-672.
Freer, Regina. 1994. "Black-Korean Conflict." In *The Los Angles Riots: Lessons for the Urban Future*, edited by Mark Baldassare, 175-203. Boulder, CO: Westview Press.
Ikemoto, Lisa. 1993. "Traces of the Master Narrative in the Story of African American/Korean American Conflict: How We Constructed 'Los Angeles'." *Southern California Law Review* 66: 1581-1598.
Jo, Moon H. 1992. "Korean Merchants in the Black Community: Prejudice among the Victims of Prejudice." *Ethnic Racial Studies* 15: 396-411.
Kang, Miliann. 1997. "Manicuring Race, Gender, and Class: Service Interactions in New York City Korean-Owned Nail Salons." *Race, Gender, and Class* 4: 143-164.
_____. 2003. "The Managed Hand: The Commercialization of Bodies and Emotions in Korean Immigrant-Owned Nail Salons." *Gender and Society* 17: 820-839.
_____. Forthcoming. "Manicuring Intimacies: Inequality and Resistance in Asian-Owned Nail Salons." In *Intimate Labors: Interdisciplinary Perspec-

tive on *Care, Sex, and Domestic Work*, edited by Eileen Boris and Rhacel Salazar Parrenas. Stanford, CA: Stanford University Press.

Kim, Barbara W., and Grace Yoo. 2009. "Immigrant Entrepreneurs: Savings for Health and Future." In *Korean Economy and Community in the 21st Century*, edited by Eui-Young Yu, Hyojoung Kim, Kyeyoung Park, and Moonsong Oh, 545-570. Los Angeles: Korean American Economic Development Center.

Kim, Claire Jean. 2009a. "Playing the Racial Trump Card: Asian Americans in Contemporary U.S. Politics." *Amerasia Journal* 26 (3): 35-66.

_____. 2000b. "The Politics of Black-Korean Conflict: Black Power Protest and the Mobilization of Racial Communities." In *Imigration and Race*, edited by Gerald Jaynes. New Haven, CT: Yale University Press.

Kim, Dae Young. 1999. "Beyond Co-Ethnic Solidarity: Mexican and Ecuadorian Employment in Korean-Owned Businesses in New York City." *Ethnic and Racial Studies* 22: 581-605.

Kim, Dae Young, and Lori Dance. 2005. "Korean-Black Relations: Contemporary Challenges, Scholarly Explanations, and Future Prospects." In *Blacks and Asians: Crossings, Conflicts, and Commonality*, edited by Hazel McFerson. Durham, NC: Carolina Academic Press.

Kim, Elaine. 1993. "Home Is Where the *Han* Is: A Korean-American Perspective on the Los Angeles Upheavals." In *Reading Rodney King/Reading Urban Uprising*, edited by Robert Gooding-Williams. New York: Routledge.

_____. 1994. "Between Black and White: An Interview with Bong Hwan Kim." In *The State of Asian America*, edited by Aguilar-San Juan, 71-100. Boston: South End Press.

Kim, Houjoung, and Sune S. Sun. 2009. "Parental Occupation and Second-Generation Korean American Ethnic Identities: The Case of Small Business Entrepreneurship." In *Korean Economy and Community in the 21st Century*, edited by Eui-Young Yu, Hyojoung Kim, Kyeyoung Park, and Moonsong Oh, 545-570. Los Angeles: Korean American Economic Development Center.

Kim, Hyung-Chan. 1976. "Ethnic Enterprise among Korean Emigrants in America." *Journal of Korean Affairs* 6: 40-58.

Kim, Illsoo. 1987. "The Koreans: Small Business in an Urban Frontier." In *New Immigrants in New York*, edited by Nancy Foner, 219-242. New York: Columbia University Press.

Kim, Kwang Chung, and Won Moo Hurh. 1985. "Ethnic Resource Utilization of Korean Immigrant Entrepreneurs in the Chicago Minority Area." *International Migration Review* 19: 82-111.

Kim, Kwang Chung, Won Moo Hurh, and Marilyn Fernandez. 1989. "Intra-Group Differences in Business Participation: Three Asian Immigrant Groups." *International Migration Review* 23: 73-95.

Kim, Kwang Chung, and Shin Kim. 2009. "Korean Business in Chicago's Southside: A Historical Overview." In *Korean Economy and Community in the 21st Century*, edited by Eui-Young Yu, Hyojoung Kim, Kyeyoung Park, and Moonsong Oh, 183-210. Los Angeles: Korean American Economic Development Center.

Kim, Richard, Kane K. Nakamura, and Gisele Fong with Ron Cabarloc, Barbara Jung, and Sung Lee. 1992. "Asian Immigrant Women Garment Workers in Los Angeles: A Preliminary Investigation." *Amerasia Journal* 18 (1): 118-119.

Kim, Taegi, and Sun Mi Chang. 2009. "Korean American Business: Clothing Industry in Los Angeles." In *Korean Economy and Community in the 21st Century*, edited by Eui-Young Yu, Hyojoung Kim, Kyeyoung Park, and Moonsong Oh, 157-182. Los Angeles: Korean American Economic Development Center.

Koch, Nadine, and H. Eric Schockman. 1994. "Riot, Rebellion, or Civil Unrest? Korean American and African American Business Communities in Los Angeles." In *Community in Crisis*, edited by George O. Totten III and H. Eric Schockman. Los Angeles: University of Southern California, Center for Multiethnic and Transnational Studies.

Lee, Dong Ok. 1992. "Commodification of Ethnicity: The Sociospatial Reproduction of Immigrant Entrepreneurs." *Urban Affairs Quarterly* 28: 258-275.

_____. 1995a. "Koreatown and Korean Small Firms in Los Angeles: Locating in the Ethnic Neighborhoods." *Professional Geographer* 47: 184-195.

_____. 1995b. "Responses to Spatial Rigidity in Urban Transformation: Korean Business Experience in Los Angeles." *International Journal of Urban and Regional Research* 19 (1): 40-54. "

Lee, Jennifer. 1998. "Cultural Brokers: Race-based Hiring in Inner-City Neighborhoods." *American Behavioral Scientist* 41: 927-937.

_____. 1999. "Retail Niche Domination among African American, Jewish, and Korean Entrepreneurs: Competition, Co-ethnic Advantage and Disadvantage." *American Behavioral Scientist* 42: 1398-1416.

_____. 2000a. "Immigrant and African American Competition: Jewish, Korean, and African American Entrepreneurs." In *Immigration Research for a New Century*, edited by Nancy Foner, Rubén G. Rumbaut, and Steve J. Gold, 322-344. New York: Russell Sage Foundation.

_____. 2000b. "Striving for the American Dream: Struggle, Success, and Intergroup Conflict among Korean Immigrant Entrepreneurs." In *Contemporary Asian America*, edited by Min Zhou and James V. Gatewood, 278-294. New York: New York University Press.

_____. 2001. "Entrepreneurship and Business Development among African Americans, Koreans, and Jews: Exploring Some Structural Differences." In *Transnational Communities and the Political Economy of New York City in the 1990s*, edited by Héctor R. Cordero-Guzmán, Robert C. Smith, and Ramón Grosfoguel. Philadelphia: Temple University Press.

_____. 2002. "From Civil Relations to Racial Conflict: Merchant-Customer Interactions in Urban America." *American Sociological Review* 67: 77-98.

_____. 2006. "Beyond Conflict and Controversy: Blacks, Jews, and Koreans in Urban America." In *Immigration and Crime: Race, Ethnicity, and Violence*,

edited by Ramiro Martinez and Abel Valenzuela. New York: New York University Press.
Lee, John Y. 1983. "A Study on Financial Structure and Operating Problems of Korean Small Businesses in Los Angeles." Los Angeles: Mid-Wilshire Community Research Center.
Liem, Ramsay, and Jinsoo Kim. 1992. "Pico Korean Workers' Struggle, Korean Americans, and the Lessons of Solidarity." *Amerasia Journal* 18 (1): 49-68.
Light, Ivan. 1980. "Asian Enterprise in America: Chinese, Japanese, and Koreans in Small Business." In *Self-Help in Urban America: Patterns of Minority Business Enterprise*, edited by Scott Cummings, 33-57. New York: Kenikart Press.
_____. 1984. "Immigrant and Ethnic Enterprise in North America." *Ethnic and Racial Studies* 7: 195-216.
_____. 1985. "Immigrant Entrepreneurs in America: Koreans in Los Angeles." In *Clamor at the Gates: The New American Immigration*, edited by Nathan Glazer, 161-178. San Francisco: ICS Press.
Light, Ivan, Richard Bernard, and Rebecca Kim. 1999. "Immigrant Incorporation in the Garment Industry of Los Angeles." *International Migration Review* 33: 5-25.
Light, Ivan, Hadas Har-Chvi, and Kenneth Kan. 1994. "Black/Korean Conflict in Los Angeles." In *Managing Divided Cities*, edited by Seamus Dunn. Newbury Park, CA: Sage Publications.
Light, Ivan, Im Jung Kwuon, and Deng Zhong. 1990. "Korean Rotating Credit Associations in Los Angeles." *Amerasia Journal* 16 (1): 35-54.
Min, Pyong Gap. 1984a. "A Structural Analysis of Korean Business in the U.S." *Ethnic Groups* 6: 1-25.
_____. 1984b. "From White-Collar Occupations to Small Business: Korean Immigrants' Occupational Adjustment." *The Sociological Quarterly* 25: 333-352.
_____. 1986-1987. "A Comparison of Korean and Filipino Immigrants in Small Business." *Amerasia Journal* 13 (1): 53-71.
_____. 1988. "Korean Immigrant Entrepreneurship: A Multivariate Analysis." *Journal of Urban Affairs* 10: 197-212.
_____. 1989. "The Social Costs of Immigrant Entrepreneurship: A Response to Edna Bonacich." *Amerasia Journal* 5 (2): 187-194.
_____. 1990. "Problems of Korean Immigrant Entrepreneurship." *International Migration Review* 24: 436-455.
_____. 1996. "The Entrepreneurial Adaptation of Korean Immigrants." In *Origins and Destinies: Immigration, Race, and Ethnicity in America*, edited by Silvia Pedraza and Rubén Rumbaut, 302-314. Belmont, CA: Wadsworth Publishing Company.
_____. 2002. "A Comparison of Pre- and Post-1965 Asian Immigrant Businesses." In *Mass Migration to the United States: Classical and Contemporary Periods*, edited by Pyong Gap Min, 285-308. Walnut Creek, CA: Altamira Press.

_____. 2006. "Major Issues Related to Asian American Experiences." In *Asian Americans: Contemporary Trends and Issues*, Second Edition, edited by Pyong Gap Min, 80-109. Thousand Oaks, CA: Pine Forge Press.

_____. 2007a. "Korean Immigrants' Concentration in Small Business, Business-Related Inter-group Conflicts, and Ethnic Solidarity." In *Handbook of Research on Ethnic Minority Entrepreneurship*, edited by Leo-Paul Dana, 212-227. Cheltenham, United Kingdom: Edward Elgar Publishing.

_____. 2007b. "Korean-Latino Relations in the Post-1965 Era." *Dubois Review* 5: 395-412.

_____. 2009. "Patterns of Korean Businesses in New York." In *Korean Economy and Community in the 21st Century*, edited by Eui-Young Yu, Hyojoung Kim, Kyeyoung Park, and Moonsong Oh, 133-156. Los Angeles: Korean American Economic Development Center.

Min, Pyong Gap, and Mehdi Bozorgmehr. 2000. "Immigrant Entrepreneurship and Business Patterns: A Comparison of Koreans and Iranians in Los Angeles." *International Migration Review* 34 (3): 707-738.

Min, Pyong Gap, Dong Wan Joo, and Young Oak Kim. 2009. "Korean Produce Retailers in New York: Their Conflicts with White Distributors and Use of Ethnic Collective Actions." In *Korean Economy and Community in the 21st Century*, edited by Eui-Young Yu, Hyojoung Kim, Kyeyoung Park, and Moonsong Oh, 485-508. Los Angeles: Korean American Economic Development Center.

Min, Pyong Gap, and Charles. Jaret. 1985. "Ethnic Business Success: The Case of Korean Small Business in Atlanta." *Sociology and Social Research* 69: 412-435.

Min, Pyong Gap, and Andrew Kolodny. 1994. "The Middleman Minority Characteristics of Korean Immigrants in the United States." *Korea Journal of Population and Development* 23: 179-202.

Nam, Young Ho, and James I. Herbert. 1999. "Characteristics and Key Success Factors in Family Business: The Case of Korean Immigrant Business in Metro-Atlanta." *Family Business Review* 12 (4): 341-352.

Norman, Alex J. 1994. "Black-Korean Relations: From Desperation to Dialogue, or from Shouting and Shooting to Sitting and Talking." *Journal of Multicultural Social Work* 3 (2): 87-99.

Oh, Joong-Hwan. 2007. "Economic Incentive, Embeddedness, and Social Support: A Study of Korean-owned Nail Salon Workers' Rotating Credit Associations." *International Migration Review* 41: 623-655.

_____. 2011. "Immigration, Cultural Adjustment, and Work Values: The Case of Korean Nail Care Workers in New York." *Development and Society* 40 (2): 261-288.

Oh, Moonsong. 2009. "The Growth and Change of Korean-Owned Businesses in the United States, 1970s-2000s." In *Korean Economy and Community in the 21st Century*, edited by Eui-Young Yu, Hyojoung Kim, Kyeyoung Park, and Moonsong Oh, 67-96. Los Angeles: Korean American Economic Development Center.

Ong, Paul, Kyeyoung Park, and Yasmin Tong. 1994. "The Korean-Black Conflict and the State." In *New Asian Immigration in Los Angeles and Global Reconstructing*, edited by Paul Ong, Edna Bonacich, and Lucie Cheng, 264-294. Philadelphia: Temple University Press.

Park, Edward J.W. 1996. "Our L.A.?: Korean Americans in the 'New' Los Angeles." In *Rethinking Los Angeles*, edited by Michael Dear, H. Eric Schockman and Greg Hise, 153-168. Thousand Oaks, CA: Sage Publications.

———. 2001. "Community Divided: Korean American Politics in Post-Civil Unrest Los Angeles." In *Asians and Latino Immigrants in a Restructuring Economy: The Metamorphosis of Southern California*, edited by Marta Lopez-Garza and David R. Diaz, 273-288. Stanford: Stanford University Press.

———. 2004. "Labor Organizing Beyond Race and Nation: The Los Angeles Hilton Case." *International Journal of Sociology and Social Research* 24 (2/8): 137-152.

———. 2009. "Korean Americans and the U.S. High Technology Industry: From Ethnicity to Transnationalism." In *Korean Economy and Community in the 21st Century*, edited by Eui-Young Yu, Hyojoung Kim, Kyeyoung Park, and Moonsong Oh, 293-314. Los Angeles: Korean American Economic Development Center.

Park, Edward J.W., and John S.W. Park. 1999. "A New American Dilemma?: Asian Americans and Latinos in American Race Relations Theorizing." *Journal of Asian American Studies* 2: 289-309.

Park, Edward J.W., and Leland T. Saito. 2000. "Multiracial Collaborations and Coalitions." In *The State of Asian Pacific America: Transforming Race Relations*, edited by Paul Ong, 435-474. LEAP Public Policy Institute and University of California, Los Angeles Asian American Studies Center.

Park, Kyeyoung. 1995. "The Reinvention of Affirmative Action: Korean Immigrants' Changing Conceptions of African Americans and Latin Americans." *Urban Anthropology* 24: 59-92.

———. 1996. "Use and Abuse of Race and Culture: Black-Korean Tension in America." *American Anthropologist* 98: 492-499.

———. 2009. "Challenging the Liquor Industry in Los Angeles." In *Korean Economy and Community in the 21st Century*, edited by Eui-Young Yu, Hyojoung Kim, Kyeyoung Park, and Moonsong Oh, 253-292. Los Angeles: Korean American Economic Development Center.

Robinson, Reginald Leamon. 1993. "'The Other against Itself': Deconstructing the Violent Discourse between Korean and African Americans." *Southern California Law Review* 67: 15-115.

Shin, Eui Hang. 2009. "The Interplay of Economy and Ethnicity: The Case of the Textile and Apparel Industry and Korean Immigrant Communities." In *Korean Economy and Community in the 21st Century*, edited by Eui-Young Yu, Hyojoung Kim, Kyeyoung Park, and Moonsong Oh, 315-348. Los Angeles: Korean American Economic Development Center.

Shin, Eui Hang, and S.K. Han. 1990. "Korean Immigrant Small-Businesses in Chicago: An Analysis of the Resource Mobilization." *Amerasia Journal* 16 (1): 39-62.

Silverman, Robert Mark. 1998. "Middleman Minorities and Sojourning in Black America: The Case of Korean Entrepreneurs on the South Side of Chicago." *Sociological Imagination* 35: 159-181.

Stewart, Ella. 1993. "Communication between African Americans and Korean Americans: Before and After the Los Angeles Riots" *Amerasia Journal* 19 (2): 23-53.

Waldinger, Roger. 1995. "When the Melting Pot Boils Over: The Irish, Jews, Blacks, and Koreans of New York." In *The Bubbling Cauldron: Race, Ethnicity, and the Urban Crisis*, edited by Michael Peter Smith and Joe R. Feagin, 265-281. Minneapolis: University of Minnesota Press.

Weitzer, Ronald. 1997. "Racial Prejudice among Korean Merchants in African American Neighborhoods." *Sociological Quarterly* 38: 587-606.

Yoon, In-Jin. 1990. "The Changing Significance of Ethnic and Class Resources in Immigrant Business: The Case of Korean Immigrant Businesses in Chicago." *International Migration Review* 25: 303-332.

———. 1995. "The Growth of Korean Immigrant Entrepreneurship in Chicago." *Ethnic and Racial Studies* 18: 315-335.

Young, Phillip K. Y. 1983. "Family Labor, Sacrifice and Competition: Korean Greengrocers in New York City." *Amerasia Journal* 10 (2): 53-71.

Yoo, Jin Kyung. 2000. "Utilization of Social Networks for Immigrant Entrepreneurship: A Case Study of Korean Immigrants in the Atlanta Area." *International Review of Sociology* 10: 347-363.

5. Family Relations, Women, the Elderly, and Social Services (Health)

Asis, Maruja Milagros. 1991. "To the United States and into the Labor Force: Occupational Expectations of Filipino and Korean Immigrant Women." Papers of the Population Institute, Paper No. 118. Honolulu: East-West Center.

Chang, Janet. 2004. "Married and Divorced Korean Immigrant Women: A Report on Their Psychological Well-being." *Amerasia Journal* 30 (1): 75-87.

Chang, J., S. Rhee, and D. Weaver. 2006. "Characteristics of Child Abuse in Immigrant Korean Families and Correlates of Placement Decision." *Child Abuse and Neglect* 30: 881-891.

Chai, Alice Yun. 1986. "Adaptive Strategies of Recent Korean Immigrant Women in Hawaii." In *Beyond the Public/Domestic Dichotomy: Contemporary Perspectives on Women's Public Live*, edited by Janet Sharistanian, 65-99. West Port, CT: Greenwood Press.

Erickson, Joan Good, Patrick J. Devlieger, and Jenny Moon Sung. 1999. "Korean-American Female Perspectives on Disability." *American Journal of Speech-Language Pathology* 8: 99-108.

Eu, Hongsook. 1992. "Health Status and Social and Demographic Determinants of Living Arrangements among the Korean Elderly." *Korea Journal of Population and Development* 21: 197-223.

Jeong, Gyung Ja, and Walter R. Schumm. 1990. "Family Satisfaction in Korean/American Marriage: An Exploratory Study of the Perception of Korean Wives." *Journal of Comparative Family Studies* 219: 325-336.

Kauh, Tae-Ock. 1997. "Intergenerational Relations: Older Korean Americans' Experience." *Journal of Cross-cultural Gerontology* 12: 245-271.

_____.1999. "Changing Status and Roles of Older Korean Immigrants in the United States." *International Journal of Aging and Human Development* 49: 213-229.

Kiefer, C.W., S. Kim, K. Choi, L. Kim, B. L. Kim, S. Shon, and T. Kim. 1985. "Adjustment Problems of Korean American Elderly." *Gerontologist* 25: 477-82.

Kim, Bok-Lim. 1972. "An Appraisal of Korean Immigrant Service Needs." *Social Casework* 57: 139-148.

_____. 1978. "Problems and Service Needs of Asian Americans in Chicago: An Empirical Study." *Amerasia Journal* 5 (2): 23-44.

_____. 1996. "Korean Families." In *Ethnicity and Family Therapy*, Second Edition, edited by Monica McGoldrick, Joe Giordano, and Nydia Garcia-Preto, 183-214. New York: Guilford Press.

Kim, Elaine H. 1998. "Men's Talk: A Korean American View of South Korean Constructions of Women, Gender, and Masculinity." In *Dangerous Women: Gender and Korean Nationalism*, edited by Elaine H. Kim and Chungmoo Choi, 67-118. New York: Routledge.

_____. 1999. "Dangerous Affinities: Korean American Feminism (En)-counter Gendered Korean and Racialized U.S. Nationalist Narratives." *Hitting Critical Mass* 6: 1-12.

Kim-Goh, Mikyong, Joe Yamamoto, and Chong Suh. 1994. "Characteristics of Asian/Pacific Islander Psychiatric Patients in a Public Mental Health System." *Asian American and Pacific Islander Journal of Health* 2: 125-132.

Kim, Jaeyop. 1999. "Marital Conflict and Violence in Korean-American Families." *Asian Journal of Women's Studies* 5: 47-68.

Kim, K., et al. 1999. "Cervical Cancer Screening Knowledge and Practices among Korean-American Women." *Cancer Nursing* 22: 297-302.

Kim, K. A., and D. J. Mueller. 1997. "Memory, Self-Efficacy, and Adaptability in Korean American Older Adults: A Collective Study of Four Cases." *Educational Gerontology* 23: 407-423.

Kim, Kwang Chung, and Won Moon Hurh. 1988. "The Burden of Double Roles: Korean Wives in the USA." *Ethnic and Racial Studies* 11: 151-167.

Kim, Kwang Chung, Won Moo Hurh, and Shin Kim. 1988. "Generational Differences in Korean Immigrants' Life Conditions in the United States." *Sociological Perspectives* 36: 258-270.

Kim, Kwang Chung, Hei Chu Kim, and Won Moo Hurh. 1979. "Division of Household Tasks in Korean Immigrant Families in the United States." *International Journal of Sociology of the Family* 9: 161-175.

Kim, Kwang Chung, Shin Kim, and Won Moon Hurh. 1991. "Filial Piety and Intergenerational Relationships in Korean Immigrant Families." *International Journal of Aging and Human Development* 33: 233-245.

Kim, K. K., et al.1993. "Nutritional Status of Chinese-, Korean-, and Japanese-American Elderly." *Journal of American Dietetic Association* 93 (12): 1416-1422.

Kim, Nadia Y. 2006. "'Patriarchy Is So Third World': Korean Immigrant Women and Migrating White Western Masculinity." *Social Problems* 53: 519-536.

Kim, Oksoo. 1999a. "Meditation Effect of Social Support between Ethnic Attachment and Loneliness in Older Korean Immigrants." *Research in Nursing & Health* 22: 169-175.

_____. 1999b. "Predictors of Loneliness in Elderly Korean Immigrant Women Living in the United States of America." *Journal of Advanced Nursing* 29: 1082-1088.

Kim, Paul, and Jung Sup Kim. 1992. "Korean Elderly: Policy, Program, and Practice Implications." In *Social Work Practice with Asian Americans*, edited by Sharlene M. Furuto, Renuka Biswas, Douglas K. Chung, Kenji Murase, and Fairial Ross-Sheriff, 227-239. Newbury Park, CA: Sage Publications.

Kim, Shin, and Kwang Chung Kim. 2001. "Intimacy at a Distance: Korean American Style: The Invited Korean Elderly and Their Married Children." In *Age through Ethnic Lenses: Caring for the Elderly in a Multicultural Society*, edited by Laura Katz Olson, 45-58. Lanham, MD: Rowman and Littlefield.

Kim, Sunah, and Lynn Rew. 1994. "Ethnic Identity, Role Integration, Quality of Life, and Depression in Korean-American Women." *Archives of Psychiatric Nursing* 8 (6): 348-356.

Kim-Goh, Mikyong, et al. 1995. "Psychological Impact of the Los Angeles Riots on Korean-American Victims: Implications for Treatment." *American Journal of Orthopsychiatry* 65: 138-147.

Kim, Yujin. 2009. "Family Caregivers on Dementia Caregiving: A Post Phenomenological Inquiry." *Journal of Gerontological Social Work* 52: 600-617.

Ko, Christine, and Henry Cohen. 1998. "Intraethnic Comparison of Eating Attitudes in Native Koreans and Korean Americans Using a Korean Translation of the Eating Attitudes Test." *Journal of Nervous and Mental Disease* 186 (10): 631-636.

Koh, James Y., and William G. Bell. 1987. "Korean Elders in the United States: International Relations and Living Arrangement." *Gerontologist* 27: 66-71.

Lee, H. Y., and Charles K. Eaton. 2009. "Financial Abuse in Elderly Korean Immigrants: Mixed Analysis of the Role of Culture on Perception and Help-Seeking Intension." *Journal of Gerontological Social Work* 52: 463-488.

Lee, H. Y., Ailee Moon, and J.E. Lubben. 2005. "Depression among Elderly Korean Immigrants: Exploring Socio-Cultural Factors." *Journal of Ethnic and Cultural Diversity in Social Work* 13: 1-26.

Lee, Jik-Joen. 1987. "Asian American Elderly: A Neglected Minority Group." *Journal of Gerontological Social Work* 9 (4): 103-116.

Lee, Mee Sook, et al. 1996. "Social Support and Depression among Elderly Korean Immigrants in the United States." *International Journal of Aging and Human Development* 42: 313-327.

Lee, S. K., et al. 2000. "Acculturation and Health in Korean Americans." *Social Science and Medicine* 51: 159-173.

Lee, Y. J., and H. Koo. 2006. "'Wild Goose Fathers' and Globalized Family Strategy for Education in Korea." *International Development Planning Review* 28: 533-553.

Lee, Y. R., and K. T. Sung. 1997. "Cultural Difference in Caregiving Motivations for Demented Parents: Korean Caregivers Versus American Caregivers." *International Journal of Aging & Human Development* 44: 115-127.

Lim, In-Sook. 1997. "Korean Immigrant Women's Challenge to Gender Inequality at Home: The Interplay of Economic Resources, Gender and Family. *Gender and Society* 11: 31-51.

Lim, Jung-Won, and Maura O'Keefe. 2009. "Social Problems and Service Needs in a Korean American Community: Perceptions of Community Residents and Community Key Informants." *Journal of Ethnic and Cultural Diversity in Social Work* 18: 182-202.

Linden, S. 1997. "Aiko: Drama Therapy in the Recovery Process of a Japanese/Korean-American Woman." *Arts in Psychotherapy* 24: 193-203.

Ludman, E. K., K.J. Kang, and L.L.Lynn. 1992. "Food Beliefs and Diets of Pregnant Korean American Women." *Journal of American Dietetic Association* 92: 1519-1520.

Min, J. W., Ailee Moon, and J. E. Lubben. 2005. "Determinants of Psychological Distress over Time among Older Korean Americans and Non-Hispanic White Elders: Evidence from a Two-Wave Panel Study." *Journal of Aging and Mental Health* 9: 210-222.

———. 2006. "Social Work Practice with Asian American Elders." In *Handbook on Aging,* edited by B. Berkman, 257-271. New York: Oxford University Press.

Min, Pyong Gap. 1984. "An Exploratory Study of Kin Ties among Korean Immigrant Families in Atlanta." *Journal of Comparative Family Studies* 15: 59-76.

———. 1988. "Korean Immigrant Families." In *Ethnic Families in America,* edited by Charles Mindel, Robert Habenstein, and Roosevelt Wright, 199-229. New York: Elsevier.

_____. 1992. "Korean Immigrant Wives' Overwork." *Korea Journal of Population and Development* 21: 23-36.

_____. 1993. "Korean Immigrants' Marital Patterns and Marital Adjustment: An Exploratory Study." In *Family Ethnicity: Strengths in Diversity*, edited by Harriette McAdoo, 287-299. Newbury Park, CA: Sage Publications.

_____. 1997. "Korean Immigrant Wives' Labor Force Participation, Marital Power, and Status." In *Women and Work: Race, Ethnicity, and Class*, edited by Elizabeth Higginbotham and Mary Romero, 176-191. Newbury Park, CA: Sage Publications.

_____. 1998a. "Korean American Families." In *Minority Families in the United States: A Multicultural Perspectives*, Second Edition, edited by Ronald L. Taylor, 189-207. Upper Saddle River, NJ: Prentice Hall.

_____. 1998b. "The Korean American Family." In *Ethnic Families in America: Patterns and Variations,* Fourth Edition, edited by Charles Mindel, Robert Habenstein, and Roosevelt Wright, Jr., 223-253. Upper Saddle River, NJ: Prentice Hall.

_____. 2001. "Changes in Korean Immigrants' Gender Role and Social Status, and Their Marital Conflicts." *Sociological Focus* 16: 201-220.

Moon, Ailee. 1996. "Predictors of More among Korean Immigrant Elderly in the USA." *Journal of Cross-Cultural Gerontology* 11: 351-367.

_____. 1999. "Elder Abuse and Neglect among the Korean Elderly in the United States." In *Understanding Elder Abuse in Minority Populations*, edited by T. Tatara, 109-118. Washington, D. C. New York: Taylor and Francis.

_____. 2006. "Working with Korean American Families." In *Ethnicity and Dementias*, Second Edition, edited by G. Geo, and D. Gallagher-Thomson, 245-262. Washington, D.C.: Taylors and Francis.

Moon, Ailee, and D. Benton. 2000. "Tolerance of Elder Abuse and Attitudes toward Third-Party Intervention among African American, Korean American, and White Elderly." *Journal of Multicultural Social Work* 8: 283-303.

Moon, Ailee, and T. Evans-Campbell. 1999. "Awareness of Formal and Informal Sources of Help for Victims of Elder Abuse among Korean American and Non-Hispanic White Elders in Los Angeles." *Journal of Elder Abuse and Neglect* 11(3): 1-23.

Moon, Ailee, and S. K. Tomita, and S. Jung-Kamei. 2001. "Elderly Mistreatment among Four Asian American Groups: An Exploratory Study on Tolerance, Victim Blaming, and Attitudes toward Third-Party Intervention." *Journal of Gerontological Social Work* 36: 159-169.

Moon, Ailee, J. Lubben, and V. Villa. 1998. "Awareness and Utilization of Community Long-Term Care Services by Elderly Koreans and Non-Hispanic White Americans." *The Gerontologist* 38: 309-316.

Moon, Ailee, and S. Rhee. 2006. "Social Work Practice with Immigrant and Refugee Elders." In *Handbook on Aging*, edited by B. Berman, 205-217. New York: Oxford University Press.

Moon, Ailee, and O. Williams. 1993. "Perceptions of Elder Abuse and Help Seeking Patterns among African-American, Caucasian-American, and Korean-American Elderly Women." *The Gerontologist* 33: 386-395.

Moon, Sungsook. 2003. "Immigration and Mothering: Two Generations of Middle-Class Korean Immigrant Women." *Gender and Society* 17: 840-860.

Na, Kyung-Hee. 1993. "Perceived Problems and Service Delivery for Korean Immigrants." *Social Work* 38 (3): 103-109.

Pang, Keum Young. 1990. "Hwabyung: The Construction of a Korean Popular Illness among Korean Elderly Immigrant Women in the United States." *Culture, Medicine and Psychiatry* 14: 495-512.

_____. 1994. "Understanding Depression among Elderly Korean Immigrants through Their Folk Illnesses." *Medical Anthropology Quarterly* 8: 209-216.

_____. 1998. "Symptoms of Depression in Elderly Korean Immigrants: Narration and the Healing Process." *Culture, Medicine and Psychiatry* 22: 93-122.

Park, Kee-Joung Yoo, and Leona M. Peterson. 1991. "Beliefs, Practices, and Experiences of Korean Women in Relation to Childbirth." *Health Care for Women International* 12: 261-269.

Park, Kyeyoung. 1998. "Attitudes toward Patient Autonomy among Elderly Korean-Americans." *Medical Anthropology Quarterly* 12: 403-423.

_____. 2000. "Sudden and Subtle Challenge: Disparity in Conception of Marriage and Gender in the Korean American Community." In *Cultural Compass: Ethnographic Explorations of Asian America*, edited by Martin Manalansan, 159-174. Philadelphia: Temple University Press.

_____. 2002. "10,000 Senora Lees: The Changing Gender Ideology in the Korean Diaspora as Reflected in the Clothing Industry." *Amerasia Journal* 28 (2): 161-180.

Pourat, N., J. Lubben, S. Wallace, and A. Moon." 1999. "Predictors of Use and Traditional Korean Healers among Elderly Koreans in Los Angeles." *The Gerontologist* 39: 711-719.

Pyke, Karen. 2000. "The Normal American Family as an Interpretive Structure of Family Life among Grown Children of Korean and Vietnamese Immigrants." *Journal of Marriage and Family* 62: 240-255.

Rhee, Siyon. 1997. "Domestic Violence in the Korean Immigrant Family." *Journal of Sociology and Social Welfare* 24: 63-77.

Rhner, Ronald, and Sandra Pettengill. 1985. "Perceived Parental Acceptance-Rejection and Parental Control among Korean Adolescents." *Child Development* 56: 524-528.

Sawyers, J.E., et al. 1992. "Gastric Cancer in the Korean-American: Cultural Implications." *Oncological Nursing Forum* 19: 619-623.

Shin, Hosung, Howin Song, Jinsook Kim, and Janice Probst. 2005. "Insurance, Acculturation and Health Service Utilization among Korean-Americans." *Journal of Immigrant Health* 7 (2): 65-74.

Shin, Kyung Rim. 1993. "Factors Predicting Depression among Korean-American Women in New York." *International Journal of Nursing Studies* 30: 415-423.

Shon, H., and Ailee Moon. 2008. "A Model for Developing and Implementing a Theory-Driven, Culture-Specific Outreach and Educational Program for Korean American Caregivers of People with Alzheimer's Disease." *Journal of Aging and Mental Health* 9: 210-222.

Sohn, Linda. 2004. "The Health and Health Status of Older Korean Americans at the 100-Year Anniversary of Korean Immigration." *Journal of Cross-Cultural Gerontology* 19: 203-219.

Sohng, Sue, and Larry D. Icared. 1996. "A Korean Gay Man in the United States: Toward a Cultural Context for Social Service Practice." In *Men of Color: A Context for Service to Homosexually Active Men*, edited by John F. Longres, 115-137. New York: Harrington Park Press/Haworth Press, Inc.

Song, Young In. 1992. "Battered Korean Women in Urban United States." In *Social Work Practice with Asian Americans*, edited by Sharlene M. Furuto, Renuka Biswas, Douglas K. Chung, Kenji Murase, and Fairial Ross-Sheriff, 213-226. Newbury Park, CA: Sage Publications.

Strom, Robert, Susan Daniels, and Seong Park. 1986. "The Adjustment of Korean Immigrant Families." *Educational & Psychological Research* 6: 213-227.

Sung, Kyu-taik. 2000. "An Asian Perspective on Aging East and West: Filial Piety and Changing Families." In *Aging in East and West: Families, States, and the Elderly*, edited by Vern Bengston, Kyung-Dong Kim, George Myers, and Ki-Soo Eun, 101-122. New York: Springer Publishing Company.

Sunoo, Sonia Shin. 1978. "Korean Women Pioneers of the Pacific Northwest." *Oregon Historical Quarterly* 79: 51-64.

Villa, V., S. P. Wallace, Ailee Moon, and J. Lubben. 1999. "A Comparative Analysis of Chronic Disease Prevalence among Older Koreans and Non-Hispanic Whites." In *Special Populations in the Community*, edited by J. G. Sebastian and A. Bushy, 217-227. Gaitherburn, MD: Aspen Publishers, Inc.

Wallace, Steven P., et al. 1996. "Health Practices of Korean Elderly People: National Health Promotion Priorities and Minority Community Needs." *Family & Community Health* 19 (2): 29-42.

Weatherspoon, A.J., et al. 1994. "Alcohol Consumption and Use Norms among Chinese Americans and Korean Americans." *Journal for Study of Alcohol* 55 (2): 202-206.

Yamamoto, Joe, Siyon Rhee, and Dong-San Chang. 1994. "Psychiatric Disorders among Elderly Koreans in the United States." *Community Mental Health Journal* 30: 17-27.

Yang, Eun Sik. 1984. "Korean Women of America: From Subordination to Partnership, 1903-1930." *Amerasia Journal* 11 (2): 1-28.

Youn, G. Y., et al. 1999. "Difference in Familism: Values and Caregiving Outcomes among Korean, Korean American, and White American Dementia Caregivers." *Psychology and Aging* 14: 355-364.

6. Ethnicity and Transnationalism

Danico, Mary Yu. 2000. "1.5 Generation: A Case Study of the Korean American Jaycee in Hawaii." *Korean and Korean American Studies Bulletin* 10 (12): 42-69
———. 2005. "Korean Identities: What Does it Mean to be Korean American in Korea?" *Transactions* 80: 115-136.
Hong, Joann, and Pyong Gap Min. 1999. "Ethnic Attachment among Second-Generation Korean Adolescents." *Amerasia Journal* 25 (1): 165-180.
Kibria, Nazli. 1997. "The Construction of 'Asian American': Reflection on Intermarriage and Ethnic Identity among Second-Generation Chinese and Korean Americans." *Ethnic and Racial Studies* 20: 77-86.
———. 1999. "College and the Notions of 'Asian American': Second Generation Chinese and Korean Americans Negotiate Race and Ethnicity." *Amerasia Journal* 25 (1): 29-52.
———. 2000. "Race, Ethnic Options, and Ethnic Binds: Identity Negotiations of Second-Generation Chinese and Korean Americans." *Sociological Perspectives* 43 (1): 77-95.
———. 2002. "Of Blood, Belonging, and Homeland Trips: Transnationalism and Identity among Second-Generation Chinese and Korean Americans." In *The Changing Faces of Home: The Transnational Lives of the Second Generation*, edited by Peggy Levitt and Mary C. Waters, 295-311. New York: Russell Sage Foundation.
Kim, Nadia Y. Forthcoming. "Finding Our Way Home: Korean Americans, 'Homeland Trips,' and Cultural Foreignness." In *Diasporic Homecomings: Ethnic Return Migrants in Comparative Perspective*, edited by Takeyuki Tsuda. Stanford, CA: Stanford University Press.
Kim, Y. Y. 1977. "Inter-ethnic and Intra-ethnic Communication: A Study of Korean Immigrants in Chicago." In *International and Intercultural Communication Annual*, edited by N. C. Jain. Falls Church, VA: Speech Communication Association.
Lee, Sara S. 2004a. "Class Matters: Racial and Ethnic Identities of Working- and Middle-Class Second-Generation Korean Americans in New York City." In *Becoming New Yorkers: Ethnographies of the New Second Generation*, edited by Philip Kasinitz, John H. Mollenkopf, and Mary C. Waters, 313-338. New York: Russell Sage Foundation.
Lee, Stacey J. 1996. "Perceptions of Panethnicity among Asian American High School Students." *Amerasia Journal* 22 (2): 109-126.
Lee, Young-Oak. 2004. "Language and Identity: An Interview with Chang-rae Lee." *Amerasia Journal* 30 (1): 215-228.

Min, Pyong Gap. 1991. "Cultural and Economic Boundaries of Korean Ethnicity: A Comparative Analysis." *Ethnic and Racial Studies* 14: 225-241.
_____. 2000. "Korean Americans' Language Use." In *New Immigrants in the United States: Background for Second Language Educators*, edited by Sandra Lee McKay and Sau-Ling Cynthia Wong, 305-332. Boston: Cambridge University Press.
Min, Pyong Gap, and Youna Choi. 1993. "Ethnic Attachment among Korean American High School Students." *Korea Journal of Population and Development* 22: 167-179.
Min, Pyong Gap, and Young Oak Kim. 2009. "Ethnic and Sub-ethnic Attachments among Korean, Chinese and Indian Immigrants in New York City." *Ethnic and Racial Studies* 32: 758-780.
Park, Keumjae. 2007. "Constructing Transnational Identities without Leaving Home: Korean Immigrant Women's Cognitive Border-Crossing." *Sociological Forum* 22: 200-218.
Park, Kyeyoung. 1991. "Conceptions of Ethnicities by Koreans: Workplace Encounter." In *Asian Americans*, edited by S. Hune, H. Kim, S. Fugita and A. Ling, 179-190. Pullman, WA: Washington State University Press.
_____. 1999a. "'I Really Do Feel I'm 1.5!' The Construction of Self and Community by Young Korean Americans." *Amerasia Journal* 25 (1): 139-164.
_____. 1999b. "'I'm Floating in the Air': Creation of a Korean Transnational Space among Korean-Latino-American Re-Migrants." *Positions: East Asia Cultures Critique* 7 (3): 667-695.
_____. 2005. "The Cultivation of Korean Immigrants on American Soil: The Discourse on Cultural Construction." In *Multiculturalism in the United States*, edited by Lorman A. Ratner and John D. Buenker, 281-297. Westport, CT: Greenwood Press.
Park, Yoon Jung. 2000-2001. "An Asian American Outside: Crossing Color Lines in the United States and Africa." *Amerasia Journal* 26 (3): 99-117.
Phillips, Earl H. 1980. "Koreans in Los Angeles: A Strategy for a University Bicultural Humanities Curriculum." *Bilingual Resources* 3 (2): 25-41.

7. Korean Community, Ethnic Organizations, and Political Development

Chang, Edward Tea. 1988. "Korean Community Politics in Los Angeles: The Impact of the Kwangju Uprising." *Amerasia Journal* 14 (1): 51-67.
_____. 1999. "The Post-Los Angeles Riot Korean American Community: Challenges and Prospects." *Korean and Korean American Studies Bulletin* 10: 6-26.
Chung, Angie Y. 2001. "The Powers That Bind: A Case Study on the Collective Bases of Coalition-Building in Post-Civil Unrest Los Angeles." *Urban Affairs Review* 37: 205-226.
_____. 2004. "Giving Back to the Community." *Amerasia Journal* 30 (1): 107-124.

———. 2005. "'Politics without the Politics': The Evolving Political Cultures of Ethnic Non-Profits in Koreatown, Los Angeles." *Journal of Ethnic and Migration Studies* 31: 911-929.

———. 2009. "Ethnic Solidarity in a Divided Community: A Study on Bridging Organizations in Koreatown." *Asian America: Forming Communities, Expanding Boundaries*, edited by Huping Ling. New Brunswick, NJ: Rutgers University Press.

———. Forthcoming. "The Geo-Ethnic Bases of Transnational Political Identities: An Analysis of Korean American Organizations in Los Angeles." *Journal of Contemporary Society and Culture*. Seoul, Korea: Institute of Social Development at Yonsei University.

Danico, Mary Yu. 2002. "The Construction and Transformation of the Koran American Community among the 1.5 Generation in Hawaii." In *Intersections and Divergences of Contemporary Asian American Communities*, edited by Linda Trinh Vo and Rick Bonus. Philadelphia: Temple University Press.

Givens, Helen Lewis. 1974. "The Korean Community in Los Angeles County." Originally presented as the author's thesis (M.A.), University of Southern California, 1939. San Francisco: R and E Research Associates.

Lee, C. 2004. "Korean Immigrants' Viewing Patterns of Korean Satellite Television and Its Role in Their Lives." *Asian Journal of Communication* 14 (1): 68-80.

Min, Pyong Gap. 2001. "Koreans: Institutionally Complete Community in New York." In *New Immigrants in New York*, Revised and Updated Edition, edited by Nancy Foner, 173-200. New York: Columbia University Press

Park, Edward J. W. 1998. "Competing Visions: Political Formation of Korean Americans in Los Angeles, 1992-1997." *Amerasia Journal* 24 (1): 41-57.

———. 1999. "Friends or Enemies?: Generational Politics in the Korean American Community in Los Angeles." *Qualitative Sociology* 24: 41-57.

———. 2001. "The Impact of Mainstream Political Mobilization on Asian American Communities: The Case of Korean Americans in Los Angeles, 1992-1998." In *Asian American Politics: Perspective, Experiences, Prospects*, edited by Gordon Chang, 285-307. Stanford, CA: Stanford University.

———. 2002. "Immigration and the Crisis of the Urban Liberal Coalition: The Case of Korean Americans in Los Angeles." In *Governing American Cities: Immigration and Urban Politics*, edited by Michael Jones-Correa, 90-108. New York: Russell Sage Foundation Press.

Roh, Kim-Nam. 1983. "Issues of Korean American Journalism." *Amerasia Journal* 10 (2): 89-102.

Yu, Eui-Young. 1983. "Korean Communities in America: Past, Present, and Future." *Amerasia Journal* 10 (2): 23-52.

Yum, June Ock. 1982. "Communication Diversity and Information Acquisition among Korean Immigrants in Hawaii." *Human Communication Research* 8 (2): 154-169.

8. Religious Practices and Religious Organizations

Abelmann, Nancy, and Shanshan Lan. 2008. "Christian Universalism and U.S. Multiculturalism: An 'Asian American' Campus Church." *Amerasia Journal* 34 (1): 65-84.

Alumkal. Antony. 1999. "Preserving Patriarchy: Assimilation, Gender Norms, and Second-Generation Korean American Evangelicals." *Qualitative Sociology* 22: 129-140.

_____. 2001. "Being Korean, Being Christian: Particularlism and Universalism in a Second-Generation Congregation." In *Korean Americans and Their Religions*, edited by Ho-Youn Kwon, Kwang Chung Kim, and R. Stephen Warner, 181-192. University Park, PA: Pennsylvania State University Press.

Cha, Peter. 2001. "Ethnic Identity Formation and Participation in Immigrant Churches: Second-Generation Korean American Experiences." In *Korean Americans and Their Religions*, edited by Ho-Youn Kwon, Kwang Chung Kim, and R. Stephen Warner, 141-156. University Park, PA: Pennsylvania State University Press.

Chai, Karen. 1998. "Competing for the Second Generation: English-Language Ministry at a Korean Protestant Church." In *Gatherings in Diaspora: Religious Communities and the New Immigration,* edited by R. Stephen Warner and Judith Wittner, 295-332. Philadelphia: Temple University Press.

_____. 2001a. "Beyond 'Strictness' to Distinctiveness: Generational Transition in Korean Protestant Churches." In *Korean Americans and Their Religions*, edited by Ho-Youn Kwon, Kwang Chung Kim, and R. Stephen Warner, 157-180. University Park, PA: Pennsylvania State University Press.

_____. 2001b. "Inter-Ethnic Religious Diversity: Korean Buddhists and Protestants in Greater Boston." In *Korean Americans and Their Religions*, edited by Ho-Youn Kwon, Kwang Chung Kim, and R. Stephen Warner, 273-294. University Park, PA: Pennsylvania State University

Chong, Kelly H. 1998. "What It Means to Be Christian: The Role of Religion in the Construction of Ethnic Identity and Boundary among Second Generation Korean Americans." *Sociology of Religion* 59 (3): 259-286.

Ecklund, Elaine Howard. 2005. "Models of Civil Responsibility; Korean Americans in Congregations with Different Ethnic Composition." *Journal for the Scientific Study of Religion* 44: 15-28.

Goette, Robert. 2001. "The Transformation of First-Generation Church into a Bilingual Church." In *Korean Americans and Their Religions*, edited by Ho-Youn Kwon, Kwang Chung Kim, and R. Stephen Warner, 125-140. University Park, PA: Pennsylvania State University Press.

Hurh, Won Moo, and Kwang Chung Kim. 1990. "Religious Participation of Korean Immigrants in the United States." *Journal of the Scientific Study of Religion* 29: 19-34.

Kim, Andrew E. 2000. "Korean Religious Culture and Its Affinity to Christianity: the Rise of Protestant Christianity in South Korea." *Sociology of Religion* 61: 117-133.

Kim, Bok In. 2001. "Won Buddhism in the United States." In *Korean Americans and Their Religions*, edited by Ho-Youn Kwon, Kwang Chung Kim, and R. Stephen Warner, 259-272. University Park, PA: Pennsylvania State University Press.

Kim, Henry H., and Ralph E. Pyle. 2004. "An Exception to the Exception: Second Generation Korean Church Participation." *Social Compass* 51 (3): 321-333.

Kim, Illsoo. 1985. "Organizational Patterns of Korean-American Methodist Churches: Denominationalism and Personal Community." In *Rethinking Methodist History: A Bicentennial Historical Consultation*, edited by Russell E. Richey and Kenneth E. Row, 228-237. Nashville, TN: Kingswood.

Kim, Jung Ha. 1996. "The Labor of Compassion: Voices of 'Churched' Korean American Women." *Amerasia Journal* 22 (1): 93-105.

_____. 2002. "Cartography of Korean American Protestant Faith Communities in the United States." In *Religion in Asian America: Building Faith Communities*, edited by Pyong Gap Min, 185-214. Walnut Creek, CA: Altamira Press.

Kim, Kwang Chung, and Shin Kim. 2001. "Ethnic Roles of Korean Immigrant Churches in the United States." In *Korean Americans and Their Religions*, edited by Ho-Youn Kwon, Kwang Chung Kim, and R. Stephen Warner, 71-94. University Park, PA: Pennsylvania State University Press.

Kim, Rebecca. 2004a. "Made in the U.S.A.: Second-Generation Korean American Campus Evangelicals." In *Asian American Youth: Culture, Identity, and Ethnicity*, edited by Jennifer Lee and Min Zhou, 235-250. New York: Routledge.

_____. 2004b. "Second-Generation Korean American Evangelicals: Ethnic, Multiethnic, or White Campus Ministries?" *Sociology of Religion* 65: 19-34.

_____. 2004c. "Asian American College Campus Evangelicals: Constructing and Negotiating Ethnic and Religious Boundaries." In *Asian American Religions: The Making and Remaking of Borders and Boundaries*, edited by Tony Carnes and Fenggang Yang, 141-159. New York: New York University Press.

Kim, Sangho J. 1975. "A Study of a Korean Church and Her People in Chicago, Illinois." San Francisco: R and E Research Associates.

Kim, Sharon. 2000. "Creating Campus Communities: Second-Generation Korean American Ministries at UCLA." In *Gen X Religions*, edited by Richard W. Flory and Donald E. Miller, 92-112. New York: Routledge.

Kim, Shin, and Kwang Chung Kim. 2000. "Korean Immigrant Churches: Male Domination and Adaptive Strategy." *Korean and Korean American Studies Bulletin* 11: 53-67.

Kim, Young Choon. 1989. "The Nature and Destiny of Korean Churches in the United States." *Journal of Social Sciences and Humanities* 67: 33-47.

Kwon, Victoria Hyonchu, Helen Rose Ebaugh, and Jacqueline Hagan. 1997. "The Structure and Functions of Cell Group Ministry in a Korean Christian Church." *Journal for the Scientific Study of Religion* 36: 247-256.

Lee, Sang Hyun. 1991. "Korean American Presbyterians: A Need for Ethnic Particularity and the Challenge of Christian Pilgrimage." In *The Diversity of Discipleship: The Presbyterians and Twentieth Century Christian Witness*, edited by Milton J. Coalter, John M. Mulder, and Louis B. Weeks, 312-330. Louisville, KY: Westminster John Knox.

_____. 1995. "Pilgrimage to Home in the Wilderness to Marginality: Symbols and Context in Asian American Theology." *Princeton Seminary Bulletin* 16 (1): 49-64.

Min, Anselm Kyongsuk. 1997. "From Autobiography to Fellowship of Others: Reflections on Doing Ethnic Theology Today." In *Journeys at the Margin*, edited by Peter Phan, 135-159. Collegeville, MN: Liturgical Press.

_____. 2000. "From Tribal Identity to Solidarity of Others: Theological Challenges of a Divided Korea." *Missiology* 27: 333-345.

Min, Pyong Gap. 1992. "The Structure and Social Functions of Korean Immigrant Churches in the United States." *International Migration Review* 26: 1370-1395.

_____. 2000. "Immigrants' Religion and Ethnicity: A Comparison of Indian Hindu and Korean Christian Immigrants in New York." *Bulletin of the Royal Institute of Inter-Faith Studies* 2: 52-70.

_____. 2005. "How Immigrant Groups Maintain Ethnicity through Religion: A Comparison of Indian Hindu and Korean Protestant Immigrants in New York." In *Immigrant Faiths: Transforming Religious Life in America*, edited by Karen Leonard, Alex Stepick, Manuel Vasquez, and Jennifer Holdaway, 99-122. Newbury Park, CA: Altamira Press.

_____. 2008. "Severe Under-Representation of Women in Church Leadership in the Korean Immigrant Community in the U.S." *Journal for the Scientific Study of Religion* 46: 225-242.

_____. 2009. "A Comparison of Korean Protestant, Catholic and Buddhist Religious Institutions." *Studies of Koreans Abroad* 20: 182-231.

Min, Pyong Gap, and Dae Young Kim. 2005. "Intergenerational Transmission of Religion and Ethnic Culture: Korean Protestants in the United States." *Sociology of Religion* 66: 263-282.

Park, Hae-Seong, Wanpen Murgatroyd, Douglas C. Raynock, and Marydee A. Spillett. 1998. "Relationship between Intrinsic-Extrinsic Religious Orientation and Depressive Symptoms in Korean Americans." *Counseling Psychology Quarterly* 11: 315-324.

Park, Julie. 2011. "I Needed to Get Out of My Korean Bubble: An Ethnographical Account of Korean American Collegians Juggling Diversity in a Religious Context." *Anthropology and Education Quarterly* 42 (3): 193-212.

Park, Kyeyoung. 1989. "'Born Again': What Does It Mean to Korean Americans In New York City?" *Journal of Ritual Studies* 3: 287-301.

Park, So-Young. 2001. "The Intersection of Religion, Race, Gender, and Ethnicity in the Identity Formation of Korean American Evangelical Women." In *Korean Americans and Their Religions*, edited by Ho-Youn Kwon, Kwang Chung Kim, and R. Stephen Warner, 193-208. University Park, PA: Pennsylvania State University

———. 2004. "'Korean American Evangelical': A Resolution of Sociological Ambivalence among Korean American College Students." In *Asian American Religions: The Making and Remaking of Borders and Boundaries*, edited by Tony Carnes and Fenggang Yang, 141-159. New York: New York University Press.

Seong, Mu. 1998. "Korean Buddhism in America: A New Style of Zen." In *The Faces of Buddhism in America*, edited by Charles S. Prebish and Kenneth Tanaka, 117-128. Berkeley and Los Angeles: University of California Press.

Shim, Steve. 1977. "Korean Immigrant Churches Today in Southern California." San Francisco: R and E Research Associates.

Shin, Eui Hang, and Hyung Park. 1988. "An Analysis of Causes of Schisms in Ethnic Churches: The Case of Korean American Churches." *Sociological Analysis* 49: 234-248.

Song, Min-Ho. 1997. "Constructing a Local Theology for a Second-Generation Korean Ministry." *Urban Mission* 15 (2): 23-34.

Suh, Sharon. 2003. "To Be Buddhist Is to Be Korean: The Rhetorical Use of Authenticity and Homeland in the Construction of the Post-Immigrant Identities." In *Revealing the Sacred in Asian & Pacific America*, edited by Jane Naomi Iwamura and Paul Spickard, 171-192. New York: Routledge.

———. 2009. "Buddhism, Rhetoric, and the Korean American Community: The Adjustment of Korean Buddhist Immigrants to the United States." In *Immigration and Religion in America: Comparative and Historical Perspectives*, edited by Richard Alba, Albert J. Raboteau, and Josh DeWind, 166-190. New York: New York University Press.

Yu, Eui-Young. 1988. "The Growth of Korean Buddhism in the United States, with Special Reference to Southern California." *Pacific World: Journal of the Institute of Buddhist Studies* 4: 82-93.

9. Children, Education, and Psychology

Byun, Myung-Sup. 1990. "Bilingualism and Bilingual Education: The Case of the Korean Immigrants in the United States." *International Journal of the Sociology of Language* 82: 109-128.

Choi, H., L. Stafford, J. C. Meininger, R. E. Roberts, and D. P. Smith. 2002. "Psychometric Properties of the DSM Scale for Depression (DSD) with Korean American Youths." *Issues in Mental Health Nursing* 23 (8): 735-756.

Choi, Y. Elsie, Janine Bempechat, and Herbert P. Ginsburg. 1994. "Educational Socialization in Korean American Children: A Longitudinal Study." *Journal of Applied Developmental Psychology* 15: 313-318.

Choi, Yoonsun. 2008. "Diversity Within: Subgroup Differences of Youth Problem Behaviors among Asian Pacific Islander American Adolescents." *Journal of Community Psychology* 36 (3): 352-370.

Choi, Yoonsun, and Benjamin B. Lahey. 2006. "Testing the Model Minority Stereotype: Youth Behaviors across Racial and Ethnic Groups." *Social Service Review* 80 (3): 419-452.

Choi, Yoonsun, Tracy Harachi, and Richard Catalano. 2006. "Neighborhoods, Family, and Substance Use: Comparisons of the Relations across Racial and Ethnic Groups." *Social Service Review* 80 (4): 675-704.

Choi, Yoonsun, and Youseung Kim. 2010. "Acculturation and the Family: Core vs. Peripheral Changes among Korean Americans." *Journal of Studies of Koreans Abroad* 21: 135-190.

Chung, R. H. G. 1995. "Sites of Race and Ethnicity in Psychological Research of Asian Americans." In *Privileging Positions: The Sites of Asian American Studies*, edited by G. Okihiro, M. Alquizola, D. Rony, and S. Wong, 413-420. Pullman, WA: Washington State University Press.

———. 2001. "Gender, Ethnicity, and Acculturation in Intergenerational Conflict of Asian-American College Students." *Cultural Diversity and Ethnic Minority Psychology* 7 (4): 376-386.

———. 2005. "Gender, Ethnicity, and Acculturation in Intergenerational Conflict of Asian-American College Students." In *Readings in Asian American Psychology*, edited by N. Zane and B. Kim. San Francisco, CA: Kendall/Hunt Publishing Company.

Golden, John. 1990. "Acculturation, Biculturalism and Marginality: A Study of Korean American High School Students." *NABE: The Journal of the National Association for Bilingual Education* 14: 93-107.

Jo, Hye-young. 2002. "Negotiating Ethnic Identity in the College Korean Language Classes." *Identities* 9: 87-115.

Johnson H., and J. Lew. 2005. "Learning to Talk: Reflections on the First-Year Faculty Seminar." In *Community in the Making: Lincoln Center Institute, the Arts, and Teacher Education*, edited by M. F. Holzer and S. Noppe-Brandon, 77-86. New York: Teachers College Press.

Jun, Suk-ho. 1984. "Communication Patterns among Young Korean Immigrants." *International Journal of Intercultural Relations* 8: 373-389.

Kennedy, E., and H. S. Park. 1994. "Home Language as a Predictor of Academic Achievement: A Comparative Study of Mexican- and Asian-American Youth." *Journal of Research and Development in Education* 27: 188-194.

Kim, Bryan S., M. M. Omizo, and D. S. Salvador. 1996. "Culturally Relevant Counseling Services for Korean American Children: A Systematic Approach." *Elementary-School-Guidance-and Counseling* 31: 64-73.

Kim, Dae Young. 2011. "The Pursuit of Elite High Schools and Colleges among Second-Generation Korean Americans." *Development and Society* 40 (2): 225-260.

Kim, Do Yeong. 2001. "Parent Traditionalism and Parent-Child Relationships, Explicit and Implicit Psychological Acculturation, and Mental Health of Korean-American Young Adults" (University of Washington). *Dissertation Abstracts International: Section B: The Sciences and Engineering* 62 (5).

Kim, Eun-Young. 1993. "Career Choice among Second-Generation Korean Americans: Reflections of Cultural Model of Success." *Anthropology and Education Quarterly* 24: 224-248.

Kim, E. 2005. "Korean American Parental Control: Acceptance or Rejection?" *Ethos* 33 (3): 347-366.

Kim, E., and K. C. Cain. 2008. "Korean American Adolescent Depression and Parenting." *Journal of Child and Adolescent Psychiatric Nursing* 21 (2): 105-115.

Kim, H., and R. H. G. Chung. 2003. "Relationship of Parenting Style to Self-Perception among Korean-American College Students." *Journal of Genetic Psychology* 164: 481-492.

Kim, K., and R. P. Rohner. 2002. "Parental Warmth, Control, and Involvement in Schooling: Predicting Academic Achievement among Korean American Adolescents." *Journal of Cross-Cultural Psychology* 33 (2): 127-140.

Lee, Hakyoon. 2010. "'I am a Kirogi Mother': Education Exodus and Life Transformation among Korean Transnational Women." *Journal of Language, Identity, and Education* 9: 250-264.

Lee, Richard M. 2005. "Resilience against Discrimination: Ethnic Identity and Other-group Orientation as Protective Factors for Korean Americans. *Journal of Counseling Psychology* 52 (1): 36-44.

Lee, Richard M., Jennifer Choe, Gina Kim, and Vicky Ngo. 2000. "Construction of the Asian American Family Conflicts Scale." *Journal of Counseling Psychology* 47 (2): 211-222.

Lew, Jamie. 2003a. "Korean American High School Dropouts: A Case Study of Their Experiences and Negotiations of Schooling, Family, and Communities," In *Invisible Children in the Society and its Schools*, edited by Sue Books, 53-66. Philadelphia: Lawrence Erlbaum.

———. 2003b. "(Re)Construction of Second-Generation Ethnic Networks: Structuring Academic Success of Korean American High School Students." In *Research on the Education of Asian Pacific Americans*, Vol. II., edited by C. C. Parks, S. J. Lee and A. L. Goodwin, 157-176. Charlotte, NC: Information Age Publishing.

———. 2004. "The 'Other' Story of Model Minorities: Korean American High School Dropouts in an Urban Context." *Anthropology and Education Quarterly* 35: 297-311.

———. 2006. "Burden of Acting Neither White nor Black: Asian American Identities in Context." *The Urban Review* 38 (5): 335-352.

_____. 2007a. "A Structural Analysis of Success and Failure of Asian Americans: A Case of Korean Americans in Urban Schools." *Teachers College Record* 109 (2): 369-390.

_____. 2007b. "Asian American Identities: Intersection of Class, Race, Schools," In *Sociology of Education: A Critical Reader*, edited by A.R. Sadovnik. New York: Routledge.

_____. Forthcoming. "Keeping the American Dream Alive: Model Minority Discourse of Asian American Children." In *Handbook of Research in the Social Foundations of Education*, edited by S. Tozer, S. Gallegos and A. Henry. New York: Routledge.

Miller, Lisa, et al. 1999. "Beliefs about Responsibility and Improvement Associated with Success among Korean American Immigrants." *Journal of Social Psychology* 139 (2): 221-227.

Park, E. J. 1994. "Educational Needs and Parenting Concerns of Korean-American Parents." *Psychological Report* 75: 559-562.

Park, Hae-Seong, Wanpen Murgatroyd, Douglas C. Raynock, and Marydee A. Spillett. 1998. "Relationship between Intrinsic-Extrinsic Religious Orientation and Depressive Symptoms in Korean Americans." *Counseling Psychology Quarterly* 11: 315-324

Park, Jung-Sun. 2004. "Korean American Youth and Transnational Flows of Popular Culture across the Pacific." *Amerasia Journal* 30 (1): 147-170.

Pyke, Karen. 2000. "'The Normal American Family' as an Interpretive Structure of Family Life among Grown Children of Korean and Vietnamese Immigrants." *Journal of Marriage and the Family* (62) 1: 240-255.

Shin, Sara, and Lesley Milroy. 1999. "Bilingual Language Acquisition by Korean School Children in New York City." *Bilingualism: Language and Cognition* 2: 147-169.

Park, Wansoo. 2009. "Acculturative Stress and Mental Health among Korean Adolescents in the United States." *Journal of Human Behavior in the Social Environment* 19: 626-634.

_____. 2009b. "Parental Attachment among Korean-American Adolescents." *Child and Adolescent Social Work* 26: 307-319.

Shin, Sung Lim A. 1999. "Contextualizing Career Concerns of Asian American Students." In *Diversity in College Settings: Directives for Helping Professionals*, edited by Yvonne M. Jenkins et al, 201-209. New York: Routledge.

Shrake, Eunai K., and Siyon Rhee. 2004. "Ethnic Identity as a Predictor of Problem Behaviors among Korean American Adolescents." *Adolescence* 39 (155): 601-623.

Tseng, V., and A. J. Fuglini. 2000. "Parent-Adolescent Language Use and Relationships among Immigrant Families with East Asian, Filipino, and Latin American Backgrounds." *Journal of Marriage and the Family* 62: 465-477.

Woo, Susie. 2004. "Online and Unplugged: Locating Korean American Teens in Cyberspace." *Amerasia Journal* 30 (1): 171-190.

Yang, Jang-Ae. 1999. "An Exploratory Study of Korean Fathering of Adolescent Children." *Journal of Genetic Psychology* 160: 55-68.

Yeh, C. J. 2003. "Age, Acculturation, Cultural Adjustment, and Mental Health Symptoms of Chinese, Korean, and Japanese Immigrant Youths." *Cultural Diversity and Ethnic Minority Psychology* 9: 34-48.

Yoo, Hyung Chol, and Richard M. Lee. 2005. "Ethnic Identity and Approach-Type Coping as Moderators of the Racial Discrimination/Well-Being Relation in Asian Americans." *Journal of Counseling Psychology* 52 (4): 497-506.

You, Byeong-Keun. 2005. "Children Negotiating Korean American Ethnic Identity through Their Heritage Language." *Bilingual Research Journal* 29: 711-721.

Zhou, Min. 2007. "Non-Economic Effects of Ethnic Entrepreneurship." In *Handbook of Research on Ethnic Minority Entrepreneurship: A Co-Evolutionary View on Resource Management*, edited by Leo-Paul Dana, 279-288. Cheltenham, United Kingdom: Edward Elgar Publishing.

_____. 2009. "How Neighborhoods Matter for Immigrant Children: The Formation of Educational Resources in Chinatown, Koreatown, and Pico Union, Los Angeles." *Journal of Ethnic and Migration Studies* 35: 1153-1179.

Zhou, Min, and Susan S. Kim. 2006. "Community Forces, Social Capital, and Educational Achievement: The Case of Supplementary Education in the Chinese and Korean Immigrant Communities." *Harvard Educational Review* 76: 1-29.

10. Health

Cho, Y., S. E. Song, and W. P. Frisbie. 2005. "Adverse Birth Outcomes among Korean Americans: The Impact of Nativity and Social Proximity to Other Koreans." *Population Research and Policy Review* 24: 263-282.

Kim, M. T., K. B. Kim, H. S. Juon, and M. N. Hill. 2000. "Prevalence and Factors Associated with High Blood Pressure in Korean Americans." *Ethnicity and Disease* 10: 364-374.

Lee, J. A., G. Yeo, and D. Gallagher-Thompson. 1993. "Cardiovascular Disease Risk Factors and Attitudes towards Prevention among Korean American Elders." *Journal of Cross-cultural Gerontology* 8: 17-33.

Lee. S. K., J. Sobal, A. Frongillo, Jr. 2000. "Acculturation and Health in Korean Americans." *Social Science and Medicine* 51: 159-173.

Lim, J. W., and J. Yi. 2009. "The Effects of Religiosity, Spirituality, and Social Support on Quality of Life: A Comparison between Korean American and Korean Breast and Gynecologic Cancer Survivors." *Oncology Nursing Forum* 36: 699-708.

Park, S., and K. S. Bernstein. 2008. "Depression and Korean American Immigrants." *Archives of Psychiatric Nursing* 22: 12-19.

Ryu, H., W. B. Young, and C. Park. 2001. "Korean American Health Insurance and Health Services Utilization." *Research in Nursing and Health* 24: 494-505.

Shin, H., H. Song, J. Kim, and J. Probst. 2005. "Insurance, Acculturation, and Health Service Utilization among Korean-Americans." *Journal of Immigrant Health* 7: 65-74.

Shin, H. S. 2000. "Patterns and Factors Associated with Health Care Utilization among Korean American Elderly." *Asian American and Pacific Islander Journal of Health* 8: 117-129.

Sohn, Y. H. 1988. "Knowledge and Use of Preventive Health Practices among Korean Women in Los Angeles County." *Preventive Medicine* 41: 167-178.

Yoo, G., and B. W. Kim. 2008. "Korean Immigrant and Health Care Access: Implications for the Uninsured and Underinsured." *Research in the Sociology of Health Care* 25: 77-94.

Yu, E. S., and W. T. Liu. 1992. "U.S. National Health Data on Asian Americans and Pacific Islanders: A Research Agenda for the 1990s." *American Journal of Public Health* 82: 1648-1652.

11. Adoptees, War Brides, and Others

Hong, S., B. S. Kim, and S. P. Kim. 1979. "Adoption of Korean Children by New York Couples: A Preliminary Study." *Child Welfare* 58: 419-427.

Huh, Nam Soon, and William J. Reid. 2000. "Intercountry, Transracial Adoption and Ethnic Identity: A Korean Example." *International Social Work* 43: 75-87.

Hurh, Won Moo. 1972. "Marginal Children of War: An Exploratory Study of American-Korean Children." *International Journal of Sociology of the Family* 2: 10-20.

Hurh, Won Moo, and Kwang Chung Kim. 1981. "Methodological Problems in Cross-Cultural Research: A Korean Immigrant Study." *California Sociologist* 4: 17-32.

Kang, Miliann. 2000. "Researching One's Own: Negotiating Co-Ethnicity in the Field." In *Cultural Compass: Ethnographic Explorations of Asian America*, edited by Martin Manalansan. Philadelphia: Temple University Press.

Kim, Bok-Lim. 1972. "Casework of Japanese and Korean Wives of Americans." *Social Casework* 53: 242-279.

_____. 1977. "Asian Wives of U.S. Servicemen: Women in Shadows." *Amerasia Journal* 4 (1): 91-116.

Kim, Chim, and Timothy Carroll. 1977. "Intercountry Adoption of South Korean Orphans: A Lawyers' Guide." *Journal of Family Law* 14: 223-253.

Kim, Eleana. 2001. "Korean Adoptee Auto-Ethnography: Refashioning Self, Family, and Finding Community." *Visual Anthropology Review* 16: 43-70.

_____. 2003. "Wedding Citizenship and Culture: Korean Adoptees and the Global Family of Korea." *Social Text* 74: 57-81.

_____. 2004. "Gathering 'Roots' and Making History in the Korean Adoptee Community." In *Local Actions: Cultural Activism, Power and Public Life,*

edited by M. Checker and M. Fishman, 208-230. New York: Columbia University Press.
———. 2005. "Wedding, Citizenship, and Culture: Korean Adoptees and the Global Family of Korea." In *Cultures of Transnational Adoption*, edited by T. A. Volkman, 49-80. Durham, NC: Duke University Press.
———. 2007a. "Our Adoptee, Our Alien: Transnational Adoptees as Specters of Foreignness and Family in South Korea." *Anthropological Quarterly* 80: 497-531.
———. 2007b. "Remembering Loss: The Koreanness of Overseas Adopted Koreans." In *International Korean Adoption: A Fifty-Year History of Policy and Practice*, edited by K. Bergquist and E. Vonk, 111-126. Hawthorne, NJ: Hawthorn Press.
Kim, H. J. 1991. "Voices from the Shadows: The Lives of Korean War Brides." *Amerasia Journal* 17 (1): 15-30.
Kim, Katherine, Elena Yu, Edwin H Chen, Jae Kyung Kim, Mary Kaufman, and Joel Purkiss. 1999. "Cervical Cancer Screening Knowledge and Practices among Korean American Women." *Cancer Nursing* 22 (4): 297-302.
Kim, Nadia Y. 2004. "A View from Below: An Analysis of Korean Americans' Racial Attitudes." *Amerasia Journal* 30 (1): 1-24.
Kim, Peter. 1980. "Behavior Symptoms of Three Transracially Adopted Asian Children: Diagnosis Dilemma." *Child Welfare* 59: 213-224.
Kim, Peter S., Sungdo Hong, and Bok Soon Kim. 1979. "Adoption of Korean Children by New York Area Couples: A Preliminary Study." *Child Welfare* 58 (7): 419-428.
Kim, Wun Jung. 1995. "International Adoption: A Case Review of Korean Children." *Child Psychiatry and Human Development* 25: 141-154.
Kim, Wun Jung, Yee-Jin Shin, and Michael P. Carey. 1999. "Comparison of Korean-American Adoptees and Biological Children of Their Adoptive Parents: A Pilot Study." *Child Psychiatry and Human Development* 29: 221-228.
Koh, Howard Kyongju, and Hesung Chun Koh. 1993. "Health Issues in Korean Americans." *Asian American and Pacific Islander Journal of Health* 1: 176-223.
Lee, Kun Jong. 2008. "Korean-Language American Literary Studies: An Overview." *Amerasia Journal* 34 (2): 14-36.
Lee, Sara S. 2004. "Marriage Dilemmas: Partner Choices and Constraints for Korean Americans in New York City." In *Asian American Youth: Culture, Identity, and Ethnicity*, edited by Jennifer Lee and Min Zhou, 285-298. Philadelphia: Temple University Press.
Messaris, Paul, and Jisuk Woo. 1991. "Image vs. Reality in Korean-Americans' Responses to Mass-Mediated Depictions of the United States." *Critical Studies in Mass Communication* 8: 74-90.
Mok, Jin Whyu, and Young Soon Yim. 1994. "The Korean-Americans' Role Perception toward the North-South Reunification Issue." *International Journal of Comparative Sociology* 35: 252-263.

Pang, Keum Young. 1989. "The Practice of Traditional Korean Medicine in Washington, D.C." *Social Science Medicine* 28 (8): 875-884.

Shiao, Jiannbin Lee, and Mia H. Tuan. 2007. "A Sociological Approach to Race, Identity, and Asian Adoption." In *International Korean Adoption: A Fifty-Year History of Policy and Practice*, edited by Betsy Vonk, Dong Soo Kim, and Marvin Feit, 155-170. Binghamton, NY: Hawthorne Press.

_____.2008a. "Korean Adoptee and the Social Context of Ethnic Exploration." *American Journal of Sociology* 113: 1023-1066.

_____. 2008b. "'Some Asian Men Are Attractive to Me, but Not for a Husband': Korean Adoptees and the Salience of Race in Romance." *Dubois Review* 5: 259-285.

_____. 2008c. "Shared Fates in Asian Transracial Adoption: Korean Adoptee Experiences of Difference in Their Families." In *Twenty-First Century Color Lines" Multiracial Change in Contemporary America*, edited by Andrew Grant-Thomas and Gary Orfield, 178-200. Philadelphia: Temple University Press.

Shiao, Jiannbin Lee, Mia H. Tuan, and Elizabeth Rienzi. 2004. "Shifting the Spotlight: Exploring Race and Culture in Korean-White Adoptive Families." *Race and Society* 7: 1-16.

Shin, Eui Hang, and Eui-Young Yu. 1984. "Use of Surname in Ethnic Research: The Case of Kim in the Korean American Population." *Demography* 21: 347-359.

Yi, Samson. 2006. "My Most Favorite Kim Bop Isn't Made Anymore." *Amerasia Journal* 32 (2): 115-120.

Yuh, Ji-Yeon. 1999. "Out of the Shadows: Camptown Women, Military Brides, and Korean (American) Communities." *Hitting Critical Mass* 6 (1): 13-34.

11. Koreans in General

Barringer, Herbert, and Sung-Nam Cho. 1989. "Koreans in the United States: A Fact Book." Honolulu: East-West Center.

Harvey, Young Sook Kim, and Soon-Hyung Chung. 1980. "The Koreans." In *People and Cultures of Hawaii: A Psychocultural Profile*, edited by John F. McDermott, Wen-Shing Tseng, and Thomas Maretzki, 135-154. Honolulu: University of Hawaii Press.

Kim, Elaine H. 1997. "Korean Americans in U.S. Race Relations: Some Considerations." *Amerasia Journal* 23 (2): 69-78.

Kim, Hyung-Chan. 1974. "Some Aspects of Social Demography of Korean Americans." *International Migration Review* 8: 23-42.

Kim, Nadia. 2004. "A View from Below: An Analysis of Korean Americans' Racial Attitudes." *Amerasia Journal* 30 (1): 1-24.

Min, Pyong Gap. 1995. "Korean Americans." In *Asian Americans: Contemporary Trends and Issues*, edited by Pyong Gap Min, 199-231. Thousand Oaks, CA: Sage Publications.

_____. 1997. "Korean Immigrants." In *American Immigrant Cultures*, edited by David Levinson and Melvin Ember, 554-563. New York: Macmillan Reference USA.

_____. 2006. "Korean Americans." In *Asian Americans: Contemporary Trends and Issues,* Second Edition, edited by Pyong Gap Min, 230-259. Thousand Oaks, CA: Pine Forge Press.

_____. 2007. "Immigrants from Korea." In *The New Americans*, edited by Mary Waters and Reed Ueda, 491-503. Cambridge: Harvard University Press.

Park, Kyeyoung. 2005a. "Koreans in the United States." In *Encyclopedia of Diaspora*, edited by Melvin Ember, Carol R. Ember, and Ian Skoggard, 993-1003. New York: Human Relations Area Files (HRAF) at Yale University.

_____. 2005b. "Korean Americans." In *Multiculturalism in the United States,* edited by Lorman A. Ratner and John D. Buenker, 281-297. Westport, CT: Greenwood Press.

Yu, Eui-Young. 1977. "Koreans in America: An Emerging Ethnic Minority." *Amerasia Journal* 4 (1): 117-131.

_____. 1983. "Korean Communities in America: Past, Present, and Future." *Amerasia Journal* 10 (1): 23-52.

Index of Topics

Asian population in the U.S. by ethnic group, 38; Asian population in Los Angeles City by ethnic group, 50; Asian population in New York City by ethnic group, 52

Brazilian *nikkeijin*, 161

Chooseok, 88, 91
a comprehensive bibliography on Korean Americans, 211-252; books and edited anthologies, 211-217; journal articles and book chapters-adoptees, war brides and others, 250-252; journal articles and book chapters-business and business-related intergroup conflicts, 224-231; journal articles and book chapters-children, education and psychology, 244-248; journal articles and book chapters-ethnicity and transnationalism, 238-239; journal articles and book chapters-family relations, women, the elderly and social services, 231-237; journal articles and book chapters-health, 248-249; journal articles and book chapters-history, 217-218; journal articles and book chapters-immigration and settlement patterns, 219-221; journal articles and book chapters-religious practices and religious organizations, 241-244; journal articles and book chapters-socioeconomic attainments and assimilation, 221-223

dongpo (ethnic Koreans), 161

ethnic identity among Korean return migrants from the U.S. and China, 161, 162-169; complications of transnationalism, 162-164; conflicts in Korean identity, 166-168; data sources, 162; diasporic ethnic enclaves, 164-166; emotional ties, 168; ethnic identities at "Home" in the U.S. and China, 159-160; literature, 161; social construction of ethnicity, 158

guyukmoim (district meeting), 87
guyuk yebae (district service), 86

hyodo kwankwang (filial tours), 85, 87

Immigration Act of 1990, 13-14, 18
the Immigration and Nationality Act of 1965, 9, 159, 195
intact vs. transnational (*kirogi*) family, see Toronto Korean Family Study of 2011

jemigyopo (Korean Americans), p.167
Joseonjok (Koreans in China), 157, 158, 160, 162, 163, 165, 166, 167, 168, 169

Korean adoptees, 20-22, 209-210
Korean-black conflicts, 203-204; see also Korean merchants, the role of middleman merchants,
Korean immigrants' religious practices, 75-101; Buddhists, 80, 83-84, 87-88, 90-91, 95-96; Catholics, 79, 82-83, 86-

87, 89-90, 94-95; cultural retention function of religious institutions, 88-91; fellowship function of religious institutions, 84-88; frequency of participation in religious institutions, 80-84; Protestants, 2, 78-79, 80-82, 84-86, 88-89, 92-93; religious affiliations, 78-80; social service function of religious institutions, 92-96; survey data on Korean immigrants' religious affiliations and participation in religious institutions, 78, 81

Korean immigration to Canada, 3-4, 104, 124-126; factors that contributed to the movement of Koreans to Canada, 105-106

Korean immigration to the U.S., 9-29; Changes in the Korean population in New York City by Borough (1990-2010); entry mechanisms, 15-22; early-study students, 26-27; immigration through specialty occupations, 18-20; Korean international students, 25-27; major contributing factors to, 10-15; proportion of female immigrants, 23; status adjusters, 24-25; temporary residents, 28-29, 59; temporary workers (H1B), 28-29, 32, 59

Korean international students' wives, 135-153; characteristics, 138-139; changes in the division of household labor, 145-151; changes in spousal relationships, 139-145; conclusion, 151-153; data and methods, 137-138; literature review, 135-137

Korean merchants; 57-69; business-related intergroup conflicts, 2, 57-58, 62-64; changes in business patterns, 60, 62-66; decrease in self-employment rate, 58-62, see also Korean immigration to the U.S., temporary residents; produce stores, 68; nail salons, 65; the role of middleman merchants, 66-68; occupational assimilation, 69-71; survey data on Korean immigrants' self-employment rate, 61

Korean population in the U.S., 9, 35-37; differences between gateway vs. non-gateway cities in the characteristics of Korean Americans, 48; distribution of Korean Americans in four regions, 38-39; distribution of Korean Americans in major metropolitan areas, 43-47; distribution of Korean Americans in major states, 40-43; Korean population in Bergen County, 54; Korean population in the Flushing area, 55; Korean population in the Los Angeles-Orange-Riverside CMSA, 48-51; Korean population in the New York-New Jersey CMSA, 51-55; multiracial Koreans, 37, 42-43

KPA (Korean Produce Association of New York), 68-69

New York Bulkwang Zen Meditation Center, 77, 87-88, 90-91, 95-96

pre-1965 native-born Koreans' authenticity dilemma 173-194;

background, 174-176; methods, 76; rejection by the Korean community and peers due to their strong in-group/out-group boundaries, 182-189; rejection by the white community due to their being racial foreigners," 177-182;

review of the literature on Korean Americans, 195-210;by chronological order (generational changes), 199-201; by topic, 201-210; overall volume, 198-199

sebae, 89, 90

second- and 1.5-generation Korean Americans; Korean American Community Foundation, 71; native-born Koreans, 37; participation in the mainstream economy, 70-71; see also ethnic identity among Korean return migrants from the U.S. and China; see also authenticity dilemma among pre-1965 native-born Koreans, 173-191

Shin Kwang Church of New York, 80, 84-86, 88-89, 92-93

social construction of ethnicity, 158-159

St. Paul Chong Ha Sang Roman Catholic Chapel, 77, 86-87, 89-91, 94-95

Toronto Korean Family Study of 2011, 104; major findings, 108-114; research method, 106-108; financial ties, 129-130; informal exchanges, 129; informal ties and contacts, 126-129; organizational participation, 130; transnational theories, 106-108, 122-124;

transnational ties of Korean immigrants in Toronto to South Korea, 121-132; cultural, emotional, and

Yanbian Korean Autonomous Prefecture, 160

Index for Authors

Abelmann, Nancy, 57, 105, 114, 203
Alba, Richard, 174
Alumkal, Antony, 75, 77
Alwin, D., 176
Azores, Tania, 137

Bailey, A. R., 123
Baker, Donald, 84, 88
Baldwin, Nancy Toman, 136, 137
Bankston, Carl, III, 95
Barberia, Lorena, 175
Basch, Linda, 105, 121, 161
Bellah, Robert, 95
Berry, John, 174
Bianchi, Suzanne M., 136, 137
Blanc-Szanton, Cristina, 105, 121, 161
Blumberg, Rae Lesser, 142, 150
Bonacich, Edna, 57
Boyd, Monica, 113

Castles, Stephen, 113
Chafetz, Janet Saltzman, 95
Chai, Alice, 199
Chai, Karen, 75, 76, 200, 209
Chang, Edward, 200
Cho, Uhn, 105
Choe, P., 174, 175
Choi, Bong-Youn, 202
Choi, Woo-Gil, 160
Chong, Kelly, 75, 174, 184, 200
Cornell, Stephen, 158
Chung, Angie, 200, 202, 208
Chung, Ruth, 200
Cummings, Bruce, 184

Danico, Mary Yu, 185
Daniels, Roger, 174
Darvishpour, Mehrdad, 135
Dolan, Jay, 95

Ebaugh, Helen Rose, 83, 95

Eckland, Elaine, 75, 95
Eckstein, Susan, 175
Eitzen, Stanley, 66
England, Paula, 136
Espiritu, Yen Le, 135, 137, 142, 147, 157

Fenton, John, 83
Foner, Nancy, 121

Gans, Herbert, 158
George, Sheba Mariam, 137
Ghosh, S., 124
Glenn, Evelyn Nakano, 135, 141, 147
Glick Schiller, Nina, 105, 121, 161
Goh-Grapes, 108
Goldring, Luin, 105
Goodstein, Laurie, 83
Gordon, Milton, 158
Grahame, Kamini, 135, 141, 147
Guarnizo, Luis E., 123

Hall, Stuart, 157
Han, Joe Jeong Ho, 121
Hao, L., 187
Hartmann, Douglass, 158
He, Jiancheng, 160
Heertz, R., 142, 150
Hertzog, Esther, 135, 141
Hiebert, Daniel, 106, 121, 122, 124, 131
Hochischild, Arlie, 136
Hondagneu-Sotelo, Pierrtte, 135, 137, 142, 150
Huang, Shirlena, 106
Hurh, Won Moo, 3, 57, 75, 78, 81, 174, 204, 205, 206
Hwang, Cindy, 190

Hyndman, J., 124
Immigration Act of 1965, 1, 35
Immigration Act of 1999, 18-20

Jacoby, T., 175
Jaworsky, Nadya, 103
Jin, Shangzhen, 160
Johnson-Sumerford, Danette, 136

Kang, Millian, 200, 204
Kanjananpan, Wilawan, 135
Kelly, P., 124, 131
Khoo, Louisa-May, 135
Kibria, Nazli, 135, 137, 142, 147, 150, 159, 161, 207
Kim, Ai Ra, 75, 209
Kim, Ann, 103, 104, 113
Kim, Bok Lim, 199
Kim, Chigon, 5, 6, 35, 206
Kim, Claire, 57, 66, 203
Kim, Dae Young, 77, 200. 205, 209
Kim, Eleana, 200, 207
Kim, H. J., 175, 197
Kim, Illsoo, 62, 75, 76, 199, 201, 202
Kim, Jung Ha, 75, 209
Kim, Katherine Youngmee, 202, 203
Kim, Kwang Chung, 57, 75, 76, 81, 83, 86, 93, 197, 199, 204, 205, 206, 209
Kim, Minjeong, 136, 137, 141
Kim, M. S., 184
Kim, Nadia, 173, 175, 183, 200, 201, 207
Kim, Rebecca, 77, 200
Kim, Rose, 159, 174, 187
Kim sample technique, 77-77
Kim, Shin, 57, 75, 76, 83, 93, 209
Kim, Song-Chul, 106
Kitano, Harry, 174
Kivisto, Peter, 122
Koo, Hagen, 106, 111, 114
Krishnamurti, Sailaja, 105

Kwak, Min-Jung, 121
Kwon, Ho-Youn, 76, 86, 197, 209
Kwon, Okyun, 76

Langlois, A., 126
Lee, Doo Hyoo, 111
Lee, Helene, 7, 157
Lee, Jennifer, 57, 66, 200, 203
Lee, Se Hwa, 7, 135
Lee, Yean-Ju, 106, 114
Lee, Youngmin, 202
Lee Shiao, Jiannbin, 210
Levitt, Peggy, 103, 105, 122, 123, 161
Lew, Jamie, 200
Ley, David, 106, 122, 124, 131
Lie, John, 57, 203
Light, Ivan, 57
Lim, In-Sook, 135, 136, 150
Liu, Haidong, 136, 141
Louie, Andrea, 159, 161

Madsen, R., 95
Mahler, S., 123
Man, Guida, 135, 136, 137
Maria, Sunaina Marr, 159
Martin, J.N., 184
Menjivar, Cecilia, 135,141
Miller, Mark, 111
Min, Pyong Gap, 5-6, 7, 9, 35, 38, 57, 58, 59, 60-62, 64, 66, 67, 68, 70, 75, 76, 81, 85,86, 92, 95,135, 136, 141,150.159, 174, 175, 187, 199, 201, 202, 203, 204, 2006, 207, 208, 209
Moon, Aili, 199, 204
Moon, Seungsook, 135

Nee, Victor, 174
Noh, Marianne, 104
Noh, Samuel, 6, 103, 104, 121

Oh, Moonsung David, 197
Oh, Sook Hee, 59, 70

Okihiro, Garry. Y., 174
Omni, Michael, 175
Ong, Aihwa, 135
Orstein, M., 126

Park, Edward, 200
Park, Hyung, 77
Park, Kyeyoung, 197, 199, 200, 202, 203
Park, Linda, 7, 173, 207
Park, Robert, 158
Park, So Jin, 112, 114
Park, So-Young, 75
Park, Wansoo, 103
Parrefia, Rhacel Salazar,135
Perista, Heloisa, 141
Pesquera, Beatriz, 137, 142, 146
Pessar, Patricia R., 135, 137, 142, 147, 150
Phinney, J. 185
Portelli, A., 176
Portes, Alejandro, 122, 123, 124, 175, 186, 187

Razin, E., 126
Rinder, Irwin, 66
Risman, Barbara J., 136
Roth, Joshua Hotaka, 161
Rumbaut, Ruben, 175, 186

Safran, William, 161
Sakamoto, Arthur, 205
Scott, J., 176
Shim, R. J., 111
Shim, T. Y., 184
Shin, Eui Hang, 77, 199
Shin, G. W., 176
Silvey, Rachel, 107
Smart, A., 123
Smart, J., 123
Song, Young In, 199, 200, 204
South, Scott, 136, 137
Spitze, Glenna, 136, 137

Stone, Pamela, 143
Suarez-Orozco, 175
Suh, Sharon, 76, 90, 208
Sullivan, W. M., 95
Swindler, A., 95
Szanton Blanc, Cristina, 105, 121

Takaki, Ronald, 174, 197
Tinker, Hugh, 68
Tipton, S.M., 95
Tsang, A. Ka, 107
Tsuda, Takeyuki, 161
Tuan, Mia, 159, 173, 174, 190, 210

Walton-Roberts, M., 124
Wang, L., 124
Warner, R. Stephen, 75, 83, 197, 209
Waters, Johanna L., 108, 110, 112, 124
Waters, Mary C., 158, 159
Weeks, Kerri, 135, 136, 137, 141
Willis, Katie., 123, 135, 136, 147
Winant, Howard, 175
Wong, Madeleine, 135, 141
Wuthnow, Robert, 95

Yamanaka, Keiko, 105
Yang, Fenggang, 83
Yanou, D., 175
Yeoh, Brenda S.A, 106, 123, 135, 136, 147
Yoo, David, 200, 202 , 207
Yoon, In-Jin, 57, 202, 203, 205
Yu, Eui-Young, 78,174, 175, 197, 199, 202
Yuh, Ji-Yeonm 202
Yun, Sung Hyun, 103

Zenner, Walter 66
Zengtgraf, Kristine M., 135
Zhou, Min, 95, 135, 137, 184

About the Contributors

The Editor:

Pyong Gap Min is a Distinguished Professor of Sociology at Queens College and the Graduate Center of the City University of New York. He also serves as Director of the Research Center for Korean Community at Queens College. The areas of his research interest are immigration, ethnic identity, ethnic business, immigrants' religious practices, and family/gender, with a special focus on Asian/Korean Americans. He is the author of five books, all focusing on Korean immigrants' experiences. They include *Caught in the Middle: Korean Communities in New York and Los Angeles* (1996), the winner of two national book awards, and *Preserving Ethnicity through Religion in America: Korean Protestants and Indian Hindus across Generations* (2010), the winner of three national book awards, one in Korea and the other two in the United States. His eight edited or co-edited books include *Encyclopedia of Racism in the United States*, 3 volumes (2005) and *Asian Americans: Contemporary Trends and Issues*, the Second Edition (2006). He received the Distinguished Career Award from the International Migration Section of the American Sociological Association in 2012. He completed his undergraduate education at Seoul National University majoring in history. He received a master's degree in history and two Ph.D. degrees, one in educational philosophy and the other in sociology, all from Georgia State University.

Contributors:

Joe Jeong Ho Han graduated from University of Toronto with a double major in Psychology and Neuroscience. He is primarily interested in transnational migration and immigrant life among Koreans. He worked at CAMH (Centre for Addiction and Mental Health) under Dr. Samuel Noh to complete the paper on "Transnational Interactions among Korean Immigrants in Toronto" and currently seeks to start a graduate studies program.

Ann H. Kim is an assistant professor of sociology at York University. Her research is largely motivated by questions related to the immigrant and ethnic integration process. She has studied the experiences of Korean immigrants in relation to ethnic entrepreneurship, living arrangements, and new destinations, and currently, she is working on two major projects, one on Korean transnational families and another on the gendered and racialized patterns of economic security among seniors. She has a forthcoming co-edited book entitled, *Korean Immigrants in Canada: Perspectives on Migration, Integration and the Family*.

Min-Jung Kwak is a human geographer who currently teaches in the Urban Studies Program at University of Toronto. Her research interests broadly cover the areas of globalization, transnational migration, immigrant entrepreneurship, urban housing and labor market issues, and family and gender relations. She has been particularly interested in the Korean Canadian communities in major Canadian cities. She has published policy reports, book chapters, and journal articles. The most recent publication includes an article published in the *Journal of International Migration and Integration*.

Helene Lee received her Ph.D. in Sociology from the University of California, Santa Barbara, and is an Assistant Professor in the Department of Sociology at Dickinson College. She is currently working on a book manuscript exploring the impact of return migration projects to the ancestral homeland (South Korea) on two diasporic Korean communities—Korean Americans and Korean Chinese (Joseonjok). Her continued research interests focus on how individuals construct and maintain complicated transnational Korean identities at the intersections of gender, ethnicity and nationality.

Se Hwa Lee is a Ph.D. candidate in Sociology at the University at Albany, State University of New York. Her research is centered on gender, family, international migration and women's leadership. Her recent paper about women's political representation was accepted with minor revisions by the *Journal of Women, Politics and Policy* (JWPP). She also serves as an occasional reviewer for JWPP. She was the Chair of the Program Scheduling Committee and a member of the Session Paneling Committee for the 2011 Eastern Sociological Society (ESS) annual meeting. She currently is working on her dissertation, titled "Korean Wild Geese Families, A New Trend of Transnational Migration: Split Household Strategies and Gender Dynamics" with the support of a dissertation scholarship from the Research Center for the Korean Community at Queens College of CUNY.

Samuel Noh currently holds an Endowed Professorship, the David Crombie Professor of Cultural Pluralism in Health, in the Department of Psychiatry at the University of Toronto. He also serves as the Co-Director of the Equity, Gender and Population Health Division Culture, Community and Health Studies Program, a post-graduate psychiatry residence training and research program. He is Senior Research Scientist at the Centre for Addiction and Mental Health, where he founded and directed a program in Social Equity and Health Research, including a post-doctoral research training program in social determinants of mental health. He has published over one-hundred articles, book chapters, and abstracts. He has delivered over two-hundred refereed presentations and invited lectures and seminal presentations.

Linda S. Park has just completed her Ph.D. program in the Department of Human Development and Family Studies at the University of Wisconsin-Madison. Her doctoral studies include two minors: Research Methods in Cultural Studies and Social Welfare with a focus on policy. Her dissertation explores issues of authenticity for second-generation Korean Americans focusing on a little-known cohort of Korean immigrants. Linda also has two master's degrees, one in Social Work and the other in Business Management & Human Resources. In 2010, she received a dissertation scholarship from the Research Center for Korean Community. She is a second-generation Korean American born in Washington, D.C. in the early 1960s. She is an active member of both Korean and Asian American communities in Madison, Wisconsin.

Wansoo Park is an associate professor at the School of Social Work, University of Windsor, Ontario, Canada. Her areas of interest in research, practice, and teaching are grounded in promoting civic engagement, social inclusion and making connections between and amongst individuals, families, institutions, communities, programs, and policies in multicultural society. She is particularly interested in the area of health and mental health among immigrant and transnational families across life span. One of her current projects is exploring ways to promote health and well-being among seniors and residents in low-income housing neighborhoods through community–university partnerships.

Dr. Sung Hyun Yun is an associate professor at the School of Social Work, University of Windsor, Ontario, Canada. As a social work scholar who works with/for the community, he has developed a series of research efforts grounded in anti-oppressive perspectives, human empowerment, transnationalism, and pro-feminist frameworks embedded in global and interdisciplinary context. His research aims not only to generate knowledge and understanding about people in need and societal challenges, but more importantly, to develop effective treatment and intervention directly applicable to social work practice. His research also highlights the importance of evidence-based and outcome-driven teaching/learning components that are judiciously integrated with effective social work practice.